Mass Communication and Journalism

For UGC-NET/SLET

Objective Type Questions

Second Edition
Revised, Updated and Enlarged

Mass Communication and Journalism

For UGC-NET/SLET

Objective Type Questions

Second Edition
Revised, Updated and Enlarged

Atlantic Research Division

ATLANTIC
PUBLISHERS & DISTRIBUTORS (P) LTD

Published by
ATLANTIC
PUBLISHERS & DISTRIBUTORS (P) LTD
7/22, Ansari Road, Darya Ganj,
New Delhi-110002
Phones : +91-11-40775252, 23273880, 23275880, 23280451
Fax : +91-11-23285873
Web : www.atlanticbooks.com
E-mail : orders@atlanticbooks.com

Branch Office
5, Nallathambi Street, Wallajah Road,
Chennai-600002
Phones : +91-44-64611085, 32413319
E-mail : chennai@atlanticbooks.com

First Edition: 2012

Printed in India at Nice Printing Press, A-33/3A, Site-IV,
Industrial Area, Sahibabad, Ghaziabad, U.P.

General Information

About the NET

The National Educational Testing Bureau of University Grants Commission (UGC) conducts National Eligibility Test (NET) to determine eligibility for lectureship and for award of Junior Research Fellowship (JRF) for Indian nationals in order to ensure minimum standards for the entrants in the teaching profession and research. The Test is conducted in Humanities (including languages), Social Sciences, Forensic Science, Environmental Sciences, Computer Science and Applications and Electronic Science.

The Council of Scientific and Industrial Research (CSIR) conducts the UGC-CSIR NET for other Science subjects, namely, Life Sciences, Physical Sciences, Chemical Sciences, Mathematical Sciences and Earth Atmospheric Ocean & Planetary Sciences jointly with the UGC. The tests are conducted twice in a year generally in the months of June and December. For candidates who desire to pursue research, the Junior Research Fellowship (JRF) is available for five years subject to fulfillment of certain conditions. UGC has allocated a number of fellowships to the universities for the candidates who qualify the test for JRF. The JRFs are awarded to the meritorious candidates from among the candidates qualifying for eligibility for lectureship in the NET. JRFs are available only to the candidates who opt for it in their application forms.

The test for Junior Research Fellowship is being conducted since 1984. The Government of India, through its notification dated 22nd July, 1988 entrusted the task of conducting the eligibility test for lectureship to UGC. Consequently, UGC conducted the first National Eligibility Test, common to both eligibility for Lectureship and Junior Research Fellowship in two parts, that is, in December 1989 and in March, 1990.

NET Schedule

UGC conducts NET twice a year, i.e., in the months of June and December. The notifications announcing the June and December examinations are published in the months of March and September respectively in the weekly journal of nation-wide circulation, viz, Employment News.

NET Results Declaration Schedule

The result of June, UGC-NET is declared generally in the month of October. Similarly December, UGC-NET result is usually declared in the month of April. The UGC-NET results published in the Employment News are also available on UGC website.

UGC-NET in Objective Mode from June, 2012 Onwards

1. The UGC-NET will be conducted in objective mode from June 2012 onwards. The Test will consist of three papers. All the three papers will consist of only objective type questions and will be held on the day of Examination in two separate sessions as under:

Session	Paper	Number of Questions	Marks	Duration
First	I	60 out of which 50 questions are to be attempted	50 × 2 = 100	1¼ Hours (09.30 a.m. to 10.45 a.m.)
First	II	50 questions all of which are compulsory	50 × 2 = 100	1¼ Hours (10.45 a.m. to 12.00 Noon.)
Second	III	75 questions all of which are compulsory	75 × 2 = 150	2½ Hours (01.30 p.m. to 04.00 p.m.)

2. The candidates are required to obtain minimum marks separately in Paper-I, Paper-II and Paper-III as given below:

Category	Minimum marks (%) to be obtained		
	Paper-I	Paper-II	Paper-III
General	40 (40%)	40 (40%)	75 (50%)
OBC	35 (35%)	35 (35%)	67.5 (45%) rounded off to 68
PH/VH/SC/ST	35 (35%)	35 (35%)	60 (40%)

Only such candidates who obtain the minimum required marks in each Paper, separately, as mentioned above, will be considered for final preparation of result.

However, the final qualifying criteria for Junior Research Fellowship (JRF) and eligibility for Lectureship shall be decided by UGC before declaration of result.

3. The syllabus of Paper-I, Paper-II and Paper-III will remain the same.

4. The candidates will be allowed to carry the carbon printout of OMR Response Sheets with them on conclusion of the examination.

5. There will be no negative marking.

Preface

The book has been designed for students preparing for UGC-NET/SLET in Mass Communication and Journalism. This second edition has been thoroughly revised, updated and sufficiently enlarged with the inclusion of many more questions in each chapter. The book is very comprehensive and covers almost all possible objective type questions on the subject. Many of the questions set in UGC-NET/SLET and various other competitive examinations in the previous years have been used for preparing this book.

In spite of our best efforts to cover all possible questions, the paper may contain some questions which are not covered in this book and can be answered only if the candidate has a thorough knowledge of the topics covered in the syllabus. For a thorough and elaborate knowledge of the subject, candidates are advised to read the following books published by Atlantic Publishers and Distributors (P) Ltd., viz. (i) *How to Become a Good Journalist,* Raza Elahi; (ii) *Trends in Networking and Communication,* Ed. Girish Kumar Srivastava and Charul Bhatnagar; (iii) *Handbook of Communication Models, Perspectives, Strategies,* Uma Narula; (iv) *Dynamics of Mass Communication: Theory and Practice*, Uma Narula; (v) *The Art and Science of Cinema,* Anwar Huda; (vi) *Advertising on the Internet: Let Your Fingers Do the Talking,* Godfrey Harris; and (vii) *Communication Models,* Uma Narula.

Atlantic Research Division

Contents

1

Communication and Journalism

1. Find the odd one out of the following:
   (a) Cable TV (b) Television
   (c) Radio (d) Newspaper
2. Find the odd one out of the following:
   (a) Perceptual variations
   (b) Lack of command
   (c) Personal emotions
   (d) Biases
3. By whom was the cultivation theory developed?
   (a) George Herbner (b) John Milton
   (c) John Done (d) Henry
4. Find the odd one out of the following:
   (a) Audio communication
   (b) Aural communication
   (c) Verbal communication
   (d) Visual communication
5. Find the odd one out of the following:
   (a) Informal communication
   (b) Formal communication
   (c) Grapevine
   (d) Gossip
6. Find the odd one out of the following:
   (a) Problem due to linguistic difference
   (b) Semantics
   (c) Barriers
   (d) Noise
7. When was the uses and gratification first introduced and by whom?
   (a) Kaif in 1955
   (b) Henary in 1950
   (c) Ehity Katz in 1959
   (d) John Hemilton in 1960
8. Which is the probability technique used in survey research?
   (a) Cluster sampling
   (b) Simple random sampling
   (c) Stratified random sampling
   (d) All of the above.
9. The non-probability technique used in survey research is
   (a) quota sample
   (b) purposive sample
   (c) accidental sample
   (d) All of the above.
10. Multi-stage sampling is also known as
    (a) stratified sampling
    (b) purposive sampling
    (c) quota sampling
    (d) cluster sampling
11. When was the first media dependency theory described?
    (a) In 1960 (b) In 1950
    (c) In 1976 (d) In 1956
12. Which sampling involves picking up of cases that are judged to be 'typical' of the population?
    (a) Purposive sampling
    (b) Quota sampling
    (c) Accidental sampling
    (d) Cluster sampling.

13. To choose the news items for the newspaper and to correct the language, spelling and remove all the unimportant sentences are the functions of
    (a) reporter
    (b) editor
    (c) writer
    (d) None of the above
14. Independent variable and dependent variable are variables of which method available to a communication researcher?
    (a) Survey Method
    (b) Content Analysis Method
    (c) Historical Method
    (d) Experimental Method.
15. ABC means
    (a) Advance Business Circulation
    (b) Advance Business Certificate
    (c) Audit Bureau of Circulation
    (d) Audit Bureau of Certificate
16. To keep only the essential parts in the picture is called
    (a) cropping
    (b) editing
    (c) edging
    (d) None of the above
17. Which composing method is also called as cold type setting?
    (a) Machine setting
    (b) Phototype setting
    (c) Hand setting
    (d) None of the above.
18. Headlines are generally given by
    (a) photographers (b) reporters
    (c) editors (d) page designers
19. A logo is an identify mark of
    (a) Person (b) Seller
    (c) Product (d) Company
20. What should be avoided while writing the masthead?
    (a) Writing in small size
    (b) Writing in a fixed place on the front page every day
    (c) Writing in distinctive bold point
    (d) All of the above.
21. Using of all elements in the population and taking a lottery to select the desired number of elements from the totality is
    (a) Cluster Sampling
    (b) Simple Random Sampling
    (c) Stratified Random Sampling
    (d) None of the above.
22. A letter written to the editor of a newspaper in response to a news item for giving one's own side of the story is
    (a) A confession (b) A reminder
    (c) A rebuke (d) A rejoinder
23. Points included in the coverage of any game are
    (a) names of players
    (b) crucial moments of the game
    (c) final score
    (d) All of the above.
24. Which of these news values are not highlighted in sports news story?
    (a) Progress in terms of statistics
    (b) Human interest
    (c) Prominence of the sports event
    (d) None of the above.
25. TRP stands for
    (a) Physical Training Institute
    (b) Physical Training Inspector
    (c) Trade Restricted Practice
    (d) Trade Recall Percentage
26. Which media would be ideal to attract the attention of children to sell chocolates to them?
    (a) TV (advertisements)
    (b) Leaflets
    (c) Radio
    (d) Newspapers.

27. What is the meaning of circulation in the parlance of the print media?
(a) Number of editions
(b) Number of copies printed
(c) Number of copies sold
(d) None of the above.

28. A journalist need not be __________ while covering an event.
(a) inquisitive (b) domineering
(c) impartial (d) meticulous

29. Which one of the following do not provide entertainment to the targeted audience?
(a) Leaflets
(b) Newspaper features
(c) TV programmes
(d) Magazines.

30. Who presented the Mathematical model of communication?
(a) Shannon and Weaver
(b) David Becham and D.J. Read
(c) Teg Blues and Tom Morri
(d) Weaver and Charles Hugg

31. What is average frequency?
(a) Total exposures in a given time period
(b) Total Exposures÷Audience Reach
(c) Audience Reach÷Total Exposures
(d) None of the above.

32. What is the job of development reporter?
(a) To inform readers, listeners and viewers about various plans.
(b) To help in creating awareness about the developmental issues.
(c) To create an atmosphere of understanding the objectives of the schemes.
(d) All of the above.

33. What do you understand by GRPs?
(a) The number of points earned by an advertising campaign.
(b) The number of readers reading an advertisement.
(c) The number of advertising insertions in one campaign.
(d) All of the above.

34. Identify the true statement.
(a) Journalist must be allowed to visit such areas as are deemed sensitive from the viewpoint of nation's defence.
(b) Communication between a person and a group is called Dyadic communication.
(c) TV is a visual media.
(d) Radio is an audio media.

35. What is Print Run?
(a) The number of copies sold by one particular retailer.
(b) Print Run + Complementary Copies.
(c) Print Run – Complementary Copies.
(d) The number of copies produced under a print order.

36. In downward communication, messages
(a) flow from the top to the bottom of the organization structure.
(b) are meant to be exchanged between the members of the top brass.
(c) flow from the bottom to the top of the organization structure.
(d) None of the above.

37. An interview is a type of
(a) mass communication
(b) dyadic communication
(c) multiadic communication
(d) None of the above.

38. Digital Audio Broadcasting (DAB) arose out of a European Project called
(a) Eureka-Eureka (b) Eureka 147
(c) Forbes 147 (d) Eureka Forbes

39. Who developed the first paper for the mankind?
(a) The Mayans (b) The Aryans
(c) The Sumerians (d) The Chinese

40. What are net sales in the parlance of book publishing?
   (a) The number of books or magazines available for sales.
   (b) The number of books or magazines sold by one retailer or bookshop.
   (c) The number of books or magazines printed by a publisher at one time.
   (d) None of the above.

41. Which of the following is not a part of seven C's of communication?
   (a) Clarity (b) Courtesy
   (c) Content (d) Consideration

42. The term "agenda setting" was introduced in
   (a) 1982 (b) 1976
   (c) 1972 (d) 1975

43. The art of listening can help a person become a good communicator. How is that so?
   (a) Patient listeners quite often win the hearts of speakers.
   (b) Good listeners can become good executives and leaders.
   (c) He would become more patient if he listens to the other person.
   (d) If he listens to the other person carefully, he would be able to understand his viewpoint with ease and thus be able to send his message to others accordingly.

44. Who was not a part of the team that developed the transistor?
   (a) Julius Lilienfeld
   (b) William Shockley
   (c) Walter Brattain
   (d) John Bardeen.

45. Find out the name of the Rishi who always carried 'Veena' with him.
   (a) Narada (b) Durvasa
   (c) Shukracharya (d) Kanwa

46. Who invented the TV?
   (a) Chester Carlson
   (b) C. Francis Jenkins
   (c) Alexander Graham Bell
   (d) John Logie Baird.

47. Which of the following is not a traditional media?
   (a) Music (b) TV
   (c) Painting (d) Literature

48. Which of the following is not a modern media?
   (a) Sculpture (b) Cinema
   (c) Radio (d) The Press

49. Which of the following is not a responsibility of the media?
   (a) Passing remarks on the personal lives of film stars.
   (b) Dissemination of the news.
   (c) Commenting on the contemporary socio-political scenario.
   (d) All of the above.

50. Silence is also a form of
   (a) Communication (b) Dissent
   (c) Protest (d) Rebellion

51. Which of the following statements is true for journals?
   (a) They feature all types of news, views, and entertaining events.
   (b) They are not prepared under the guidance of expert editors, writers and researchers but by journalists and freelance writers from the open market.
   (c) They are not a part of the print media.
   (d) They concentrate on industry-specific, stream-specific or trade-specific issues, which are defined before hand.

52. Cinema is a/an
   (a) audio media
   (b) print media

(c) visual media
(d) audiovisual media

53. The MMS is a/an
(a) audio media
(b) visual media
(c) audiovisual media
(d) None of the above.

54. Which of these news values are not highlighted in sports news story?
(a) Human interest
(b) Prominence of the sports event
(c) Progress in terms of statistics
(d) None of these

55. The Conditional Access System (CAS) allows the viewers to
(a) interact with TV channels through the set-up boxes.
(b) cut down the costs of televsion viewing.
(c) select TV channels of their choice.
(d) None of the above.

56. Dyadic communication is the transfer of messages from a person
(a) to a mass audience
(b) to another person and vice versa
(c) to a group of persons
(d) None of the above.

57. Spiral of silence model is associated with
(a) Donald Show (b) Mellombs
(c) Nacolle Neuman (d) None of these

58. Which of the following cannot be delivered to a mass audience through the currently used media vehicles?
(a) Products
(b) Information
(c) Music
(d) All of the above.

59. Which of the following is true for informal communication?
(a) It disseminates information at high speed.
(b) It enhances performances of people through the use of grapevine.
(c) It promotes harmony and resolves many problems.
(d) None of the above.

60. Which of the following would not give us city information?
(a) Seminar (b) PA system
(c) TV (d) Radio

61. Which organisation decides the rates of cellular phone services and land line service in India?
(a) The Telecom Regulatory Authority of India (TRAI).
(b) The VSNL.
(c) The Department of Telematics (DoT).
(d) The Ministry of Industry, Government of India.

62. Why is the repetition of a message necessary?
(a) The audience needs to be informed about the product, scenario or concept time and again, lest they should forget it altogether.
(b) Costs come down as the messages are sent through the same vehicle, it is a commercial decision.
(c) Messages must be repeated, else what the advertising firms and TV/radio stations would sit idle.
(d) Repeated advertisements create an image of the media in the minds of the targeted audience.

63. What is a media brief?
(a) A checklist for media planners to help them prepare a media plan for a client organisation.
(b) A type of media vehicle.
(c) Expenditure done on a media campaign that has been executed.
(d) None of the above.

64. A media brief includes
(a) seasonality/time of introduction of the product/service.
(b) broad set of objectives.
(c) geography/location of the targeted markets.
(d) All of the above.

65. Which of the following is not a part of seven C's of communication?
(a) Curiosity (b) Clarity
(c) Channels (d) Content

66. What is a house journal?
(a) It is a private in house magazine that is circulated among the members of a firm, industry, or trade, and it conveys the views of the management or other people working in that firm/industry/trade.
(b) It is a low-cost edition of a top-selling magazine that is sold to specific market niches at a low cost.
(c) It is a magazine of a publishing group that is given free of cost to some readers.
(d) None of the above.

67. What is a media plan?
(a) A costing sheet for a media brief.
(b) Another name for an advertising campaign.
(c) A blueprint of execution schedule of an advertising campaign.
(d) An annexure of a media brief.

68. TRPs of TV serials are calculated on a
(a) daily basis
(b) weekly basis
(c) fornightly basis
(d) monthly basis.

69. Which of the following is not a responsibility of the media?
(a) Passing remarks on the personal lives of film stars
(b) Dissemination of the news
(c) Commenting on the contemporary socio-political scenario
(d) All the above

70. Reach and frequency of an advertisement is calculated by studying the targeted audience over a period of
(a) 4 months (b) 6 weeks
(c) 4 weeks (d) 3 months

71. What is the difference between the WAP and Bluetooth?
(a) The WAP is an analog technology whereas Bluetooth is a digital technology.
(b) The WAP is used by cellular phone users to surf through the Net whereas Bluetooth facilitates data exchange without wires and cables.
(c) The WAP is a wireless technology whereas Bluetooth is a wire-based technology.
(d) The WAP and Bluetooth are the same.

72. When was colour TV transmission started in India?
(a) In 1979 (b) In 1980
(c) In 1982 (d) In 1986

73. Which of the following is not a mass communication exercise?
(a) An Internet website use multimedia presentation techniques to promote RMCGS
(b) A radio announcer gives news in brief at 10.00 am on the FM channel
(c) A van moves about in a village and a PA system aboard the van tells the villagers about the risks of acquiring AIDS
(d) A salesman's talks to his client over telephone and asks for payment

74. What does the book review correspondent do?

(a) He interacts with the authors of various books but does not review books.
(b) He only screens the books and picks up the one that would be reviewed by another person.
(c) He organises the book review panel.
(d) He reviews the books that are given to him for this purpose.

75. Bar charts and histograms are often used to represent economic data. Which media are using them nowadays?
(a) Only magazines
(b) Only TV
(c) TV, newspaper, catalogues, and brochures
(d) All types of media.

76. SEBI stands for
(a) Securities and Exchange Board of India
(b) Software Export of India
(c) Services Evaluation Board of India
(d) South East Broadcast Incorporated

77. What is junk mail?
(a) In the parlance of TV viewing, it refers to the receipt of phone calls by a VJ.
(b) In the parlance of radio broadcast, it refers to the receipt of phone calls by a Radio Jockey.
(c) In the parlance of postal services, it refers to the receipt of sales letters and mailers.
(d) In the parlance of Internet operations, it refers to the receipt of pornographic and other socially irrelevant messages in an e-mail box.

78. Which media does not make the use of eyes and ears simultaneously?
(a) TV advertisements
(b) SMS
(c) MMS
(d) Cinema

79. When was the first TV station set up in India?
(a) August 1949; Kolkata
(b) November 1958; Mumbai
(c) September 1959; Delhi
(d) January 1963; Delhi.

80. Identify the true statement.
(a) The DD reaches 60 per cent of the Indian populace.
(b) The number of Internet connections is rising fast in our country.
(c) Retention of the message is better in the print media than in the audio-visual media.
(d) Editors in the parlance of the print media are different from correspondents.

81. Who started *The Tribune*?
(a) Master Tara Singh
(b) Prem Bhatia
(c) Dyal Singh Majithia
(d) James Augustus Hicky

82. Mass communication
(a) is more effective than dyadic communication so far as reach is concerned.
(b) is an impersonal tool for delivering information to the masses.
(c) does not need technology-based media vehicles.
(d) is meant for delivering messages to the residents of a city.

83. Compared to girls, the mean length of sentences uttered by boys is
(a) Less (b) More
(c) Superior (d) Equal

84. We can use Internet for
(a) interacting with many net surfers through Internet Relay Chat (IRC).
(b) sending and receiving e-mail.

(c) sending SMS messages to many people at the same time through PC-to-phone messaging tools.
(d) All of the above.

85. Speech disorder refers to a serious defect in
(a) Articulation (b) Pronunciation
(c) Stammering (d) Cooing

86. Books are also mass communication tools, because
(a) they use state-of-the-art printing techniques and the presentations are better than those of the audio-visual method.
(b) they entertain people.
(c) they are subject-specific.
(d) they disseminate information and data among millions.

87. Live telecasts are covered by TV channels with the help of
(a) low-power transponders
(b) OB vans
(c) mobile TV vans
(d) None of the above.

88. The acquisition of language is highly
(a) a rough process.
(b) a complicated process.
(c) a simple process.
(d) a complex process.

89. A journalist should not have which of the following traits?
(a) The wisdom to give the right direction to his journalistic pursuits.
(b) A drive for developing relations with powerful people to grind his own axe.
(c) An ability to contact those people who are not willing to talk to him.
(d) A keen sense of judgment to find out the real cause of an accident.

90. Who is a crime reporter?
(a) A journalist who writes news, views and articles about the crime scenario.
(b) A person who keeps in touch with the CBI and gives vital facts to the press about its operations.
(c) A person who gives information to the media about police operations.
(d) A journalist who covers the news related to criminal courts.

91. In an Internet network,
(a) there cannot be more than three nodes connected to the main computer system.
(b) only one Internet connection is needed and other nodes of the network can use it.
(c) connectivity is given by an ISP located in India.
(d) None of the above.

92. In the beginning of a child's life, crying is only a
(a) Stimulation (b) Response
(c) Reflex Action (d) Reflex Arc

93. What is the full form of CATV?
(a) Conductor for Antenna Television
(b) Conduit for Antenna Television
(c) Community Access Television
(d) Community Action Televised View

94. Which one of the following messages can be sent to the mass audience at very low cost?
(a) The news of expansion of the union ministry.
(b) Information about the screening of a new movie in city theatres.
(c) An advertisement of potato chips.
(d) A schedule of the polio campaign.

95. When a person says, "This is a beautiful car", his language is obviously serving

(a) Tact function
(b) Ecolic behaviour
(c) Autoclitic behaviour
(d) Textual behaviour

96. Which of the following is not a mass communication exercise?
(a) A salesman talks to his client over telephone and asks for payment.
(b) A van moves about in a village and a PA system aboard the van tells the villagers about the risks of acquiring AIDS.
(c) A radio announcer gives news in brief at 10:00 a.m. on the FM channel.
(d) An Internet website uses multimedia presentation techniques to promote its products.

97. Identify the true statement.
(a) Journalist must be allowed to visit such areas as are deemed sensitive from the viewpoint of a nation's defence.
(b) Communication between a person and a group is called dyadic communication.
(c) Radio is an audio media.
(d) TV is a visual media.

98. Osgood has developed a technique of deciphering meaning and of measuring its various aspects. This technique is known as
(a) Scale Discrimination Technique
(b) Cumulative Scaling Technique
(c) Disguised Technique
(d) Semantic Differential Technique (SDT)

99. Which of the following is not an advantage of TV?
(a) The audience remain glued to TV and hence, they do not do much physical work.
(b) The audience remain glued to TV and hence, they learn a lot about products/services/concepts/news that are telecast on the same.
(c) Live coverage is done by many TV channels.
(d) Information given by it is current and up-to-date.

100. According to Osgood, a connotative meaning is
(a) Unidimensional
(b) Tridimensional
(c) Multidimensional
(d) Bidimensional

101. Identify the true statement.
(a) Journals are general magazines with no industry-specific sets of information.
(b) Mark Tully never worked for the BBC.
(c) In a star network, all the modes are connected to a common centre or node.
(d) James Murdoch belongs to the Zee-Turner group.

102. A Russian psychologist held that children's speech is essentially a social phenomenon and that it may have nothing to do with thinking. Who is he?
(a) Koutilya (b) L.P. Pavlov
(c) Sechenov (d) Vigotsky

103. Identify the true statement.
(a) Editors in the parlance of the print media are different form correspondents.
(b) Retention of the message is better in the print media than in the audio-visual media.
(c) The number of Internet connections is dwindling in our country.
(d) The DD reaches less than 60 per cent of the Indian populace.

104. Special correspondents are invariably

(a) not keen to dabble into the fields of regional, national, and global politics.
(b) told to write on economy, industry and the basic sciences.
(c) highly educated journalists.
(d) well connected in the highest echelons of (political) power.

105. Chomsky's major contribution to cognitive psychology was his
(a) Theory of Pronunciation
(b) Theory of Syllables
(c) Theory of Recitation
(d) Theory of Grammar

106. Identify the true statement.
(a) The full form of CNN is California Network and News.
(b) *The National Herald* once belonged to the TOI group.
(c) A faulty telephone line is a barrier to communication.
(d) Semantics is the technique of forming new words and phrases.

107. The term Press normally does not include
(a) Newspapers
(b) Journals
(c) Magazines
(d) Internet websites

108. Who viewed that the major problem in understanding a language is to derive deep structure from the surface structure of the sentence?
(a) Skinner (1957)
(b) Chomsky (1959)
(c) Brown (1973)
(d) None of the above

109. Who was killed by militants in Pakistan?
(a) Pradeep Bhatia
(b) Shivani Bhatnagar
(c) Shivani Jajodia
(d) Daniel Pearl

110. *Sun* is a tabloid being published from
(a) Gothenburg (b) London
(c) San Francisco (d) Kolkata

111. A science correspondent should have an academic background in
(a) the social sciences
(b) journalism and feature writing
(c) an engineering stream
(d) the basic sciences

112. Dance is a very refined and artistic form of
(a) Verbal communication
(b) Non-verbal communication
(c) Language
(d) Both verbal and non-verbal communication

113. A group discussion is a form of
(a) mass communication
(b) dyadic communication
(c) multiadic communication
(d) None of the above.

114. The behaviouristic approach to language, "Circular Reflex Theory" was formulated by
(a) L.B. Whorf (b) LP. Pavlov
(c) J.B. Watson (d) E.B. Molt

115. In order to deliver the message to the right set of audiences
(a) the duration of the message is increased in one particular advertisement.
(b) the number of insertions per week (in a media vehicle) is increased.
(c) market segmentation is done.
(d) market testing is done.

116. "The media mould the tastes and preferences of the audience." Do You agree with this statement?
(a) No! People's tastes and static preferences are static.
(b) Yes! Fully.

(c) No! Most of the people support or nurture those tastes and preferences that have gelled in their minds since their childhood years.
(d) Partially! Some people are receptive to the messages while some others are not. Tastes and preferences do change but according to the socio-economic conditions of the audience. Complete transformation of tastes is a fallacy.

117. A behaviourist explained language in terms of verbal habit formation. Who is he?
(a) LP. Pavlov (b) EX. Thorndike
(c) C. Hull (d) J.B. Watson

118. What is Internet Addiction Disorder?
(a) It is the change in the behaviour of an Internet user due to consistent use of Internet based services; such a user becomes secluded, depressed and easily angry.
(b) It is a state of discontent that arises due to faulty transmission of e-mail massages.
(c) It is the change in the psyche of children because of their addiction to the Net.
(d) None of the above.

119. While taking abroad learning theory approach, Slobin believed that in the early acquisition of language
(a) imprinting plays a vital role.
(b) identification plays a vital role.
(c) imitation plays a leading role.
(d) introjection plays a vital role.

120. In which year, the first commercial company for the manufacture of radio equipment, The Wireless Telegraph & Signal Company Ltd. (England) was set up?
(a) 1899 (b) 1897
(c) 1889 (d) 1885

121. Who has revealed in his theory of intellectual development that language is acquired as a "mode of action"?
(a) R. Brown (b) H.H. Clark
(c) Jean Piaget (d) J.V. Irwin

122. WHA was an experimental station located in the University of
(a) Oxford (b) J.N.U.
(c) Harvard (d) Wisconsin

123. Which of the following does not fall in the category of higher frequencies?
(a) Gigahertz (1,000,000,000, cycles per second)
(b) Kilohertz (1000 cycles per second)
(c) Sinzahertz (50,000 cycles per second)
(d) Megahertz (1,000,000 cycles per second).

124. The mechanism of language acquisition reveals that a child learns to use language by observing the speech of others. This is known as
(a) Imitation
(b) Operant Conditioning
(c) Observational Learning
(d) None of the above

125. Which of the following is true for the communication model of Schramm?
(a) Decoding has been replaced
(b) Context of stimuli has been used
(c) Noise and feedback has been added
(d) Encoding has been replaced.

126. Which of the following is based on the fact that powerful media are modified by group relations?
(a) The reception model
(b) The publicity model
(c) The transmission model
(d) The expressive model.

127. According to Piaget, egocentrism is the hindrance to

(a) Conservation
(b) Motor development
(c) Emotional development
(d) Cognitive development

128. Interpersonal communication is
(a) communication with public.
(b) communication with crowd.
(c) communication with one's own mind.
(d) communication between two individuals.

129. Which of the following enhances performances of people through the use of grapevine?
(a) Informal communication
(b) Intrapersonal communication
(c) Formal information
(d) None of the above.

130. The very word 'language' came from the Latin word "Lingua" which means
(a) Teeth (b) Tongue
(c) Throat (d) Larynx

131. *Lokmat* is being published in three languages. Languages are
(a) Bengali, Hindi and Kannada
(b) English, Hindi and Bengali
(c) Marathi, English and Hindi
(d) Kannada, Gujarati and Marathi

132. Which of the following is a noise factor?
(a) Five senses
(b) Perceptual variations
(c) External element that hinders the process of communication
(d) All of the above.

133. Following crying, children make explosive sounds commonly known as
(a) Cluttering (b) Slurring
(c) Cooing (d) Lisping

134. Which of the following is in correct order?
(a) Sender → information → message coding → sender's background
(b) Information → sender → sender's background → message coding
(c) Massage coding → sender's background → sender → information
(d) None of the above.

135. Who called his mass communication theory as "cultivation of dominant image patterns"?
(a) George Gerbner
(b) Donald L. Shaw
(c) Maxwell McCombs
(d) None of the above.

136. Delayed speech is an indication of
(a) Retardation
(b) Communication
(c) Growth
(d) Development

137. Who classified his theories on the basis of world's national media systems?
(a) Melvin DeFleur
(b) George Gerbner
(c) Sandra Ball Rokeach
(d) Siebert and others

138. Communication needs a
(a) receiver (b) channel
(c) sender (d) All of the above

139. Stammering and stuttering are common among
(a) school going children.
(b) girls than boys.
(c) boys than girls.
(d) young children.

140. Communication helps in
(a) integration (b) persusasion
(c) entertainment (d) All of the above

141. Intrapersonal communication is
(a) where more than two persons are involved.

(b) person-to-person contact.
(c) talking to oneself.
(d) None of the above.

142. Which of the communication has an emotional appeal?
(a) Group communication
(b) Intrapersonal communication
(c) Interpersonal communication
(d) None of the above.

143. Audience and feedback are the two main components of
(a) interpersonal communication
(b) mass communication
(c) intrapersonal communication
(d) None of the above.

144. A very intricate, complex and refined tool of communication is
(a) Language (b) Gesture
(c) Posture (d) Smiling

145. Speaker-Speech-Audience are the elements of whose model of communication?
(a) Harold Lasswell
(b) Claude Shannon
(c) Wilbur Schramm
(d) Aristotle

146. Who introduced the concept of noise in model of communication?
(a) George Gerbner
(b) Claude Shannon and Warren Weaver
(c) Wilbur Schramm
(d) Charles E. Osgood

147. Which model refers to Gatekeeper' concept?
(a) Bruce Westley and MacLean's
(b) George Gerbner's
(c) Shannon and Weaver's
(d) Theodore Newcomb's

148. B.F. Skinner postulates that the acquisition of language behaviour is very much controlled by the occurrence of
(a) Cognition (b) Latent Learning
(c) Reinforcement (d) Place Learning

149. In the parlance of audio-visual media, what do you understand by the term reach?
(a) The product of frequency and the average household size.
(b) The number of people/households watching a soap during a given six-month period.
(c) The number of people/households exposed to an advertising campaign during a given time frame.
(d) None of the above.

150. A seller of an electronic device gives a small booklet to his customers at the time of sale of that device. What is the name of this booklet?
(a) Technical Booklet
(b) User's Manual
(c) Catalogue
(d) Brochure

151. In a particular stage of Piaget's cognitive development, the children reveal everything according to them. They think everything in terms of their own point of view and do not regard other's opinion as valid. What is this called?
(a) Egocentrism
(b) Centration
(c) Circular reaction
(d) Adaptation

152. Which stage of Interpersonal communication lowers our social guard a little?
(a) The Phatic Stage
(b) The Intermediate Stage
(c) The Intimate Stage
(d) The Personal Stage.

153. The 'Audit Bureau of Circulations' was established in

(a) 1951 (b) 1948
(c) 1939 (d) 1935

154. Readership surveys were firstly conducted by
(a) *The Hindu*
(b) *Reader's Digest*
(c) *The Times of India*
(d) All of the above

155. When was colour TV transmission started in India?
(a) In 1986 (b) In 1979
(c) In 1980 (d) In 1982

156. What is the name of that continent which first published the newspaper in the world?
(a) Australia (b) Asia
(c) Europe (d) Africa

157. On March 11, 1702, the first daily newspaper appeared in London called
(a) *Sun* (b) *Daily Courant*
(c) *Mirror* (d) *Morning Port*

158. Who is the eighteenth century's most important journalist?
(a) Anne Green
(b) John Milton
(c) Abraham Lincoln
(d) Daniel Defoe

159. Who started the *Father* and *Spectator*?
(a) James Ford
(b) John Milton
(c) Steele and Addison
(d) Henry Ford

160. A four year old child was asked—"What does the moon do?" "The moon is following me where I go"—came the answer from the child. This is an illustration of
(a) Egocentrism
(b) Reversibility
(c) Centration
(d) Transductive Reasoning

161. The age of satellite communication began in the year
(a) 1962 (b) 1964
(c) 1966 (d) 1974

162. Aurobindo was the editor of
(a) *Harijan* (b) *Pioneer*
(c) *Vande Mataram* (d) *Chronicle*

163. Which of the following is/are called as fourth estate?
(a) Print media
(b) Visual media
(c) Electronic media
(d) All of the above.

164. Which of the following ranks first in the total publications in India?
(a) Fortnightlies (b) Monthlies
(c) Dailies (d) Weeklies

165. In his theory, B.F. Skinner has postulated that our linguistic habits are determined by
(a) Biological factors
(b) Social factors
(c) Environmental or Reinforcing factors
(d) Psychological factors

166. Highest number of newspapers published in India are in
(a) Urdu (b) Bengali
(c) Hindi (d) English

167. In India, which state ranks first with the large number of newspapers publishing?
(a) Madhya Pradesh
(b) Delhi
(c) Maharashtra
(d) Uttar Pradesh

168. Largest circulated single edition daily newspaper in India is
(a) *Malayala Manorama*
(b) *The Hindustan Times*
(c) *The Times of India*
(d) *The Hindu*

169. Daily newspapers are published in all main languages except
(a) Kashmiri (b) Manipuri
(c) Nepali (d) Konkani

170. PIB stands for
(a) Public Information Bureau
(b) Press Information Bureau
(c) Personnel Information Bureau
(d) Press Institute of Bombay

171. Which of the following cities publishes maximum newspapers?
(a) Chennai (b) Kolkata
(c) Delhi (d) Mumbai

172. Knowledge tends to create more knowledge is the thesis behind
(a) the circular model
(b) the helical model
(c) the telephone model
(d) the spiral of silence model

173. The largest number of newspapers in English are published from
(a) Chennai (b) Kolkata
(c) Delhi (d) Mumbai

174. Largest circulated periodical in India is
(a) *Saras Salil*
(b) *Kumudham*
(c) *Malayala Manorma*
(d) *The Hindu Weekly Magazine*

175. Largest circulated periodical is in
(a) Malyalam (b) Tamil
(c) Hindi (d) English

176. Which of the following was considered as 'Gagging Act'?
(a) Vernacular Press Act
(b) Press (Emergency) Powers Act, 1931
(c) Indian Penal Code
(d) Indian Press Code

177. Majority of the newspapers in India are owned by
(a) societies
(b) joint stock companies
(c) trusts
(d) individuals

178. In which year was the Commercial Broadcasting Service of AIR was introduced?
(a) In 1967 (b) In 1968
(c) In 1966 (d) In 1965

179. Wireless telegraphy was developed by
(a) Heinrich Hertz
(b) James Watt
(c) Thomas Alva Edison
(d) Guglielmo Marconi

180. Who gave the following definition of mass communication—who says what in which channel to whom with what effect?
(a) Socrates
(b) Harold D. Lasswell
(c) Aristotle
(d) Harold J. Laskie

181. Who presented the 'Mathematical' model of communication?
(a) Weaver and Charles Hugg
(b) David Becham and D.J. Reed
(c) Teg Blues and Tom Morrison
(d) Shannon and Weaver

182. When and what was started by Balashastri Jambhekar?
(a) Anglo – Rajasthani in 1850
(b) Anglo – Gujarati in 1890
(c) Anglo – Assami in 1832
(d) Anglo – Marathi in 1932

183. Aristotlean model of communication does not have
(a) feedback (b) listeners
(c) speaker (d) speech

184. In which year the Supreme Court of India declared that 'the airwaves are the public property'?

(a) 1994 (b) 1995
(c) 1992 (d) 1993

185. The following English newspapers crossed hundred years except one. Which is the newspaper?
(a) *The Hindu*
(b) *The Statesman*
(c) *The Times of India*
(d) *Hindustan Times*

186. Select the correct sequence in descending order in respect of the circulation of Indian newspapers.
(a) Hindi, English, Malyalam
(b) English, Malyalam, Hindi
(c) English, Hindi, Malyalam
(d) Hindi, Malyalam, English

187. Among Indian languages which of the following publications ranks in top after Hindi?
(a) Malyalam (b) Urdu
(c) Marathi (d) Bengali

188. Oldest English daily of India is
(a) *Statesman*
(b) *The Times of India*
(c) *The Tribune*
(d) *The Hindu*

189. Who wrote *Mass Media and National Development*?
(a) Everett Rogers
(b) Johannes Gutenberg
(c) Daniel Lerner
(d) Wilbur Schramm

190. World's first newspaper *Acta Diurna* belonged to which country?
(a) Germany (b) Rome
(c) USA (d) France

191. Mahatma Gandhi was the editor of
(a) *Young India* (b) *Harijan*
(c) *Indian Opinion* (d) All of the above

192. Which of following follows the pattern of 'Tabloid Press'?
(a) *The Times of India*
(b) *Mid-Day*
(c) *The Hindu*
(d) *The Asian Age*

193. When was the moving transmission of TV started?
(a) 1985 (b) 1987
(c) 1990 (d) 1993

194. Which kind of the discussions give an insight into a person's interactive skills in a group, etc.?
(a) Group discussion
(b) Public discussion
(c) Personal discussion
(d) None of the above.

195. Who installed the first steam printing press?
(a) John Walter (b) John Dome
(c) Johan Milton (d) John Walter II

196. Which is most effective communication model that identifies the source message, content, channel, audience, etc.?
(a) Harold Lasswell's model
(b) Schramm's Interactive model
(c) Brown's Holographic model
(d) None of the above.

197. Which of the following is a later adaptor of new camp model and addresses itself particularly to various formal media related to mass communication?
(a) Westley and MacLean's model
(b) Theodore model
(c) George model
(d) None of the above.

198. Kill in media language means ______ .
(a) move (b) eliminate
(c) hold (d) shoot

199. A model which sees communication essentially as a process of transmission.

(a) Weaver's model
(b) Gerbner's model
(c) Theodore model
(d) None of the above

200. Who is the author of the play *Theory of Mass Communications*?
(a) Horace Meweomb
(b) William Stephenson
(c) W.L. Rivers
(d) George Gerbner

201. When was the normative theory of mass communication introduced first?
(a) In 1950 (b) In 1956
(c) In 1963 (d) In 1957

202. Who added development media theory and democratic media theory in 1980?
(a) Harold Lasswell
(b) Wilbur Schramm
(c) Marshall McLuhan
(d) Denis McQuail

203. *Aaj Lucknow* the Hindi daily is published by ________.
(a) Kothari Prakashan Ltd.
(b) Gomti Prakashan Ltd.
(c) Sandesh Ltd.
(d) Tutu Bose

204. In which parts the mass media is divided?
(a) Savvy and media
(b) Open and closed and media
(c) Print and electronic media
(d) None of the above.

205. According to whom mass exists only in the minds of elite?
(a) Michael Charlton
(b) Raymond Williams
(c) James Lull
(d) None of the above.

206. This newspaper was vernacular in origin but overnight it became English because of the enactment of Vernacular Press Act of 1878.
(a) *Bengalee*
(b) *Patrika*
(c) *Amrita Bazar Patrika*
(d) *Anand Bazar Patrika*

207. In which year was Indian Institute of Mass Communication established?
(a) 1978 (b) 1970
(c) 1965 (d) 1960

208. Select the wrong statement regarding newspaper circulation.
(a) Small : upto 25,000 copies
(b) Medium : between 25,001 and 75,000 copies
(c) Big : more than 75,000 copies
(d) None of the above

209. A Bromide paper is used in
(a) Camera (b) Laser Printing
(c) Photography (d) Both (b) and (c)

210. Which is the largest selling newspaper (Hindi daily) in Rajasthan and Madhya Pradesh?
(a) *Dainik Bhaskar*
(b) *Dainik Jagaran*
(c) *Rajasthan Patrika*
(d) *Navbharat Times*

211. As December 2010, how many people use Internet in India?
(a) 37 million
(b) 75 million
(c) over 100 million
(d) None of the above.

212. Which country publishes maximum number of dailies in the world?
(a) Japan (b) UK
(c) USA (d) India

213. A psychoanalyst has emphasized the importance of need gratifications in the development of language. Who is he?
(a) Sigmund Freud (b) Otto Rank
(c) Anna Freud (d) Ferenczi

214. Of the following television channels, all are owned by one particular company except one. Which is that?
(a) Gemini TV (b) Kairali TV
(c) Sun TV (d) Surya TV

215. In how many parts the theories of communication can be divided?
(a) One (b) Three
(c) Four (d) Five

216. Which of the following is the function of the 'Mass Media'?
(a) Advertising
(b) Entertainment
(c) Information
(d) All of the above.

217. What has made it possible to beam programme across frontiers to diffferent parts of the world?
(a) Only long wave
(b) Short wave and long wave broadcasing
(c) Short wave
(d) Medium wave

218. Who differentiated between 'hot and cold' messages?
(a) Wilbur Schramm
(b) Val Gielgud
(c) Marshall McLuhan
(d) Raymond Williams

219. In the early eighteenth century which of the following presented all the preconditions for the rapid growth of a newspaper growth?
(a) African colonies
(b) English colonies
(c) Indian colonies
(d) American colonies

220. Major source of revenue of newspaper is
(a) Subsidies
(b) Advertisements
(c) Selling newspaper
(d) None of the above

221. Which of the following was given in inscriptions on walls of temples and in copper plates and through victory coins and writings on rocks?
(a) Anything (b) Clothes
(c) Money (d) News

222. Robert Coles and Samuel Pecke were the most prominent publishers of
(a) *Boston Newsletter*
(b) *Coranto*
(c) *Diurnal*
(d) *The Times*

223. The National Film Archive of India (NFAI) located in
(a) New Delhi (b) Kolkata
(c) Mumbai (d) Pune

224. What is called the fourth stage of the newsbook?
(a) Coranto (b) Mercury
(c) Gazette (d) Diurnal

225. What is MIFF related to?
(a) Writing industry
(b) Film industry
(c) Drama industry
(d) None of the above.

226. The title of the cartoon column in *The Hindu* is
(a) Counterpoint
(b) You said it
(c) All in the game
(d) Business as usual

227. Who was the chairman of the Draft Akash Bharti Bill, 1978?
(a) V. Sharda Prasad
(b) I.D. Tiwari
(c) B.G. Verghese
(d) B.I. Ram Mohan Rao

228. Jhumpa Lahiri won Pulitzer prize under arts category for her novel
(a) *Wings of fire*
(b) *Insider*

(c) *Interpreter of Maladies*
(d) *The Namesake*

229. Daniel Pearl who was killed in Pakistan after the collapse of Taliban in Afghanisation was the reporter for
(a) *Wall Street Journal*
(b) *CNN*
(c) *New York Times*
(d) *BBC*

230. Identify the true statement.
(a) Leaflets and small documents can be printed on a mini offset press.
(b) A hoarding is an audio-visual medial.
(c) Mr. H.K. Dua had never worked for *The Hindustan Times*.
(d) Newspapers use poor quality newsprint because they are not to import high-quality newsprint.

231. Which one of the following is a mismatch?
(a) *The Indian Express* - Screen
(b) *The Times of India* - Filmfare
(c) *The Hindu* - Frontline
(d) *Hindustan Times* - Femina

232. Which one of the following is a mismatch?
(a) POGO–Fashion channel
(b) ESPN–Sports channel
(c) NDTV–News channel
(d) HBO–Movie channel

233. _______ is unmodulated—sound track made by recording silence with the microphone circuit open when commentary is recorded.
(a) Beta Card (b) Boom
(c) Buzz Track (d) Beta Came

234. Selective retention in communication implies
(a) retain only what one would like to
(b) retain the message in full
(c) retain only visuals
(d) retain only verbal messages

235. Identify the correct pair of Newspaper and its language:
(a) *Deshabimani*–Oriya
(b) *Eenadu*–Telugu
(c) *Navbharat Times*–Gujarati
(d) *Thanthi*–Marathi

236. Which paper is published by 'Sadhu Singh Hamdard' Trust?
(a) *Ajit Samachar*
(b) *Singh Hamdard Samachar*
(c) *Central Chronicle*
(d) *Hamdard Samachar*

237. Identify the correct pair
(a) Gujarat–Charkula
(b) Tamil Nadu–Villupattu
(c) Uttar Pradesh–Garba
(d) Karnataka–Lavani

238. Identify the correct sequence of the following media in order of their evolution:
(a) Radio, Television, Newspaper, Cinema
(b) Newspaper, Radio, Cinema, Television
(c) Newspaper, Cinema, Radio, Television
(d) Radio, Cinema, Newspaper, Television

239. Who enforced the Vernacular Press Act?
(a) Queen Victoria
(b) East India Company
(c) Lord Canning
(d) Lord Lytton

240. The statistics show that which of the following language newspapers, circulation is receding:
(a) Hindi (b) English
(c) Urdu (d) Marathi

241. In the second model of communication of Wilbur Schramm, the encoder was also the
(a) decoder (b) transmitter
(c) source (d) signal

242. The concept of print-on-demand (POD) is associated with
(a) newspapers (b) magazines
(c) housejournals (d) books

243. What is NFDC?
(a) National Film Development Corporation
(b) National Fashion of Designing Center
(c) National Federation of Development Council
(d) None of the above

244. The largest media house in the world is
(a) Sony
(b) Disney
(c) AOL Time Warner
(d) Viacom CBS

245. The annual Guillermo Cano World Press Freedom Prize by UNESCO in 2011 was given to
(a) Razl Rivero, Cuba
(b) Ahmad Zeidabadi, Iran
(c) May Chidiac, Lebanon
(d) Amira Hass, Israel

246. Babbling is considered as
(a) Explosive Speech
(b) Symbolic Speech
(c) Dramatic Speech
(d) Gestures

247. Which India newspaper is published from the United Kingdom?
(a) *The Hindu*
(b) *The Times of India*
(c) *The Statesman*
(d) *Asian Age*

248. Which single edition daily has the largest circulation in India?
(a) *Malayalam Manorama*
(b) *The Hindu*
(c) *Ananda Bazar Patrika*
(d) *Dina Malar*

249. Journalist James Gordon Bennett was associated with
(a) *New York Herald*
(b) *The Times*
(c) *New York Times*
(d) *The Times of India*

250. Which of the following statements is true for journals?
(a) They gives all types of news, views, and entertaining events.
(b) They are not prepared under the guidance of expert editors, writers and researchers but by journalists and freelance writers from the open market.
(c) They are not a part of the print media.
(d) They concentrate an industry-specific, stream-specific or trade-specific issues, which are defined before hand.

251. In theoretical assessment, communication is equated with
(a) Language (b) Invention
(c) Diffusion (d) Culture

252. 'Black Box' effect theory is related to
(a) Advertising
(b) Public Relations
(c) Communication
(d) Printing Technology

253. *The Tribune* was first established at
(a) Patiala (b) Amritsar
(c) Shimla (d) Lahore

254. Temporary blocking of words is called
(a) Stammering (b) Lisping
(c) Stuttering (d) R.R. Slurring

255. The combined circulation of newspapers, according to the latest report of the RNI is
(a) Less than 5 crores
(b) Between 5-10 crores
(c) Between 10-15 crores
(d) More than 15 crores

256. The mediaperson who has written the book *The Island of Blood* is
   (a) Barkha Dutt
   (b) Malini Parthasarathy
   (c) Kalpana Sharma
   (d) Anita Pratap

257. *West Side Plus* is the weekly English Newspaper published by ____________ .
   (a) The Tribune Trust
   (b) Ademan Ltd.
   (c) Bennett Coleman and Co. Ltd.
   (d) Indian Express Mumbai Ltd.

258. A set of standards for determining the structure of a true newspaper was formulated for the first time by
   (a) Benjamin Harris
   (b) Otto Groth
   (c) Thomas Emmel
   (d) Nathaniel Butler

259. One of the long-term and indirect influences of mass communication is
   (a) traditionalisation
   (b) socialisation
   (c) contemporisation
   (d) routinisation

260. Length of communication is a barrier to
   (a) reception (b) understanding
   (c) acceptance (d) transmission

261. Identify the true statement.
   (a) The programmed Ankhon Dekhi is sponsored by Doordarshan.
   (b) The world this week was hosted by Sriniwasan Jain when it was started during the nineties.
   (c) The government plans to send all children to school by 2015 AD.
   (d) Deepak Chourasia is a news reporter of the print media.

262. Lasswell's model of communication was further improved by
   (a) Wilbur Schramm
   (b) Elihu Katz
   (c) Braddock
   (d) David Berlo

263. It is expected that news breeds
   (a) entertainment (b) expectation
   (c) learning (d) news

264. An amount of information which reduces uncertainty by half is called
   (a) One bit (b) One gesture
   (c) One thought (d) One posture

265. Dow Jones is associated with the Indian newspaper
   (a) *Mint*
   (b) *Financial Express*
   (c) *Economic Times*
   (d) *Economic and Political Weekly*

266. Libertarianism was born during
   (a) the Age of Conflict
   (b) the Age of Reason
   (c) the Age of Darkness
   (d) the Age of Industrialisation

267. Identify the chronological order of the following:
   (a) photography, telegraphy, telephone, film
   (b) photography, film, telegraphy, telephone
   (c) photography, telegraphy, film, telephone
   (d) telegraphy, photography, telephone, film

268. Lower organisms use—
   (a) Language
   (b) Verbal means of communication
   (c) Non-verbal means of communication
   (d) Both verbal and non-verbal means of communication

269. The first person to use the term 'gate keeper' in communication was

(a) Kurt Lewin
(b) C.D. MacDougale
(c) Ralph Webb
(d) J.E. Walsh

270. The concept of positivism is found in
(a) transnational communication
(b) developmental communication
(c) intercultural communication
(d) organisational communication

271. Identify the true statement.
(a) Reality TV is owned by Zee-Turner.
(b) A four-colour advertisement is cheaper to produce than half-tone advertisements.
(c) The mass audience can be contracted through multiadic communication modes.
(d) Style and content are the two vital elements of any media.

272. The history of authoritarian theory can be traced to
(a) Aristotle (b) Stuart Mill
(c) Adam Smith (d) Plato

273. Sky News is owned by
(a) L.N.Mittal (b) Ted Turner
(c) Rupert Murdoch (d) John Kelly

274. The CPU consists of
(a) Control unit
(b) Arithmetic and logic unit
(c) Memory
(d) All the above

275. Identify the correct sequence of the contributions of the following communication scholars
(a) Wilbur Schramm, Harold Lasswell, Shannon and Weaver, E.M. Rogers.
(b) Shannon and Weaver, E.M. Rogers, Wilbur Schramm and Harold Lasswell.
(c) Harold Lasswell, E.M. Rogers, Wilbur Schramm, Shannon and Weaver.
(d) Harold Lasswell, Shannon and Weaver, Wilbur Schramm, E.M. Rogers.

276. In the context of communication, congruity refers to
(a) truth (b) agreement
(c) false (d) imbalance

277. The language of mathematics is exclusively
(a) Non-verbal (b) Verbal
(c) Connotative (d) Denotative

278. The model which helps to locate the attribution and construction of meaning with the receiver
(a) expressive (b) ritual
(c) publicity (d) reception

279. The Indian media group which has tied up with the Reuters
(a) *The Tribune*
(b) *Anand Bazar Patrika*
(c) *Malayala Manorama*
(d) *The Times of India*

280. The interaction which involves transmitting and receiving ideas, information, directives, etc. is known as
(a) Sociability
(b) Socialization Process
(c) Gregariousness
(d) Communication Behaviour

281. The well-known sequence 'Odessa Steps' appears in
(a) *Mother*
(b) *War and Peace*
(c) *Battleship Potemkin*
(d) *Diary of a Country Priest*

282. Find the correct order of communication models in their chronological years
(a) FEX Dance - Lasswell - Osgood and Schramm - Shannon and Weaver.
(b) Shannon and Weaver - Lasswell - Osgood and Schramm - FEX Dance.

(c) Shannon and Weaver - Osgood and Schramm - Lasswell - FEX Dance.
(d) Lasswell - Shannon and Weaver - Osgood and Schramm - FEX Dance.

283. Two step flow model of media influence was given by
(a) Mc Coomf
(b) J. Willson
(c) Katz and Lazassted
(d) Shaw

284. The element that distorts or disrupts a message being sent from a sender to a receiver is
(a) cognitive (b) medium
(c) noise (d) resonance

285. The process of controlling the flow of information is
(a) media event (b) media strategy
(c) frequenting (d) gatekeeping

286. Different studies on language development of children reveal that socio-economic status of children influences vocabulary size but not
(a) verbal development.
(b) emotional development.
(c) syntactic development.
(d) grammatical development.

287. The leading financial publication *Wall Street Journal* has been acquired by
(a) Bill Gates
(b) Rupert Murdoch
(c) Ted Turner
(d) Knight-Ridder

288. DNA is a joint venture of
(a) Zee TV and STAR TV
(b) Zee TV and *Dainik Bhaskar*
(c) Zcc TV and *Dainik Jagran*
(d) Zee TV and Doordarshan

289. Who among the following is a Celebrated Cartoonist?
(a) Bachi Karkaria (b) Abu Abraham
(c) Aravind Adiga (d) Sevanti Ninan

290. What is the spectrum width of Airtel in Delhi?
(a) 17.1 Mhz (b) 6.2 Mhz
(c) 9.8 Mhz (d) 10.0 Mhz

291. Identify the single most significant trend in Indian Newspaper Industry
(a) Better distribution
(b) Use of interesting type faces
(c) Dominance of language newspapers
(d) Changing editorial styles

292. The newspaper recently launched under the editorship of M.J. Akbar is
(a) *The India Observer*
(b) *The Sunday Guardian*
(c) *The India Mail*
(d) *The India Mirror*

293. The hypothesis which states that the structure of a language determines thought-processes and behaviour patterns and that it serves as a sort of mould for values and other motives and styles of thinking is known as
(a) Whorpian hypothesis
(b) Osgoodian hypothesis
(c) Chomsky hypothesis
(d) Centril hypothesis

294. In the semiotic theory of communication, any organising system of signs is referred to as a/an
(a) code (b) signal
(c) symbol (d) icon

295. Find out the correct sequence of Union Ministers of Information and Broadcasting.
(a) Sardar Patel - B.V. Keshar - Indira Gandhi - R.R. Diwakar.
(b) Sardar Patel - R.R. Diwakar - B.V. Keshar - Indira Gandhi.

(c) Indira Gandhi - Sardar Patel - R.R. Diwakar - B.V. Keshar.
(d) B.V. Keshar - R.R. Diwakar - Sardar Patel - Indira Gandhi.

296. Who stated in his theory that there are two major functions of language—"Mand" function and "Tact" function?
(a) Kurt Lewin (b) B.F. Skinner
(c) E.L. Thoradike (d) Clark H. Hull

297. The first Indian newspaper to have a readers' editor is
(a) *The Times of India*
(b) *The Hindu*
(c) *The Hindustan Times*
(d) *The Pioneer*

298. The first ever language newspaper in India was started in
(a) Bombay Presidency
(b) Madras Presidency
(c) Gujarat
(d) Bengal

299. The component of the CPU which is responsible for performing calculations is called
(a) Control Unit (b) A.L.U.
(c) V.D.U. (d) None of the above

Directions: Questions 300 to 304 are of multiple statement type. Choose the correct answers from the code given below the statements.

300. Identify the true statements.
1. Nil feedback is also a feedback.
2. The receiver must have competence in the sender.
3. The action to be taken by the sender does not depend upon the response of receiver.
4. Communication should not concentrate on the present needs of the receiver.

Codes:
(a) 1 and 2 (b) 1 and 3
(c) 2 and 4 (d) 3 and 4

301. According to Leland Brown, the advantages of grapevine communication are
1. It saves time
2. It gets immediate responses
3. It provides useful feedback for decision-making
4. It generates ideas and suggestions that may prove helpful.

Codes:
(a) 1, 2 and 3 (b) 1, 2 and 4
(c) 2, 3 and 4 (d) 1, 2, 3 and 4

302. According to DeFleur and Ball-Rokeach, the communication levels which are used in human communication are
1. Intra-personal communication
2. Dyadic communication
3. Multiyadic communication
4. Group communication

Codes:
(a) 1 and 2 (b) 1, 2 and 3
(c) 2, 3 and 4 (d) 1, 2, 3 and 4

303. Dyadic or interpersonal communication is
1. highly personal
2. result-oriented in most of the cases
3. designed to have 100 per cent reach

Codes:
(a) 1 only (b) 2 only
(c) 1 and 2 (d) 1, 2 and 3

304. Institutional communication is
1. mainly motivated by profit
2. designed to analyse moral values
3. affected by politicians only
4. the only way of educational training

Codes:
(a) 1 only (b) 4 only
(c) 2 and 4 (d) 2 and 4

Directions: Questions 305 to 328 are of matching type. Match List-I with List-II and select the correct answer using the codes given below the lists.

305. **List-I** / **List-II**

(A) Noise — 1. Problems due to differences
(B) Barriers — 2. Problems due to disturbance
(C) Semantics — 3. The science of meanings
(D) Information — 4. It is encoded

Codes:	A	B	C	D
(a)	2	1	3	4
(b)	2	1	4	3
(c)	4	3	2	1
(d)	1	2	3	4

306. **List-I** / **List-II**

(A) Intrapersonal — 1. Dyadic
(B) Interpersonal — 2. Multiadic
(C) Intragroup — 3. Association
(D) Intergroup — 4. Within the mind

Codes:	A	B	C	D
(a)	2	3	4	1
(b)	1	3	2	4
(c)	1	2	3	4
(d)	4	1	2	3

307. **List-I** / **List-II**

(A) Print media — 1. Books
(B) Broadcast media — 2. TV
(C) Telecommunication — 3. Telephone

Codes:	A	B	C
(a)	3	2	1
(b)	1	2	3
(c)	2	3	1

308. **List-I**

(A) Transmission model
(B) Expressive model
(C) Publicity model
(D) Reception model

List-II

1. Fundamentalist perspective
2. Ritual model
3. Display and Attention model
4. Semiology and discourse analysis

Codes:	A	B	C	D
(a)	4	2	3	1
(b)	1	2	3	4
(c)	1	3	4	2
(d)	1	3	2	4

309. **List-I (Communications)**

(A) The process of meaningful interactions
(B) A process of transmitting ideas
(C) A field of knowledge
(D) The exchange of information and the transmission of meaning

List-II (Thinkers)

1. Katz and Kahn
2. Kelly
3. Brown
4. McFarland

Codes:	A	B	C	D
(a)	3	2	1	4
(b)	4	3	2	1
(c)	1	2	3	4
(d)	2	1	4	3

310. **List-I** / **List-II**

(A) Biases — 1. Personal barrier
(B) Cue meanings — 2. Semantic barrier
(C) Class conflict — 3. Organization structure barrier
(D) Space — 4. Technical Barrier

Codes:	A	B	C	D
(a)	1	2	3	4
(b)	4	3	2	1
(c)	2	3	1	4
(d)	3	2	4	1

311. **List-I (Satellite)** / **List-II (Countries Covered)**

(A) 2E (wide beam) — 1. India
(B) 2C (Expanded beam) — 2. Parts of Russia

(C) PAS-4/PAS-10 3. Parts of Europe
(D) 2DT/Thaicom-3 4. India and neighbouring countries

Codes:	A	B	C	D
(a)	4	3	2	1
(b)	3	4	1	2
(c)	2	3	4	1
(d)	1	2	3	4

312. List-I / List-II

(A) Audio media 1. Sculptures
(B) Visual media 2. Magazines
(C) Print media 3. TV
(D) Traditional media 4. Radio

Codes:	A	B	C	D
(a)	4	3	2	1
(b)	2	3	4	1
(c)	1	2	3	4
(d)	3	4	2	1

313. **List-I (Books)**

(A) *Decline of the West*
(B) *Social and Cultural Dynamics*
(C) *Future Shock*
(D) *Mind and Society*

List-II (Authors)

1. VilfredoPareto
2. Oswald Spengler
3. Pitirim Sorokin
4. Alvin Toffler

Codes:	A	B	C	D
(a)	2	3	4	1
(b)	2	3	1	4
(c)	1	2	3	4
(d)	3	2	1	4

314. List-I (Specific Subjects) / List-II (Magazines)

A. Women 1. *Telematics*
B. Children 2. *Celebrity*
C. Detective 3. *Dakshata*
D. Computers 4. *Target*

Codes:	A	B	C	D
(a)	4	1	3	2
(b)	3	1	2	4
(c)	3	2	1	7
(d)	2	4	3	1

315. **List-I (Newspapers)**

(A) *Malayalam Manorama*
(B) *Sandesh*
(C) *The Telegraph*
(D) *The Tribune*

List-II (States)

1. Kolkata
2. Chandigarh
3. Gujarat
4. Kerala

Codes:	A	B	C	D
(a)	2	3	1	4
(b)	3	2	1	4
(c)	4	3	1	2
(d)	4	2	1	3

316. **List-I (Directors)**

(A) Anil Sharma
(B) Ananth Narayan Mahadevan
(C) Rituparno Ghosh
(D) Sanjay Gupta

List-II (Movies)

1. *Raincoat*
2. *Ab tumhare Hawale waten Sathiyo*
3. *Dil Mange More*
4. *Musafir*

Codes:	A	B	C	D
(a)	2	3	1	4
(b)	3	4	2	1
(c)	2	3	4	1
(d)	3	1	2	4

317. List-I (Newspapers) / List-II (States)

(A) *Divya Bhaskar* 1. Maharashtra
(B) *Lokmat* 2. Gujarat

(C) *Dinamani* 3. Karnataka
(D) *Prajavani* 4. Tamil Nadu

Codes:	A	B	C	D
(a)	2	1	4	3
(b)	3	1	2	4
(c)	2	3	1	4
(d)	4	2	3	1

318. **List-I (Producers)** **List-II (Movies)**
(A) Karanjohar 1. *Black*
(B) Sajid Nadiadwala 2. *Kal Ho Naa Ho*
(C) Sanjay Leela Bhansali 3. *Mujhse Shaadi Karogi*
(D) Boney Kapoor 4. *Bewafee*

Codes:	A	B	C	D
(a)	2	3	1	4
(b)	3	4	2	1
(c)	2	3	4	1
(d)	3	1	2	4

319. **List-I (Personalities)** **List-II (Media)**
(A) Rajdeep Sardesai 1. *Times of India*
(B) Subhash Chandra 2. *ETV*
(C) Samir Jain 3. *CNN-IBN*
(D) Ramoji Rao 4. *Zee TV*

Codes:	A	B	C	D
(a)	1	3	4	2
(b)	4	1	3	2
(c)	3	4	1	2
(d)	1	3	2	4

320. **List-I (Models)** **List-II (Authors)**
(A) Circular (i) Elisabeth Neumann
(B) Helical (ii) Riley and Riley
(C) Ritual (iii) Frank Dance
(D) Spiral of Silence (iv) Wilbur Schramm

Codes:	A	B	C	D
(a)	3	2	1	4
(b)	4	3	2	1
(c)	1	2	4	3
(d)	2	4	3	1

321. **List-I (Editors)** **List-II (Publications)**
(A) Shekhar Bhatia 1. *India Today*
(B) Rahul Joshi 2. *Outlook*
(C) Vinod Mehta 3. *The Economic Times*
(D) Prabhu Chawla 4. *The Hindustan Times*

Codes:	A	B	C	D
(a)	4	3	2	1
(b)	3	2	1	4
(c)	2	1	4	3
(d)	1	2	3	4

322. **List-I (Authors)** **List-II (Concepts)**
(A) Daniel Bell 1. Austrian School
(B) J. Habermas 2. Third wave
(C) Alvin Toffler 3. Post-industrial society
(D) Joseph Schumpeter 4. Public sphere

Codes:	A	B	C	D
(a)	1	3	4	2
(b)	2	1	3	4
(c)	1	2	4	3
(d)	3	4	2	1

323. **List-I (Books)**
(A) *Warrior of the Fourth Estate*
(B) *Future Shock*
(C) *The Road Ahead*
(D) *The Passing of the Traditional Society*

List-II (Authors)
1. Bill Gates
2. B.G. Verghese
3. Daniel Lerner
4. Alvin Toffler

Codes:	A	B	C	D
(a)	3	4	1	2
(b)	2	1	4	3
(c)	2	4	1	3
(d)	4	3	2	1

324.

List-I (Books)	List-II (Authors)
(A) *India's Newspaper Revolution*	1. Walter Lippmann
(B) *Public Opinion*	2. Vanita Kohli
(C) *Small is Beautiful*	3. Thomas C. Friedman
(D) *Indian Media Business*	4. Robin Jeffrey
(E) *The World is Flat*	5. Schumacher

Codes:	A	B	C	D	E
(a)	3	2	1	4	5
(b)	2	4	5	1	3
(c)	5	4	2	1	3
(d)	4	1	5	2	3

325. **List-I (Communication model)**

(A) Sociological view of communication
(B) Spiral of Silence
(C) Agenda-Setting
(D) Dependency
(E) Selective gate-keeping

List-II (Author)

1. McCombs and Shaw
2. DeFleur
3. Riley and Riley
4. Galtung and Ruge
5. Noelle-Neumann

Codes:	A	B	C	D	E
(a)	3	5	1	2	4
(b)	4	1	5	2	3
(c)	1	3	4	5	2
(d)	3	1	5	4	2

326.

List-I (Communication Models)	List-II (Authors)
(A) Mathematical Model	1. Frank Dance
(B) Helical Model	2. E. Noelle-Neumann
(C) ABX Model	3. Shannon and Weaver
(D) Spiral of Silence	4. T. Newcomb

Codes:	A	B	C	D
(a)	4	3	2	1
(b)	3	1	4	2
(c)	2	4	1	3
(d)	1	2	3	4

327.

List-I	List-II
(A) Udaya TV	1. Bengali
(B) OTV	2. Telugu
(C) TV5	3. Kannada
(D) Star Anand	4. Odiya

Codes:	A	B	C	D
(a)	3	2	1	4
(b)	4	1	2	3
(c)	4	3	1	2
(d)	3	4	2	1

328.

List-I (Books)	List-II (Authors)
(A) *Development of Underdevelopment*	1. Daniel Bell
(B) *Communication Networks*	2. Manuel
(C) *Post-Industrial*	3. E.M. Rogers and D.L. Kincaid
(D) *The Rise of the Network Society*	4. Andre Gunder Frank

Codes:	A	B	C	D
(a)	2	1	4	3
(b)	3	4	2	1
(c)	4	3	1	2
(d)	1	2	3	4

Directions: Questions 329 to 342 consist of two statements, one labelled as 'Assertion' (A) and the other labelled as 'Reason' (R). You are to examine these two statements carefully and decide if the Assertion (A) and the Reason (R) are individually true and if so, whether the Reason is a correct explanation of the Assertion. Select your answer to these questions using the codes given below:

(a) Both (A) and (R) are true and (R) is the correct explanation of (A).
(b) Both (A) and (R) are true but (R) is not the correct explanation of (A).
(c) (A) is truth but (R) is false.
(d) (A) is false but (R) is true.

329. **Assertion (A):** Development communication is not a tool but a product.

Reason (R): Development communication is a goal-oriented concept.

330. **Assertion (A):** According to Gandhiji, media is secondary instrument in the field of spreading literacy in India.

Reason (R): He thought that the basic needs were more necessary than media advertisements for literacy among rural Indians.

331. **Assertion (A):** Children hate news.

Reason (R): They love cartoons, dance shows, and movies.

332. **Assertion (A):** Most of the people like to watch TV.

Reason (R): TV programmes provide entertainment to the targeted audience.

333. **Assertion (A):** English newspaper readers are of higher education and social status.

Reason (R): Because of their education they are well placed in society and keen to know about public affair.

334. **Assertion (A):** Communication is the basic survival need of human beings.

Reason (R): Communication builds relationships.

335. **Assertion (A):** The ratio between circulation and readership of newspapers is not a constant factor.

Reason (R): Circulation is always less than the readership.

336. **Assertion (A):** Communication has power value.

Reason (R): Those who possess power of communication try to control and those who do not, try to acquire it.

337. **Assertion (A):** Unlike mass communication, semiology prefers a microscopic approach.

Reason (R): In semiology, the emphasis is on deconstruction of texts with surgical precision.

338. **Assertion (A):** Authoritarian theory can justify advance censorship and punishment for deviation from rules laid down by political authorities.

Reason (R): The theory was likely to be observed in dictatorial regimes, under conditions of military rule of foreign occupation and even during states of extreme emergency in democratic societies.

339. **Assertion (A):** Relative to participant receivers, observers represent lesser independence with senders. They offer a distinctive perspective devoid of perpetual bias, cognitive load, relational engagement and conversational demands.

Reason (R): Sender participants do not possess greater ability to make discrimination than participant receivers who are occupied with conversational responsibilities.

340. **Assertion (A):** Newcomb's model implies that any communication system may be characterized by a balance of forces. And any change in any part of the system will lead to strain towards balance and symmetry.

Reason (R): Because imbalance or lack of symmetry is psychologically uncomfortable and generates internal pressure to restore balance.

341. **Assertion (A):** Participatory communication implies people's participation in production process from the stage of idea to reception of final message.

Reason (R): Messages created through participatory mode do not address the needs of the audience.

342. **Assertion (A):** The convergence model of communication removed biases of non-linear models of communication.

Reason (R): Because the convergence model was derived from the basic concepts of information theory, cybernetics and general systems theory.

ANSWERS

1. (d)	2. (b)	3. (a)	4. (d)	5. (b)	6. (b)
7. (c)	8. (d)	9. (d)	10. (d)	11. (c)	12. (a)
13. (b)	14. (d)	15. (c)	16. (a)	17. (b)	18. (c)
19. (d)	20. (a)	21. (b)	22. (d)	23. (d)	24. (d)
25. (c)	26. (a)	27. (c)	28. (b)	29. (a)	30. (a)
31. (b)	32. (d)	33. (c)	34. (d)	35. (d)	36. (a)
37. (b)	38. (b)	39. (d)	40. (c)	41. (c)	42. (b)
43. (d)	44. (a)	45. (a)	46. (d)	47. (b)	48. (a)
49. (a)	50. (a)	51. (d)	52. (d)	53. (c)	54. (d)
55. (c)	56. (b)	57. (c)	58. (a)	59. (b)	60. (a)
61. (a)	62. (a)	63. (a)	64. (d)	65. (a)	66. (a)
67. (c)	68. (b)	69. (a)	70. (c)	71. (b)	72. (c)
73. (d)	74. (d)	75. (c)	76. (a)	77. (d)	78. (b)
79. (c)	80. (d)	81. (c)	82. (b)	83. (a)	84. (d)
85. (b)	86. (d)	87. (b)	88. (b)	89. (b)	90. (a)
91. (b)	92. (c)	93. (c)	94. (a)	95. (a)	96. (a)
97. (b)	98. (d)	99. (a)	100. (c)	101. (c)	102. (d)
103. (a)	104. (d)	105. (d)	106. (c)	107. (d)	108. (b)
109. (d)	110. (b)	111. (d)	112. (b)	113. (c)	114. (d)
115. (c)	116. (d)	117. (d)	118. (a)	119. (c)	120. (b)
121. (c)	122. (d)	123. (c)	124. (c)	125. (c)	126. (c)
127. (d)	128. (c)	129. (a)	130. (b)	131. (c)	132. (c)
133. (c)	134. (b)	135. (a)	136. (a)	137. (d)	138. (d)
139. (c)	140. (d)	141. (c)	142. (c)	143. (b)	144. (a)
145. (d)	146. (b)	147. (a)	148. (c)	149. (c)	150. (b)
151. (a)	152. (d)	153. (b)	154. (d)	155. (d)	156. (c)

157. (b)	158. (d)	159. (c)	160. (a)	161. (a)	162. (c)
163. (d)	164. (d)	165. (c)	166. (c)	167. (d)	168. (d)
169. (a)	170. (b)	171. (c)	172. (c)	173. (a)	174. (c)
175. (d)	176. (a)	177. (d)	178. (a)	179. (b)	180. (d)
181. (a)	182. (d)	183. (d)	184. (b)	185. (a)	186. (b)
187. (a)	188. (c)	189. (b)	190. (b)	191. (d)	192. (b)
193. (a)	194. (a)	195. (d)	196. (a)	197. (b)	198. (b)
199. (c)	200. (b)	201. (d)	202. (c)	203. (b)	204. (b)
205. (c)	206. (d)	207. (d)	208. (a)	209. (d)	210. (c)
211. (a)	212. (b)	213. (d)	214. (b)	215. (d)	216. (c)
217. (c)	218. (d)	219. (d)	220. (b)	221. (c)	222. (b)
223. (d)	224. (b)	225. (c)	226. (c)	227. (c)	228. (a)
229. (d)	230. (a)	231. (a)	232. (a)	233. (c)	234. (b)
235. (b)	236. (a)	237. (c)	238. (b)	239. (d)	240. (a)
241. (d)	242. (c)	243. (a)	244. (b)	245. (d)	246. (c)
247. (c)	248. (a)	249. (a)	250. (d)	251. (c)	252. (d)
253. (d)	254. (a)	255. (d)	256. (a)	257. (c)	258. (d)
259. (a)	260. (d)	261. (a)	262. (d)	263. (a)	264. (a)
265. (b)	266. (b)	267. (d)	268. (c)	269. (a)	270. (c)
271. (a)	272. (d)	273. (c)	274. (d)	275. (d)	276. (b)
277. (d)	278. (d)	279. (d)	280. (d)	281. (b)	282. (d)
283. (c)	284. (c)	285. (d)	286. (d)	287. (b)	288. (b)
289. (b)	290. (d)	291. (d)	292. (b)	293. (a)	294. (a)
295. (b)	296. (b)	297. (b)	298. (d)	299. (b)	300. (a)
301. (d)	302. (d)	303. (d)	304. (a)	305. (a)	306. (d)
307. (b)	308. (b)	309. (b)	310. (a)	311. (d)	312. (a)
313. (a)	314. (d)	315. (c)	316. (a)	317. (a)	318. (a)
319. (c)	320. (b)	321. (a)	322. (d)	323. (c)	324. (d)
325. (a)	326. (b)	327. (d)	328. (c)	329. (d)	330. (a)
331. (b)	332. (a)	333. (c)	334. (b)	335. (b)	336. (a)
337. (c)	338. (a)	339. (a)	340. (a)	341. (c)	342. (b)

2

Media and the Society

1. In which parts the mass media is divided?
   (a) Libertarian media
   (b) Print and electronic media
   (c) Savvy media
   (d) None of these
2. The Kashmiri women participate in the Rauf dance to welcome
   (a) the snowfall.
   (b) a guest who has come from abroad.
   (c) a new arrival in the family.
   (d) the arrival of spring in the Kashmir valley.
3. Who started the life as a translator in Deccan Star?
   (a) Ranade
   (b) Karsondas Mulji
   (c) Bal Gangadhar Tilak
   (d) Desmukh
4. Asgari Bai was a popular
   (a) Kheyal singer
   (b) Dhrupad singer
   (c) Bharatnatyam dancer
   (d) Kathak dancer
5. Radio broadcasting commenced in India in
   (a) 1930 (b) 1936
   (c) 1934 (d) 1927
6. What is the difference between print media and broadcasting media?
   (a) Print media use hackneyed printing techniques but broadcast media always use latest telecasting and broadcasting techniques.
   (b) Print media are space-oriented but broadcast media are time-oriented.
   (c) Print media take care of all the issues but the broadcast media do not.
   (d) Print media are very expensive but the broadcast media are not.
7. Which of the following is not a public service broadcasting concept?
   (a) Impartiality and fairness
   (b) Editorial independence
   (c) Media diversity
   (d) Cultural equality and identity.
8. National Channel of All India Radio was inaugurated in
   (a) 1988 (b) 1991
   (c) 1955 (d) 1982
9. Which of the following is not an exponent of Odissi?
   (a) Sonal Mansingh
   (b) Birju Maharaj
   (c) Madhavi Mudgal
   (d) Sanyukta Panigrahi
10. Young India was later renamed as
    (a) Navjivan (b) Harijan
    (c) Kalyan (d) None of the above
11. The New World Information and Communication Order (NWICO), which has been mentioned in the ten clauses of the International Principles of Professional Ethics in Journalism (UNESCO) lays stress on

(a) the need for decolonisation and democratisation of information and communication.
(b) the need to set up news agencies like the NANAP and CANA.
(c) respect for the people of underprivileged classes of the West.
(d) None of the above.

12. Colour transmission was started by Doordarshan in
(a) 1984 (b) 1986
(c) 1976 (d) 1982

13. Who wrote Silent Spring?
(a) Dr. R.H. Richharia
(b) Rachel Carson
(c) Claude Alvares
(d) None of the above.

14. Which of the following theories believes that the mass media are being used as the stooges of the rich capitalists to exploit the weak poor masses?
(a) The New Normative Theory
(b) The Social Responsibility Theory
(c) The Information Society Theory
(d) The Maxist Theory of Media and Society.

15. Who founded the Indian Express?
(a) Ashok Jain
(b) Lala Jagat Narayan
(c) Arun Shourie
(d) Ramnath Goenka

16. Which of the following is not a social function of the media under the sub-head correlation?
(a) Socialising.
(b) Forging and maintaining commonality of values.
(c) Setting orders of priority and signalling relative status.
(d) Consensus building.

17. Given that traditional media have fallen into disuse, how would you revive their old glory?
(a) Forcibly teaching dance forms and music to little children so that they develop a habit to consume such media.
(b) Use modern and electronic media to execute a pull strategy and supplement this strategy with the USP of our old cultural values and ethics.
(c) Use of academic curricula in schools and colleges that essentially include the study of such media.
(d) None of the above.

18. "AIR" was called Akashwani in
(a) 1960 (b) 1972
(c) 1947 (d) 1927

19. What is the major problem of the Press in India?
(a) To check communal writings by the Press.
(b) To check political writings by the Press.
(c) To check invasion into individual's privacy by the Press.
(d) All of the above.

20. In which year was the world's first news agency founded?
(a) 1835 (b) 1846
(c) 1850 (d) 1856

21. In which writer's words the newspaper is historian reporter, analyst, communicator, salesmen and advocate?
(a) Indian writer (b) English writer
(c) American writer (d) African writer

22. In which year was the United Press Association founded?
(a) 1903 (b) 1907
(c) 1908 (d) 1909

23. In which year Internatinal News Service (INS) marged with United Press Associations?
(a) 1950 (b) 1954
(c) 1956 (d) 1958

24. Name the journal, which was composed by Karsadas Mulji in 1852.
(a) Stri Bodh (b) Kiran
(c) Satya Prakash (d) Marathi

25. Which news agency is a post-war successor to the Agence Havas?
(a) Agence France-Presse
(b) TASS
(c) Reuters
(d) Associated Press

26. When was the journal The Induprakash got published by Ranade?
(a) 1861 (b) 1950
(c) 1850 (d) 1870

27. The fundamental difference characterising class differences relates to the distinction between
(a) the propertied and the property-less.
(b) the elite and the commoners.
(c) the rentiers and the enterpreneurs.
(d) the manual workers and professionals.

28. Who wrote The Deccan Star?
(a) Raja Ram Mohan Roy
(b) Mulji
(c) Bal Gangadhar Tilak
(d) Wasudeo Balwant

29. The difference between the number of people coming into the area and those going out of that area is called
(a) net migration
(b) gross migration
(c) volume of migration
(d) natural migration

30. The reason for low levels of literacy among the rural women of India is
(a) shortage of schools in rural areas.
(b) low speed of spread of audio-visual tools of communication.
(c) social taboos and beliefs of the rural masses.
(d) lack of adequate communication tools.

31. Who was the great social reformer between 1884 and 1891?
(a) Ranade
(b) B. Behram Malabari
(c) Bal Gangadhar Tilak
(d) Mulji

32. A child watches a TV commercial and demands a chocolate or snack that is promoted by this commercial. What is the impact of this advertising campaign on the family, to which this child belongs?
(a) The eating habits of the child are spoiled and hence, the family suffers due to his demands for such types of costly snacks and chocolates.
(b) The family has to spend more on the chocolate or snacks and hence, its budget goes haywire.
(c) The child is impressed by the campaign but the family remains aloof to it.
(d) None of the above.

33. What are the features of Deccan Star?
(a) Misery (b) Political matter
(c) Obristian spirit (d) Socialisation

34. Quite often, women read an advertisement in a newspaper and rush to buy products advertised in that advertisement. What type of purchase are they doing in this context?
(a) Planned
(b) Impulsive
(c) Planned but slightly impulsive
(d) None of the above.

35. Dadabhai Naoroji's own monthly journal was published on?
(a) March 1, 1950 (b) May 10, 1921
(c) Feb. 1, 1982 (d) Feb. 10, 1890

36. Advertising can help in
(a) increasing the needs of a limited number of targeted audience.
(b) improving the economy of a small region.
(c) promoting only products and services.
(d) promoting products, services and concepts, which are devoted to social issues, environment and societal transformation.

37. Name the journal, which was composed by Dadabhai.
(a) The Passage to India
(b) The Voice of India
(c) The Spectator Club
(d) The Blinman

38. The government has used print, visual and audio-visual media to drive home the concept that girls are also a part of the family. What is the basic issue that the government is trying to address through such campaigns?
(a) Improvement in the quality of working life (QWL)
(b) Gender equality
(c) Human rights
(d) Societal growth.

39. Why did Malabari organised country-wide agitation?
(a) For keeping child unmarried
(b) For abolishing the child remarriage
(c) For starting the child remarriage
(d) None of the above

40. What is the impact of print media on the people?
(a) They have led to a new kind of revolution in which, the people have been motivated to buy only the products and services advertised by such media.
(b) They have made people more materialistic and ambitious, as the advertisements make them more demanding.
(c) They have made people knowledgeable, materialistic and industrious, as the news, views and advertisements targeting them and their specific need through have zeroed in appropriate features.
(d) None of the above.

41. Who helped the "Sarvjanik Sabha" of Poona to organize the conference of journalists working on language papers?
(a) Darsondas Mulji
(b) Behram Malabari
(c) Bal Gangadhar Tilak
(d) Ranade

42. Why TV is better than radio?
(a) The announcers of radio stations do not present their programmes well but TV announcers are more adept at doing so because they are 'visible'.
(b) TV has national networks and cable TV systems but radio does not.
(c) The TV sets carry a tag of prestige along with them but radio sets do not.
(d) TV is an audio-visual medium and hence, more effective but radio is only an audio medium and hence, does not get the desired responses from the audience.

43. What was the major effect of the mushroom growth of cable and satellite television advertising?
(a) They earned huge profits
(b) They popularized India
(c) They got many awards
(d) None of the above

44. Urban poverty has been reduced due to the advent of the media. Do you agree with this statement?

(a) Yes! The media gives them knowledge of various kinds. Hence, they become alert to the economic environment and try to reap rich benefits from it.
(b) Yes! Advertisements have made them ambitious of buying and using products and services.
(c) No! The media have given them a limited number of opportunities in urban areas.
(d) All of the above.

45. A media audience would be a participative community if we consider communication to be a
(a) mean for production.
(b) social good.
(c) merchandise.
(d) None of the above.

46. How the media change political loyality of people?
(a) The media give false news and views about the political parties and governments.
(b) The media support only those parties and governments from whom, they get moral, legal and financial support.
(c) Newspapers, TV channels and magazines give facts, views and news about political parties and governments, which are assimilated by the masses.
(d) All of the above.

47. "Media audience" is the masses that need to be indoctrinated if communication is the mean for
(a) Social service (b) Merchandise
(c) Propaganda (d) None of these

48. Doordarshan channels have nearly 95 per cent reach in India. But private TV channels have better viewership and impact on the audience. Why did the DD loose its sheen?
(a) Good quality (and affluent) sponsors are not available to the DD. But private channels have the support of various corporate groups.
(b) The government plans to telecast only traditional art forms, news, political events and a few (Friday) movies.
(c) Old programmes are being telecast. The announcers are old and lack creative thoughts in their presentations. Other TV channels are more glossy. The DD is using traditional music and simple studios to sell its software.
(d) Corporate firms like Zee, Sony and Star can spend a lot of money in promoting their respective channels. On the other hand, the DD is cash-strapped.

49. Who defined an audience as a "conventionalized crowd"?
(a) Philosophers (b) Staticians
(c) Psychologists (d) Sociologists

50. In South India, the chief exponents of Bharata Natyam were
(a) kings and their princes.
(b) people living in urban centres of the south.
(c) local tribal groups.
(d) devadasis.

51. Janet Cooke was awarded for
(a) Gandhi Peace Prize
(b) Bharat Ratna
(c) Pulitzer Prize
(d) Noble Prize

52. The themes of the Manipuri dance form are based on the
(a) rituals of tribal groups of Manipur.
(b) history of the entire north-eastern region.
(c) life of a great king of Manipur.
(d) life of Lord Krishna.

53. Which is the responsibility of the reporters?
(a) Responsibility towards research department
(b) Responsibility towards sources
(c) Responsibility towards reader and society
(d) All of the above

54. The folk dance, Kavadi, is devoted to
(a) Godess Sita (b) Goddess Kali
(c) Lord Murugan (d) Lord Ayyappa

55. Which of the following is not a type of Indian dances?
(a) Fusion dance (b) Classical dance
(c) Folk dance (d) Tribal dance

56. The total number of puranas are many, but praminent among them are
(a) 4 (b) 16
(c) 18 (d) 20

57. The example of eventuality that could be considered as a civil contempt of court is
(a) to publish certain particulars about the accused, during the pendency court proceedings against him.
(b) a news item casting aspersious by implication, on the character of a sitting judge of the court.
(c) failure of a defendant to comply with a court's order to pay a punitive sum of money towards a fine.
(d) Both (a) and (c).

58. It has been alleged that the media have helped increase western influences over the youth, children, and the masses at large. How can we protect the moral values of our society, given that we are also a part of the mad materialistic system that perpetuates this type of media influences?
(a) We can use the media to step up our campaigns for informing the masses about the relevance of our culture and values. The Western influences can go along with our media rhetoric.
(b) We can educate the masses, through the same media, about the magnanimity of our cultural and moral values and norms. We must contiue to impinge upon the minds of such audience so that they do not forget what we really are.
(c) We can stop harmful media altogether so that the masses remain cut off from their ill effects.
(d) We can tell the media to send only those messages to the audience that are in tune with our moral values; other messages can be carefully censored.

59. Gandhiji started "Harijan movement" in
(a) 1931 (b) 1932
(c) 1929 (d) 1930

60. In Yakshagana, a form of Indian folk theatre, the chief narrator is known as the
(a) Songadya (b) Konnagi
(c) Bhagavata (d) Sutradhar

61. Despite the efforts of the media, the Sati problem still remains alive in Rajasthan. What should be done to eliminate this dogma?
(a) The media must educate the masses to come out of the Dark Age.
(b) The media are not responsible for this type of evils. They should continue to keep the people informed about this practice.
(c) Societal transformation is not possible overnight, so enough time should be given to the media to transform the thoughts and attitudes of the people.
(d) None of the above.

62. Vividh Bharti in AIR was started in
    (a) 1982 (b) 1985
    (c) 1957 (d) 1967

63. Which is not the quality of a reporter?
    (a) A nose for news
    (b) Editing interviews for use
    (c) Team spirit
    (d) Outgoing nature

64. Who got the Upnishads translated into Persian?
    (a) Dara Shikoh
    (b) Bhadur Shah Zafar
    (c) Jahangir
    (d) Aurangzeb

65. A defamation is committed buy the following
    (a) gestures and gossip.
    (b) written words and cartoons.
    (c) spoken words and photographs.
    (d) All the above.

66. Kariyala, a folk drama of Himachal Pradesh, is known for its
    (a) humour and social criticism.
    (b) narration of wars of the ancient era.
    (c) tragic love themes.
    (d) praise of lord Rama.

67. The fundamental difference characterising class differences relates to the distinction between
    (a) elite and commoners.
    (b) the propertied and the propertyless.
    (c) the rentier and the enterpreneure.
    (d) the manual worker and professionals.

68. Mark out the Indian type of family
    (a) Consanguineous
    (b) Matrilineal
    (c) Polyandrous
    (d) Conjugal

69. Which of the following is most important in Gandhi's concept of state?
    (a) Body politic. (b) Society
    (c) Individual (d) Law

70. A corporation or a firm can file a legal case when its
    (a) property and business are affected.
    (b) individual members of the corporation are affected.
    (c) top management is affected.
    (d) None of the above

71. What is repugnant to the Gandhian State?
    (a) To submit to the bad laws
    (b) Not to accept the supremacy of state
    (c) To follow the laws
    (d) Not to follow the laws.

72. Leader was launched in 1909 in Allahabad by
    (a) Motilal Nehru (b) Gandhiji
    (c) Pt. M.M. Malviya (d) Pt. J.L. Nehru

73. The caste system was role-oriented. Which of the following statements you think is correct?
    (a) Society was divided into the role groups.
    (b) It gave an humble role to shudras.
    (c) The role of an individual depended on his merit.
    (d) The role of every group was fixed.

74. Reservation for Scheduled Castes is provided in proportion to their
    (a) populationty
    (b) low ritual positions
    (c) social backwardness
    (d) economic necessities

75. Exception in filing a case in the court on behalf of a defamed person can be made in the case of
    (a) Seliot and lunatic (b) Minor
    (c) Sick (d) All the above

76. The non-fraternal polyandry is in existence in the

(a) Nayars of Malabarty
(b) Toda of Nilgiri
(c) Kot of Kerala
(d) Khasis of Meghalaya

77. Adelphic or fraternal polyandry is in practice in the
(a) Santhals (b) Gangu tribe
(c) Nayars (d) Khasi tribe

78. The instance in which the comment cannot be deemed as a 'flair comments'
(a) when a judge is described as being incompetent.
(b) when improper motives are attributed to the judge of a case.
(c) when a judgement on a case is stated to be arbitrary.
(d) All of the above.

79. Who is a Dvija?
(a) One who has been initiated as a student, and has gone through the formal course of study.
(b) One born in the family of a Vaishya.
(c) One born in the family of Kshatriya.
(d) One born in the family of Shudra.

80. Legislative provision for intercaste-marriage in India was first provided by
(a) The Special Marriage Act, 1872
(b) The Gains of Learning Act, 1930
(c) The Hindu Marriage Act, 1955
(d) None of the above.

81. Adelphic or Fraternal polyandry is in practice in the
(a) Gangu tribe (b) Santhals
(c) Khasi tribe (d) Nayars

82. Levirate marriage is
(a) marriage with the brother's daughter.
(b) marriage with deceased husband's brother.
(c) marriage between cross cousins.
(d) marriage with the daughter of the sister.

83. Why are alcoholism, drug addiction, and tension common in industrial cities?
(a) Due to loss of emotional security
(b) Due to frustration
(c) Due to value conflicts
(d) All of the above.

84. The total number of Puranas is ____ and the total number of the Vedas is ____.
(a) 18, 19 (b) 18, 4
(c) 6, 18 (d) 18, 10

85. Which set of goods are exchanged under the Kula?
(a) Wheat and clothes
(b) Rice and fish
(c) Necklaces and armlets
(d) Salt and sheep

86. Which of the following statements about Sanskritisation is correct?
(a) It is an exogenous source of change.
(b) It is a process of positional change.
(c) It is a process of structural change.
(d) It started with the advent of British Rule in India.

87. What Gandhiji thought the most important for a state?
(a) Individual (b) Society
(c) Body politic (d) Law

88. The practice of Pratiloma and Anuloma marriage indicates that
(a) the inter-caste marriages were not completely unknown.
(b) marriage was not sacramental.
(c) the caste system was rigidly followed.
(d) inter-caste marriages were discouraged.

89. Superstition and everything else connected with it greatly influence the villager and he sticks to it. Why?
(a) Because he is illiterate and ignorant of his true heritage.
(b) In his helplessness, he draws confidence from it.

(c) Because he is orthodox.
(d) Because he is ignorant.

90. Which of the following is not an exponent of Odissi?
(a) Sonal Mansingh
(b) Birju Maharaj
(c) Madhavi Mudgal
(d) Sanyukta Panigrahi

91. Community projects
(a) are more official and less local and more formal than basic.
(l m at the involvement of the village ɔmmunity with the village development.
(c) are an attempt to bring about a social and economic transformation of village life through the efforts of the people themselves.
(d) aim at effecting the required changes in the social and economic fields.

92. Publication of court proceedings are restricted by
(a) Section 14 of the Official Secrets Act, 1923, empowers the court to hold the proceedings of a case or any part there of in camera.
(b) Section 228A of IPC which prohibits publications of the names of victims of certain sexual crimes.
(c) Section 33 of Special Marriage Act, 1954, requires the proceedings under the act to be held in camera if either party to the case whishes so, or if the court so directs.
(d) All of the above.

93. Who, mainly, encourage the dependency behaviour of children?
(a) Brothers (b) Fathers
(c) Parents (d) Mothers

94. Which factors among the following have not weakened the caste system?
(a) The policy of reservations
(b) The Constitution
(c) The quick means of transport
(d) Modernisation

95. Which of the following is not a public service concept?
(a) Impartiality and fairness
(b) Editorial independence
(c) Diversity
(d) Cultural quality and identity

96. 'Reporting' which deals with the subject matter where an attempt is being made to hide the truth from the people is
(a) Interpretative (b) Crime
(c) Investigative (d) Objective

97. The first stage of psychosexual development of children is known as
(a) Phallic stage (b) Anal stage
(c) Genital stage (d) Oral stage

98. What does 'a nose for news' mean?
(a) Publish crime reports
(b) Space for news
(c) Senses material for news
(d) None of the above.

99. In his psychoanalytic theory, Freud said that two psychological phenomena emerge during any stage of psychosexual development and these are
(a) Frustration and Regression
(b) Aggression and Regression
(c) Fixation and Frustration
(d) Fixation and Regression

100. Which of the following is not a part of traditional media of India?
(a) Radio broadcast
(b) Sculptures of Khajuraho
(c) Puppet theatre
(d) Folk dances

101. Which of the following theories believes that the mass media are being used as the

stages of the rich capitalists to export the weak poor masses?
(a) The New Normative Theory
(b) The Social Responsibility Theory
(c) The Information Society Theory
(d) The Maxist Theory of Media and Society

102. When excessive frustration occurs in any of the psychosexual stages, the libidinal energy may remain locked in the erogeneous zone from which the child obtains pleasure in that particular stage. This is known as
(a) Regression (b) Aggression
(c) Fixation (d) Projection

103. Who started the Saharanpur Gharana in Indian classical music?
(a) Khalifa Mohammad Zama
(b) Ustad Wazir Khan
(c) Tansen
(d) Nathan Khan

104. Which of the following is not a social function of the media under the sub-head correlation?
(a) Forging and maintaining commnality of values
(b) Socialising
(c) Consensus building
(d) Setting orders of priority and signalling relative status

105. To return to an earlier mode of obtaining satisfaction when frustrated or anxious is known as
(a) Projection (b) Regression
(c) Fixation (d) Aggression

106. Which of the following is not a type of Indian dance?
(a) Fusion dance (b) Classical dance
(c) Folk dance (d) Tribal dance

107. Which of the following statements about Sanskritisation is correct?
(a) It is an exogenous source of change.
(b) It is a process of positional change.
(c) It is a process of structural change.
(d) It started with the advent of British Rule in India.

108. Nowadays, in India, the migration trend is in favour of a/an
(a) urban family
(b) the Hindu undivided family (HUF)
(c) joint family
(d) independent family

109. In which year was the contempt of court Act enacted?
(a) 1972 (b) 1973
(c) 1971 (d) 1970

110. In his study of the three "twice-born" castes of Rajasthan, Carstairs has given some information about
(a) Child-rearing practices
(b) Prejudices
(c) Attitude
(d) Social learning

111. A reporter is responsible towards
(a) sources
(b) news organization
(c) society
(d) All of the above

112. Minturn and Lambert have studied the child-rearing practices in India as a part of a cross-cultural research and the study was conducted in the Rajput caste in a village of
(a) Bihar
(b) Rajasthan
(c) Himalaya Valley
(d) Uttar Pradesh

113. In Indian context, mass culture is
(a) very much traditional
(b) dynamic and progressive
(c) dominated by capitalism
(d) All of the above.

114. Which of the following is a work of Pareto?
(a) *Mind and Society*
(b) *Society: A Drama*
(c) *Frustration*
(d) *New World*

115. Whiting and Child label the early period of children as the
(a) period of indulgence.
(b) period of socialization.
(c) period of intelligence.
(d) period of social recognition.

116. Which of the following statements is not true?
(a) During Rigvedic period, women were not allowed to attend sabhas and samitis.
(b) The term 'Gawisthi' is used for war in Rigveda.
(c) A sabha was a council of elders.
(d) Rigveda is the oldest Vedic Text.

117. In 1946, the World Service of ______ was created.
(a) UPI (b) AFP
(c) Reuters (d) Associated Press

118. Which of the following is not a mode, according to Schramm, through which the media can help in national development?
(a) By helping in decision-making
(b) By providing food to the poor
(c) By teaching
(d) By acting as watchman

119. Child-rearing practices pertaining to feeding, weaving and toilet training are called
(a) Adlerian variables in socialization.
(b) Erikson's variables in socialization.
(c) Freudian variables in socialization.
(d) Jungian variables in socialization.

120. Which of the following is not true?
(a) Mass media can lessen the population growth.
(b) Mass media can raise aspirations.
(c) Mass media can focus attention.
(d) All of the above.

121. The book *Childhood and Society* was written by
(a) Erik Erikson (1963)
(b) Otto Rank (1910)
(c) Sigmund Freud (1912)
(d) Alfred Adler (1908)

122. Scientifically, the term radio means
(a) the method through which all signals could be conveyed and controlled simultaneously.
(b) conversion of radiation waves into mechanical strategy.
(c) the usage of radiation and detection of signal propagated through space as electromagnetic wave to communicate.
(d) None of the above.

123. According to Erikson's Ego Psychology, the first stage of psychosexual development begins with the child's encounter between his instincts and the demands of society. This is called
(a) Muscular-anal stage
(b) Young adulthood
(c) Latency stage
(d) Oral-sensory stage

124. Which of the following is a true statement?
(a) DAVP stressed the need to educate the girl child.
(b) DAVP was organised by WTO.
(c) DAVP issued advertisements in newspapers and on television.
(d) a and c both are true.

125. According to Piaget, preoperational period is sometimes referred to as

(a) Preconceptual stage
(b) Sensori-motor period
(c) Concrete operations
(d) Formal operations

126. Question to which a written answer is deemed to have been laid on the 'Table of the House' after the question hour is
(a) Starred (b) Short Notice
(c) Unstarred (d) Both (b) and (c)

127. According to whom, mass media are primarily moulders of society as well as reflectors of it?
(a) Harold Lasswell
(b) Denis McQuail
(c) George Gerbner
(d) Wilbur Schramm

128. Egocentrism is a major hinderance to
(a) the emotional development of children.
(b) the intellectual development of children.
(c) the cognitive development of children.
(d) the language development of children.

129. Ethical concepts change with
(a) situation (b) time
(c) place (d) All of the above

130. Question to which a member desires an oral answer is
(a) Short-Notice (b) Starred
(c) Unstarred (d) None of these

131. What influences the attitudes?
(a) Appeals through communication
(b) Value symbols
(c) Events
(d) All of the above

132. "Centration" means the child's habit of attending to one salient aspect of a problem neglecting other ones, thus distorting
(a) Learning (b) Reasoning
(c) Imagination (d) Personality

133. Long hours of TV watching are affecting our children. Which one of the following is not an ill-effect in this context?
(a) Children are becoming obese as they do not move out of their homes.
(b) Eye strain leads to weak eyes of children.
(c) Parents can do important tasks while their children are busy with the idiot box.
(d) Children are able to amass more knowledge (and with an amazing ability) than they should.

134. Journalists are like
(a) Photographers (b) Publishers
(c) Painters (d) Writers

135. "Reversibility" means the ability of the child to maintain equivalence in spite of change in the
(a) Emotional field (b) Imaginative field
(c) Perceptual field (d) Intellectual field

136. The 'watchdog of democracy' is
(a) the press (b) music CDs
(c) cinema (d) newspapers

137. In which year INS decided to merge with AP?
(a) 1957 (b) 1960
(c) 1958 (d) 1956

138. Who has designed an experiment to demonstrate the formation of norms in the laboratory?
(a) Rogers (1951) (b) Richards (1957)
(c) Sherif (1936) (d) Miller (1958)

139. PIB stands for
(a) Public Information Bureau
(b) Press Information Bureau
(c) Personal Information Bureau
(d) Press Institute of Bombay

140. Which news-agency is a post war successor to the Agency Havas?

(a) TASS
(b) Agency France Presse
(c) Associated
(d) Reuters

141. The method of studying social structures based on affection or attraction is known as
(a) Sociometry
(b) Social conformity methods
(c) Social attitude test
(d) Sociogram

142. Which of the following conditions gives characterization to primary groups?
(a) Small size of group
(b) Lasting nature of the bond
(c) A close physical proximity
(d) All of the above.

143. Sometimes an individual stands on the boundary between two groups. He feels uncertain about his status in both. In such circumstances, he is called a
(a) Boarderline Man (b) Marginal Man
(c) Boundary Man (d) Line Man

144. Two-step flow model of media influence was given by
(a) Melvin De Fleur
(b) Gabriel Weimann
(c) Katz and Lazarsfeld
(d) Swen Windahl

145. Social role is imposed on the individual by
(a) the nation (b) the group
(c) the society (d) the culture

146. "Media is used by individuals to connect or disconnect themselves from others." Said by
(a) Katz, Gurevitch and Hass
(b) Karl Erik Rosengren
(c) Hamilton and Franklin
(d) Franklin and John Dawson

147. Assimilation and accommodation are
(a) complimentary to each other.
(b) concepts which have no experimental background.
(c) opposite to each other.
(d) vague concepts.

148. Who is the writer of the book named the *Medium is the Message*?
(a) Marshall McLuhan
(b) R.K. Narayan
(c) Wilbur Schramm
(d) None of the above.

149. From the following, who emphatically told that sucking is not only the source of obtaining nutrition but is also a source of pleasure?
(a) Erikson (b) Carl Jung
(c) Sigmund Frued (d) Alfred Adler

150. Usually people's interaction with media is
(a) Unquestioning
(b) Homogeneous
(c) Inactive
(d) All of the above

151. When was the journal *Stribodhi* got published?
(a) 1920 (b) 1720
(c) 1850 (d) 1857

152. Large and highly diverse groups that represent the broad cross-section of the society form the ________ audience.
(a) general
(b) specialised
(c) elite
(d) None of the above.

153. Which Hindi news weekly was edited by Atal Bihari Vajpayee before he entered politics?
(a) *Hindustan* (b) *Bharat*
(c) *Panchajanya* (d) *Matribhoomi*

154. "They have high status in the society. Their number is small but their influence is strong." This is with reference to what kind of audience?
(a) Specialised (b) Elite
(c) General (d) None of these.

155. In which type of socialization, there is no direct contact but the influence of society operates through the media like the newspaper, cinema, books and other agencies?
(a) Indirect Socialization
(b) Latent Socialization
(c) Direct Socialization
(d) Free Socialization

156. Who called our society as a 'dramatised' society?
(a) James Augustus Hicky
(b) Marshall McLuhan
(c) Johannes Gutenberg
(d) Raymond Williams

157. Peculiarities of writing style that the court reporter usually has to adopt are
(a) no need to note down every word that is uttered.
(b) major decisions, points of issue and comments need to be recorded in one's notes.
(c) the defendant must never be addressed as the guilty one.
(d) All of the above.

158. What influence the attitudes?
(a) Events
(b) Appeals through communicat ι.n
(b) Value symbols
(d) All of the above.

159. Whenever an imitation is successful, the child is rewarded and this strengthens the child's response. This is called
(a) Eco-cultural crisis
(b) Social learning
(c) Social norm
(d) Social reinforcement

160. In which newspaper did Gandhi write: "I have taken up journalism not for its sake, but merely as an aid to what I have conceived to be my mission in life."
(a) *The Madras Standard*
(b) *Young India*
(c) *Bangalee*
(d) *Bombay Chronicle*

161. The name of the newspaper that Gandhiji brought out in South Africa was
(a) Independent (b) Foreign Indian
(c) Indian Opinion (d) My Country

162. The situation in which an individual believes that other persons hold differing and incompatible expectations about how he should perform a particular role is known as
(a) Status incompatibility
(b) Role incompatibility
(c) Group status
(d) Group norm

163. Small newspapers have progressed rapidly because of
(a) rise in people's purchasing power
(b) cost of newspaper has gone down
(c) newspapers have become viewspaper
(d) newspapers are being sold as product

164. Who is the 18th century's most important journalist?
(a) Dafoe
(b) Alexander
(c) John Milton
(d) Abraham Lincoln

165. Which of the following does not contribute to the 'credibility' of the press?
(a) Sensationalism
(b) Impartiality
(c) Accuracy
(d) Believability

166. Registrar of Newspapers for India (RNI) started functioning in
(a) July 1956 (b) September 1951
(c) October 1954 (d) August 1960

167. The correct sequence of archetypal elements of folk tales is
(a) hero, object, donor, receiver
(b) object, receiver, hero, donor
(c) donor, receiver, object, Hero
(d) object, hero, receiver, donor

168. The congnitive domain of media is related to audience
(a) Preference (b) Composition
(c) Values (d) Intellect

169. The infant is born as
(a) an antisocial being.
(b) a non-social biological being.
(c) a social being.
(d) a social biological being.

170. A system of meaning in language is referred to as
(a) Grammar (b) Semantics
(c) Allegory (d) Diction

171. "A social value or norm is standardised in the course of human interaction to those aspects of life that have some consequence in the scheme of things of the particular group." Who has given the above statement?
(a) Janis (1953) (b) Jackson (1958)
(c) Kelly (1955) (d) Sherif (1956)

172. The sound pattern of communicative language is termed as
(a) Notation (b) Inter-diction
(c) Phonology (d) Voice control

173. Press Trust of India was founded in
(a) 1947 (b) 1952
(c) 1942 (d) 1949

174. People use mass media for four main purposes. The correct sequence of listed functions (Blumler and Katz) are
(a) Obtaining information, personal identification, social interaction, entertainment.
(b) Social interaction, obtaining information, entertainment, personal identification.
(c) Personal identification, social interaction, entertainment, obtaining information.
(d) Entertainment, obtaining information, personal identification, social interaction.

175. Socialization is a product of
(a) Learning (b) Intelligence
(c) Motivation (d) Imitation

176. The four basic effects that media produce in sequence are
(a) Amplification, retrieval, displacement, conversion.
(b) Conversion, retrieval, amplification, displacement.
(c) Amplification, retrieval, displacement, conversion.
(d) Amplification, displacement, retrieval, conversion.

177. When was the normative theory of mass communication introduced first?
(a) In 1956 (b) In 1950
(c) In 1963 (d) In 1953

178. In communication, dispersal and fragmentation of society is considered a
(a) side effect
(b) centrifugal effect
(c) centripetal effect
(d) direct effect

179. The concept which is of great help in understanding social behaviour is
(a) Prejudice
(b) Social learning
(c) Socialization
(d) Attitude

180. The outside world depicted by the media are consequences of
(a) antecedent conditions
(b) classical conditions
(c) precedent conditions
(d) controlled conditions

181. The factual information in mass media is often referred to as
(a) news information
(b) relational information
(c) content information
(d) channel information

182. In earlier days, socialization was restricted to
(a) procedures of bringing up children.
(b) procedures of taking care of schoolgoing children.
(c) procedures of bringing up animals.
(d) procedures of educating children.

183. The dominant cultural conversation is always limited to
(a) Poverty
(b) Pleasure
(c) Promises made
(d) Consumer products

184. The theory of psychoanalysis reveals that the basic driving forces of behaviour in the social development of the child are assumed to be
(a) Imitated (b) Inherited
(c) Learnt (d) Taught

185. What do you think the community projects have not come to be?
(a) It aims at the involvement of the village community with the village uplift.
(b) It is more official and less local and it is more formal than basic.
(c) It is an attempt to bring about a social and economic transformation of village life through the efforts of the people themselves.
(d) It aims at effecting the required changes in the social and economic fields.

186. The application of the general social learning theory to the acquistion of a new behaviour as a result of media portrayals is the basis of
(a) identification theory
(b) conflict theory
(c) modelling theory
(d) positivist theory

187. Jean Piaget has formulated a theory of
(a) language development of children.
(b) cognitive development of children.
(c) play in children.
(d) social development of children.

188. The phrase the people's right to know was coined by
(a) Harold Cross (b) Kent Cooper
(c) ElieAbel (d) William Rivers

189. According to Sears, it is through dependence that the process of
(a) substitution develops.
(b) learning develops.
(c) indentification develops.
(d) projection develops.

190. Find out the correct sequence of four forms of power in society in relation to media
(a) economic, political, coercive, symbolic.
(b) political, symbolic, economic, coercive.
(c) symbolic, coercive, political, economic.
(d) coercive, symbolic, political, economic.

191. With the growth of the child, the socializing process is increasingly affected by the action of the persons outside
(a) the society (b) the culture
(c) the family (d) the school

192. Find the correct order of films that were released
(a) *Mera Naam Joker - Sahib Bibi Aur Gulam - Waqt - Coolie.*
(b) *Sahib Bibi Aur Gulam - Waqt - Mera Naam Joker - Coolie.*
(c) *Waqt - Sahib Bibi Aur Gulam - Mera Naam Joker - Coolie.*
(d) *Sahib Bibi Aur Gulam - Mera Naam Joker - Waqt - Coolie.*

193. The child becomes dependent on the mother because
(a) she satisfies his psychological needs.
(b) she satisfies his social needs.
(c) she satisfies his biological needs.
(d) she satisfies his affiliative motive.

194. Demographics refer to the examination of the characteristics of the audience such as
(a) Attitudes
(b) Opinions
(c) Social and economic
(d) Feelings

195. The transmission of messages from one person to another is known as
(a) personal transaction.
(b) symbolic representation.
(c) interpersonal communication.
(d) personal correspondence.

196. The modern busy consumer lifestyle results in
(a) Positioning (b) Cocooning
(c) Cognition (d) Hyperbole

197. The latent content of the communicative process refers to
(a) social perception and social learning.
(b) social obligation.
(c) social perception.
(d) the attitudes and motivation.

198. A theory that suggests that the impact of two or more media is stronger than using either medium alone is called
(a) Media message effect
(b) Media usage effect
(c) Media survey effect
(d) Media multiplier effect

199. Which of the following tribes not follow the Anader form of marriage?
(a) Brihor (b) Gond
(c) Oraon (d) Ho

200. The system of "Transactional analysis" was first developed by
(a) Kelley and Kelman
(b) King and Kelman
(c) Henry and Helson
(d) Berne and Harris

201. Denotative meaning is the common dictionary meaning whereas connotative meaning refers to
(a) Concealed meaning
(b) Adverse meaning
(c) Emotional meaning
(d) Semantic

202. Which is most important department in newspaper?
(a) Administration (b) Press
(c) Editorial (d) Advertising

203. The system of transactional analysis assumes that each person has three components in his personality, the personality, the parent, the child, the adult and that each of these three components influences our
(a) Daily work
(b) Daily correspondence
(c) Daily transaction
(d) Daily routine

204. Identify the correct chronological order of films:
(a) *Guddi-Bhumika-Rajniganda-Kaagaj ke Phool.*
(b) *Kaagaj ke Phool-Guddi-Rajniganda-Bhumika.*

(c) *Rajniganda-Guddi-Kaagaj ke Phool-Bhumika.*

(d) *Bhumika-Guddi-Kaagaj ke Phool-Rajniganda.*

205. The sole agent of socialization of a child in the early childhood is

(a) Culture (b) Peer group
(c) Society (d) Family

206. The logic that something is true because it has always been true is seen in the method of

(a) Tenacity (b) Intuition
(c) Authority (d) Scientific

207. Clinically, thumb sucking is taken as a sign of maladjustment in the child. But its seriousness depends on

(a) the culture in which the child lives.
(b) the weight of the child.
(c) the age of the child.
(d) the height of the child.

208. Which of the following traditional forms of communication uses rasa, tal, laya and bhava?

(a) Yatra (b) Baoli
(c) Pala (d) Kuchipudi

209. Which of the following ranks first in the total publications in India?

(a) Monthlies (b) Fortnightlies
(c) Dailies (d) Weeklies

210. Identify the correct chronological sequence of the release of the following:

(a) *Citizen Kane–Bicycle Thieves–Nanook of the North–Birth of a Nation.*
(b) *Birth of a Nation–Bicycle Thieves–Citizen Kane–Nanook of the North.*
(c) *Nanook of the North–Birth of a Nation–Citizen Kane–Bicycle Thieves.*
(d) *Birth of a Nation–Nahook of the North–Citizen Kane–Bicycle Thieves.*

211. The theory of "Psychosexual development of children" was advanced by

(a) Sigmund Freud (b) Otto Rank
(c) Alfred Adler (d) Carl Jung

212. Ritual is a form of communication which has a structured sequence of

(a) Iconisation (b) Symbolic acts
(c) Mutuality (d) Dissipation

213. What is the oldest evidence of Chinese printing?

(a) Pride and Prejudice (b) Nobel
(c) Diamond Sutra (d) Meghdoot

214. Sigmund Freud emphasized the crucial importance of toilet training to the development of

(a) child's emotion.
(b) child's intelligence.
(c) child's personality.
(d) child's socialization.

215. Which of the following Satyajit Ray films had the story written by Rabindranath Tagore?

(a) *Charulatha* (b) *Sadgati*
(c) *Ganashatru* (d) *Agantuk*

216. Press Information Bureau is a

(a) Photo and Picture Division of Indian Government
(b) Central Agency of Government of India for Dissemination of Information on Government
(c) Publication Division of Indian Government
(d) Research and Reference Division of Indian Government

217. Case studies of children referred to child guidance clinic show that in nearly half of the children bladder and bowel training had started

(a) in school going stage.
(b) prematurely.

(c) in the late childhood.
(d) in adulthood.

218. Which of the following is a major cause for digital divide?
(a) High speed networks
(b) Biometric data storage
(c) Illiteracy
(d) Computer games

219. Who installed the first steam printing press?
(a) John Walter I (b) John Dome
(c) John Milton (d) John Walter II

220. The behaviour of toilet training like other behaviours of children depends on
(a) neuro-muscular maturation.
(b) motor organs.
(c) motor coordination.
(d) sensori-motor coordination.

221. Sequence in historical changes in perspectives on media influence.
(a) Negotiated influence – limited effects – all powerful – long term effects.
(b) All powerful – limited effects – long term effects – negotiated influence.
(c) Limited effects – all powerful – negotiated influence – long term effects.
(d) All powerful – long term effects – negotiated influence – limited effects.

222. When was the first international film festival held in India?
(a) In the year of 1963
(b) In the year of 1972
(c) In the year of 1960
(d) In the year of 1952

223. Why is M.F. Hussain known?
(a) For best cooking
(b) For best photography
(c) For best paintings
(d) For best writings

224. Research evidences of Sears et al. (1957) have revealed that in 87 per cent of the case studies, the mothers started bowel training by the time the child was
(a) 12 months old (b) 3 months old
(c) 5 months old (d) 20 months old

225. The first radio station was set up in
(a) Tokyo, Japan (b) Pitterburg, U.S.
(c) London, UK (d) None of above

226. As the child grows older, overt aggression
(a) Decreases
(b) Increases
(c) Vanishes
(d) Becomes haphazard

227. Who owns the newspaper The Hindu?
(a) Benett and Coleman Co. Ltd.
(b) P.G. Pawar
(c) K.K. Birla
(d) Kasturi & Sons

228. "Frustration-aggression hypothesis" was developed by
(a) Asch and his co-workers
(b) Barker and his co-workers
(c) Carter and his co-workers
(d) Dollard and his co-workers

229. What was established in India in later half of 19th century?
(a) PTI (b) UNI
(c) Anglo Indian Press (d) None of these

230. Who opened the telegraph office at Achen in Holland?
(a) Reuter
(b) Peter
(c) Coilliom Cowper
(d) John Abraham

231. "Frustration-aggression hypothesis" was developed by Dollard et al. (1939) to explain
(a) the theory of frustration.
(b) the theory of repression.

(c) the theory of aggression.
(d) the theory of regression.

232. When was the film division established in India?
(a) In 1920 (b) In 1959
(c) In 1960 (d) In 1948

233. In how many parts the communication is divided?
(a) Six (b) Nine
(c) Four (d) Five

234. Nepa mill in Madhya Pradesh under the central public sector started on
(a) 26 April 1956
(b) 26 Jan 1950
(c) 15 April 1950
(d) 16 March 1960

235. When did the earliest newspaper started in Calcutta from?
(a) 1826 (b) 1819
(c) 1850 (d) 1849

236. Who became the first Information and Broadcasting minister after Independence?
(a) B.R. Ambedkar
(b) Jawaharlal Nehru
(c) Sardar Patel
(d) Radha Krishnan

237. Where is the headquarter of Photo Division is located?
(a) Chennai (b) Hyderabad
(c) Mumbai (d) New Delhi

238. Department of Information and Broadcasting was set up in
(a) 1940 (b) 1942
(c) 1941 (d) 1928

239. Which of the following news agencies is different from others?
(a) PTI (b) IANS
(c) UNI (d) ANI

240. The first Indian daily newspaper in English was
(a) *Bombay Times* (b) *Indian Mirror*
(c) *Times of India* (d) *The Hindu*

241. In India the first news bulletin was introduced in
(a) 1938 (b) 1936
(c) 1932 (d) 1942

242. Who made the first silent feature film in India?
(a) Dhundiraj Govind Phalke
(b) N.G. Chitra
(c) R.G. Torney
(d) Both (a) and (b)

243. Hindu Patriot was started in Calcutta in 1853 by
(a) Joseph Convad
(b) Girish Carnard
(c) Subhas Chandra Bose
(d) Girish Chandra Ghose

244. Robert Knight founded the *Statesman* in the year
(a) 1875 (b) 1876
(c) 1873 (d) 1874

Directions: Questions 245 to 249 are of matching statement type. Choose the correct answer from the codes given below the statements.

245. Which of the following are basic in Indian Society on the basis of which a region is demarcated?
1. Cultural and linguistic factors
2. Historical and administrative factors
3. Political aspiration of people

Codes:
(a) 1 and 2 (b) 1 and 3
(c) 2 and 3 (d) 1, 2 and 3

246. Who amongst the following are associated with Backward Caste movement in India?
(1) Sri Narayana Guru
(2) B. R. Ambedkar
(3) Jyotiba Phule

Codes:

(a) 1 and 2 (b) 1 and 3
(c) 2 and 3 (d) 1, 2 and 3

247. According to Denis McQuail,
1. Culture is collectively formed and retained
2. It is always dynamic
3. It is not open to symbolic expression
4. It can be communicated over time and space

Codes:

(a) 1, 2 and 3 (b) 1, 2, and 4
(c) 2, 3 and 4 (d) 1, 2, 3 and 4

248. Which of the following are the Millennium development goals given by NHDR?
1. To ensure environmental stability
2. To reduce child mortality
3. To improve maternal health
4. To achieve universal primary education

Codes:

(a) 1 and 2 (b) 3 and 4
(c) 2, 3 and 4 (d) 1, 2, 3 and 4

249. Which of the following are attributes of a caste?
1. Endogamy 2. Exogamy
3. Ritual status 4. Culture

Codes:

(a) 1, 2 and 3 (b) 1, 2 and 4
(c) 1, 3 and 4 (d) 2, 3 and 4

Directions: Questions 250 to 264 are of matching type. Match List-I with List-II and select the correct answer using the codes given below the lists.

250. **List-I (Societies)** **List-II (Dominant)**

(A) Folk 1. Humanaim
(B) Industrial 2. Individualism
(C) Feudal 3. Fealty
(D) Post-industrial 4. Associationalism
5. Collectivism

Codes:	A	B	C	D
(a)	3	1	5	2
(b)	3	4	1	2
(c)	1	3	2	5
(d)	5	2	3	4

251. **List-I (Social Institutions)** **List-II (Places)**

(A) Kibbutzim 1. New Guinea
(B) Kula 2. Australia
(C) Potlatch 3. Israel
(D) Polyandry 4. India
5. The USA

Codes:	A	B	C	D
(a)	3	1	5	4
(b)	5	1	2	3
(c)	4	3	1	5
(d)	3	2	5	4

252. **List-I (Terms)** **List-II (Sense)**

(A) Attitudes 1. Rules
(B) Beliefs 2. Acts repeated again and again
(C) Habits 3. Personal truth
(D) Customs 4. Basic orientation for or against

Codes:	A	B	C	D
(a)	4	3	2	1
(b)	2	3	4	1
(c)	1	2	3	4
(d)	3	4	1	2

253. **List-I (Tribes)** **List-II (States)**

(A) Santhals 1. Madhya Pradash
(B) Bhils 2. Jharkhand
(C) Garos 3. Meghalaya
(D) Gonds

Codes:	A	B	C	D
(a)	1	2	1	3
(b)	2	2	3	3
(c)	1	1	2	2
(d)	2	1	3	1

254. **List-I**

A. Endogamy
B. Patriarchal family
C. Karta
D. Anuloma

List-II

1. Head of the family
2. Marriage outside the caste
3. Marriage inside the group
4. Male is the head of the family
5. Marriage of upper caste of man with a lower caste woman

Codes:	**A**	**B**	**C**	**D**
(a)	3	4	1	5
(b)	2	5	4	3
(c)	3	4	1	5
(d)	5	4	1	2

255.

List-I (Traditional Medium)	**List-II (States)**
(A) Pandavani	1. Himachal Pradesh
(B) Tal-maddale	2. Maharashtra
(C) Karayila	3. Chhattisgarh
(D) Gondhal	4. Karnataka

Codes:	**A**	**B**	**C**	**D**
(a)	2	3	4	1
(b)	3	1	4	2
(c)	2	4	1	3
(d)	3	4	1	2

256.

List-I (Folk Media)	**List-II (States)**
(A) Burrakatha	1. Karnataka
(B) Tamasha	2. Kerala
(C) Yakshagana	3. Andhra Pradesh
(D) Kathakali	4. Maharashtra

Codes:	**A**	**B**	**C**	**D**
(a)	3	4	1	2
(b)	4	1	2	3
(c)	3	2	1	4
(d)	1	3	4	2

257.

List-I (Films)	**List-II (Directors)**
(A) *Bombay*	1. Shyam Benegal
(B) *Manthan*	2. Satyajit Ray
(C) *Apur Sansar*	3. Aparna Sen
(D) *36 Chowringhee Lane*	4. Mani Ratnam

Codes:	**A**	**B**	**C**	**D**
(a)	2	1	4	3
(b)	4	1	2	3
(c)	1	3	2	4
(d)	1	2	4	3

258. **List-I (Book)**

(A) Television: The Critical View
(B) Culture Inc
(C) Seeing and Believing
(D) Desperately Seeking Audience

List-II (Authors)

1. Herbert Schiller
2. GregPhilo
3. IenAng
4. Horace Newcomb

Codes:	**A**	**B**	**C**	**D**
(a)	2	3	4	1
(b)	3	2	1	4
(c)	1	3	2	4
(d)	4	1	2	3

259.

List-I (Personalities)	**List-II (Films)**
(A) Satyajit Ray	1. *Swami*
(B) Adoor Gopalakrishnan	2. *Subhas Chandra Bose*
(C) Shyam Benegal	3. *Agantuk*
(D) Girish Karnard	4. *Anantam*

Codes:	**A**	**B**	**C**	**D**
(a)	3	4	2	1
(b)	4	3	1	2
(c)	2	1	3	4
(d)	1	4	3	2

260. **List-I (Folk Media)** — **List-II (States)**

(A) Yakshagana — 1. Haryana
(B) Burrakatha — 2. Maharashtra
(C) Tamasha — 3. Karnataka
(D) Saang — 4. Andhra Pradesh

Codes:	**A**	**B**	**C**	**D**
(a)	1	2	3	4
(b)	3	4	2	1
(c)	2	4	1	3
(d)	4	3	1	2

261. **List-I (Folk Media)** — **List-II (States)**

(A) Yakshagana — 1. Jammu and Kashmir
(B) Jatva — 2. Karnataka
(C) Nautanki — 3. West Bengal
(D) Bhand Pather — 4. Uttar Pradesh

Codes:	**A**	**B**	**C**	**D**
(a)	2	3	4	1
(b)	1	4	2	3
(c)	3	2	1	4
(d)	4	3	1	2

262. **List-I (Directors)** — **List-II (Films)**

(A) Sergi Eisenstein — 1. *The Bicycle Theives*
(B) D.W. Griffith — 2. *Nanook of the North*
(C) Victoria de Sica — 3. *Battleship Potemkin*
(D) Robert Flaherty — 4. *Birth of a Nation*

Codes:	**A**	**B**	**C**	**D**
(a)	2	4	1	3
(b)	1	3	2	4
(c)	4	2	3	1
(d)	3	4	1	2

263. **List-I (Directors)** — **List-II (Films)**

(A) Guru Dutt — 1. *Do Bigha Zameen*
(B) BimalRoy — 2. *Abhimaan*
(C) Mehboob Khan — 3. *Pyaasa*
(D) Hrishikesh Mukherjee — 4. *Mother India*

Codes:	**A**	**B**	**C**	**D**
(a)	1	4	3	2
(b)	4	2	3	1
(c)	3	1	4	2
(d)	2	1	3	4

264. **List-I (Folk Media)** — **List-II (States)**

(A) Bhaona — 1. Maharashtra
(B) Tamasha — 2. Kerala
(C) Garba — 3. Gujarat
(D) Kathakali — 4. Assam

Codes:	**A**	**B**	**C**	**D**
(a)	4	1	3	2
(b)	3	2	1	4
(c)	3	4	2	1
(d)	2	4	3	1

Directions: Questions 265 to 303 consist of two statements, one labelled as 'Assertion' (A) and the other labelled as 'Reason' (R). You are to examine these two statements carefully and decide if the Assertion (A) and the Reason (R) are individually true and if so, whether the Reason is a correct explanation of the Assertion. Select your answers to these questions using the code given below:

(a) Both (A) and (R) are true and (R) is the correct explanation of (A).
(b) Both (A) and (R) are true but (R) is not the correct explanation of (A).
(c) (A) is true but (R) is false.
(d) (A) is false but (R) is true.

265. **Assertion (A):** Nowadays, caste is no bar to the choice of occupations.

Reason (R): Indian democracy guarantees its people freedom in the choice of occupations.

266. **Assertion (A):** The average annual growth rate of population is normally less than the exponential growth rate.

Reason (R): Population does not grow by constant increment of people.

267. **Assertion (A):** It cannot be claimed that the incidents of atrocities on and oppression of Harijans have been totally eliminated, but these have gone down substantially as compared to those in the past.

Reason (R): For ensuring justice to Harijans, strict orders were given to the district authorities to take immediate action against those indulging in atrocities on Harijans.

268. **Assertion (A):** People do not join a cult but rather follow particular theories or prescribed ways of behaviour.

Reason (R): Members are usually allowed to maintain other religious connections.

269. **Assertion (R):** Caste discrimination is nowadays not observed in public life.

Reason (R): The upper castes have stopped practicing caste discrimination.

270. **Assertion (A):** People consciously or sub-consciously work to limit mental discomfort through three selective processes that are interrelated to each other.

Reason (R): When people are bombarded with new sets of information, they experience mental discomfort.

271. **Assertion (A):** Media motivates people.

Reason (R): Motivation is a major task of mass media.

272. **Assertion (A):** Toynbee is a follower of cyclic theory of evolution.

Reason (R): Toynbee saw the fate of great civilisations in terms of birth, growth, decay and death.

273. **Assertion (A):** The average annual growth rate of population is normally less than the exponential growth rate.

Reason (R): Population does not grow by constant increment of people.

274. **Assertion (A):** Media can educate the people.

Reason (R): It provides new informations related to various fields.

275. **Assertion (A):** Spencer felt that the struggle for survival rewarded the talented and energetic and eliminated the lazy and unfit.

Reason (R): Spencer was influenced by Darwin's theories of organic evolution.

276. **Assertion (A):** According to symbolic interaction theory, the masses give meanings to things.

Reason (R): The masses are motivated by media.

277. **Assertion (A):** Social mobility is the movement of individuals or groups from one social stratum to another.

Reason (R): The degree to which systems of stratification are open or closed depends on the extent of social mobility.

278. **Assertion (A):** Monogamy is the most common form of marriage in the contemporary society.

Reason (R): Status of women get enhanced through monogamy.

279. **Assertion (A):** The cultures of the dominant class controls the dominant meanings.

Reason (R): The structure of relations between classes perpetuates itself by reproducing its characteristics in the domain of culture.

280. **Assertion (A):** Protests by schedulded castes against the practice of untouchability and atrocities have increased.

Reason (R): Their action have stirred the government machinery to enforce law and order stictly.

281. **Assertion (A):** Lifestyle determines life chances.

Reason (R): The class position of the individual enhances or diminishes his life chances.

282. **Assertion (A):** There is a considerable ethno-linguistic diversity in India.

Reason (R): This prohibits equal opportunity.

283. **Assertion (A):** Cities are the confluence of races, cultures and people.

Reason (R): Cities are the centres of innovation.

284. **Assertion (A):** Modernisation goes hand in hand with education, mass communication, urbanisation and political participation.

Reason (R): Dominance of the cultural influences from the West changes tradition elsewhere.

285. **Assertion (A):** Traditional media are most intimate with the masses and command an immense variety of forms.

Reason (R): Traditional media are imbibed with in the socio-cultural system of the society.

286. **Assertion (A):** A house journal is not a periodical publication which tries to establish regular communication between an organisation and its internal and external publics.

Reason (R): A house journal creates a sense of belongingness among its internal public.

287. **Assertion (A):** Anti-hero movies are very popular in India.

Reason (R): Indians love vengeance and tragic end.

288. **Assertion (A):** Mass media mostly provide the contents of audience choice.

Reason (R): Media persons suffer from pluralistic ignorance and hence, this arrangement.

289. **Assertion (A):** Sex and violence in Indian movies are graphically increasing these days.

Reason (R): Indian society is violent and loves to see more and more violence on the screen.

290. **Assertion (A):** Content of media effectively influences the subject matter of the group communication in the society.

Reason (R): Content of media is the mirror image of the society.

291. **Assertion (A):** Media help only to maintain the status quo in the society.

Reason (R): Media are the subsystems of social, political and economic systems.

292. **Assertion (A):** Media penetration has reached its peak in India.

Reason (R): The user-friendly technology has helped the media to spread fast.

293. **Assertion (A):** Indian cinema survives on star value.

Reason (R): It is rooted in Indian history and culture.

294. **Assertion (A):** Big newspapers with their local editions have become more local newspapers than what they are supposed to be.

Reason (R): The readers want more local news than national or regional news.

295. **Assertion (A):** Word of mouth can spread like a wild fire. If the subject and content are right, it can burst into spontaneous combustion as an entire forest may suddenly be over run by a conflagration. Through word of mouth, rumour and innuendo may spread with extreme speed and spontaneity if the subject is close to the emotions of people.

Reason (R): More than thoughts, feelings most quickly take wings on word of mouth.

296. **Assertion (A):** The term culture is characterized by something collective and shared with others. It may not have symbolic form of expression, but have pattern, and order, and devoid of evaluative dimensions.

Reason (R): The most general and essential attribute of culture is communication, since culture could not develop, survive, extend and generally succeed without communication.

297. **Assertion (A):** Often the primary aim of mass media is neither to transmit particular information nor to write a public in some expression of culture belief or values, but simply to catch and hold visual or aural attention.

Reason (R): The message of ritual communication is usually latent and ambiguous, depending on associations and symbols which are not chosen by the participants but made available in culture.

298. **Assertion (A):** Within the space in which reality is played out, the media institutions provide media audiences with information, images, stories and impressions, sometimes according to their own purposes and logic, sometimes guided by other social institutions.

Reason (R): Mediation can be a purely neutral process and that it will not have any consistent biases.

299. **Assertion (A):** The market finds that violence and sex draw larger audiences, therefore commercial entertainment offerings tend to dominate the media.

Reason (R): The market makes money by programming that yields negative externalities that improve bottom line and consequently ignores positive public sphere by the media.

300. **Assertion (A):** The mass media audience is neither organised nor self-acting.

Reason (R): Anonymity is the major factor that contributes to this situation.

301. **Assertion (A):** It is strongly believed that there is 'casting couch' in Bollywood.

Reason (R): Talent is not the only criterion for entry and success in Bollywood.

302. **Assertion (A):** There is an increasing trend of telecasting more and more reality shows by Indian Television Channels.

Reason (R): Because reality shows attract larger viewership.

303. **Assertion (A):** India churns out a large number of commercial films from its dream factories with very little focus on creative innovation.

Reason (R): The Indian film industry is managed by unskilled and untrained manpower and driven by the aspirations of black money holders.

ANSWERS

1. (b)	2. (d)	3. (d)	4. (b)	5. (d)	6. (b)
7. (a)	8. (a)	9. (b)	10. (b)	11. (a)	12. (d)
13. (b)	14. (d)	15. (d)	16. (b)	17. (b)	18. (b)
19. (a)	20. (a)	21. (c)	22. (b)	23. (d)	24. (c)
25. (a)	26. (a)	27. (a)	28. (d)	29. (a)	30. (c)
31. (b)	32. (a)	33. (c)	34. (b)	35. (c)	36. (d)
37. (b)	38. (b)	39. (b)	40. (c)	41. (d)	42. (d)
43. (a)	44. (b)	45. (b)	46. (c)	47. (c)	48. (c)
49. (d)	50. (d)	51. (c)	52. (d)	53. (d)	54. (c)
55. (a)	56. (c)	57. (c)	58. (a)	59. (b)	60. (c)
61. (a)	62. (c)	63. (b)	64. (a)	65. (d)	66. (a)
67. (b)	68. (a)	69. (c)	70. (a)	71. (d)	72. (c)
73. (d)	74. (a)	75. (d)	76. (a)	77. (d)	78. (d)
79. (a)	80. (d)	81. (b)	82. (b)	83. (b)	84. (b)
85. (d)	86. (b)	87. (c)	88. (a)	89. (a)	90. (b)
91. (c)	92. (d)	93. (d)	94. (a)	95. (a)	96. (c)
97. (d)	98. (c)	99. (d)	100. (a)	101. (d)	102. (c)
103. (a)	104. (a)	105. (b)	106. (a)	107. (b)	108. (d)
109. (c)	110. (a)	111. (d)	112. (d)	113. (a)	114. (a)
115. (a)	116. (a)	117. (d)	118. (b)	119. (c)	120. (a)
121. (a)	122. (c)	123. (d)	124. (a)	125. (a)	126. (c)
127. (b)	128. (c)	129. (d)	130. (b)	131. (d)	132. (b)
133. (d)	134. (c)	135. (c)	136. (a)	137. (c)	138. (c)
139. (b)	140. (b)	141. (a)	142. (d)	143. (b)	144. (c)
145. (b)	146. (a)	147. (a)	148. (a)	149. (c)	150. (d)
151. (d)	152. (a)	153. (c)	154. (b)	155. (a)	156. (d)
157. (d)	158. (d)	159. (d)	160. (b)	161. (c)	162. (b)
163. (a)	164. (a)	165. (a)	166. (a)	167. (a)	168. (d)
169. (b)	170. (b)	171. (d)	172. (c)	173. (a)	174. (a)
175. (a)	176. (b)	177. (c)	178. (b)	179. (c)	180. (d)
181. (b)	182. (a)	183. (b)	184. (b)	185. (c)	186. (c)
187. (b)	188. (b)	189. (c)	190. (a)	191. (c)	192. (b)
193. (c)	194. (c)	195. (c)	196. (b)	197. (d)	198. (d)

199. (a)	200. (d)	201. (c)	202. (c)	203. (c)	204. (b)
205. (d)	206. (a)	207. (c)	208. (d)	209. (c)	210. (d)
211. (a)	212. (b)	213. (c)	214. (c)	215. (a)	216. (b)
217. (b)	218. (c)	219. (a)	220. (a)	221. (a)	222. (d)
223. (c)	224. (d)	225. (b)	226. (a)	227. (d)	228. (d)
229. (c)	230. (a)	231. (c)	232. (d)	233. (b)	234. (a)
235. (a)	236. (c)	237. (d)	238. (c)	239. (d)	240. (b)
241. (b)	242. (a)	243. (d)	244. (a)	245. (c)	246. (d)
247. (b)	248. (d)	249. (a)	250. (d)	251. (a)	252. (a)
253. (d)	254. (a)	255. (d)	256. (a)	257. (b)	258. (d)
259. (a)	260. (b)	261. (a)	262. (d)	263. (c)	264. (a)
265. (d)	266. (c)	267. (b)	268. (c)	269. (b)	270. (a)
271. (c)	272. (a)	273. (c)	274. (a)	275. (a)	276. (a)
277. (c)	278. (c)	279. (b)	280. (c)	281. (a)	282. (b)
283. (c)	284. (d)	285. (a)	286. (b)	287. (d)	288. (c)
289. (c)	290. (c)	291. (d)	292. (d)	293. (c)	294. (a)
295. (b)	296. (b)	297. (b)	298. (c)	299. (a)	300. (a)
301. (a)	302. (a)	303. (c)			

3

Journalism as a Profession

1. The Press Council set up under the Act of 1965 functioned till
   (a) January 1975 (b) December 1975
   (c) January 1976 (d) December 1976
2. Can a reporter use the news, for his personal commercial usage, after he has given it to his employer?
   (a) May be, he can take the permission from him to use it for his personal commercial operation.
   (b) Yes, but after the news has been published and also, if he has altered its content, style, and presentation.
   (c) Yes, it is allowed by the law.
   (d) No, he cannot.
3. Freedom of press is granted under which Article of the Indian Constitution
   (a) 21(1)(a) (b) 21(4)
   (c) 19(1)(a) (d) 19(2)(a)
4. ESPN is a channel owned by the
   (a) Walt Disney Company
   (b) CNN Group
   (c) ZEE Telefilms Group
   (d) None of the above.
5. Should a journo use his contact, who is a highly placed government official, for getting his personal work done?
   (a) Yes! However, he must talk to his boss and take his permission before asking that contact person for a favour.
   (b) No! He may lose his job and his contact person may also be given such an order by the government.
   (c) Yes! That is why, he may have developed this contact.
   (d) No! It is illegal.
6. The birthplace of Indian Journalism was
   (a) Mumbai (b) New Delhi
   (c) Chennai (d) Kolkata
7. The TV channel, National Geographic was launched in partnership and distribution with
   (a) Zee TV
   (b) BBC
   (c) Ted Turner group
   (d) Star TV
8. MTV India, the India specific operations of MTV started in
   (a) 1996 (b) 1997
   (c) 1998 (d) 1999
9. Bipin Chandra Pal founded
   (a) *Bengalee* (b) *New India*
   (c) *Bande Mataram* (d) Both (b) and (c)
10. In which one of the following media, the reader is not an active consumer of news or information?
    (a) TV (b) Book
    (c) Newspaper (d) Internet
11. If TV can be likened to a daily newspaper, cinema can be likened to a
    (a) Poem (b) Short Story
    (c) Novel (d) Manager
12. Who started the newspaper *National Herald*?

(a) Indira Gandhi
(b) Rajiv Gandhi
(c) Motial Nehru
(d) Jawaharlal Nehru

13. Which TV channels tagline is "Khabar Wahi Jo Sach Dikhaye"?
(a) DD News (b) NDTV India
(c) Star News (d) ZEE News

14. What is pluralism?
(a) It is a ruling of an autocratic ruler that forces the masses (under his control) to choose a number of media for collecting information.
(b) It is a social structure that allows and assures the distribution of multiple messages.
(c) It refers to a society in which people can choose the media vehicles according to their tastes and preferences.
(d) None of the above.

15. Which of the following was considered as 'Gagging Act'?
(a) Vernacular Press Act
(b) Press (Emergency) Powers Act 1931
(c) Indian Penal Code
(d) Indian Press Code

16. Who stated, "Freedom always entails an obligation, whether it is a nation's freedom or individual's freedom or a group freedom or the freedom of the Press"?
(a) Jawaharlal Nehru
(b) Professor N.G. Ranga
(c) Mahatma Gandhi
(d) Winston Churchill

17. Konkani, Manipuri, and Nepali were added to the Eight Schedule of the Constitution by the
(a) Seventy-first (Amendment) Act
(b) Seventy-fifth (Amendment) Act
(c) Seventy-seventh (Amendment) Act
(d) None of the above.

18. Raja Ram Mohan Roy edited
(a) *Bangadutta*
(b) *Mirat-ul-Akhbar*
(c) *Samvad Kaumudi*
(d) All of the above

19. When we convert an event into a news, we come across the issue of topicality at Level 3 of the process of conversion. Which one of the following is not an element of topicality?
(a) News compared with other news/ stories that are around
(b) Time sensitivity
(c) Currently valid news
(d) Time frame

20. Find the odd man out from among the following
(a) Prabhu Chawla
(b) Deepak Chaurasia
(c) Appon Menon
(d) Rajesh Badal

21. Who was the editor of *Indian Sociologist* published from London?
(a) Shyamji Krishna Verma
(b) S.N. Benerjee
(c) Devendranth Tagore
(d) Taraknath Das

22. *Lokmat* is being published in three languages. They are
(a) Bengali, Hindi, and Kannada
(b) Kannada, Gujarati, and Marathi
(c) English, Hindi, and Bangla
(d) Marathi, English, and Hindi

23. The coverage by various media of the murder case of poetess Madhumita Shukla was an example of
(a) Crime reporting
(b) Yellow journalism

(c) Sensational journalism
(d) Depth journalism

24. *Hindu Patriot* was started in Calcutta in 1853 by
(a) Joseph Convad
(b) Girish Carnad
(c) Subhash Chandra Bose
(d) Girish Chandra Bose

25. The CVO is a joint venture of the Hinduja group and the
(a) Cable Master Group
(b) ZEE Telefilms
(c) Star Group
(d) AV Birla Group

26. Who amongst the following works for Aaj Tak?
(a) Kishore Ajwani
(b) Richa Aniruddha
(c) Sheetal Rajput
(d) Rahul Kanwal

27. It is obvious that in a private firm, the editor would publish only that information, which is acceptable to his bosses. How would he convince his bosses to publish a news item that they do not like to be published?
(a) He can convince them that the news in question is likely to be published by the rival newspapers and that they should publish it first to kill competition.
(b) He can tell them that the news should be published (even if they do not like it) in the interest of journalism ethics and for the benefit of the society.
(c) He can tell them that if they do not do so, he would put in his papers.
(d) All of the above.

28. Kalinath Ray was arrested and jailed for two years, he was the editor of
(a) *Bombay Chronicle* (b) *Pioneer*
(c) *Mid-day* (d) *Tribune*

29. What a good or morally upright journalist should not do?
(a) Offer some incentive to an interviewee so that he could give information (a cold drink would suffice).
(b) Collection of information from a blazing battlefront.
(c) Collection of information by sneaking into the office or home of the target.
(d) Use of PR in a government office.

30. Aurobindo was the editor of
(a) *Chronicle* (b) *Pioneer*
(c) *Vande Matram* (d) *Harijan*

31. A TV journo is not responsible for
(a) managing his juniors.
(b) taking care of the personal grievances of the subject under his focus.
(c) managing or protecting the camera.
(d) leading his crew from the front to collect the news.

32. Tilak is connected with the newspaper
(a) *India* (b) *Hindustan*
(c) *Bande Marram* (d) *Maratha*

33. The meaning of the term 'offence' has been given in
(a) The General Clauses Act, 1897
(b) Freedom of Information Act, 2002
(c) Both (a) and (b)
(d) Article 361 of the Constitution

34. Who was called a 'flighting editor' by Gandhi?
(a) Frank Moraes
(b) M. Chalpati Rau
(c) K. Rama Rao
(d) None of the above

35. Which of the following statements is false?

(a) In today's context, we can assume that Freedom of the Press is the extension of the citizen's right to freedom of speech and expression.
(b) Freedom of expression rarely helps an individual in participating in decision-making.
(c) "In the development of Indian politics and public opinion, which has taken place since 1920, the Indian Press has played a significant part", averred the Simon Commission.
(d) Kesari and Kranti were two famous papers prior to independence.

36. The Hutchins Report led to the
(a) Press subsidies
(b) Establishment of Press Councils
(c) Anti-monopoly legislation
(d) All of the above

37. What is your opinion about the paparazzi syndrome?
(a) It is better to extend help to a subject in distress (or near the verge of death) than to encroach upon his privacy.
(b) It is immoral to shoot a subject who is dying.
(c) The law of the land may not allow the paparazzi to track down and follow the vehicles of celebrities.
(d) The celebrities like lady Diana ought not to be covered by photographers and journos.

38. Find the odd woman out from among the following
(a) Soni Sangwan (b) Nalini Singh
(c) Tavleen Singh (d) Shobha De

39. The Indian Institute of Mass Communication does not have a branch at
(a) Madurai (Tamil Nadu)
(b) Jhabua (Madhya Pradesh)
(c) Kottayam (Kerala)
(d) Dhenkanal (Orissa)

40. Who established the Persian newspaper *Miratul-ul-Akhbar*?
(a) Raja Ram Mohan Roy
(b) G.K. Gokhale
(c) B.G. Tilak
(d) None of the above

41. Daniel Pearl worked for the following publication.
(a) *The Wall Street Journal*
(b) *New York Times*
(c) *Washington Review*
(d) *Chicago Tribune*

42. Who was the last Governer General of India?
(a) Ravindra Nath Tagore
(b) Bal Gangadhar Tilak
(c) C. Rajgoplachari
(d) Bhim Rao Ambedkar

43. Which article of the Universal Declaration of Human Rights (1948) explains the concept of an individual's privacy?
(a) Article 10
(b) Article 10(a)
(c) Article 12
(d) None of the above.

44. The thinker who called his mass communication theory as "Cultivation of dominant image patterns" was
(a) Gerbner (b) Davidson
(c) McCombs (d) Shaw

45. The first draft on the Right to Information was prepared by the
(a) PCI in 1996
(b) Parliament in 1996
(c) Supreme Court in 1998
(d) PCI in 1998

46. Where the mechanical and organizational basis was being laid for the popular newspaper of the 20th century
(a) Africa and England
(b) China and South Africa

(c) America and Europe
(d) England and Europe

47. Which one of the following is most perishable?
(a) A newspaper
(b) A magazine
(c) A book
(d) All the above are equally perishable

48. Before criticising a political bigwig, the jonrno should (preferably)
(a) talk to the PA that political bigwig and through him, the political bigwig himself.
(b) send the critique to the press without consulting any person.
(c) talk to his boss first.
(d) ask that political bigwig first.

49. The sales manager of a TV station may not possess which of the following traits?
(a) Earning trust of the client.
(b) Pre-production planning tactics.
(c) Self-motivation.
(d) Knowledge about the software of his TV station.

50. On what publications the ISBN is used for reference?
(a) Weeklies (b) Books
(c) Magazines (d) Newspapers

51. According to Article 19(2) of Indian Constitution, the state can impose reasonable restrictions on the exercise of the freedom of expression and speech in the interests of
(a) the security of the state
(b) public order
(c) friendly relations with foreign states
(d) All of the above

52. Television and All India Radio were separated in the year
(a) 1925 (b) 1976
(c) 1973 (d) 1974

53. According to Article 361A of Indian Constitution
(a) a person desirous of obtaining information shall make a request in writing or through electronic means, to the concerned Public Information Officer, specifying the particulars of the information sought by him.
(b) all the citizens have the right to freedom of speech and expression.
(c) no person shall be liable to any proceedings, civil or criminal, in court, in respect of the publication of a substantially true report of the proceeding in either House of the Parliament, unless it is proved that the publication is made with malice.
(d) None of the above.

54. The code and other restriction on broadcasting are based on
(a) Clause 4
(b) Clause 5
(c) Clause 3
(d) Clause 2 or Article 19 of the Indian Constitution

55. Which of the following is an example of network media?
(a) Newspaper
(b) TV
(c) Telephone
(d) Video Conferencing

56. Which one of the following statements is correct?
(a) Neo-classical thinkers were revolutionaries.
(b) Neo-classical thinkers were against existing privileges.
(c) Neo-classical thinkers justified the existing social order.
(d) None of the above.

57. Which one of the following statements is true?

(a) Meri Baat was a popular chat show on ZEE News.
(b) Photographer Pradeep was killed in a bomb blast by the ULFA militants.
(c) The media must be managed by the state because through the actions/directors of the state, a nation can manage her media most effectively and sans chaos.
(d) It is a custom to give trade discount to retailers in the book publishing business. It may range from 30 to 50 per cent on the list price.

58. Which one of the following statements is correct?
(a) Due to lack of rigid party discipline the members often vote against the bills sponsered by the leaders of their own party.
(b) The political parties in USA do not possess any clear-cut ideologies or programme.
(c) There is laxity of discipline among the members of the political parties in USA.
(d) All of the above.

59. When was the PII established?
(a) In 1960 (b) In 1963
(c) In 1969 (d) In 1974

60. The political parties in USA have provided an elaborate organisation due to
(a) separation of powers.
(b) frequent elections.
(c) the enormous size of the country.
(d) Both (a) and (b).

61. Which Constitutional Amendment Bill added four languages to the Eighth Schedule of our Constitution?
(a) Eighty-ninth (b) Ninety-second
(c) Ninety-third (d) Ninety-ninth

62. The members of the Republic an Party of USA are drawn from the following sections. Which one of these has been wrongly listed?
(a) Commerce Magnates
(b) Planters
(c) Industrialists
(d) Financial Magnates

63. The MEN is owned by
(a) Modi Entertainment Network Ltd.
(b) Jain Studios Ltd.
(c) Asianet Communications (P) Ltd.
(d) Living Media India Ltd.

64. What is the most outstanding contribution of the political parties in the working of the political system in USA?
(a) They have contributed to the success of federal system in USA and promoted cordial relations between the Centre and the states.
(b) They have greatly helped in reducing the rigours of the theory of separation of powers.
(c) Both (a) and (b).
(d) None of the above.

65. Sony Entertainment Television (SET) was launched in India
(a) October 1995 (b) October 1996
(c) November 1997 (d) December 1999

66. The political parties in USA are
(a) the result of gradual evolution.
(b) the creation of the Constitution.
(c) an extra-constitutional growth.
(d) None of the above.

67. Who can be associated with MTV Bakra?
(a) Cyrus Broacha (b) Jaspal Bhatti
(c) Sajid Khan (d) Tunaaz Karim

68. Which one of the following unit of party organisation in USA is the lowest?

(a) Precincts (b) City
(c) Award (d) None of these

69. Which of the following is not an advantage of using a stringer (freelancer)?
(a) He can fill up for staff members who may be sick or on leave.
(b) He is cost-effective in the sense that he would be paid only if his report is printed or broadcast.
(c) He enhances the group cover of the station.
(d) He is less accountable than the staff personal of the TV, radio, or newspaper organisation.

70. At the apex of the party organisation in USA stands
(a) National Committee
(b) All State Committee
(c) Country Central Committee
(d) None of the above

71. Under the Indian Press Act (1910), the definition of the term seditions publication was widened. However, it did not include the writings against
(a) the British monarch
(b) executive officers
(c) judges
(d) Indian princes

72. Which one of the following statements about the Communist Party of erstwhile Soviet Union is correct?
(a) The party played significant role not only in the government but also in the social, economic and cultural life of the country.
(b) It is the only political party which existed in the country.
(c) The USSR constitution recognised the dominant and monopolistic position of the party.
(d) All of the above.

73. "Freedom of information is a fundamental human right." Which of the following explicitly mentions this statement?
(a) The Indian Press Act (1910)
(b) The Defence of India Act (1939)
(c) The UN Resolution 59, Para 1
(d) The Protection of Publications Proceedings (1950) of Indian Constitution.

74. Which one of the following statements regarding organisation of the Communist Party of USSR is correct?
(a) Its primary organ was known as cell or nuclei.
(b) It was highly organised political party.
(c) It had a pyramidical character.
(d) All of the above.

75. Which of the following is not a social purpose to be served by the freedom of expression?
(a) Reduction in the capacity of an individual to participate in the decision-making process.
(b) Maintenance of a reasonable balance between society and social change.
(c) Discovery of truth for an individual.
(d) Self-attainment of an individual.

76. Which one of the following was the main function of the primary organisation of the Communist Party of Soviet Union?
(a) To help the higher organs of the party in the implementation of their decisions.
(b) To establish contact with general public and propagate communist ideology.
(c) To strengthen labour discipline and inspire the workers to give their best to attain the targets of plans.
(d) All of the above.

77. What is bleed?

(a) Two colours mix with each other in an area to create a new colour.
(b) A photograph with wrapped-around text above, below, and beside it.
(c) The binding of the book is in PB.
(d) The illustration or photograph extends to the extreme edge of the page.

78. Which one of the following features of the erstwhile USSR Communist Party has been wrongly listed?
(a) It believed in mass enrollment of members.
(b) It worked in complete secrecy.
(c) It worked in close co-operation with the government.
(d) It did not permit any criticism of the party leadership.

79. Who is a cub?
(a) The managing editor of a magazine.
(b) An untrained reporter.
(c) The assistant to the (chief) news editor in a newspaper set-up.
(d) A short-story writer.

80. Which of the following is the foremost responsibility of all media firms?
(a) They must earn profits to sustain themselves in the markets.
(b) They must remain sensitive to the aspirations and information needs of the masses.
(c) They must manage their internal affairs with finesse.
(d) They must create such content as may last longer in the markets.

81. Which one of the following features of All Union Congress of the Communist Party of erstwhile USSR has been wrongly listed?
(a) All major party decisions were taken by this organisation.
(b) It was the central organisation of the party.
(c) It met once a year and took stock of the activities of the party and planned its future programme.
(d) None of the above.

82. What is RO?
(a) Review Over: the article has been edited and can be sent to the press.
(b) Reverse Off: convert the recto into verso and vice versa.
(c) Run On: let the line or paragraph continue along with the previous one.
(d) None of the above.

83. Which one of the following has been wrongly listed as a feature of the Communist Party of Soviet Union?
(a) The party represented only the workers and peasants.
(b) The party operated on the principle of collective leadership.
(c) The party enjoyed a constitutional status.
(d) It was characterised by rigid party discipline.

84. What is an ambush interview?
(a) The journo takes the help of security personal to identify the subject for the purpose of interviewing him.
(b) The journo catches a subject unaware in full view of the camera.
(c) The journo encounters the militants in a remote area in the area of operation of those militants.
(d) The journo interviews the militants in a TV studio.

85. The principle of democratic centralism on the basis of which the Communist Party of USSR operated implied
(a) in the Communist Party the power was concentrated in the hands of the top party leaders and the ordinary members could not raise voice against their decisions.

(b) all the members of the party were elected.
(c) the decisions of the party were taken by the higher organisation and the lower organisation faithfully carried them out.
(d) All of the above.

86. The Vernacular Press Act (1878) was also called
(a) Coercive Control Law
(b) Full Control Law
(c) Lytton's Act
(d) Gagging Act

87. When was the office of the Registrar of Newspapers for India (RNI) started?
(a) 1 July 1956
(b) 4 June 1956
(c) 1 July 1954
(d) 4 June 1955

88. Under the gamut of the Official Secrets Act (1923), the Indian government defined the term secret as communication to the enemy in the form of a
(a) Model (b) Plan
(c) Password (d) All of the above

89. In which year was the National film Archives of India established?
(a) 1964 (b) 1966
(c) 1960 (d) 1962

90. When was the Official Secrets Act misused in India?
(a) It was used to prevent Baba Amte from entering Mumbai.
(b) It was used to prevent non-government activists from going to the Parliament.
(c) It was used to prevent non-government anti-dam activists from accessing the Narmada Sardar Sarovar Dam.
(d) It was never misused against any private organisation or NGO.

91. When was the National Film Development Corporation established?
(a) 1984 (b) 1986
(c) 1980 (d) 1982

92. Which of the following is an example of Media Footle?
(a) A VJ explaining the details of clothes worn by a singer whose song would be played next.
(b) A TV anchor asking the guest why he joined politics.
(c) An expert in a subject describing the cause of an event on TV.
(d) A TV newscaster asking a police officer how the train accident took place.

93. In which year was the Commercial Broadcasting Service of AIR was introduced?
(a) 1967 (b) 1968
(c) 1966 (d) 1965

94. The Freedom of Information Act was passed in the United Kingdom in
(a) March 1998 (b) November 2000
(c) April 2002 (d) January 2008

95. What changes have taken place in the role of the Communist Party of Russia since the adoption of policy of *perestroika* (reconstruction) and *glasnost* (openness) by Gorbachev?
(a) Party's working was made more democratic and greater freedom of internal criticism was permitted.
(b) Efforts were made to separate the party from state.
(c) Membership of the party was thrown open to all.
(d) Both (a) and (b).

96. The first multilingual TV network of India was
(a) Gemini (b) ZEE
(c) Jain (d) Etc.

97. Which of the following is not a desirable quality in a reporter or sub-editor?
(a) Curiosity (b) Gift of the gab
(c) News sense (d) Speed

98. Switzerland possesses
(a) bi-party system.
(b) multi-party system.
(c) a party-less system of government.
(d) single party-dominated system.

99. A newspaper's news desk can receive news from its own journos, news agencies, and
(a) the Net.
(b) previous issues of the newspaper.
(c) the masses.
(d) competitors.

100. Which one of the following statements regarding political parties in Switzerland is correct?
(a) The political parties in Switzerland are moderate and conservative.
(b) The political parties in Switzerland are organised on Cantonal basis.
(c) The political parties in Switzerland do not follow any rigid party programme.
(d) All of the above.

101. It has been stated many times that the editorial policy of a newspaper should be based on fairness and accuracy. Besides, other principles of journalistic ethics are also attached to this policy to give a larger-than-life edifice to it (the policy). Why is that so, given that most of the newspapers are engaging themselves in yellow journalism?
(a) The confidence of the masses in a newspaper can be built only if it defines a rational pious editorial policy and implements it in its day-to-day operations.
(b) The masses are impressed by the difficult but seemingly powerful words in the editorial policy, and they read the newspaper with altruism because the policy is worth its weight in gold.
(c) The government wants the newspaper to add such clauses to the policy statement as should look good and society-oriented.
(d) The top brass wants the newspaper to adhere to a finely defined code of journalistic ethics.

102. What are the reasons for the absence of spirit of strife among the political parties in Switzerland?
(a) Absence of class conflict among the various sections of society.
(b) Absence of religious antagonism.
(c) Absence of economic disparities.
(d) All of the above.

103. The Freedom of Information Act was made operational in Australia in
(a) 1981 (b) 1982
(c) 1992 (d) 1993

104. The political parties in Switzerland play quite an ineffective role because of
(a) their loose organisation and lack of necessary funds.
(b) the short duration of the sessions of legislature.
(c) lack of patronage with the political parties.
(d) All of the above.

105. Which Act has made education a Fundamental Right for children in the age group of 6 to 14 years?
(a) The Constitution (86th) Amendment Act (2002)
(b) The Constitution (89th) Amendment Bill (2003)
(c) The Constitution (94th) Amendment Act (2006)
(d) None of the above.

106. The Liberal Party of Switzerland is
   (a) opposed to the Republican System.
   (b) in favour of laissez faire.
   (c) the youngest party of the country.
   (d) All of the above.

107. The magazine *Dataquest* is owned by
   (a) Bennett Coleman and Company Ltd.
   (b) Living Media India Ltd.
   (c) Cyber Media (India) Ltd.
   (d) The Ross Muraka group

108. Who is the director of Entertainment Television Network Private Ltd.?
   (a) Yogesh Radha Krishna
   (b) James Murdoch
   (c) Anthony D'Siiava
   (d) Prannay Roy

109. The magazine *Express Computer* is published by
   (a) Indian Express Newspapers (Bombay) Ltd.
   (b) The GD Goenka group
   (c) The Aditya Vikram Birla group
   (d) IQ Tech Media Pvt Ltd.

110. The Catholic Conservative Party of Switzerland is
   (a) against the protection of the interests of propertied classes.
   (b) in favour of protecting the interests of the church.
   (c) opposed to corporate state.
   (d) opposed to all the above.

111. The Second Press Commission has suggested that Section 5 of the Official Secrets Act be
   (a) scrapped (b) modified
   (c) strengthened (d) None of these

112. Radical Democratic Party of Switzerland is
   (a) a supporter of the cause of church.
   (b) supporter of devices of direct democracy.
   (c) against state intervention in economic affairs.
   (d) None of the above.

113. The guiding principle of the Press Council of India is to
   (a) bargain better salary deal for journalists.
   (b) safeguard the journalists from the government's arbitrary and irrational acts.
   (c) take appropriate action against any journalist who violates the journalistic ethics.
   (d) Both (b) and (c).

114. The Socialist Democratic Party of Switzerland stands for
   (a) merger of various like-minded political parties to achieve political stability.
   (b) bringing about socialism without using revolutionary methods.
   (c) doing away with the devices of direct democracy.
   (d) All of the above.

115. The Foreign Direct Investment in an Indian newspaper or magazine can be up to
   (a) 19 per cent (b) 26 per cent
   (c) 50 per cent (d) 51 percent

116. France is known for
   (a) multi-party system.
   (b) party-less system.
   (c) single party dominance.
   (d) bi-party system.

117. The First Press Council was set up in
   (a) 1946 (b) 1956
   (c) 1966 (d) 1976

118. What a good or morally upright journalist should not do?
   (a) Use of PR in a government office.
   (b) Offer of some incentive to an interviewee so that he could give

information (a cold drink would suffice).

(c) Collection of information from a blazing battlefront.

(d) Collection of information by sneaking into the office or home of the target.

119. The term of the Press Council is

(a) 6 years (b) 5 years
(c) 4 years (d) 3 years

120. Which one of the following features of the French Party System has been wrongly listed?

(a) Wide differences in ideology of various political parties.

(b) Complete harmony between members of the party inside and outside the legislature.

(c) Lack of rigid party discipline.

(d) Majority of the parties in France are organised on regional rather than national basis.

121. A relieving member of the Press Council

(a) can be renominated as many times as the chairman desires.

(b) can be renominated only three times.

(c) can be renominated for a second and final term.

(d) cannot be renominated at all.

122. Neo-classical theory of development became necessary

(a) due to fear of revolution created by the preachings of Marx.

(b) due to all the above reasons.

(c) due to technological and resource discoveries of the nineteenth century.

(d) due to fast deteriorating condition of the workers in Europe.

123. The Press Council of India consists of

(a) a director and 25 members.

(b) a secretary general and 30 members.

(c) a chairman and 28 members.

(d) a president, a convenor and 28 members.

124. The chairman of Press Council of India is selected by a committee consisting of

(a) person chosen by the members of the Council from among themselves

(b) Chairman of Rajya Sabha

(c) Speaker of Lok Sabha

(d) All of the above.

125. Franchise means

(a) right to vote granted to women.

(b) right to vote granted to me'

(c) vote.

(d) right to vote.

126. A civil contemptor

(a) cannot be sentenced only be detained for six months.

(b) can be sentenced for one year and fined 50 thousand rupees.

(c) can be imprisoned for at least 10 years.

(d) None of the above.

127. Electorate means

(a) the nominated members of Parliament.

(b) the candidates who actually contest the elections.

(c) the body of voters.

(d) the elected representatives of people.

128. Punishment for violating the Copyright Act may be

(a) fine.

(b) imprisonment up to one year.

(c) may be both (a) and (b).

(d) can be any of the above.

129. Suffrage means

(a) right to vote granted to people with property.

(b) right to vote granted to all without discrimination.

(c) enactment of bad laws which cause suffering to common people.
(d) the right to vote.

130. Which is the oldest feature agency operating in India?
(a) Indian Press Agency
(b) United News of India
(c) Gemini Features
(d) India News and Feature Alliance

131. Universal Adult Franchise means
(a) right to vote granted to citizens who pay taxes.
(b) right to vote granted to all university graduates.
(c) right to vote granted to all adult citizens.
(d) right to vote granted to all men.

132. The PIB has its headquarters at
(a) Kolkata (b) Chennai
(c) Delhi (d) Mumbai

133. One of the strong opponents of the universal adult franchise was
(a) Rousseau (b) J.S. Mill
(c) Marx (d) Laski

134. In which year was the National film Archives of India established?
(a) 1966 (b) 1964
(c) 1962 (d) 1960

135. Who said that universal adult franchise is not really universal?
(a) Gettell (b) Garner
(c) Laski (d) Gilchrist

136. In which year was the Commercial Broadcasting Service of AIR was introduced?
(a) 1968 (b) 1967
(c) 1966 (d) 1965

137. The Universal Adult Franchise is a feature of
(a) Totalitarian system
(b) Democratic system
(c) All systems
(d) None of the above

138. Where is the Film and Television Institute of India situated?
(a) Pune (b) Chennai
(c) Delhi (d) Mumbai

139. Which of the following is not a desirable quality in a reporter or sub-editor?
(a) Curiosity (b) Gift of the gab
(c) News sense (d) Speed

140. Which section of IPC defines the offence of defamation?
(a) 489 (b) 490
(c) 498 (d) 499

141. Universal Adult Franchise is justified on the ground that
(a) it gives power to the elected representatives of people.
(b) it gives practical shape to the principle of popular sovereignty.
(c) it leads to rule by ignorants.
(d) it makes the Parliament very powerful.

142. In which year was Indian Institute of Mass Communication established?
(a) 1970 (b) 1968
(c) 1965 (d) 1960

143. One of the chief defects of Universal Adult Franchise is
(a) it leads to rule by ignorants.
(b) it lays emphasis on the principle of equality.
(c) it protects the rights of minorities.
(d) it gives chance to a common man to be associated with the decisions of the government.

144. National Film Awards in India were established in which year?
(a) 1956 (b) 1954
(c) 1952 (d) 1950

145. The Freedom Information Act was passed in Britain in
(a) April 2002 (b) March 1998
(c) January 2003 (d) November 2000

146. Women suffrage means
(a) right to vote granted to graduate women.
(b) right to vote granted to those women who have undergone political suffering.
(c) right to vote granted to all adult women.
(d) right to vote granted to adult married women.

147. The Films Division is the re-established from which British organisation?
(a) Information Films of India
(b) Film Finance Corporation
(c) Indian Broadcasting Company
(d) Publications Division

148. One of the arguments in favour of women suffrage is
(a) political alertness leads to better understanding between husband and wife.
(b) women require greater protection and safeguards.
(c) it destroys the feminine qualities.
(d) women learn the art of government which proves helpful in the management of family affairs.

149. When was the office of the Registrar of Newspapers for India (RNI) started?
(a) 1 July 1956 (b) 4 July 1956
(c) 1 July 1957 (d) 4 June 1958

150. One of the arguments advanced against women suffrage is
(a) women are ill-fitted to represent their own interests.
(b) women would lose many of their feminine qualities.
(c) menfolk can represent the interests of women better.
(d) their participation in the political life would lead to corruption.

151. When was Television introduced in India?
(a) 5 September 1958
(b) 15 September 1959
(c) 21 September 1959
(d) 1 September 1960

152. Women in England got franchise on equal terms with men in
(a) 1911 (b) 1688
(c) 1950 (d) 1928

153. Who pleaded that there should be two Parliaments to deal with the economic and political problems
(a) J.S. Mill (b) Marx
(c) Henry Webbs (d) G.D.H. Cole

154. When was the National Film Development Corporation established?
(a) 1986 (b) 1984
(c) 1982 (d) 1980

155. Joint electorate is a system in which
(a) elections are held simultaneously for the central and state legislatures.
(b) seats are allotted to various communities in proportion to their strength.
(c) seats are reserved for various interests.
(d) there is no reservation of seats for any one.

156. Who made the registration of newspapers compulsory in 1835?
(a) John Adams
(b) Lord Lytton
(c) Lord William Bentick
(d) Sir Charles Metcalfe

157. Direct election means
(a) people cannot authorise their representatives to caste vote on their behalf.

(b) the voters directly take part in the election of their representatives.
(c) people assemble at one place and elect their representatives by voice vote.
(d) people can suggest the name of their representative on their own.

158. In which year was the *Amrit Bazar Patrika* first published?
(a) 1875 (b) 1870
(c) 1868 (d) 1867

159. Which one of the following is most perishable?
(a) A magazine
(b) A newspaper
(c) A book
(d) All the above are equally perishable.

160. Broadcasting subject is under the
(a) State List
(b) Concurrent List
(c) Union List
(d) None of the above

161. The chief defect of direct election is
(a) it has no educative value.
(b) it is not in keeping with democratic principles.
(c) it promotes aversion towards public affairs.
(d) representatives are responsive to public opinion.

162. The meaning of the term offence has been given in
(a) Article 361
(b) Freedom of Information Bill
(c) The General Clauses Act (1897)
(d) Both (a) and (c)

163. Constituency means
(a) the division of the country into electoral areas for the purpose of conducting the elections.
(b) the areas of the country as defined in the constitution.
(c) a law according to which the territory is divided into a number of units for the purpose of elections.
(d) None of the above.

164. Which of the following is not the code of journalistic ethics?
(a) Always be true towards your parents
(b) Respect for the law
(c) Truth and accuracy
(d) Respect for individual privacy

165. A single-member constituency means
(a) a constituency from which a number of candidates may contest but only one member is elected.
(b) a constituency from which only one candidate contests the election.
(c) a constituency from which a candidate is returned unopposed.
(d) None of the above.

166. Which of the following is not correctly matched?
(a) Slug: A poor work in reporting.
(b) Yellow Journalism: Publication specializing in stories that are sensational or grossly exaggerated and dealing generally with sex, crime and gossip.
(c) Work and Turn: Printing one side of a sheet and turning it over from left to right using the same side guides and plate for the second side.
(d) Wove Paper: A paper having a uniform unlined surface with a smooth finish.

167. One of the chief merits of single member constituencies is
(a) local interests are given precedence over national interests.
(b) minority may get over representation.

(c) people have a very limited choice in the selection of their representatives.
(d) intimate relationship is possible between the electors and the representative.

168. Constitution Amendment Bill requires the support of how many members of the Lok Sabha actually present and voting?
(a) Two-third
(b) Half of the house
(c) One-fourth
(d) One-third

169. One of the main defects of the single-member constituencies is
(a) every region gets adequate representation in the Parliament.
(b) people's choice regarding representative is narrowed.
(c) intimate relationship is not possible between the elector and representative.
(d) intimate relations are possible between the electors and the representative.

170. Under which rule, can a member raise any issue which he thinks is of public interest?
(a) Rule 355 (b) Rule 365
(c) Rule 377 (d) Rule 385

171. Multi-member constituency means
(a) when several members are elected from the same constituency.
(b) constituency from which a number of candidates contest but only one of them is finally elected.
(c) constituency from which a number of candidates contest but only two of them are finally elected.
(d) None of the above.

172. Motion which enables a member to draw the attention of the government to matter of public importance is
(a) Call Attention Motion
(b) No-confidence Motion
(c) Adjournment Motion
(d) None of the above.

173. Should the government fully privatize the media?
(a) No, the government should only provide sound infrastructure to the media but let them operate freely, sans any restrictions.
(b) Yes, in a country like India, the masses ought to be informed about important social, environmental, health, and moral issues, which may not be the priority areas for private media conglomerates.
(c) No, this is the era of free market economy.
(d) Yes, the government must also earn through the media.

174. What is meant by the word 'stringer'?
(a) A person who resides in a far off place and is attached to newspaper and is paid fixed amount.
(b) A full-time journalist.
(c) A freelance journalist who is not paid a fixed amount.
(d) None of the above.

175. Minority representation means
(a) representation to propertied classes which form a minority of the total community.
(b) representation to persons below the age of adulthood, so that they may be able to protect the interests of the minors.
(c) representation to the various minorities present in a state.
(d) None of the above.

176. Which of the following is not correctly matched?

(a) Run: An online story
(b) Short: A short item; a filler
(c) Schedule: A list of assignments
(d) Scoop: An exclusive story for a newspaper for which a reporter lives laborious life

177. Proportional representation is a method of representation which
(a) provides representation to all the political parties.
(b) provides representation to each group of party in proportion to its voting strength.
(c) provides votes to the people keeping in view their property.
(d) provides extra votes to the educated people.

178. Which of the following is not correctly matched?
(a) Round-up: A comprehensive story
(b) Play: Story
(c) Retainer: Amount paid to retain the use of correspondent who may not necessarily be filing copy all the time
(d) Rewrite Man: A writer (usually a sub) for a newspaper or agency

179. The two prominent schemes of proportional representation are
(a) Reservation of Seats and Direct Election.
(b) Direct Election and Communal Representation.
(c) Hare Scheme and List System.
(d) Universal Adult Franchise and Direct Elections.

180. Which of the following is not correctly matched?
(a) Lebel: Any defamatory statement expressed in writing, printing or other visible form
(b) Leader: Editorial
(c) Routing: Systematic arrangement of news
(d) Leg-man: A reporter who gathers but does not write the news

181. Under the Hare Scheme, every voter enjoys
(a) one vote less than the number of seats to be filled up.
(b) only two votes.
(c) one effective role.
(d) as many votes as there are seats to be filled.

182. Which of the following is not correctly matched?
(a) Kill: Elimination of news material at any stage in the processing
(b) Lead: Headline
(c) Human Interest: Story about human or emotional appeal but not necessarily hard news
(d) None of the above.

183. The quota under the Hare Scheme is determined by
(a) the number of votes is fixed by law before the election is held.
(b) the number of votes is decided by all the contesting candidates before the election.
(c) dividing the total number of votes by two.
(d) dividing the total number of valid polled votes by the number of seats to be filled up plus one and by adding one to the quotient.

184. Which of the following is not correctly matched?
(a) Tailpiece: A paragraph with finishing touches
(b) Tip: A small bit of information that could lead to a news story
(c) Syndicate: An organisation that sells articles and features on behalf of a writer
(d) Beat: A special kind of story

185. Under single transferable vote system, each voter can
(a) indicate one preference less than the seats to be filled up.
(b) indicate as many preferences as there are candidates to be elected.
(c) indicate only two preferences.
(d) indicate only one preference.

186. A science reporter can do justice to any write up by
(a) adopting a lucid style of writing
(b) referring to one's personal glossary of science
(c) verifying its facts
(d) All of the above

187. Under the List System, there are
(a) multi-member constituencies.
(b) single-member constituencies.
(c) two-member constituencies.
(d) None of the above.

188. Which is not the quality of a science technology reporter?
(a) A narrow network of acquaintance among the scientists and technologists of the region.
(b) An analytical mind that will not accept anything at face value.
(c) A perceptive mind that thrives on a keen awareness.
(d) An inherent scientific temper.

189. Under the List System, each voter enjoys
(a) one vote less than total number of seats to be filled up.
(b) two votes.
(c) only one vote.
(d) as many votes as there are seats to be filled up.

190. To choose the news items for the newspaper and to correct the language, spelling and remove all the unimportant sentences are the functions of
(a) Sub-editor
(b) Writer
(c) Reporter
(d) None of the above

191. Under the List System, each voter
(a) can indicate preference for candidates in the list for which he votes.
(b) can prepare his own list from amongst the candidates.
(c) votes for the list as a whole.
(d) can pick up candidates from various lists.

192. Headlines are generally given by
(a) Reporter (b) Page designer
(c) Both (a) and (b) (d) Sub-editors

193. Under the List System, the list of the contesting candidates is prepared by
(a) the Election Commissioner.
(b) mutual consent of the political parties contesting elections.
(c) each political party.
(d) the voters.

194. What is the job of development reporter?
(a) To inform readers, listeners and viewers about various plans.
(b) To create an atmosphere of understanding the objectives of the schemes.
(c) To help in creating awareness about the developmental issues.
(d) All of the above.

195. The Limited Vote Plan, which is a scheme for minority representation, entitles each voter to cast
(a) one vote less than the seats to be filled up.
(b) all his votes in favour of any single candidate.
(c) only one vote.
(d) as many votes as there are candidates to be elected.

196. To be a successful development reporter, one should
   (a) encourage 'mouthpiece writing'.
   (b) keep a desk diary.
   (c) foster a wide range of contacts.
   (d) maintain a reference manual.

197. The concept of an individual's privacy has been explained in
   (a) Article 10 (a) of Universal Declaration of Human Rights (1948).
   (b) Article 10 of Universal Declaration of Human Rights (1948).
   (c) Article 12 of Universal Declaration of Human Rights (1948).
   (d) None of these.

198. Which of the following is not correctly matched?
   (a) Exclusive: A story that no other newspaper has for that day, a scoop.
   (b) Editor: Owner of the firm.
   (c) Embargo: A deadline for the release of a story.
   (d) Editorial: The editor's opinion or comment on events.

199. The Limited Vote Plan is defective insofar as it
   (a) provides representation to large minorities only.
   (b) provides no representation to the minorities.
   (c) provides representation to small minorities alone.
   (d) provides representation to the majorities alone.

200. Which of the following is not correctly matched?
   (a) PM's: Afternoon papers.
   (b) Play: The display given to a story or a picture. Most editors talk of playing a story, rather than playing it up or down.
   (c) AM's: A mediator.
   (d) Overset: Types left over form an edition. Usually wasted; in tightly-knit news department cause for editorial ire.

201. The three important schemes for representation of minorities are
   (a) Universal Adult Franchise, Secret Ballot and Functional Representation.
   (b) Limited Vote Plan, Cumulative Vote Plan and Reservation of Seats.
   (c) Proportional Representation, Territorial Representation and Communal Representation.
   (d) None of the above.

202. Which of the following is not correctly matched?
   (a) Spread: Field of reporter.
   (b) Running Story: A chronological story of an event topped by successive leads as the news changes.
   (c) Routing: Removing the unwanted metal from non-printing areas of a plate.
   (d) Run: A reporter's beat.

203. The Cumulative Voting Plan, which gives to each voter as many votes as there are seats to be filled up, requires the voter
   (a) not to cast all his votes in favour of any one candidate.
   (b) to divide the votes amongst the candidates.
   (c) to cast all his votes in favour of one candidate.
   (d) give all votes to one candidate or divide them between two or more candidates according to his choice.

204. Which of the following is not correctly matched?
   (a) Byline: First two lines of a story.
   (b) Turn: A lengthy story that does not all go on page one and has to be

placed in an inside page with another headline, when it is said to "turn".

(c) Top: The reference to a story that should go in single column at the top of a page.

(d) Trim: To cut a story down to its essentials.

205. *National Call* was started by

(a) Pathan Joseph (b) K.N. Guruswami
(c) Rubi Karanjia (d) J.N. Sahni

206. Points included in the coverage of any game are

(a) crucial moments of the game
(b) final score
(c) names of players
(d) All of the above

207. The Party Control Committee of the Communist Party in the erstwhile USSR was concerned with

(a) punishment of members of the party who violated the party discipline or worked against the directives of the party.
(b) the enrollment of the members of the party.
(c) the maintenance of discipline in the party.
(d) Both (a) and (c).

208. Which of these news values are not highlighted in sports news story?

(a) Human interest
(b) Prominence of the sports event
(c) Progress in terms of statistics
(d) None of the above

209. What should be avoided while writing the masthead?

(a) Write in distinctive bold point
(b) Write in a fixed place on the front page every day
(c) Write in small size
(d) None of the above.

210. Who stated, "Freedom always entails in obligation, whether it is a nation's freedom or an individual's freedom or a group freedom of the Press"?

(a) Professor N.G. Ranga
(b) J.L. Nehru
(c) Lord Linlithgo
(d) N.V.L. Narasimha Rao

211. Should the media be owned and controlled by the government?

(a) Yes, the government must also earn through the media.
(b) Yes, in a country like India, the masses ought to be informed about important social environmental, health, and moral issues, wnicn may not be the priority areas for private media conglomerates.
(c) No, this is the era of free market economy.
(d) No, the government should only provide sound infrastructure to the media but let them operate freely, sans any restrictions.

212. Who is considered as the champion of Indian journalism?

(a) James Augustus Hickey
(b) Madan Mohan Malviya
(c) M.K. Gandhi
(d) Ram Mohan Roy

213. While all news is information, all information is not news. Which one of the following examples best exemplifies this statement?

(a) Mr. Obma shall unit India in 2010; Mr. Obama is the President of the USA.
(b) Mr. Obama is the President of the USA; Mr. Obama is 49 years of age.
(c) Mr. Obama is the 44th President of the USA; Mr. Obama was a Sendor from Illinois.
(d) All of the above.

214. What is Hold Over?
   (a) A radio programme that has been postponed to another date.
   (b) A typeset copy that can be used at a later date.
   (c) A TV broadcast that has been banned by the state.
   (d) A proof of a book that has been kept pending for some time.

215. Which of the following is not a social purpose to be served by the freedom of expression?
   (a) Reduction in the capacity of an individual to participate in the decision-making process.
   (b) Maintenance of a reasonable balance between society and social change.
   (c) Discovery truth for an individual.
   (d) Self-attainment of an individual.

216. What was the impact of the Press Council Repeal Act (1976)?
   (a) The First Press Council was abolished.
   (b) The Second Press Council was abolished.
   (c) The Third Press Council was abolished.
   (d) Mrs. Gandhi allowed the Press to print whatever it wanted to.

217. Which one of the following has been wrongly listed as a Youth Organisation of the Communist Party of erstwhile Soviet Union?
   (a) Young Pioneers (b) Politbureau
   (c) Little Octoberist (d) Komsomols

218. The promoter of Sun TV is
   (a) Kalanidhi Maran
   (b) Ramoji Rao
   (c) Shekhar Kapur
   (d) Sunhash Chandra

219. Who repealed the Vernacular Press Act?
   (a) Lord Rippon (b) Lord Curzon
   (c) Lord Lytton (d) Lord Irvin

220. The National Institute of Health and Family Welfare, New Delhi was set up under the
   (a) Press Council Repeal Act (1976).
   (b) Constitution (First Amendment) Act (1951).
   (c) Societies Registration Act (XXI) of 1860.
   (d) Press Council Bill (1977).

221. The newspaper *Independent* was started by
   (a) Syed Hussain
   (b) Motilal Nehru
   (c) Jawaharlal Nehru
   (d) Mahatma Gandhi

222. The government's monopoly on broadcasting rests in which Article of the Indian Constitution?
   (a) Article 234 (b) Article 246
   (c) Article 256 (d) Article 336

223. East India Company introduced censorship for the first time in
   (a) 1790 (b) 1795
   (c) 1780 (d) 1786

224. The lead (news) should answer
   (a) When and where
   (b) Why and how
   (c) Who and what
   (d) All of the above

225. Annie Besant edited
   (a) *Young India* (b) *Common Wheel*
   (c) *New India* (d) Both (b) and (c)

226. Which is the quality of a news?
   (a) Accuracy (b) Balance
   (c) Clarity (d) All of the above

227. Which reporting goes behind the news and brings out the truth?
   (a) Crime (b) Investigative
   (c) Objective (d) Interpretative

228. *Bombay Chronicle* was edited by
(a) Bal Gangadhar Tilak
(b) Km. Jogalekar
(c) Firoz Shah Mehta
(d) Srinivas Shashtri

229. James Silk Buckingham edited
(a) *Calcutta Chronicle*
(b) *Calcutta Gazette*
(c) *Calcutta Express*
(d) *Calcutta Times*

230. 'Reporting' which deals with the subject-matter where an attempt is being made to hide the truth from the people is
(a) interpretative (b) crime
(c) investigative (d) objective

231. ____ was given in inscriptions on walls of temples and in copper plates and through victory coins and writings on rocks.
(a) News (b) Clothes
(c) Money (d) Any thing

232. What does 'a nose for news' mean?
(a) Senses material for news
(b) Publish crime reports
(c) Space for news
(d) None of the above.

233. Where the news was mainly carried by the word of mouth?
(a) Canada (b) France
(c) Europe (d) England

234. Which is not the quality of a reporter?
(a) Editing interviews for use
(b) A nose for news
(c) Team spirit
(d) Outgoing nature

235. 'Tabloid Journalism' is also called
(a) White Journalism
(b) Yellow Journalism
(c) Red Journalism
(d) None of the above

236. Which country is the main origin of newspaper?
(a) Europe (b) France
(c) Australia (d) Africa

237. According to Shelton Gunaratne, development journalism involves in
(a) Constructive criticism
(b) Analytical interpretation
(c) Subtle investigation
(d) All of the above

238. What is the oldest evidence of Chinese printing?
(a) Pride and prejudice (b) Nobel
(c) Diamond Sutra (d) Meghdoot

239. How many key departments are there in any newspaper?
(a) Three (b) Four
(c) Five (d) None of these

240. Peculiarities of the language used in sports writing are
(a) war references like 'kill' are avoided.
(b) sports jargon itself finds mention only on a low key.
(c) report is written for general reader.
(d) All of the above.

241. When was started the Diamond Sutra?
(a) 525 AD (b) 1425 AD
(c) 465 AD (d) 868 AD

242. Which is not the style used in sports writings?
(a) Discovering of new angle
(b) Professional Approach
(c) Both (a) and (b)
(d) Write lengthy articles

243. In which century the metal type printing machine in mainz was made?
(a) 9th century (b) 15th century
(c) 16th century (d) 18th century

244. Points included in the coverage of any game are

(a) names of players
(b) crucial moments of the game
(c) final score
(d) All of the above

245. In how many pages did the newsletter run?
(a) Twelve pages (b) Seventeen pages.
(c) Four pages (d) Eight pages

246. Which of these news values are not highlighted in sports news story?
(a) Progress in terms of statistics
(b) Human interest
(c) Prominence of the sports event
(d) None of the above

247. Robert Coles and Samuel Pecke were the most prominent publishers of
(a) *Coranto* (b) *India Today*
(c) *Diurnal* (d) *The Times*

248. What is the job of development reporter?
(a) To inform readers, listeners and viewers about various plans.
(b) To create an atmosphere of understandings the objectives of the schemes.
(c) To help in creating awareness about the development issue.
(e) All of the above.

249. Which article of the Indian Constitution provides the provisions relating to freedom of speech and expression?
(a) 14 (b) 18
(c) 19 (d) 36

250. What created a pressure world within journalism?
(a) Monitor (b) TV
(c) Radio (d) Telegraph

251. A defamation is committed by the
(a) spoken words and photographs
(b) gestures and gossips
(c) written words and cartoons
(d) All of the above

252. Which is the oldest feature agency operating in India?
(a) Compass Features
(b) Indian Press Agency
(c) Indian News and Feature Alliance
(d) Gemini Features

253. After a defamation has been committed, the case is to be filed in the court by
(a) the aggrieved person
(b) his lawyer only
(c) any person who knows him
(d) any of his family members

254. A corporation or a firm can file a libel case when its
(a) top management is affected.
(b) property and business are affected.
(c) individual members of the corporation are affected.
(d) None of the above.

255. What created further divisions and demacrations in the newspaper?
(a) The invention of mobile and monitor
(b) The invention of radio and TV
(c) The invention of telegraph and telegram
(d) The invention of TV and phone

256. Exception in filing a case in the court on behalf of a defamed person can be made in the case of
(a) Lunatic (b) Minor
(c) Sick (d) All of the above

257. The instance in which the comment cannot be deemed as a 'fair comment'.
(a) When a judge is described as being incompetent.
(b) When improper motives are attributed to the judge of a case.
(c) When a judgement on a case is stated to be arbitrary.
(d) All of the above.

258. Who installed the first steam printing press?
(a) John Walter I (b) John Dome
(c) John Milton (d) John Walter II

259. The main function of the Youth Organisation of the Communist Party of Soviet Union was
(a) to popularise the ideology of Man and Lenin among the youth.
(b) to co-operate with the government in the formulation and implementation of policies.
(c) to enroll new members to the party.
(d) Both (a) and (b).

260. The example of eventuality that could be considered as civil contempt of court is
(a) a news item casting aspersions, by implication, on the character of sitting judge of the court.
(b) to publish certain particulars about the accused during the pendency court proceedings against him.
(c) failure of a defendant to comply with a court's order to pay a punitive sum of money towards a fine.
(d) All of the above.

261. Why is M.F. Hussain known?
(a) For best cooking
(b) For worst health
(c) For best paintings
(d) For best writings

262. Publication of court proceedings are restricted by
(a) Section 33 of Special Marriage Act, 1954, which requires the proceedings under the act to be held in camera if either party to the case wishes so, or if the court so directs.
(b) Section 14 of the official Secrets Act, 1923, which empowers the court to hold the proceedings of a case or any part there of in camera.
(c) Section 228-A of IPC which prohibits publication of the names of victims of certain sexual crimes.
(d) All of the above.

263. When was the uses and gratification first introduced and by whom?
(a) Kaifin 1955
(b) Henaryin 1950
(c) Ehitu Katzin 1959
(d) John Hemilton in 1960

264. Question to which a member desires an oral answer is
(a) Unstarred (b) Short Notice
(c) Starred (d) None of the above

265. "Media is used by individuals to connect or disconnect themselves from others." Who said this?
(a) Katz, Gure vitch and Hass
(b) Townfile, Crown
(c) Hemilton Franklin
(d) Franklin John Henery

266. Question to which a written answer is deemed to have been laid on the 'Table of the House' after the question hour is
(a) Unstarred
(b) Short Notice
(c) Starred
(d) None of the above.

267. When was the first media dependency theory described?
(a) In 1960 (b) In 1950
(c) In 1976 (d) In 1956

268. Constitution Amendment Bill requires the support of how many members of the Lok Sabha actually present and voting?
(a) Half of the House (b) Two-third
(c) One-fourth (d) One-third

269. Motion, which enables a member to draw the attention of the government, to development of public importance?

(a) Adjournment Motion
(b) Call Attention Motion
(c) No-confidence Motion
(d) None of the above.

270. Journalists are like
(a) Publishers (b) Photographers
(c) Painters (d) Writers

271. Which is most effective communication model that identifies the source message, content, channel, audience, etc.?
(a) Donne Honey model
(b) Brown model
(c) Harold Laswel model
(d) None of these

272. Milton's views on press freedom is referred to as
(a) Star chamber
(b) Areopagitica
(c) Authoritarian
(d) Social responsibility

273. In India, after how many years of the death of a writer, the copyright on his book ends?
(a) 30 years (b) 40 years
(c) 50 years (d) 60 years

274. A later adaptor of newcamp model and addresses itself particularly to various formal media related to mass communication.
(a) Theodore model I
(b) George model
(c) Westley and Mclean model
(d) None of these

275. What was dealt with in Feroze Gandhi Act?
(a) Publication of parliamentary proceedings.
(b) Publication of court proceedings.
(c) Science Reporting.
(d) Sports Reporting.

276. The commission appointed to investigate Tehelka.com exposures is
(a) Justice Chawla Commission
(b) Justice Jayachandra Reddi Commission
(c) Justice Bharucha Commission
(d) Justice Venkataswami Commission

277. A model which sees communication essentially as a process of transmission.
(a) Gerbner's model
(b) Theodore model
(c) Mc model
(d) None of these

278. Right to life and Personal Liberty is guaranteed by Indian Constitution's:
(a) Article 21 (b) Article 14
(c) Article 19(a) (d) Article 17(b)

279. What ethical principle of journalism demands that reporters identify where their information comes from and that they do not use anonymous sources?
(a) Fairness to all (b) The truth
(c) Objectivity (d) Attribution

280. Freebies are described as
(a) writing for jazz journalism
(b) obscene stories
(c) special favours to media persons
(d) precision journalism

281. When was the normative theory of mass communication introduced first?
(a) In 1956 (b) In 1950
(c) In 1963 (d) In 1957

282. A writing is not libellous, if it is a fair comment on a matter of
(a) media interest
(b) editor's interest
(c) public interest
(d) corporate interest

283. Any violation of the freedom of speech and expression by a government law or order can be challenged under Article

(a) 29 (b) 30
(c) 31 (d) 32

284. Which of the following is true in the case of working journalists?
(a) They are entitled to rights under the Industrial Disputes Act, 1947.
(b) They are entitled to rights under the Industrial Employment (Standing Orders) Act, 1946.
(c) They are entitled to the rights under the Employee's provident funds Act, 1952.
(d) They are not entitled to gratuity under the working Journalists and Miscellaneous provisions Act, 1955.

285. Who added development media theory and democratic media theory in 1980?
(a) John Hemilton (b) Shakespeare
(c) Mcmillan (d) Mcquail

286. The information model of journalism was advocated by
(a) John Miller
(b) John Fiske
(c) George Herbert Mead
(d) Ernest Barmann

287. According to the Indian Constitution, Article 19 can be suspended during the period of
(a) Cabinet formation
(b) Budget presentation
(c) Judicial enquiry
(d) Emergency

288. The Wage Boards for working journalists are constituted from time to time by
(a) the INS
(b) the Labour Board
(c) the Central Government
(d) the State Governments

289. In which parts the mass media is divided?
(a) Savvy media
(b) Libertarian media
(c) Print and electronic media
(d) None of these

290. The period of limitation to initiate a proceeding for contempt of court is
(a) One year (b) Two years
(c) Three years (d) Four years

291. The US President who introduced the fire side chats with media persons was
(a) Harry Truman
(b) Theodore Roosevelt
(c) Eisenhower
(d) Franklin Roosevelt

292. Which day is celebrated as the Press Freedom day?
(a) May 3 (b) September 22
(c) June 1 (d) August 9

293. Truth is not a defence in cases involving
(a) Criminal libel (b) Civil libel
(c) Slander (d) Official secrets

294. News deadlines have become constant because of
(a) News media
(b) Television
(c) Radio
(d) Evening newspapers

295. Children's Film Society of India was established in
(a) In 1990 (b) In 1959
(c) In 1955 (d) In 1966

296. The Supreme Court of India is a court of record, according to the Indian Constitution's
(a) Article 125 (b) Article 127
(c) Article 129 (d) Article 131

297. The ideal of independence in reporting is described as
(a) a pressure (b) an influence
(c) a firewall (d) a control

298. A multi-member constituency is better than single-member constituency because

(a) it is easy for the poor man to contest elections.
(b) it ensures more stable ministries.
(c) it provides greater freedom to the people in selecting their representatives.
(d) it encourages the growth of a number of political parties.

299. Section 132 A of the Indian Evidence Act, 1872, protects
(a) personal privacy
(b) official informers
(c) police informers
(d) information sources

300. Which of the following Article in the Constitution of India deals with the reasonable restrictions on freedom of speech and expression?
(a) Article 19(1)(a)
(b) Article 19(1)(b)
(c) Article 19(2)
(d) Article 19(3)

301. When was the film division established in India?
(a) In 1920 (b) In 1970
(c) In 1960 (d) In 1948

302. Which of the following rights was described by B.R. Ambedkar as the "heart and soul" of the Constitution?
(a) Right to freedom of religion
(b) Right to property
(c) Right to equality
(d) Right to constitutional remedies

303. 'Working Journalists Act' was introduced in
(a) 1947 (b) 1950
(c) 1955 (d) 1960

304. Which part of the Constitution of India deals with citizenship?
(a) I (b) II
(c) III (d) IV

305. What is MIFF?
(a) Dramma industry
(b) Writing indusry
(c) Film industry
(d) None of these

306. Which of the following does not contribute to the 'credibility' of the press?
(a) Impartiality (b) Believability
(c) Sensationalism (d) Accuracy

307. Currently, yellow journalism is overshadowed by a new term
(a) red journalism
(b) black journalism
(c) green journalism
(d) grey journalism

308. The Universal Adult Franchise is an indication of the principle of the
(a) Popular sovereignty
(b) National sovereignty
(c) Legal sovereignty
(d) Political sovereignty

309. Which of the following is an exception provided under the Copyright Act of India?
(a) For academic research
(b) For commercial production
(c) For profit through sales
(d) For performance before paid audience

310. Westerstahl conceptualised scheme to achieve objectivity in reporting. Which is the correct scheme?
(a) Truth – relevance – non-partisanship – neutrality.
(b) Truth – cognition – balance – neutrality.
(c) Truth – relevance – balance – emotion.
(d) Truth – cognition – balance – sensation.

Directions: Questions 311 to 318 are of multiple statement type. Choose the correct answer from the codes given below the statements.

311. Consider the following statements about the political parties in USA—
1. Political parties in USA possess more elaborate organisation than possessed by the political parties in other countries.
2. Membership of political parties in USA is largely determined by the attachment of the ancestors to a particular party.
3. USA political parties are dominated by the local bosses.
4. The USA political parties are dominated by the national party leaders.

Of the above statements—
(a) 1, 2 and 4 are correct
(b) 1, 3 and 4 are correct
(c) 1, 2 and 3 are correct
(d) 2, 3 and 4 are correct

312. Consider the following statements regarding the party system in Switzerland—
1. Political parties in Switzerland are not organised on the basis of social, political and economic principles.
2. There is no opposition party in Switzerland because all the parties are provided proportional representation in the government.
3. The political parties in Switzerland are an extra-constitutional growth.
4. The political parties in Switzerland possess an elaborate organisation.

Of the above statements—
(a) 1, 2 and 4 are correct
(b) 1, 3 and 4 are correct
(c) 1, 2 and 3 are correct
(d) 2, 3 and 4 are correct

313. Consider the following statements about the political parties in Switzerland—
1. There are no basic issues which divide the political parties in Switzerland.
2. The presence of various devices of direct democracy in Switzerland has made the political parties less active.
3. Dominance of government by a single party has rendered the other political parties ineffective.
4. The executive in Switzerland does not need the support of the majority party to keep itself in power.

Of the above statements
(a) 1, 2 and 4 are correct
(b) 1, 3 and 4 are correct
(c) 1, 2 and 3 are correct
(d) 2, 3 and 4 are correct

314. Journalists
1. Collect information.
2. Elicit opinion from the masses.
3. Select the programmes for broadcasting.
4. Write on socio-political matters only.

Codes:
(a) 1 and 2 (b) 1, 2 and 3
(c) 1, 3 and 4 (d) 2, 3 and 4

315. Consider the following statements—
1. USA has bi-party system.
2. Political parties in USA are not organised on the basis of any political, social and economic principles.
3. There are no doctrinal differences between the two political parties of USA.
4. The political parties in USA work in tight mould of discipline.

Of the above statements—
(a) 1, 3 and 4 are correct
(b) 2, 3 and 4 are correct

(c) 1, 2 and 3 are correct
(d) 1, 2 and 4 are correct

316. Which of the following are correctly matched?
1. Late News: News that arrives too late to make the front page
2. Lead: Beginning of a story
3. Ears: Boxes on either side of the nameplate on PP 1 of a newspaper that usually carry advertisements in India
4. Edition: Remake or revision of some of the pages of a newspaper.

les:
(a) 1 and 4 (b) 2 and 4
(d) 1, 2, 3 and 4 (c) 2, 3 and 4

317. Consider the following statements regarding the defamation
1. The statement must be defamatory
2. The statement must refer to the plaintiff
3. The statement must be made with malicious intentions
4. The statement must be false

Which of these statements are correct?

Codes:
(a) 1 and 2 (b) 3 and 4
(c) 1, 2 and 4 (d) 1, 2, 3 and 4

318. Consider the following statements—
1. Leadership plays a dominant role in the formation and working of the political parties in France.
2. There exist wide differences in the ideology of the political parties in France.
3. In France, a large number of parliamentary groups exist in the Parliament which have no relationship with the parties outside.
4. In France, the political parties are organised on national basis.

Of the above statements—
(a) 1, 2 and 4 are correct
(b) 1, 3 and 4 are correct
(c) 1, 2 and 3 are correct
(d) 2, 3 and 4 are correct

Directions: Questions 319 to 322 are of matching type. Match List-I with List-II and select the correct answer using the codes given below the lists.

319.

List-I	List-II
(A) Bank	1. Inside information
(B) Banner	2. Headline
(C) Agate	3. Part of a headline
(D) Dope	4. Unit for measurement of lines

Codes:	A	B	C	D
(a)	4	3	1	2
(b)	3	2	4	1
(c)	2	3	4	1
(d)	1	2	3	4

320.

List-I (Articles)	List-II (Provisions)
(A) Art. 19(1)(a)	1. Freedom of speech
(B) Art. 19(1)(b)	2. Freedom to assemble
(C) Art. 19(1)(c)	3. Freedom to form associations
(D) Art. 19(1)(d)	4. Freedom of movement

Codes:	A	B	C	D
(a)	2	3	4	1
(b)	3	4	1	2
(c)	4	1	2	3
(d)	1	2	3	4

321.

List-I (Terms)	List-II (Meanings)
(A) Cub	1. Inside information
(B) AM's	2. Territory assigned to a reporter

(C) Beat 3. Morning paper's
(D) Dope 4. An untrained newsman

Codes:	A	B	C	D
(a)	2	3	4	1
(b)	4	3	2	1
(c)	1	2	3	4
(d)	3	4	1	2

322.

List-I	List-II
(A) Indian Telegraph Act	1. 1933
(B) Indian Wireless Act	2. 1957
(C) Copyright Act	3. 1885

Codes:	A	B	C
(a)	1	2	3
(b)	1	3	2
(c)	3	1	2
(d)	2	1	3

Directions: Questions 323 to 342 consist of two statements, one labelled as 'Assertion' (A) and the other labelled as 'Reason' (R). You are to examine these two statements carefully and decide if the Assertion (A) and the Reason (R) are individually true and if so, whether the Reason is a correct explanation of the Assertion. Select your answers to these questions using the codes given below:

(a) Both (A) and (R) are true and (R) is the correct explanation of (A).
(b) Both (A) and (R) are true but (R) is not the correct explanation of (A).
(c) (A) is true but (R) is false.
(d) (A) is false but (R) is true.

323. **Assertion (A):** You cannot write for every magazine that you may come across.

Reason (R): Knowledge in a particular field and your interest and abilities decide what kind of magazine you can write for.

324. **Assertion (A):** The CAS is not operational in major parts of the four metropolises.

Reason (R): The masses have cold shouldered this technology as well as the directives of the state.

325. **Assertion (A):** Nowadays caste is no bar to the choice of occupation.

Reason (R): Indian democracy guarantees it people freedom in the choice of occupation.

326. **Assertion (A):** Leg-man is a reporter who does not write the news.

Reason (R): Leg-man runs around in the pursuit of news.

327. **Assertion (A):** Indian President cannot interfere in the government's day-to-day affairs.

Reason (R): Indian President is executive head of the union but not the leader of the members of Parliament.

328. **Assertion (A):** It is a fact that 'the Indian press is free, but not independent'.

Reason (R): No longer the editor and his team enjoy the freedom of choice in terms of contents and opinions, a consequence of new media technology.

329. **Assertion (A):** The cross media ownership in India is a reality.

Reason (R): Many large newspaper houses have diversified into other media like television, film, radio and Internet.

330. **Assertion (A):** Embedded journalism is unethical.

Reason (R): Embedded media persons are bound to project the employer's point of view.

331. **Assertion (A):** Objectivity in reporting is not achievable, and hence, it should not be attempted.

Reason (R): Giving space to all shades of opinion is good journalisam.

332. **Assertion (A):** Most media persons comply with the policies of respective media organisations.

Reason (R): Because they fear institutional authority and sanctions.

333. **Assertion (A):** Beats are nothing but a strategy of rewards to journalists.

Reason (R): Beats are hierarchical and classified in relation to performance and policy compliance.

334. **Assertion (A):** The Right to Information has made the Indian democracy vibrant.

Reason (R): Transparency is the key to the success of any democracy.

335. **Assertion (A):** The media have obligations to society, and media ownership is a public trust. News media should be truthful, accurate and objective. They should provide a forum for ideas and should be free but self-regulated.

Reason (R): Codes of ethics, professional standards and intervention of the society may unlikely to ensure media obligation and fairness.

336. **Assertion (A):** The Supreme Court in 1995 passed the judgement that the broadcast media should be under the control of the public as distinct from government.

Reason (R): Airwaves do not belong to private enterprises.

337. **Assertion (A):** The increasing share of large corporations in cultural production leads to further constriction of the 'public sphere'.

Reason (R): There is growing pressure on the independence of the professionals who work within the media industries.

338. **Assertion (A):** There is a growing tendency among newspapers to editorialise in news reports, sensationalise news and not identify sources of the news reports.

Reason (R): The ubiquitous word 'sources' is used to cover speculation and biased writing.

339. **Assertion (A):** Women in print media are largely confined to covering soft news.

Reason (R): Women journalists lack the networks, access to positions of authority, and family and social environment to succeed in mainstream journalism.

340. **Assertion (A):** Professionalism is not very strongly developed within the media organizations and employees have relatively little autonomy in relation to management and owners.

Reason (R): Codes of ethics invariably address some harm or offence caused to an individual or group and cannot usually exert strong pressure on powerful media.

341. **Assertion (A):** Indian journalism is fast moving towards tabloidisation like its western counterparts.

Reason (R): Because there is no law of privacy in India to prevent its invasion.

342. **Assertion (A):** Subliminal advertising is rampant in Indian media and is unchecked.

Reason (R): The self-regulatory mechanism in the form of code of ethics has proved ineffective.

ANSWERS

1. (b)	2. (b)	3. (c)	4. (a)	5. (a)	6. (d)
7. (d)	8. (a)	9. (d)	10. (a)	11. (c)	12. (d)
13. (b)	14. (b)	15. (a)	16. (a)	17. (a)	18. (d)
19. (a)	20. (a)	21. (a)	22. (d)	23. (a)	24. (d)
25. (a)	26. (d)	27. (b)	28. (d)	29. (c)	30. (c)
31. (b)	32. (d)	33. (b)	34. (c)	35. (b)	36. (d)
37. (a)	38. (b)	39. (a)	40. (a)	41. (a)	42. (c)
43. (c)	44. (a)	45. (a)	46. (c)	47. (a)	48. (d)
49. (b)	50. (b)	51. (d)	52. (a)	53. (c)	54. (d)
55. (d)	56. (c)	57. (d)	58. (d)	59. (b)	60. (d)
61. (b)	62. (d)	63. (a)	64. (c)	65. (a)	66. (c)
67. (a)	68. (a)	69. (d)	70. (a)	71. (a)	72. (d)
73. (c)	74. (d)	75. (a)	76. (d)	77. (d)	78. (a)
79. (b)	80. (b)	81. (c)	82. (c)	83. (a)	84. (b)
85. (d)	86. (c)	87. (a)	88. (d)	89. (a)	90. (c)
91. (c)	92. (a)	93. (a)	94. (b)	95. (d)	96. (c)
97. (b)	98. (d)	99. (a)	100. (d)	101. (a)	102. (d)
103. (b)	104. (d)	105. (a)	106. (b)	107. (c)	108. (a)
109. (a)	110. (b)	111. (a)	112. (b)	113. (d)	114. (b)
115. (b)	116. (a)	117. (c)	118. (d)	119. (d)	120. (b)
121. (c)	122. (c)	123. (c)	124. (d)	125. (d)	126. (a)
127. (c)	128. (d)	129. (d)	130. (d)	131. (c)	132. (c)
133. (d)	134. (b)	135. (d)	136. (b)	137. (b)	138. (a)
139. (b)	140. (d)	141. (b)	142. (c)	143. (a)	144. (b)
145. (d)	146. (c)	147. (a)	148. (b)	149. (a)	150. (b)
151. (b)	152. (d)	153. (c)	154. (d)	155. (d)	156. (d)
157. (b)	158. (c)	159. (b)	160. (c)	161. (d)	162. (d)
163. (a)	164. (a)	165. (a)	166. (a)	167. (d)	168. (a)
169. (b)	170. (c)	171. (a)	172. (a)	173. (c)	174. (a)
175. (c)	176. (a)	177. (b)	178. (b)	179. (c)	180. (c)
181. (c)	182. (b)	183. (d)	184. (d)	185. (b)	186. (d)
187. (a)	188. (a)	189. (d)	190. (a)	191. (c)	192. (d)
193. (c)	194. (d)	195. (a)	196. (a)	197. (c)	198. (b)

199. (a)	200. (c)	201. (b)	202. (a)	203. (d)	204. (a)
205. (d)	206. (d)	207. (d)	208. (d)	209. (c)	210. (b)
211. (b)	212. (d)	213. (a)	214. (b)	215. (a)	216. (b)
217. (b)	218. (a)	219. (a)	220. (c)	221. (b)	222. (b)
223. (b)	224. (d)	225. (d)	226. (d)	227. (d)	228. (c)
229. (a)	230. (c)	231. (a)	232. (a)	233. (c)	234. (a)
235. (b)	236. (a)	237. (d)	238. (c)	239. (c)	240. (d)
241. (d)	242. (d)	243. (b)	244. (d)	245. (d)	246. (d)
247. (c)	248. (d)	249. (c)	250. (d)	251. (d)	252. (c)
253. (a)	254. (b)	255. (c)	256. (d)	257. (d)	258. (a)
259. (d)	260. (c)	261. (c)	262. (c)	263. (c)	264. (c)
265. (a)	266. (a)	267. (c)	268. (b)	269. (b)	270. (c)
271. (c)	272. (b)	273. (d)	274. (c)	275. (a)	276. (d)
277. (a)	278. (a)	279. (d)	280. (c)	281. (c)	282. (c)
283. (d)	284. (c)	285. (d)	286. (c)	287. (d)	288. (c)
289. (c)	290. (a)	291. (d)	292. (a)	293. (a)	294. (b)
295. (c)	296. (c)	297. (c)	298. (c)	299. (d)	300. (c)
301. (d)	302. (d)	303. (c)	304. (b)	305. (c)	306. (c)
307. (c)	308. (a)	309. (a)	310. (a)	311. (c)	312. (c)
313. (a)	314. (a)	315. (c)	316. (c)	317. (c)	318. (c)
319. (b)	320. (d)	321. (b)	322. (c)	323. (a)	324. (a)
325. (a)	326. (a)	327. (a)	328. (c)	329. (a)	330. (a)
331. (d)	332. (b)	333. (d)	334. (a)	335. (b)	336. (a)
337. (c)	338. (a)	339. (d)	340. (c)	341. (b)	342. (d)

4

History of Print and Broadcast Media

1. Who amongst the following has not received the prestigious Dada Saheb Phalke Award?
   (a) Yash Chopra
   (b) Hrishikesh Mukherjee
   (c) N.T. Rama Rao
   (d) Majrooh Sultanpuri

2. What created further divisions and democrations in the newspaper?
   (a) The discovery of mobile and monitor.
   (b) The discovery of radio and TV.
   (c) The discovery of telegraph and telegram.
   (d) The discovery of T.V. and phone.

3. Who amongst the following is associated with parallel cinema?
   (a) Govind Nihalani
   (b) Mukesh Rishi
   (c) Prakash Mehra
   (d) Shah Rukh Khan

4. The role of Pallavi, in the family serial, *Kahani Ghar Ghar Ki*, was played by
   (a) Sweta Tiwari
   (b) Parvati
   (c) Shweta Razdaan
   (d) Shweta Kwatra

5. When was the film division established in India?
   (a) In 1920 (b) In 1970
   (c) In 1960 (d) In 1948

6. One of the problems of small newspapers is
   (a) the difficulty in getting patronage of regional markets.
   (b) poor printing.
   (c) the difficulty in the collection of news and data.
   (d) poor contents.

7. In the movies of the yore, there used to be as many as 15-20 songs in a Hindi movie. What could be the reason for this phenomenon?
   (a) The audience demanded it.
   (b) Artists, especially singers, sang freely.
   (c) Love of the Indians for music and dance.
   (d) Mellifluous voices of singers of those times.

8. Which of the following magazines is exclusively dedicated to travel and tourism?
   (a) *Savvy* (b) *Vogue*
   (c) *Famina* (d) *Go Now*

9. Who amongst the following is (or was) not a famous newsreader of the AIR?
   (a) Pratima Puri
   (b) Lotika Ratnam
   (c) Ramanuj Prasad Singh
   (d) Devki Nandan Pandey

10. Doordarshan started its operations in Delhi in

(a) 1932 (b) 1954
(c) 1959 (d) 1968

11. *Bombay Samachar* daily newspaper started in
(a) 1849 (b) 1847
(c) 1822 (d) 1850

12. According to the British Film Institute, the best movie of Asia is
(a) *Raise the Red Lauterm*
(b) *Mother India*
(c) *The Seven Samurai*
(d) *Sholay*

13. Till date, the only one Indian costume designer to be awarded an Oscar is
(a) J.J. Valaya
(b) Manish Malhotra
(c) Ritu Beri
(d) Bhanu Athaiya

14. The oldest *Janmabhoomi* a weekly newspaper started publishing from?
(a) 1948 (b) 1949
(c) 1947 (d) 1950

15. Which movie was made by M.F. Hussain with Madhuri Dixit in the lead role?
(a) *Gaja Gamini*
(b) *Monsoon Wedding*
(c) *Meenaxi*
(d) *Talaash*

16. The costliest ever film made in India is
(a) *Hum Aapke Hain Kaun*
(b) *Drona*
(c) *Sholay*
(d) None of the above

17. The Research and Reference Division does not publish the following book/periodical.
(a) *Development Digest*
(b) *Disha*
(c) *India 2000*
(d) *Diary*

18. The Press Information Bureau has ______ Regional Offices and ______ Branch Offices/Information Centres for dissaminating information in India.
(a) 6; 32 (b) 8; 35
(c) 7; 29 (d) 10; 27

19. When was the Second Press Council set up?
(a) 1965 (b) 1970
(c) 1975 (d) 1979

20. *Chaman* newspaper is
(a) Kannada (b) Tamil
(c) Rajasthani (d) Kashmiri

21. Who was the Chairman of the First Press Council of India?
(a) Swarn Singh
(b) J.R. Mudholkar
(c) V.K.R.V. Rao
(d) R.S. Sarkaria

22. Colour TV was introduced in India in the year
(a) 1985 (b) 1983
(c) 1982 (d) 1959

23. Sandeep Chowta is a
(a) producer (b) music director
(c) choreographer (d) art director

24. *Vighyan Mikshepam*, which was published in 1940, is in
(a) Malyalam (b) Hindi
(c) Tamil (d) Urdu

25. During the decade of the seventies, the total number of movies made in India was
(a) nearly 9,700 (b) nearly 7,200
(c) nearly 5,300 (d) nearly 2,300

26. The Editor in Chief of *Malayala Manorama* is
(a) Mammon Mathew
(b) Jacob Mathew
(c) N. Ram
(d) S. Raman

27. The famous movie *Deewar* was based on the life of
    (a) Haji Mastan
    (b) Daword Ibrahim
    (c) Chhota Rajan
    (d) None of the above.
28. *Khalsa Samachar* started from
    (a) Tamil Nadu (b) Pakistan
    (c) Punjab (d) Rajasthan
29. As per the report of the First Press Commision,
    (a) small newspapers were doing extremely well in local pockets and so, growing in terms of number.
    (b) newspaper concentration was prominent only in four metropolises, state capitals and other important cities.
    (c) growth of print media was witnessed at a faster pace than that of electronic media.
    (d) All of the above.
30. Among Indian languages, which of the following publications ranks in top after Hindi?
    (a) Malyalam (b) Urdu
    (c) Marathi (d) Bengali
31. The term TRP stands for
    (a) Television Rating Point
    (b) Television Related Purchase
    (c) Television Rating Profile
    (d) Television Regression Profile
32. The owner of Balaji Telefilms is
    (a) Shashi Kapoor
    (b) Ekta Kapoor
    (c) Jitendra
    (d) Vinod Khanna
33. Over the years, the number of dailies has increased. Comment about the statement is
    (a) May be true (b) Can't be ascertained
    (c) True (d) False
34. Who started *Amrita Bazar Patrika* in 1868?
    (a) Moti Lal Ghosh and Sisir Ghosh
    (b) Navin Chandra Rai
    (c) Harish Chandra Mukherjee
    (d) B.K. Bhatt and M.M. Ghosh
35. In 2010, the number of TV channels in the country was
    (a) 150 (b) 225
    (c) 395 (d) 515
36. The Fourth Estate is a name generally given to the Press, but previously, it was the name given to
    (a) the Press of England.
    (b) the news of the agency, Reuters.
    (c) the Press Regulation Authority of the USA.
    (d) the elite writers of Europe.
37. The AIR broadcasts its programmes in ________ languages and ________ dialects.
    (a) 24; 146 (b) 22; 120
    (c) 18; 156 (d) 12; 138
38. The Second Press Commission was appointed by the government on
    (a) June 11, 1976
    (b) June 12, 1976
    (c) May 18, 1977
    (d) None of the above.
39. Select the wrong statement regarding newspaper circulation.
    (a) Big: more than 75,000 copies
    (b) Small: upto 25,000 copies
    (c) Medium: upto 75,000 copies
    (d) None of the above
40. The Chairman of the tenth Press Council is
    (a) Mr. Justice G.N. Ray
    (b) Mr. Justice P.B. Sawant

(c) Mr. Justice A.S. Ananad
(d) None of the above.

41. The Film Certification Appellate Tribunal (FCAT)
(a) gives funds for the production of Hindi feature films.
(b) is a watchdog organisation of the Government of India that takes care of the needs of the Indian viewers.
(c) gives certificates of clearance to foreign video films.
(d) hears appeals against any order of the CBFC.

42. What would be the major feature of local broadcasting (in the parlance of radio transmission)?
(a) Education, information and entertainment according to needs.
(b) Chiefly entertainment.
(c) Chiefly education but entertaining programmes to be broadcast from time to time.
(d) None of the above.

43. The Satellite Instructional Television Experiment (SITE) was inaugurated in
(a) March 1981 (b) August 1979
(c) December 1977 (d) August 1975

44. The satellite used to launch the SITE was
(a) ATS-6 (b) INSAT 1-A
(c) VSAT-2 (d) Soyuz T-6

45. According to Section 13 of the Press Council Act (1978), the objects of the Press Council are the following:
(a) To help newpapers and news agencies to maintain their independence.
(b) To build up a code of conduct for newspapers, news agencies and journalists.
(c) Both (a) and (b).
(d) None of the above.

46. Who is the father of Marathi Journalism?
(a) K.T. Ranade
(b) Bal Shastri Jambekar
(c) Bal Gangadhar Tilak
(d) M.C. Kelkar

47. Which of the following is not a problem being faced by the print media?
(a) Poor availability in metropolitan areas of India.
(b) Invasion of cable TV and DTH.
(c) Rising costs of production.
(d) Language problems.

48. In August 1983, INSAT-1B was launched in its orbit by the following space shuttle
(a) Columbia (b) Atlantis
(c) Challenger (d) Endeavour

49. The tenure of the First Press Council was
(a) 1 year (b) 3 years
(c) 5 years (d) 6 years

50. Which was the year of inauguration of the Times of India?
(a) 1826 (b) 1856
(c) 1861 (d) 1878

51. Femina, a non-news fortnightly, is published by
(a) Express Publications Ltd.
(b) Express Publication (Bombay Ltd.)
(c) Benett Coleman & Co. Ltd.
(d) Hindustan Times Group

52. Who is deemed as the father of Indian Journalism?
(a) S.N. Banerjee
(b) Devendra Nath Ghosh
(c) Dadabhai Nauroji
(d) J.A. Hicky

53. Which newspaper was started as a Bengali paper but later, changed into an English paper?
(a) *Mirqi-ul-Akhbar*
(b) *Amrita Bazar Patrika*

(c) *Indian Mirror*
(d) *Kesari*

54. Who pioneered the newspaper publication in India?
(a) James Augustus Hicky
(b) M.A.K. Halliday
(c) Harold Pinter
(d) Ian Hilly

55. What does "Stop Press" mean?
(a) Some news or articles are sent to press and printed while the newspaper is going through the stage of printing; this addition is done at the end of the newspaper or book in most of the cases.
(b) The printing press is stopped for a few minutes.
(c) Some material to be printed is taken out and printed at a later stage.
(d) All of the above.

56. The National Film Archive of India (NFAI) was set up in
(a) 1960 (b) 1962
(c) 1964 (d) 1969

57. The first newspaper in India was
(a) *Young India* (b) *Bengal Gazette*
(c) *Harijan* (d) *Sevak*

58. The Pioneer was started in Allahabad in the year
(a) 1865 (b) 1876
(c) 1890 (d) 1901

59. In 2009, India produced a total of how many films on celluloid?
(a) 222 (b) 1,405
(c) 1498 (d) 2961

60. Largest circulated periodical in India is
(a) *Kumudham*
(b) *Saras Salil*
(c) *Malayala Manorama*
(d) *The Hindu* weekly magazine

61. In India, the frequency of FM channels varies form
(a) 70-80 MHz
(b) 422.4-500 kHz
(c) 88-108 MHz
(d) None of the above.

62. *Bengal Gazette alias Calcutta General Adviser* came out in January
(a) 28, 1779 (b) 28, 1782
(c) 29, 1780 (d) 30, 1781

63. The Directorate of Film Festivals (DFF) was set up under the Ministry of Information and Broadcasting in the year
(a) 1968 (b) 1973
(c) 1983 (d) 1992

64. Bal Gangadhar Tilak was associated with
(a) *Bombay Times* (b) *Indian Gazette*
(c) *Hindu* (d) *Maratha*

65. DD Bharati is available through the following satellite.
(a) PAS-10 (b) INSAT 1-B
(c) PAS-4 (d) INSAT-1E

66. Which newspaper was taken over by Raja Ram Mohan Roy to propagate his ideas?
(a) *Kesari*
(b) *Desabhakta*
(c) *Sudharak*
(d) *Samvad Kaumudi*

67. The News Division of the DD (in Delhi) is supported by ____ Regional News Units (RNUs).
(a) 20 (b) 21
(c) 22 (d) 23

68. The approximate number of TV households in 2010, was
(a) 82 million (b) 90 million
(c) 100 million (d) 125 million

69. Who started *Dharamvir* from Africa in 1912?

(a) Bhawani Dayal Sanyasi
(b) Mahtama Ananad Swami
(c) Madanjit
(d) None of the above.

70. In India which state ranks first with the large number of newspaper publishing?
(a) Uttar Pradesh (b) Delhi
(c) Maharashtra (d) Madhya Pradesh

71. Which was the first movie of Abhishek Bachchan?
(a) *Refugee*
(b) *Shararate*
(c) *Kabhi Khushi Kabhi Gham*
(d) *Dhoom.*

72. During the infancy stage of Indian cinema, Raja Harishachandra was made in Hindi (in 1899). But another movie, *Satyawadi Raja Harishachandra*, was made in
(a) Bengali (b) Telugu
(c) Malayalam (d) Kannada

73. The editor of *Kudi Arasu* was
(a) K. Karunanidhi
(b) E.V. Ramaswamy Naicker
(c) Rajaji
(d) C. Annadurai

74. The first movie of south India was
(a) *Bhuwan Shome*
(b) *Shankarcharya*
(c) *Alam Ara*
(d) *Keechak Wadham*

75. In which year the Newspaper (Price and Pages) Act was passed?
(a) 1961 (b) 1966
(c) 1951 (d) 1956

76. The gamut of yellow journalism does not include
(a) live coverage of news and events.
(b) smear campaigns.
(c) slime games.
(d) mud-slinging exercises.

77. Daily newspapers are published in all main language except
(a) Manipuri (b) Kashmiri
(c) Nepali (d) Konkani

78. Which one of the following was not a guideline of the First Press Council for the Press?
(a) Employment of intemperate and unrestrained language in the presentation of news or views even as a piece of literary flourish, or for the purpose of emphasis.
(b) Expansion of operations of the Press by adding more magazines or newspapers to the existing set of media of a group.
(c) Scurrilous and untrue attacks on communities or individuals, particularly when they are accompanied by charges attributing misconduct to them due to their being members of a particular community or caste.
(d) Distortion or exaggeration of facts or incidents in relation to communal matters, or giving currency to unverified rumours, suspicions or interference, as if they were facts and base their comments on them.

79. Which of the following magazines is exclusively dedicated to travel and tourism?
(a) *Vogue* (b) *Savvy*
(c) *Femina* (d) *Go Now*

80. Which of the following cities publishes maximum newspapers?
(a) Kolkata (b) Chennai
(c) Delhi (d) Mumbai

81. The Second Press Commission was headed by
(a) P.K. Goswami (b) Prem Bhatia
(c) Arun Shourie (d) K.K. Mathew

82. The first talking movie, *Alam Ara*, had ________ songs in it.
(a) 5 (b) 7
(c) 15 (d) 16

83. The Indian Cinematograph Act was passed in the year
(a) 1909 (b) 1910
(c) 1918 (d) 1921

84. The largest number of newspapers in English published from
(a) Kolkata (b) Chennai
(c) Delhi (d) Mumbai

85. Who amongst the following was not a member of the First Press Commission?
(a) Jaipal Singh Singh
(b) Acharya Narendra Dev
(c) A.R. Bhat
(d) B.D. Jatti

86. *Indian Standard* was renamed *New India* in
(a) 1912 (b) 1913
(c) 1910 (d) 1911

87. Which is the only movie in which, Rajesh Khanna acted along with Jaya Bhaduri?
(a) *Anand* (b) *Aradhana*
(c) *Guddi* (d) *Bawarchi*

88. One of the recommendations of the First Press Commission was to
(a) make every newspaper a separate unit so that profits and losses could be ascertained.
(b) curtail the freedom of the Press during emergency days.
(c) appoint two chairmen for itself instead of one.
(d) increase the number of newspapers in urban areas.

89. Largest circulated periodical is from
(a) Malayalam (b) Tamil
(c) Hindi (d) English

90. What is a "typed image" in the parlance of Indian cinema?
(a) Actors and actresses do not get roles that are worthy of them.
(b) They are told to change their personalities after their films flop at the box office.
(c) They are told to act is casting couches.
(d) They get only those roles that have been performed by them previously.

91. What would be the major feature of local broadcasting in the parlance of radio transmission?
(a) Chiefly entertainment.
(b) Chiefly education but entertaining programmes to be broadcast from time to time.
(c) Education, information and entertainment according to the needs of the local populace.
(d) None of the above.

92. Majority of the newspaper in India is owned by
(a) Joint Stock Companies
(b) Trust
(c) Individuals
(d) Societies

93. The UNI launched Univarta (in Hindi) in
(a) April 1979 (b) August 1980
(c) June 1982 (d) May 1982

94. Which of the following journals/magazines are published by the Publications Division of the Ministry of Information and Broadcasting?
(a) *Ajkal*
(b) *Yojana*
(c) *Kurukshetra*
(d) All of the above

95. 'Varta' is a news agency owned by
(a) PTI
(b) Hindustan Samachar

(c) Indian Government
(d) UNI

96. The Research Reference and Training Division looks after the training aspect of the
(a) Indian Information Service
(b) Indian Administrative Service
(c) Indian Forest Service
(d) Indian Revenue Service

97. The Fourth Estate is a name generally given to the Press, but previously, it was the term applied to
(a) lawyers
(b) the queen of England
(c) the proletariat
(d) All of the above

98. Largest circulated government publication is
(a) *Employment News*
(b) *Suraksha*
(c) *Yojana*
(d) *Kurukshetra*

99. The office of the UNI is located at
(a) KG Marg, New Delhi
(b) Ballard Estate, Mumbai
(c) Veer Savarkar Marg, Mumbai
(d) Rafi Marg, New Delhi

100. In order to promote good cinema in India, the
(a) Ministry of Information and Broadcasting was created.
(b) NFDC was scrapped in 1975.
(c) NFDC was formed in 1975.
(d) None of the above.

101. The first Hindi newspaper was
(a) *Sudhakar* (b) *Aj*
(c) *Prajamitra* (d) *Odund Martand*

102. Which one was the first newspaper of the USA to become electronic on July 1, 1980?
(a) *The Columbia Despatch*
(b) *Time*
(c) *Popular Science*
(d) *Future*

103. In August 1983, INSAT-1B was launched in its orbit by the space shuttle
(a) Endeavor (b) Challenger
(c) Atlantis (d) Columbia

104. Which language pioneered language journalism in India?
(a) Bengali (b) Tamil
(c) Hindi (d) Marathi

105. "They have high status in the society. Their number is small but their influence is strong." This is with reference to what kind of audience?
(a) Specialised
(b) Elite
(c) General
(d) None of the above

106. Hindu's sports magazine is
(a) *Cricket Star* (b) *Sportstar*
(c) *Cricket Today* (d) *Sports Today*

107. Which is the method used for receiving information in market based feedback system?
(a) Media Review
(b) Audience Decision Making
(c) Direct Feedback
(d) All of the above

108. The first newspaper published in Malayalam language was
(a) *Deen Bandhu*
(b) *Deshabhimani*
(c) *Malayala Manorama*
(d) *Vigyan Nikeshapan*

109. Who differentiated between 'hot' and 'cool' media?
(a) Wilbur Schramm
(b) Raymond Williams

(c) Val Henry
(d) Marshall McGielgud Luhan

110. When was the first printing press established in India?
(a) 1674 (b) 1672
(c) 1670 (d) 1671

111. When an object is moved farther away, we tend to see it as more or less invariant in size. This is due to
(a) Colour Constancy
(b) Size Constancy
(c) Brightness Constancy
(d) Shape Constancy

112. What is the other name of Hicky's *Bengal Gazette*?
(a) *Bengal Harkarv*
(b) *The Bengal News*
(c) *Calcutta General Advertise*
(d) *Bengal Journal*

113. When was the first press ordinance issued?
(a) 1826 (b) 1825
(c) 1824 (d) 1823

114. Which country publishes maximum number of dailies in the world?
(a) Japan (b) UK
(c) USA (d) India

115. In which language was *Amrita Bazar Patrika* first published before changing over to English language?
(a) Bengali (b) Punjabi
(c) Urdu (d) Hindi

116. *The Times of India* came into being with the amalgamation of which of these papers?
(a) *The Bombay Times* and *The Courier*
(b) *The Standard* and *The Telegraph*
(c) Both (a) and (b)
(d) *The Standard* and *The Bombay Times*

117. G. Subramani Aiyar was the editor of
(a) *Hindustan Times* (b) *Statesman*
(c) *Times of India* (d) *Hindu*

118. To be a successful development reporter, one should
(a) keep a desk diary.
(b) encourage 'mouthpiece writing'.
(c) maintain a reference material.
(d) foster a wide range of contacts.

119. Who called our society as a 'dramatised' society?
(a) James Augustus
(b) Johannes Gutenberg
(c) Marshall McLuhan
(d) Raymond Williams

120. The following English newspapers crossed hundred years except one, which is the newspaper?
(a) *Hindustan Times* (b) *Statesman*
(c) *Times of India* (d) *Hindu*

121. Closed ended type of question are questions calling for
(a) agree-disagree answers.
(b) multiple choice type of responses.
(c) simple 'yes-no'.
(d) All of the above.

122. When was censorship introduced on Indian Press?
(a) 1792 (b) 1793
(c) 1794 (d) 1795

123. In open-ended question, the respondent is provided with
(a) multiple type answers.
(b) objective type answers.
(c) no answers.
(d) None of the above.

124. Select the correct sequence in descending order in respect of the circulation of Indian newspaper.
(a) Hindi, Malayalam, English
(b) English, Malayalam, Hindi

(c) English, Hindi, Malayalam
(d) Hindi, English, Malayalam

125. The advantage of interviewing over questionnaire is
(a) it posses great flexibility.
(b) it yields a better sample of the population.
(c) the method can be used with illiterates.
(d) All of the above.

126. The name given to the first radio programme journal was
(a) *The Indian Listener*
(b) *Akashvani*
(c) *India Radio Times*
(d) None of the above.

127. When was the name All India Radio adopted?
(a) January 8, 1935 (b) June 8, 1936
(c) June 10, 1936 (d) April 8, 1937

128. Which of the following newspaper has "India's National Newspaper" on its masthead?
(a) *The Hindu* (b) *Indian Express*
(c) *Times of India* (d) *Hindustan Times*

129. When was the first National Orchestra set up, with Pandit Ravi Shankar as its conductor?
(a) 1952 (b) 1954
(c) 1956 (d) 1958

130. When was the channel 'Yuva Vani' started in Delhi?
(a) 1976 (b) 1969
(c) 1968 (d) 1967

131. Where was the highest AIR station set-up in 1971?
(a) Leh (b) Mumbai
(c) Nainital (d) Shimla

132. *Frontline* is the publication of
(a) Indian Express Group
(b) Hindustan Times Group
(c) Kasturi & Sons
(d) Bennet & Coleman

133. Who enforced the Vernacular Press Act?
(a) Queen Victoria
(b) East India Company
(c) Lord Canning
(d) Lord Lytton

134. When was the Bombay TV centre inaugurated?
(a) 1972 (b) 1974
(c) 1976 (d) 1978

135. When were educational programmes by UGC started on TV?
(a) 1984 (b) 1983
(c) 1982 (d) 1980

136. Who, amongst the following, is associated with parallel cinema?
(a) Govind Nihalani
(b) Mukesh Rishi
(c) Aksnay Kumar
(d) Prakash Mehra

137. When was the moving transmission of TV started?
(a) 1989 (b) 1987
(c) 1986 (d) 1985

138. When were the Bombay and Calcutta stations inaugurated by the Indian Broadcasting Company?
(a) 1926 (b) 1927
(c) 1928 (d) 1930

139. In which year did Doordarshan started its five metro channels?
(a) 1996 (b) 1995
(c) 1994 (d) 1993

140. First Indian daily to be published from Delhi was
(a) *The Hindustan Times*
(b) *The Statesman*
(c) *The Indian Express*
(d) *The Pioneer*

141. Which committee criticised the Doordarshan for concentrating on the North for its programme contents?
(a) Joshi Committee
(b) Chandra Committee
(c) Verghese Committee
(d) None of the above.

142. Heinrich Hertz who founded the theory of radio waves which helped in the process of broadcasting was
(a) German (b) American
(c) French (d) British

143. In 1915, Edgar Rubin introduced the idea of
(a) Physiological Nystagmus
(b) Hallucination
(c) Figure and Ground
(d) Phiphenomenon

144. Wireless telegraphy was developed by
(a) Thomas Alva Edison
(b) Guglielmo Marconi
(c) J.C. Maxwell
(d) Heinrich Hertz

145. Akash Bharati Broadcast Trust was recommended by
(a) Verghese Committee
(b) Advani Committee
(c) Ashok K. Chandra Committee
(d) None of the above.

146. Till date, only one Indian costume designer has been awarded an Oscar. His or her name is
(a) Monisha Bajaj (b) J.J. Valaya
(c) Ritu Beri (d) Bhanu Athaiya

147. In which year, Delhi Broadcasting station was set-up?
(a) 1982 (b) 1954
(c) 1944 (d) 1936

148. Who wrote the poem "Akashvani"?
(a) M.K. Gandhi (b) R.N. Tagore
(c) H.R. Bachchan (d) S.K. Dey

149. Broadcasting subject falls under the
(a) Concurrent list
(b) Changes from time to time
(c) State list
(d) Union list

150. Which of the following was the recommendation of Chandra Committee?
(a) Starting of commercial broadcasting
(b) Autonomy to Radio and TV
(c) Both (a) and (b)
(d) None of the above.

151. The first experimental radio transmission was made in India in
(a) April 1905 (b) March 1907
(c) January 1909 (d) August 1921

152. In 1902, the first song recorded on a gramophone record was at
(a) Coronation Theatre, Bombay
(b) Classic Theatre, Calcutta
(c) Urdu, Calcutta
(d) None of the above

153. *Statesman* was founded by
(a) Robert Knight
(b) Robert MacMohan
(c) Robert Browning
(d) Robert Frost

154. The MEN Interactive Network Ltd. was started by Modi Entertainment Network Limited. It was incorporated in
(a) 1995 (b) 1996
(c) 1998 (d) 1999

155. In which year Dr. Frank Conrad, a research engineer, opened the first commercially licensed radio station KDKA?
(a) 1920 (b) 1926
(c) 1933 (d) None of these

156. The first demonstration of television in real sense was made in
(a) 1923 (b) 1924
(c) 1925 (d) 1926

157. When was the first Press Council is abolished?
(a) On January 1, 1976
(b) On January 26, 1976
(c) On December 12, 1976
(d) On December 18, 1976

158. The Press Information Bureau has ______ Regional Offices and Branch Offices/Information Centres in India.
(a) 1230 (b) 835
(c) 729 (d) 1024

159. When was the PTI-Bhasha launched?
(a) In 1980 (b) In 1986
(c) In 1989 (d) In 1994

160. The "Yuvavani" Services was started in 1969. It caters to the young audience from the age of
(a) ten up wards
(b) six up wards
(c) fifteen up wards
(d) twenty-one up wards

161. "Chanda Committee" was set to review the functioning of
(a) Panchyati Raj System
(b) Autonomy to North-East States
(c) broadcasting system in India
(d) None of the above.

162. Who is the Chief Editor of *The Hindustan Times*?
(a) Prabhu Chawala (b) N.C. Menon
(c) Soni Sangwan (d) Veer Sanghvi

163. In which year television was separated from Akashvani and renamed as "doordarshan"?
(a) 1979 (b) 1976
(c) 1972 (d) 1965

164. When was the first TV station set up in India?
(a) August 1949, Kolkata
(b) September 1959, Delhi
(c) January 1963, Delhi
(d) November 1968, Mumbai

165. Which of the following Act stated that the Press Council was being abolished because it was not able to carry on its functions effectively to achieve the objects for which it was established?
(a) The Constitution (fourty-third Amendment) Act
(b) The Parasar Bharati Act
(c) Press Council Bill
(d) Press Council Repeal Act

166. Marathi newspaper was started in 1932 by
(a) Bal Shastri Jambhekar
(b) Mohan Das
(c) Bal Gangadhar Tilak
(d) None of these

167. The first news bulletin went on air from Bombay station in
(a) July, 1927 (b) Oct., 1936
(c) April, 1939 (d) July, 1943

168. Who is the head of the News Services Division?
(a) Director General
(b) Managing Director
(c) Directional officer
(d) Editor-in-charge

169. What is the total number of bulletins put out by the News Service Division of AIR from the various radio stations every day?
(a) 300 (b) 284
(c) 265 (d) 131

170. *Morning Post* belonged to
(a) America (b) Mumbai
(c) India (d) London

171. India's largest News Agency is
(a) UTI (b) UNI
(c) PTI (d) IANS

172. India made its first Satellite Instructional Television Experiment (SITE) in
(a) 1968-69 (b) 1970-71
(c) 1972-73 (d) 1975-76

173. When was 'Prasar Bharati', the autonomous Broadcasting Corporation of India, was set up?
(a) 15th August 1992
(b) 26th Jan., 1996
(c) 23rd Nov., 1997
(d) None of the above.

174. Tamil daily, *Dinamani*, was started in
(a) 1936 (b) 1937
(c) 1934 (d) 1935

175. In which year Registrar of Newspapers for India came into being?
(a) 1942 (b) 1947
(c) 1952 (d) 1956

176. How many editions does *The Times of India* have in English?
(a) Four (b) Six
(c) Eight (d) Ten

177. Who said "Newspaper should be both a daily teacher and a daily tribune"?
(a) Jawaharlal Nehru
(b) Edwin Emery
(c) Joseph Pulitzer
(d) Chester Barnard

178. The NFAI was set up in
(a) 1957 (b) 1960
(c) 1989 (d) 1964

179. Who wrote the book The Press and America?
(a) Abraham Lincoln
(b) Richard Nixon
(c) Edwin Emery
(d) Joseph Pulitzer

180. A successful freelance journalist must not have
(a) identified an area.
(b) developed a link between the various newspapers or magazines.
(c) love for writing.
(d) a weak writing skill.

181. The FCAT
(a) gives funds for the production of Hindi feature films.
(b) is a watchdog organisation of the Government of India that takes care of the needs of the Indian viewers.
(c) gives certificates of clearance to foreign video films.
(d) hears appeals against the decision of the CBFC.

182. *Deccan Herald* was started in the year
(a) 1940 (b) 1941
(c) 1948 (d) 1949

183. *National Call* was started by
(a) K.N. Guruswami
(b) Pothan Joseph
(c) J.N. Sahni
(d) Rusi Karanjia

184. Which paper was started by Chittaranjan Das in Bengal?
(a) Foreword
(b) Forward
(c) Swarajya
(d) Free Press Journal

185. *Prajamitra* appeared in
(a) Chennai (b) Lahore
(c) Kolkata (d) Delhi

186. Gandhiji started *Harijan* in
(a) 1932 (b) 1933
(c) 1935 (d) 1937

187. *Independent* was started by
(a) Jawaharlal Nehru
(b) Gandhiji
(c) Motilal Nehru
(d) Lal Bahadur Shastri

188. *Navjivan* was started by
(a) Kalanath Shastri
(b) Gandhiji
(c) Moti Lal Nehru
(d) Jawaharlal Nehru

189. S. Kasturiranga Iyengar, a lawyer, become the editor of the *Hindu* in
(a) 1907 (b) 1908
(c) 1905 (d) 1906

190. *Young India* was later renamed as
(a) *Navjivan* (b) *Harijan*
(c) *Kalyan* (d) None of these

191. Leader was launched in 1909 in Allahabad by
(a) Pt. J.L. Nehru
(b) Gandhiji
(c) Pt. M.M. Malviya
(d) Moti Lal Nehru

192. *The Morning Post* was published from
(a) Bombay (b) Chicago
(c) Madras (d) London

193. Tamil daily *Makkal Kural* appeared in Madras in
(a) 1972 (b) 1973
(c) 1970 (d) 1971

194. Kalinath Roy was arrested and jailed for two years, he was the editor of
(a) *Pioneer*
(b) *Bombay Chronicle*
(c) *Mid-Day*
(d) *The Tribune*

195. Which committee recommended a franchise system for promoting local radio for education and development?
(a) The Verghese Committee (1978)
(b) The Heeraman Committee (1978)
(c) The Chanda Committee (1978)
(d) None of the above.

196. The first local/community experiment with FM facility was conducted in
(a) Nagercoil (b) Delhi
(c) Chennai (d) Mumbai

197. S.S. Vasan of Tamil Nadu started a perodical in 1924, was
(a) *Ananda Murti* (b) *Anand Sahitya*
(c) *Ananda Vikatan* (d) None of the above

198. The Prasar Bharati Bill was introduced in the Lok Sabha in the year
(a) 1978 (b) 1979
(c) 1980 (d) 1987

199. The name of the first commercial communication satellite was
(a) Peacock (b) New Galaxy
(c) Blue Bird (d) Early Bird

200. Television and All India Radio were separated in the year
(a) 1976 (b) 1975
(c) 1974 (d) 1973

201. SITE is an experiment on
(a) Agriculture
(b) Rural Development
(c) Communication
(d) Environment

202. Metro Entertainment Channel (DD-2) was introduced in
(a) 1990 (b) 1988
(c) 1984 (d) 1980

203. Which committee strongly recommended granting broadcast franchises to educational institutes?
(a) The Malabari Committee
(b) The Verghese Committee
(c) The Bachhawat Committee
(d) The Hunter Committee

204. Al Hilal marked a turning point in the history of Urdu journalism was edited by
(a) Syed Hussain
(b) Moulana Abul Kalam Azad
(c) Ram Chandra
(d) Maulana Nasir Ali

205. What has made it possible to beam programmes across frontiers to different parts of the world?
(a) Short wave and Long wave broadcasting
(b) Short wave
(c) Medium wave
(d) Only long wave

206. Reversible goblet is a favourite demonstration of
(a) a size-contour reversal.
(b) a shape-size reversal.
(c) a focus-margin reversal.
(d) a figure-ground reversal.

207. Which of the following was the first newspaper of India?
(a) *Bengal Gazette*
(b) *The Hindu*
(c) *Maratha*
(d) *The Times of India*

208. *Bengal Journal* was first published in the year
(a) 1832 (b) 1792
(c) 1786 (d) 1785

209. A simpler form of stroboscopic motion is
(a) Phi-Phenomenon
(b) Hallucination
(c) Psychokinesis
(d) Autokinetic Effect

210. *The Statesman* was published from
(a) Delhi (b) Madras
(c) Calcutta (d) Bombay

211. First rotary linotype machine was installed by
(a) *The Statesman*
(b) *Hindustan Times*
(c) *The Hindu*
(d) *The Times of India*

212. Empiricists (Barkeley, Locke) maintained that we learn our ways of perceiving through
(a) Learning (b) Experiene
(c) Motivaton (d) Eyes

213. When was the 'Indian and Eastern Newspaper Society' (IENS) set up?
(a) 1923 (b) 1930
(c) 1939 (d) 1948

214. To which state the Lokmat group of newspapers belongs to?
(a) Bihar
(b) Madhya Pradesh
(c) Orissa
(d) Maharashtra

215. In which year was the Contempt of Court Act enacted?
(a) 1962 (b) 1963
(c) 1970 (d) 1971

216. William James characterised the perception of an infant as a
(a) Stimulation of nerve cells in the eyes.
(b) Stimulation of rods and cones.
(c) Blooming buzzing confusion.
(d) Haphazard stimulation of nerve cells.

217. The British Government in India set up the 'Central Bureau of Public Information' in
(a) 1900 (b) 1912
(c) 1923 (d) 1942

218. First of all which country made the paper?
(a) USA (b) India
(c) UK (d) China

219. Behaviourists have
(a) no theory of thinking.
(b) no theory of perception.
(c) no theory of learning.
(d) no theory of memory.

220. What was made from the mixture of campblack and resin or gum ?
(a) Ink (b) Scale
(c) Pen (d) Rubber

221. The second stage in the development of newspapers consisted of a series of 'Relations' published in the form of

(a) Coranto (b) Bhaskar
(c) The Diurnals (d) None of these

222. The process by which the eyes get prepared to see very dimlight is known as
(a) Brightness Adaptation
(b) Colour Adaptation
(c) Light Adaptation
(d) Dark Adaptation

223. Who printed the greatest number of corantos?
(a) Greek (b) Italian
(c) Dutch (d) Germans

224. The current broadcasting policy is based on
(a) The AIR code of 1968
(b) The AIR code of 1970
(c) The AIR code of 1972
(d) None of the above

225. The partially colour blind people are known as
(a) Dichromats (b) Achromats
(c) Colour Blind (d) Blind

226. The Code and other restrictions on broadcasting are based on ______ of Article 19 of the Indian Constitution.
(a) Clause 2 (b) Clause 3
(c) Clause 4 (d) Clause 5

227. The World Communication Year (1983) was sponsored by
(a) UNICEF (b) UNESCO
(c) European Union (d) United Nations

228. Totally colour blind people are otherwise known as
(a) Monochromats (b) Colour Blind
(c) Dichromats (d) Achromats

229. Which committee recommended establishment of a Broadcasting Corporation?
(a) The Montague Committee
(b) The Verghese Committee
(c) The Chandran Committee
(d) The Chanda Committee

230. When was the first International Film Festival held in India?
(a) In the year of 1963
(b) In the year of 1972
(c) In the year of 1960
(d) In the year of 1952

231. Which committee recommended the setting up of a National Broadcast Trust (Aakash Bharti)?
(a) The Naidu Committee
(b) The Verghese Committee
(c) The Chanda Committee
(d) None of the above.

232. The phenomenon of sifting from one picture to another is known as
(a) Attention Rivalry
(b) Perception Rivalry
(c) Retina Rivalry
(d) Eyes Rivalry

233. Which committee suggested that Doordarshan should devote at least 20 per cent of total broadcasting time on each channel to socially relevant programmes?
(a) The Verghese Committee
(b) The Varadan Committee
(c) The Naidu Committee
(d) The Chanda Committee

234. Since first IFFI, how many festivals have been held in India?
(a) 33 (b) 50
(c) 44 (d) 48

235. The Ram Vilas Paswan Consultative Committee was set up in the year
(a) 1997 (b) 1996
(c) 1995 (d) 1994

236. When the lens cannot bulge out to the extent necessary due to muscular defects, the individual suffers from

(a) Astigmatism (b) Double Vision
(c) Farsightedness (d) Myopia

237. Tilak is connected with the paper
(a) *India* (b) *Hindustan*
(c) *Vande Mataram* (d) *Maratha*

238. *Sunday*, a weekly, from the Anand Bazar Patrika Group was launched in 1970 under the editorship of
(a) M.J. Akbar
(b) Arun Shourie
(c) Jamanadas Bajaj
(d) None of the above

239. Due to the irregularities in the formation of the lens or the cornea, the object viewed will be partly clear and partly blurred. This occurs when the individual suffers from
(a) Ratinal disparity
(b) Astigmatism
(c) Colour blindness
(d) Distraction

240. Who was called a 'fighting editor' by Gandhi?
(a) Frank Moraes
(b) M. Chalpati Rao
(c) K. Rama Rao
(d) None of the above.

241. *Frontline* made appearance in the year
(a) 1987 (b) 1986
(c) 1983 (d) 1981

242. The length of car number has reference to
(a) Focus and Margin
(b) Span of Attention
(c) Focus of Consciousness
(d) Shifting of Attention

243. Which newspaper was founded by six young men, all in their twenties, in Madras on September 20, 1878?
(a) *Hindustan Times*
(b) *The Hindu*
(c) *Anand Bazar Patrika*
(d) None of the above.

244. When was the television service at the Delhi Kendra inaugurated?
(a) Aug. 15, 1959 (b) Nov. 25, 1958
(c) Sept. 20, 1958 (d) Sep. 15, 1959

245. Sensations of movement from inside our bodies are called
(a) Interoception (b) Sensation
(c) Proprioception (d) Attention

246. In how many states was the SITE (Satellite Instructional Television Experiment) programmes launched?
(a) 6 (b) 5
(c) 3 (d) 2

247. Indian agencies are a part of
(a) UNI (b) NANA
(c) ANA (d) None of these

248. When was the first English newspaper, *Bengal Gazette* published?
(a) 1795 A.D. (b) 1790 A.D.
(c) 1780 A.D. (d) 1770 A.D.

249. Sensation increases by a constant amount each time the stimulus is doubled. This is called
(a) Mallinoswki Law
(b) Webber-Fechner Law
(c) Lewin-Zeigamik Effect
(d) Lewin-Prentice Effect

250. Who is known as the father of Indian language journalism in India?
(a) Swami Vivekananda
(b) Raja Ram Mohan Roy
(c) V.D. Savarkar
(d) Bhupendra Nath Dutta

251. Import of newsprint, including glazed newsprint was put under Open General Licence (OGL) in
(a) 1998 (b) 2000
(c) 1992 (d) 1995

252. The experiments which tell us about the relationship between the intensity of stimulus and the consequent changes in the intensity of sensation are included in
(a) Parapsychology
(b) Psychophysics
(c) Psychoanalysis
(d) Gestalt Psychology

253. Why did Central Government start the national film awards in 1954?
(a) To demote the artistic endeavour.
(b) To make default the artistic endeavour of film.
(c) To promote the artistic endeavour of the film personalities.
(d) None of the above.

254. At the time of Independence, only three agencies—AFP, AP and Reuter—were working in India. These agencies are of
(a) India
(b) Canada
(c) UK
(d) None of the above

255. The study on the Zulu tribes of Africa revealed that the Zulu individuals would be less susceptible to the
(a) Zollner Illusion
(b) Figure-Ground Phenomenon
(c) Muller-Lyer Illusion
(d) Ponzo Illusion

256. What was founded by a group of newspapers in 1961 to provide competition to PTI?
(a) DPA (b) NANAP
(c) UNI (d) AFP

257. When was the News Control Order passed?
(a) In 1960 (b) In 1975
(c) In 1962 (d) In 1950

258. Nepa Mill in Madhya Pradesh under the central public sector commenced production in
(a) March 1960 (b) Jan 1959
(c) April 1957 (d) April 1956

259. A complete change of vitreous humour occurs approximately once in
(a) every one hour.
(b) every two hours.
(c) every three hours.
(d) every four hours.

260. When was the Newsprint Control Order passed?
(a) In 1960 (b) In 1961
(c) In 1962 (d) In 1965

261. When did the earliest newspaper started in Calcutta from?
(a) 1826 (b) 1819
(c) 1850 (d) 1849

262. Who was the Chairman of the Drafting Committee of Akash Bharati Bill, 1978?
(a) Ram Mohan Rao
(b) I.D. Tiwari
(c) B.G. Verghese
(d) V Sharda Prasad

263. The theory of colour perception which seems to be the most acceptable one today is called the
(a) Confusion Theory
(b) Young-Helmholtz Theory
(c) Retinex Theory
(d) Perspective Theory

264. The first newspaper published from Mumbai was
(a) *Bombay Samachar*
(b) *Bombay Times*
(c) *The Times of India*
(d) *Bombay Herald*

265. The first Kannad newspaper *Mangaloora Samachara* was published in
(a) 1844 (b) 1847
(c) 1850 (d) 1843

266. The first Indian daily newspaper in English was
(a) *Indian Mirror*
(b) *Bombay Times*
(c) *The Times of India*
(d) *The Hindu*

267. Who developed the "Retinex Theory" of colour perception?
(a) Edward Herring
(b) Edwin Land
(c) Thomas Young
(d) Hermann Von Helmholtz

268. Who was the editor of *Indian Sociologist* published from London?
(a) S.N. Banerjee
(b) Shyamji Krishna Varma
(c) Devendranath Tagore
(d) Taraknath Das

269. First evening paper in India was
(a) *Calcutta Mail* (b) *Mid-Day*
(c) *Madras Mail* (d) *Bombay Mail*

270. Who received Nobel Prize for his research on the mechanisms of the cochlea?
(a) Pronko (b) Turnbull
(c) Stratton (d) Von Bekesy

271. *Kranti*, published in 1927, is connected with
(a) S.V Ghate (b) S.S. Mirajkar
(c) K.N. Joglekar (d) All of the above

272. Department of Information and Broadcasting was set up
(a) 1941 (b) 1940
(c) 1939 (d) 1938

273. The condition of nightblindness is a consequence of
(a) Defective cones
(b) Defective retina
(c) Rhodopsin deficiency in rods
(d) Defective rods

274. 'Commercials' were introduced on All India Radio in
(a) 1972
(b) 1968
(c) 1967
(d) None of the above

275. Which is the largest selling newspaper (Hindi daily) in Rajasthan and Madhya Pradesh?
(a) *Navbharat Times*
(b) *Dainik Jagaran*
(c) *Rajasthan Patrika*
(d) *Dainik Bhaskar*

276. In which year Radio's National Channel was inaugurated?
(a) 1988 (b) 1990
(c) 1992 (d) 1993

277. As compared with cones, rods appear to be more sensitive to
(a) Shorter wavelengths
(b) Any wavelengths
(c) Longer wavelengths
(d) Both shorter and longer wavelengths

278. 'Lassa Kaul' award is given by
(a) *India Today*
(b) *Akashvani*
(c) *Hindustan Times*
(d) *The Times of India*

279. In 1961, India's first school television service was commissioned at
(a) Delhi (b) Madras
(c) Bombay (d) Calcutta

280. The alteration in the comparative sensitivity of the retinal apparatus which accompanies change in the level of light energy is known as
(a) Scotopic Vision
(b) Visual Acuity
(c) Purkinje Effect
(d) Dark Adaptation

281. India made its first Satellite Instructional Television Experiment (SITE) in
(a) 1990-91 (b) 1988-89
(c) 1978-79 (d) 1975-76

282. Which country is the largest film producer in the world?
(a) China (b) England
(c) India (d) America

283. 'Doordarshan-India' the International Channel is in operation from
(a) 1997 (b) 1996
(c) 1995 (d) None of these

284. An increase in sensitivity of retina owing to absence of stimulation in darkness is known as
(a) Visual Acuity
(b) Photopic Vision
(c) Dark Adaptation
(d) Scotopic Vision

285. The name given to the first radio programme was
(a) Akashvani
(b) India Radio Times
(c) The Indian Listener
(d) None of the above

286. The decrease in sensitivity of the eye which occurs on account of its stronger stimulation is known as
(a) Scotopic Vision
(b) Visual Acuity
(c) Light Adaptation
(d) Photopic Vision

287. When were the Bombay and Calcutta stations inaugurated by the Indian Broadcasting Company?
(a) 1927 (b) 1928
(c) 1929 (d) 1930

288. When was the name All India Radio adopted?
(a) January 8, 1935 (b) June 8, 1936
(c) June 10, 1937 (d) April 8, 1938

289. In cone adaptation experiment, test field is strictly limited to the
(a) Retina (b) Rod-free fovea
(c) Cone-free fovea (d) Cornea

290. When was the first National Orchestra set-up with Pandit Ravi Shankar as its conductor?
(a) 1952 (b) 1954
(c) 1965 (d) 1971

291. PIB is recently connected to ____ regional centers by video conferencing system.
(a) 50 (b) 60
(c) 25 (d) 26

292. PTI stands for
(a) Physical Training Institute
(b) Physical Training Inspector
(c) Prime Time Instroction
(d) Press Trust of India

293. Reaction to powerful light, primarily by cones, is called
(a) Colourless Vision
(b) Visual Acuity
(c) Photopic Vision
(d) Scotopic Vision

294. Wage board for working journalists was set up after recommendations of
(a) First Press Commission
(b) Second Press Commission
(c) Journalists Union
(d) Non of the above

295. Who started the newspaper *National Herald*?
(a) Rajiv Gandhi
(b) Indira Gandhi
(c) Motilal Nehru
(d) Jawaharlal Nehru

296. Visual reaction of the dark adapted eye to very feeble light is called

(a) Visual Acuity
(b) Colourless Vision
(c) Photopic Vision
(d) Scotopic vision

297. East India Company introduced censorship for the first time in
(a) 1790 (b) 1795
(c) 1800 (d) 1806

298. Visual angle varies inversely with
(a) Length of cones (b) Brightness
(c) Light (d) Acuity

299. Which of the following was considered as 'Gagging Act'?
(a) Press (Emergency) Powers Act, 1931
(b) Vernacular Press Act
(c) Indian Penal Code
(d) India Press Code

300. Ability to discriminate fine differences in visual detail or visual sharpness is otherwise known as
(a) Visual Acuity
(b) Colourless Vision
(c) Photopic Vision
(d) Scotopic Vision

301. Press Council was constituted under the recommendations of the Press Commission in
(a) 1986 (b) 1977
(c) 1971 (d) 1966

302. Intensity multiplied by its duration brings about a constant perceptual effect. Let "I" stands for light intensity and "T" for time or duration, then IXT = C, where "C" is constant perceptual effectiveness. This above principle is called
(a) Evans Principle
(b) Landis Principle
(c) Roscoe-Bunsen Law
(d) Hess and Polt Law

303. G. Subramania Iyer was the editor of
(a) *Statesman*
(b) *The Times of India*
(c) *The Hindu*
(d) *Hindustan Times*

304. Cases of yellow-blue colour blindness are
(a) mostly found in men.
(b) maximum.
(c) exceedingly Rare.
(d) mostly found in children.

305. This newspaper was vernacular in origin but overnight it became English because of the enactment of Vernacular Press Act of 1878.
(a) *Anand Bazar Patrika*
(b) *Naya Bazar Patrika*
(c) *Amrit Bazar Patrika*
(d) *Bengalee*

306. "Interest is latent attention and attention is interest in action." This statement deals with the
(a) shifting of attention.
(b) objective determinants of attention.
(c) span of attention.
(d) subjective determinants of attention.

307. In India, Englishman William Bolts made the first attempt for the publication of newspapers
(a) 1768 (b) 1772
(c) 1776 (d) 1780

308. "It is not a different process, it is just attention to irrelevant stimuli that are not a part of the main assigned task." Then what is it?
(a) Span of attention
(b) Voluntary attention
(c) Distraction
(d) Shifting of attention

309. What was started by Balshastri Jambhekar?

(a) Anglo-Marathi newspaper in 1832
(b) Anglo-Gujarati newspaper in 1850
(c) Anglo-Assami newspaper in 1832
(d) Anglo-Rajasthani newspaper in 1850

310. Simultaneous focussing on two separate activities is otherwise known as
(a) Division of attention
(b) Distraction
(c) Span of attention
(d) Shifting of attention

311. Who was the editor of *Indu Prakash*, a journal which was published in 1861?
(a) Vishnu Shastri Pandit
(b) Mahadev Govind Ranade
(c) Bal Gangadhar Tilak
(d) Gopal Rao Deshmukh

312. When familiar large objects look smaller than they are known to be, they are regarded as being at a distance. This is an instance of what is called
(a) Scotopic Vision
(b) Photopic Vision
(c) Visual Acuity
(d) Linear Perspective

313. When was the journal *Stribodhi* published?
(a) In 1780 (b) In 1790
(c) In 1850 (d) In 1857

314. Movement Parallax is a monocular cue of distance or depth and for this reason it is also called
(a) Scotopic Vision
(b) Photopic Vision
(c) Monocular Parallax
(d) Visual Acuity

315. Name the journal which was composed by Karsandas Mulji in 1852.
(a) *Maratha* (b) *Kiran*
(c) *Satya Prakash* (d) *Stribodh*

316. Certain alterations in the colour of objects occur depending upon their relative distances from the observer. For this reason, distant hills look blue on account of the light rays travelling through haze. This illustrates
(a) Aerial Perspective
(b) Scotopic Vision
(c) Linear Perspective
(d) Visual Acuity

317. Name the hero of the language press during the period 1845-83.
(a) Dwarkanath Tagore
(b) Manmohan Ghosh
(c) Christo Paul
(d) Vasudev Balwant Phadke

318. A set of depth cues of the nature of some sort of arrangement of proportional rise and fall in compactness of designs which is related to perspectives is called
(a) Gradients (b) Perspectives
(c) Rods (d) Cones

319. The apparent displacement of an object resulting from an actual change of observer's position is known as
(a) Scotopic Vision (b) Parallax
(c) Photopic Vision (d) Acuity

320. The phenomenon of 'induced movement' occurs when there is some real movement which is attributed to
(a) a wrong object
(b) a substitute object
(c) a right object
(d) a real object

321. When was the Bombay TV centre inaugurated?
(a) 1972 (b) 1974
(c) 1975 (d) 1976

322. When were educational programmes by UGC started on TV?

(a) 1983 (b) 1984
(c) 1987 (d) 1988

323. In which year did Doordarshan started its five metro channels?
(a) 1991 (b) 1992
(c) 1993 (d) 1994

324. According to Woodworm (1938), the first systematic experiment that attempted to measure the span of apprehension was carried out by
(a) Jastrow (b) Jevons
(c) Hersey (d) Paulham

325. The first experiment to measure span of attention (apprehension) was designed by
(a) Jevons in 1871
(b) Watkins in 1973
(c) Coren and Porac in 1979
(d) Coren and Girgus in 1978

326. Which committee recommended separation of AIR and Television?
(a) Verghese Committee
(b) Joshi Committee
(c) Chanda Committee
(d) None of the above.

327. Who was/were the subject(s) in Jevon's first experiment on span of apprehension?
(a) A friend of Jevons
(b) The wife of Jevons
(c) Boys from different SES
(d) Jevons himself

328. Who is known as the 'Father of Indian Cinema'?
(a) Ardeshir Irani
(b) Dada Saheb Phalke
(c) Raj Kapoor
(d) Nonc of the above

329. The first person to document the existence of the sensory register and to explore its properties was
(a) Paulham (1887)
(b) O'comer (1958)
(c) Hersey (1936)
(d) George Sperling (1960)

330. When was the first talki feature film made?
(a) 1933 (b) 1932
(c) 1931 (d) 1930

331. From his experiments of sensory register, Sperling suggested that there is some visual trace available to the subject that prolongs the life of the image. He calls this visual trace as the
(a) Attending Information Centre
(b) Apprehension Information Centre
(c) Sensory Information Centre
(d) Perceptual Information Centre

332. Which is the oldest feature agency operating in India?
(a) Gemini Features
(b) Indian Press Agency
(c) Indian News and Feature Alliance
(d) Compass Features

333. In 1976, Neisser introduced a term for "Sensory Information Store." That term is called as
(a) Margin (b) Focus
(c) Extensity (d) Icon

334. The PIB has its headquarters at
(a) Chennai (b) Kolkata
(c) Mumbai (d) Delhi

335. When was the office of the Registrar of Newspapers for India (RNI) started?
(a) 1 July 1956 (b) 4 June 1956
(c) 4 June 1955 (d) 1 July 1954

336. When tachistoscope exposures are short and there is no post exposure masking field, we can be fairly sure that the subject is actually reading the stimulus
(a) from the short-term memory storage.
(b) from the long-term memory storage.

(c) from the icon rather than from the visual image itself.
(d) from the image.

337. Press Council of India has how many members?
(a) 28 (b) 27
(c) 26 (d) 25

338. In which year was the National Film Archives of India established?
(a) 1964 (b) 1966
(c) 1968 (d) 1970

339. In which year was the Commercial Broadcasting Service of AIR was introduced?
(a) In 1967 (b) In 1968
(c) In 1969 (d) In 1970

340. A basis on which one stream of information can be segregated and attended to while others can be ignored is known as
(a) Tympanic Membrane
(b) Eustachian Tube
(c) Basilar Membrane
(d) Channel

341. Where is the Film and Television Institute of India situated?
(a) Pune (b) Chennai
(c) Delhi (d) Mumbai

342. The Film Institute of India was created in the premises of old Prabhat film studio in
(a) Kolkata (b) Hyderabad
(c) Pune (d) Mumbai

343. The most important school of psychology which has contributed a lot toward perception is
(a) Functionalistic School
(b) Structuralistic School
(c) Gestalt Psychology
(d) Behaviouristic School

344. What was established in India in the latter half of nineteenth century?
(a) PTI
(b) UNI
(c) Anglo-Indian Press
(d) None of the above

345. Who made a silent feature film *Pundalik*?
(a) Baburao Pai
(b) N.G. Chitra and R.G. Torney
(c) Dadasaheb Phalke
(d) None of the above

346. Autokinetic movement does not occur if there is a fixed
(a) Illusion
(b) Frame of Reference
(c) Distance between Stimulus and the Eye
(d) Vision

347. When was *Pundalik* movie released?
(a) On February 26, 1921
(b) On March 26, 1920
(c) On May 18, 1915
(d) On May 18, 1912

348. The second Press Commission was formed in
(a) 1979 (b) 1972
(c) 1971 (d) 1967

349. The first news agency of India was
(a) United News of India (UNI)
(b) Free Press of India (FPI)
(c) Press News Bureau (PNB)
(d) Press Trust of India (PTI)

350. Hue, saturation and brightness are the conventional terms which are used to characterise the attributes of
(a) Light (b) Darkness
(c) Brightness (d) Colours

351. The first Press Commission was appointed in
(a) 1950 (b) 1951
(c) 1952 (d) 1952

352. Who among the following was the chairman of the first Press Commission?
(a) Justice J.S. Rajadhyaksha
(b) J. Natrajan
(c) Dr. V.K.R.V. Rao
(d) Dr. C.P. Ramaswami Aiyer

353. Who was the Chairman of the second Press Commission?
(a) P.V. Gadgil
(b) Rajendra Mathur
(c) Justice K.K. Mathew
(d) Girilal Jain

354. The important part of the inner ear for hearing is the snail-shaped
(a) Round Window (b) Cochlea
(c) Auditory Nerve (d) Oval Window

355. Who among the following was the member of second Press Commission?
(a) Ranbir Singh
(b) Prof. H.K. Paranjape
(c) Amrita Pritam
(d) All of the above.

356. The most primitive and oldest feature of music is
(a) Rhythm (b) Song
(c) Harmony (d) Melody

357. When was the first Radio Station inaugurated?
(a) 1900s (b) 1910s
(c) 1920s (d) 1930s

358. Phiphenomenon is a form of
(a) Scotopic Vision
(b) Illusion
(c) Stroboscopic Motion
(d) Photopic Vision

359. Bal Gangadhar Tilak edited
(a) *Kesari* (b) *Maratha*
(c) Both (a) and (b) (d) *Gyan Prakash*

360. Which one of the following is not a principle of Organization of Perception?
(a) The Law of Pragnaz
(b) The Law of Contrast
(c) The Law of Proximity
(d) The Law of Similarity

361. Who founded the Indian Languages Newspapers Association?
(a) Mahatma Gandhi
(b) Bal Gangadhar Tilak
(c) Mammen Mappillai
(d) Amritlal Seth

362. Alcohol is/an
(a) Effective Stimulus
(b) Depressant
(c) Stimulant
(d) Sensory Stimulus

363. Who is known as Indian Gutenberg?
(a) James Augustus Hicky
(b) John de Bustamante
(c) John Bosco
(d) Col. James Todd

364. The name given to the cone pigments is
(a) Ganglian Cells (b) Rhodopsin
(c) Idopsin (d) Bipolar Cells

365. Who is considered as the champion of Indian journalism
(a) Madan Mohan Malaviya
(b) James Augustus Hicky
(c) M.K. Gandhi
(d) Raja Ram Mohan Roy

366. Ishihara test is meant for testing
(a) Principal Complementary Colour
(b) Visual Experience
(c) Colourblindness
(d) Wavelengths

367. Mahatma Gandhi was the editor of
(a) *Young India*
(b) *Harijan*
(c) *Indian Opinion*
(d) All of the above

368. Young-Helmholtz theory of colour vision can otherwise be called
(a) Ladd-Franklin Theory
(b) Scientific Validity Theory
(c) Trichromatic Theory
(d) Opponent Process Theory

369. UNI for Univarta and PTI for
(a) PTI-Hindi (b) Varta
(c) PTI Varta (d) Bhasha

370. Urdu News Service was started for the first time in India by
(a) UNI (b) IANS
(c) PTI (d) IRNA

371. When your friend is at a distance, certainly he looks smaller than when he is standing close to you. But you do not think that really he is smaller or shorter. The size of familiar objects does not change with distance. As your friends comes closer to you from a distance, you do not think that he is getting larger and larger. This is an illustration of
(a) Height Constancy
(b) Binocular Vision
(c) Object Constancy
(d) Size Constancy

372. NFDC headquarters are located at
(a) Mumbai (b) Chennai
(c) New Delhi (d) Bengaluru

373. When Mahatma Gandhi was in South Africa he started which newspaper?
(a) *Young India* (b) *Indian Opinion*
(c) *Reformer* (d) *Hindustan*

374. A continuous small tremor of the eyes is known as
(a) Physiological Nystagmus
(b) Acuity
(c) Rod-cone break
(d) Purkinje Effect

375. The editor of *Kudiyarasu* was
(a) E.V Ramasamy Naicker
(b) M.G. Ramachandran
(c) C.N. Annadurai
(d) K. Karunanidhi

376. Annie Besant edited
(a) *New India*
(b) *Common Wheel*
(c) Both (a) and (b)
(d) *Young India*

377. The eye is sensitive to wavelengths of light that range from about
(a) 200 to about 300 nm
(b) 160 to about 200 nm
(c) 380 to about 760 nm
(d) 300 to about 500 nm

378. Raja Ram Mohan Roy edited
(a) *Sambad Kaumudi*
(b) *Banga Dutta*
(c) *Mirat-ul-Akhbar*
(d) All of the above

379. Different wavelengths produce the experience of different
(a) Lights (b) Hues
(c) Brightness (d) Colours

380. In which year was the BBC world service started in India?
(a) 1995 (b) 1993
(c) 1991 (d) 1990

381. In which year was the Asian Television Network started?
(a) 1992 (b) 1993
(c) 1994 (d) 1995

382. The Scott is Philosopher Thomas Reid (1710-96) has first developed the distinction between
(a) Audition and Vision
(b) Vision and Recurrent Inhibition
(c) Sensation and Attention
(d) Sensation and Perception

383. Kristo Das Pal was the editor of
(a) *Deshmukh* (b) *Dainik Jagran*
(c) *Hindu Patriot* (d) *Hindu*

384. Military Gazette belonged to
(a) Lahore (b) Rawalpindi
(c) Peshawar (d) Delhi

385. Robert Knight founded *The Statesman* in the year
(a) 1871 (b) 1872
(c) 1873 (d) 1875

386. Helmholtz's theory of space perception centred around the concept of
(a) Recurrent Inhibition
(b) The Static Sense
(c) Unconscious Inference
(d) Mechanism of Vision

387. *Indian Economist* was started by
(a) G. Subramania Iyer
(b) Kristo Das Pal
(c) Robert Knight
(d) Robert Dahl

388. The *Indian Daily Mail* was closed down in
(a) 1933 (b) 1934
(c) 1935 (d) 1937

389. Rundol Lotze (1817-81) assumed that mind is inherently capable of
(a) Perceiving Depth
(b) Perceiving Brightness
(c) Perceiving Space
(d) Perceiving Size

390. Chintamani is connected with
(a) *Indian Daily Mail*
(b) *Frontline*
(c) *Pioneer*
(d) *Leader*

391. *The Current* was started by
(a) Bennett and Coleman
(b) D.F. Karaka
(c) C.Y. Chintamani
(d) Gopala Krishna Gokhale

392. Indian Cinematograph Act was passed in
(a) 1971 (b) 1968
(c) 1965 (d) 1952

393. The National Film Archive of India was set up under the ministry of
(a) Finance
(b) Parliamentary Affairs
(c) Human Resource Development
(d) Information and Broadcasting

394. Who defined apperception as the awareness of any conscious content that is clearly comprehended or grasped?
(a) J.B. Watson
(b) Kurt Lewin
(c) Ratliff
(d) Wilmhelm Wundt

395. The Song and Drama Division set up in 1954 is a unit of
(a) Doordarshan
(b) Publication Division
(c) All India Radio
(d) None of the above

396. When was the first printing press established in India?
(a) 1676 (b) 1674
(c) 1670 (d) 1662

397. Harvey Carr defined perception as the cognition of a present object in relation to
(a) some acts of adjustment.
(b) recurrent inhibition.
(c) simultaneous contrast.
(d) some acts of stimulation.

398. A relieving member of the Press Council
(a) can be renominated as many times as the chairman desires.
(b) has to be renominated three times.
(c) cannot be renominated at all.
(d) can be renominated for a second and final term.

399. Gestalt Psychology looks upon the world as
(a) Neuro-physiological
(b) Neurological
(c) Psychological
(d) Psychophysical

400. The Press Council of India consists of
(a) A director and 25 members
(b) A secretary-general and 30 members
(c) A chairman and 28 members
(d) A president, a convenor and 28 members

401. The Chairman of Press Council of India is selected by a committee consisting of
(a) Speaker of Lok Sabha.
(b) Person chosen by the members of the council from among themselves.
(c) Chairman of Rajya Sabha.
(d) All of the above.

402. Which principle states that because Gestalten are isomorphic to stimulus patterns, they may undergo extensive changes without losing their identities?
(a) Transposition
(b) Autokinetic Effect
(c) Simultaneous Contrast
(d) Recurrent Inhibition

403. Sponsored programmes were introduced in Vividh Bharati from
(a) June 1971 (b) May 1970
(c) April 1969 (d) March 1968

404. Prasar Bharati is also known as
(a) Broadcasting Corporation of India
(b) Broadcasting Association of India
(c) Broadcasting Centre of India
(d) Indian Broadcasting Authority

405. "Memory is a dynamic process in which traces undergo progressive changes according to some principles of organization that govern original perception."
This definition of memory was given by
(a) Gestalt Psychologists
(b) Psychoanalysts
(c) Structuralists
(d) Behaviourists

406. Which of the following committees recommended that Broadcasting Corporation should be established by an Act of Parliament in which its objectives should be clearly laid down?
(a) The Subramaniam Committee
(b) The Chanda Committee
(c) The Krishna Committee
(d) The Verghese Committee

407. Who defined 'perception' as the process of maintaining contact with the world?
(a) Herring (b) Gibson
(c) Helmholtz (d) Lorrin A. Riggs

408. According to Chanda Committee how many members should be there in the Board of Governors?
(a) No more than seven
(b) No more than six
(c) No more than five
(d) None of the above

409. How many members did the Verghese Committee recommend in its Board of Trustees (or Nyasi Mandal)?
(a) 13 members (b) 12 members
(c) 10 members (d) 9 members

410. When the sense organs are oriented towards the environment and are actively seeking information, we call
(a) Distraction
(b) Obtained Perception
(c) Illusion
(d) Hallucination

411. What is the oldest evidence of Chinese printing?
(a) *Confucian Canon*
(b) *Confucian Analects*

(c) *Diamond Sutra*
(d) *Meghdoot*

412. The perception which arises from the skin, nose, ears, eyes or other organs is called
(a) Hallucination
(b) Imposed Perception
(c) Obtained Perception
(d) Illusion

413. The National Film Development Corporation Limited (NFDC) was incorporated in
(a) 1960 (b) 1970
(c) 1975 (d) 1980

414. When was the Directorate of Film Festivals (DFF) set up by the Government of India?
(a) In 1970 (b) In 1971
(c) In 1972 (d) In 1973

415. The distinction between "Obtained and Imposed Perception" was brought out by
(a) Riggs (b) Gibson
(c) Helmholtz (d) Herring

416. What is the work of NFDC?
(a) To encourage the high budget films.
(b) To encourage the concept of low budget films.
(c) To complete the high budget films.
(d) To discourage the concept of low budget films.

417. One psychologist has developed a theory of colour vision as well as a theory of hearing. Who is he?
(a) Hubel (b) N.R. Carlson
(c) Wiesel (d) Helmholtz

418. *Mirat-ul-Akbar* belonged to
(a) Aurobindo Ghosh
(b) Maulana Abul Kalam Azad
(c) Raja Ram Mohan Roy
(d) Syed Abdulla Brelvi

419. The gestalt concept of equilibrium is expressed by the law of
(a) Continuity (b) Similarity
(c) Proximity (d) Pragnaz

420. Who was the owner of *The Hindu*?
(a) K.R. Iyengar
(b) Surendranath Banerjee
(c) Mahatma Gandhi
(d) Motilal Ghosh

421. Which committee was established in 1996 to have another look at the Prasar Bharati Act and to suggest amendments?
(a) The Chand Committee
(b) The Nitish Sengupta Committee
(c) The Verghese Committee
(d) The Ram Vilas Paswan Committee

422. The 'Law of Closure' reflects the idea of striving for
(a) Continuity (b) Good Figure
(c) Good Contour (d) Completion

423. The STAR TV channel was launched in India in the year
(a) 1992 (b) 1991
(c) 1989 (d) 1987

424. What is NFDC?
(a) National Film Development Corporation
(b) National Fashion Designing Centre
(c) National Federation of Development Council
(d) None of the above

425. Which law of organization in perception has become a principle of temporal contiguity in the learning theory?
(a) The Law of Proximity
(b) The Law of Good Figure
(c) The Law of Similarity
(d) The Law of Pragnaz

426. The Nagercoil Experiment in local community radio with FM was conducted on

(a) October 30, 1984
(b) December 30, 1986
(c) September 30, 1987
(d) November 30, 1987

427. The chairman of the press council of India is appointed for the term of
(a) One year (b) Two years
(c) Three years (d) Four years

428. The contrast between a dynamic field and a mechine was brought out by
(a) Helmholtz (b) W.G. Kohler
(c) Kurt Koffka (d) Wertheimer

429. The first Press Council Act was passed in
(a) 1966 (b) 1987
(c) 1965 (d) 1980

430. Sometimes it is very difficult to find an empty seat in a dark cinema hall. We bump against people and sometimes try to sit on them after entering to the dark hail in a sunny afternoon. After a brief span of time, we may adapt to darkness and see. This is an example of
(a) Brightness Constancy
(b) Colour Constancy
(c) Depth Perception
(d) Dark Adaptation

431. Indian Press has witnessed a _____ growth over the past few decades
(a) two-tier (b) three-tier
(c) four-tier (d) five-tier

432. The oldest surviving newspaper of India is
(a) *The Statesman*
(b) *The Times of India*
(c) *Malayalam Manorama*
(d) *Mumbai Samachar*

433. The Gestalt Psychologists learned their "Principles of Organization" from the study of
(a) Attention
(b) Insightful Learning
(c) Consciousness
(d) Sensory Experience

434. Which recommendation of Chanda Committee was adopted by the Union government?
(a) AIR be converted into a corporation.
(b) Commercial broadcasting in electronic media.
(c) New method of recruitment and financial management.
(d) Introduction of different satellite channels.

435. Reinforcing factors in perceptual organization are analogous to the
(a) The Law of Effect
(b) Reinforcement of a conditioned response
(c) The Law of Exercise
(d) Both (a) and (b)

436. Which of the following statutes has not been enforced?
(a) The Cable Television Network (Regulation) Act, 1995.
(b) The Telecom Regulating Authority of India Act, 1997.
(c) The Information Technology Act, 2000.
(d) The Right to Information Act, 2002.

437. Wavelength is obtained by dividing the speed of the light by the
(a) Illumination (b) Colour
(c) Frequency (d) Brightness

438. Identify the correct sequence of launching the satellites from the following
(a) INTELSAT-INSAT 1A-INTERSPUTNIK-EARLY BIRD.
(b) EARLY BIRD–INTELSAT–INTERSPUTNIK–INSAT 1A.

(c) INSAT 1A–EARLY BIRD–INTERSPUTNIK–INTELSAT.
(d) INTERSPUTNIK–INSAT 1A EARLY BIRD–INTELSAT

439. For constancy to operate in the world of normal objects, the more distant features must be
(a) projected in sufficient light.
(b) clearly spaced.
(c) perceptually expanded.
(d) clearly visualised.

440. The first nationalist news agency Swaminath of Sadanand was established at
(a) New Delhi (b) Bombay
(c) Hyderabad (d) Lucknow

441. Outline or boundary of an object is called
(a) Brightness (b) Ground
(c) Figure (d) Contour

442. The Newspaper (Price Control) Act, 1972 was in force for
(a) One year (b) Two years
(c) Three years (d) Four years

443. The Radio Farm Forums were the experiments conducted in
(a) Bangladesh (b) Sri Lanka
(c) Nepal (d) India

444. Prolongation or renewal of a sensory experience after the stimulus has ceased to affect the sense organ is called
(a) Autokinetic Effect
(b) Hallucination
(c) Illusion
(d) Afterimage

445. The correct sequence of launching 24 hours news channels in India is
(a) NDTV-BBC-CNN-Aaj Tak
(b) CNN-BBC-Aaj Tak-NDTV
(c) BBC-CNN-NDTV-Aaj Tak
(d) BBC-NDTV-CNN-Aaj Tak

446. The committee that suggested the division of Samachar news agency was headed by
(a) B.G. Verghese (b) Kuldip Nayyar
(c) Arun Shourie (d) Sham Lal

447. A familiar study on perception which has shown that the poor children overestimated the size of coins to a greater degree than wealthy children, was done by
(a) Mc Ginnis
(b) Dember
(c) Bruner and Goodman
(d) Murray

448. The printing press was introduced in India during
(a) The thirteenth century
(b) The fourteenth century
(c) The fifteenth century
(d) The sixteenth century

449. The chronological sequence of the establishment of the following newspapers is
(a) *The Statesman-The Times of India-The Hindu-The Indian Express.*
(b) *The Hindu-The Times of India-The Statesman-The Indian Express.*
(c) *The Times of India-The Statesman-The Hindu-The Indian Express.*
(d) *The Hindu-The Indian Express-The Times of India-The Statesman.*

450. Camouflage is the deliberate confusion of
(a) Figure and Ground
(b) Phiphenomenon
(c) Illusion and Hallucination
(d) Stroboscopic Motion

451. The chronological sequence of the chairpersons of press council is
(a) R.S. Sarkaria-P.B. Sawant-K. Jayachandra Reddy-G.N. Ray.
(b) K. Jayachandra Reddy-R.S. Sarkaria-G.N. Ray-P.B. Sawant.

(c) G.N. Ray-K. Jayachandra Reddy-P.B. Sawant-R.S. Sarkaria.
(d) G.N. Ray-R.S. Sarkaria-K. Jayachandra Reddy-P.B. Sawant.

452. The protective colouration of many animals is an example of
(a) Reversible Figures
(b) Phiphenomenon
(c) Figure and Ground
(d) Camouflage

453. Write the proper sequence of the Indian press laws given here in terms of their historicity.
(a) Official Secrets Act, Copyright Act, Contempt of Courts Act, Right to Information Act.
(b) Contempt of Courts Act, Copyright Act, Official Secrets Act, Right to Information Act.
(c) Copyright Act, Right to Information Act, Contempt of Courts, Official Secrets Act.
(d) Right to Information Act, Official Secrets Act, Contempt of Courts Act, Copyright Act.

454. *The Searchlight* was a newspaper published from
(a) Kolkata (b) Mumbai
(c) Guwahati (c) Patna

455. Sense organs in the muscles, tendons and joints tell us about the position of our limbs and the state of tension in the muscles. They serve the sense called
(a) Vision (b) Auditory Sense
(c) Kinesthesis (d) Transduction

456. The newspaper group in India that has obtained the largest number of licences to launch FM radio stations is
(a) *Dainik Jagaran* (b) *Hindustan*
(c) *Dainik Bhaskar* (d) *Nayee Dunia*

457. The *Samchar Darpan* was a publication of
(a) the Baptist mission
(b) the Wesleyan mission
(c) the Danish mission
(d) the Scottish mission

458. The process of converting physical energy into nervous system activity is called
(a) Inhibition (b) Transduction
(c) Transmission (d) Nerve Impluse

459. Identify the correct chronological order:
(a) cable, video, satellite, e-mail
(b) satellite, cable, video, e-mail
(c) e-mail, cable, satellite, video
(d) cable, video, e-mail, satellite

460. Identify the correct chronological sequence of the following:
(a) AINEC, INS, ILNA, Editor's Guild
(b) INS, AINEC, Editor's Guild, ILNA
(c) Editor's Guild, INS, AINEC, ILNA
(d) ILNA, Editor's Guild, AINEC, INS

461. The first European who attempted to bring out a newspaper in India was
(a) James Augustus Hicky
(b) James Silk Buckingham
(c) William Carey
(d) William Bolts

462. Receptor cells convert physical energy into an electric voltage or potential called
(a) Vestibular Sense
(b) Spike Potential
(c) Receptor Potential
(d) Generator Potential

463. The body which represents the Indian Newspaper publishers is
(a) AINEC (b) NUJ
(c) IFWJ (d) INS

464. The committee which looked into the problems of small newspapers in India was headed by

(a) Justice Rajyadhaksha
(b) B.G. Verghese
(c) R.R. Diwakar
(d) Kuldip Nayar

465. Whether it is the receptor potential itself or some other voltage, the electrical event that triggers nerve impulses is known as the
(a) Generator Potential
(b) Spike Potential
(c) Nerve Impulse
(d) Receptor Potential

466. Identify the correct chronological order of places where Doordarshan launched its operations
(a) New Delhi-Kolkata-Mumbai
(b) New Delhi-Chennai-Mumbai
(c) New Delhi-Mumbai-Kolkata
(d) Chennai-Mumbai-New Delhi

467. Identify the correct chronological order of dailies when they were launched
(a) *The Hindustan Times-The Hindu-Amrit Bazaar Patrika-Bombay Chronicle*
(b) *The Hindu-Bombay Chronicle-Amrit Bazaar Patrika-The Hindustan Times*
(c) *Amrit Bazaar Patrika-The Hindu-Bombay Chronicle-The Hindustan Times*
(d) *Bombay Chronicle-The Hindu-The Hindustan Times-Amrit Bazaar Patrika*

468. The entire range of wavelengths is called the
(a) Photosensitive Area
(b) Blind Spot
(c) Electromagnetic Spectrum
(d) Visible Spectrum

469. Identify the correct chronological order of the following
(a) *Udant Martand-Samachar Darpan-Gospel Magazine-Digdarshan*
(b) *Digdarshan-Samachar Darpan-Gospel Magazine-Udant Martand*
(c) *Samachar Darpan-Udant Martand-Digdarshan-Gospel Magazine*
(d) *Gospel Magazine-Digdarshan-Samachar Darpan-Udant Martand*

470. The tendency to perceive a line that starts in one way as continuing in the same way is called the principle of
(a) Continuation (b) Closure
(c) Similarity (d) Proximity

471. Identify the correct chronological sequence of committees
(a) P.C. Joshi-MacBride-Varadan-Sengupta
(b) Varadan-Sengupta-MacBride-P.C. Joshi
(c) MacBride-P.C. Joshi-Sengupta-Varadan
(d) MacBride-P.C. Joshi-Varadan-Sengupta

472. Identify the correct chronological sequence of magazines that were launched
(a) *India Today-The Week-Frontline-Outlook*
(b) *The Week-India Today-Outlook-Frontline*
(c) *Outlook-India Today-The Week-Frontline*
(d) *India Today-Frontline-The Week-Outlook*

473. The idea that we may be 'ready' and 'primed for' certain kinds of sensory input is known as
(a) Sensory System
(b) Mood
(c) Set
(d) Cognitive Style

474. Find the correct sequence of TV channels when they were established in India
(a) Zee TV-Star World-Sony TV-Discovery Channel
(b) Zee TV-Sony TV-Discovery Channel-Star World
(c) Zee TV-Star World-Sony TV-Discovery Channel
(d) Sony TV-Zee TV-Star World-Discovery Channel

475. The spatial-frequency theory maintains that form vision depends on the firing pattern of brain cells that respond to variations in the rates of change in brightness from
(a) spinalcord to brain.
(b) one part of the brain to another.
(c) one part of a visual scene to another.
(d) temporal lobe to frontal lobe.

476. Which committee was set up to re-examine the Prasar Bharati Act?
(a) Varadan Committee
(b) Chanda Committee
(c) Sengupta Committee
(d) Verghese Committee

477. In India, the first newspaper mean for publication was announced by William Bolts in
(a) 1778 (b) 1782
(c) 1780 (d) 1776

478. The first radio broadcast in India was in
(a) 1911 (b) 1921
(c) 1931 (d) 1941

479. Which BBC correspondent was expelled from India during the state of emergency declared in 1975?
(a) Charles Wheeler
(b) Andrew Whitehead
(c) Mark Tully
(d) David Loyn

480. The receptors for taste are specialized cells gouped together in little clusters known as
(a) Taste Buds
(b) Tongue
(c) Sweet Glands
(d) Taste Nerves

481. Identify the correct sequence of the following TV transmission technologies in the order of their emergence.
(a) DTH, VHF, Cable, Satellite Cable
(b) Satellite cable, VHF, DTH, Cable
(c) Cable, VHF, Satellite Cable, DTH
(d) VHF, Cable, Satellite Cable, DTH

482. Which of the following is the correct sequence of television soaps according to their telecast?
(a) Hum Log, Ramayana, Mahabharat, Buniyaad
(b) Hum Log, Buniyaad, Mahabharat, Ramayana
(c) Hum Log, Buniyaad, Ramayana, Mahabharat
(d) Buniyaad, Hum Log, Ramayana, Mahabharat

483. The audible range for human beings is from about
(a) 400 hertz to about 4000 hertz
(b) 600 hertz to about 6000 hertz
(c) 20 hertz to about 20,000 hertz
(d) 300 hertz to about 3000 hertz

484. The first Director of News of All India Radio was
(a) Lionel Fielden
(b) Charles Barns
(c) G.C. Awasthy
(d) Ahmed Shah Bokhari

Directions: Questions 485 to 488 are of multiple statement type. Choose the correct answer from the codes gives below the statements.

485. Which of the following statements are true?
1. The Press Council Act was passed in 1965
2. A Press Council was appointed in July, 1966
3. The first Press Commission gave its report on June 30, 1968
4. The First Press Council started its operations from July 14, 1954

Codes:

(a) 1 and 2 (b) 2 and 3
(c) 1, 2 and 4 (d) 2, 3 and 4

486. Which of these is false?
1. A developmental TV report should include a lot of field based footages.
2. 'Sustainable Development' means more industrialisation.
3. Television relies heavily on the words of a reporter than the visuals.

Codes:

(a) Both 1 and 3 (b) 1 only
(c) 3 only (d) Both 2 and 3

487. According to the communication convergence Act, 2001, programme means
1. television or radio programme including
2. Advertising or sponsorship
3. Whether or not of a commercial kind
4. broadcast programming shall be construed accordingly

Which of these statement(s) is/are correct

Codes:

(a) 1 and 2 (b) 1, 3 and 4
(c) 4 only (d) 1, 2, 3 and 4

488. According to Information Technology Act, 2000, "Electronic Record" means the information relating to

(1) Data based computer
(2) Data record or data generated image
(3) Sound stored, received or sent in an electronic form
(4) Microfilm or computer generated micro fiche

Which of these statement(s) is/are correct?

Codes:

(a) 1 only (b) 2 and 3
(c) 4 only (d) 2, 3 and 4

Directions: Questions 489 to 500 are of matching type. Match List-I with List-II and select the correct using the codes gives below the lists.

489. **List-I**

(A) Ramacharitmanasa
(B) Ramayana
(C) Srimadbhagavadgita
(D) Ranganatha Ramayana

List-II

1. Vyasa
2. Gonabudda Reddy
3. Tulasidasa
4. Valmiki

Codes:	A	B	C	D
(a)	2	3	4	1
(b)	3	4	1	2
(c)	4	3	2	1
(d)	1	2	3	4

490.

List-I	List-II
(A) Copyright Act	1. 1956
(B) Young Persons Act	2. 1947
(C) Press Council Act	3. 1957
(D) Industrial Disputes Act	4. 1965

Codes:	A	B	C	D
(a)	4	2	2	3
(b)	3	1	4	2
(c)	1	2	3	4
(d)	2	3	3	1

491. **List-I (Channel)** **List-II (Satellite)**

List-I (Channel)	List-II (Satellite)
(A) STAR TV	1. ASIASAT-1
(B) MTV	2. INTELSAT-703
(C) ASIANET	3. Panam SAT-4
(D) ETV	4. INTELSAT-704

Codes:	A	B	C	D
(a)	1	3	2	4
(b)	4	2	3	1
(c)	1	2	3	4
(d)	4	3	2	1

492. **List-I (Persons)** **List-II (Publications)**

List-I (Persons)	List-II (Publications)
(A) C.R. Irani	1. Kesari
(B) Bal Gangadhar Tilak	2. Mirat-ul-Akbar
(C) Raja Ram Mohan Roy	3. The Hindu
(D) Kasturi Ranga Iyengar	4. The Statesman

Codes:	A	B	C	D
(a)	4	1	2	3
(b)	2	4	1	3
(c)	1	3	2	4
(d)	4	2	1	3

493. **List-I (TV Shows)** **List-II (Channels)**

List-I (TV Shows)	List-II (Channels)
(A) Indian Idol	1. NDTV
(B) Walk the Talk	2. Sony
(C) Devil's Advocate	3. Star one
(D) Great Indian Laughter show	4. CNN-IBN

Codes:	A	B	C	D
(a)	1	3	4	2
(b)	2	3	1	4
(c)	2	1	4	3
(d)	3	4	2	1

494. **List-I (News Agencies)**
(A) Associated Press of India
(B) Press Trust of India
(C) Free Press of India
(D) Samachar Bharathi

List-II (Personalities associated with)
1. Krishnakanth
2. S. Sadanand
3. Kasturi Srinivasan
4. K.C. Roy

Codes:	A	B	C	D
(a)	1	2	3	4
(b)	2	3	1	4
(c)	4	3	2	1
(d)	3	4	1	2

495. **List-I (Newspapers)** **List-II (Years)**

List-I (Newspapers)	List-II (Years)
(A) Anand Bazaar Patrika	1. 1920
(B) Sakal	2. 1923
(C) Mathrubhoomi	3. 1922
(D) Aaj	4. 1932

Codes:	A	B	C	D
(a)	1	2	3	4
(b)	4	2	1	3
(c)	1	4	2	3
(d)	3	1	4	2

496. **List-I (Acts)**
(A) Official Secrets Act
(B) Press and Registration of Books Act
(C) Right to Information Act
(D) Cable Networks (Regulation) Act

List-II (Years of enactment)
1. 1923 2. 1995
3. 2005 4. 1867

Codes:	A	B	C	D
(a)	2	1	4	3
(b)	1	4	3	2
(c)	4	3	2	1
(d)	3	2	1	4

497. **List-I (Journalists)**
(A) Chalapathi Rau
(B) B.G. Verghese

(C) Ravindra Kumar
(D) Arun Shourie

List-II (Newspaper associated with)

1. *The Indian Express*
2. *The Statesman*
3. *The National Herald*
4. *The Times of India*

Codes:	A	B	C	D
(a)	2	4	3	1
(b)	1	2	4	3
(c)	3	1	2	4
(d)	4	3	2	2

498. **List I (Newspaper)**

A. *Bombay Darpan*
B. *Mumbai Vartman*
C. *Jam-e-Jamshed*

List II (Year of Establishment)

1. 1850
2. 1830
3. 1831

Codes:	A	B	C
(a)	3	1	2
(b)	2	3	1
(c)	1	2	3
(d)	2	1	3

499.

List-I (Launch of Stations/Programmes)	List-II (Years)
(A) Vividh Bharati	1. 1984
(B) First Local Radio Station	2. 1977
(C) First FM Station	3. 1969
(D) Yuvavani Programme	4. 1957

Codes:	A	B	C	D
(a)	1	2	4	3
(b)	2	4	3	1
(c)	4	1	2	3
(d)	3	4	1	2

500.

List I (Newspaper)	List II (Journalist)
A. *Sandhya*	1. Aurobindo Ghose
B. *Jugantar*	2. B.B. Upadhayaya
C. *Bande Matram*	3. B.N. Dutt

Codes:	A	B	C
(a)	2	3	1
(b)	1	3	2
(c)	2	1	3
(d)	3	1	2

Directions: Question 501 consists of two statements one labelled as 'Assertion' (A) and the other labelled as 'Reason' (R). You are to examine these two statements carefully and decide if the Assertion (A) and the Reason (R) are individually true and if so, whether the Reason is a correct explanation of the Assertion. Select your answers to this questions using the codes given below:

(a) Both (A) and (R) are true and (R) is the correct explanation of (A).
(b) Both (A) and (R) are true but (R) is not the correct explanation of (A).
(c) (A) is true but (R) is false.
(d) (A) is false but (R) is true.

501. **Assertion (A):** Classical China was conservative and stable.

Reason (R): Classical China vested supreme authority in the very old people.

ANSWERS

1. (c)	2. (c)	3. (a)	4. (d)	5. (d)	6. (d)
7. (c)	8. (d)	9. (a)	10. (c)	11. (c)	12. (d)
13. (d)	14. (c)	15. (a)	16. (d)	17. (b)	18. (b)
19. (d)	20. (d)	21. (b)	22. (c)	23. (b)	24. (a)
25. (c)	26. (a)	27. (a)	28. (c)	29. (b)	30. (b)
31. (a)	32. (b)	33. (c)	34. (a)	35. (d)	36. (a)
37. (a)	38. (c)	39. (d)	40. (a)	41. (d)	42. (a)
43. (d)	44. (a)	45. (c)	46. (b)	47. (a)	48. (c)
49. (b)	50. (c)	51. (c)	52. (d)	53. (b)	54. (a)
55. (a)	56. (c)	57. (b)	58. (a)	59. (d)	60. (b)
61. (c)	62. (c)	63. (b)	64. (d)	65. (a)	66. (d)
67. (d)	68. (d)	69. (a)	70. (a)	71. (a)	72. (a)
73. (b)	74. (d)	75. (d)	76. (a)	77. (b)	78. (b)
79. (d)	80. (c)	81. (a)	82. (b)	83. (c)	84. (c)
85. (d)	86. (b)	87. (d)	88. (a)	89. (c)	90. (d)
91. (c)	92. (c)	93. (d)	94. (d)	95. (d)	96. (a)
97. (d)	98. (a)	99. (d)	100. (c)	101. (d)	102. (a)
103. (b)	104. (a)	105. (b)	106. (b)	107. (d)	108. (d)
109. (d)	110. (a)	111. (b)	112. (c)	113. (d)	114. (a)
115. (a)	116. (c)	117. (d)	118. (b)	119. (d)	120. (a)
121. (d)	122. (d)	123. (c)	124. (d)	125. (d)	126. (c)
127. (b)	128. (a)	129. (a)	130. (b)	131. (a)	132. (c)
133. (d)	134. (a)	135. (a)	136. (a)	137. (b)	138. (b)
139. (d)	140. (a)	141. (a)	142. (a)	143. (c)	144. (b)
145. (a)	146. (d)	147. (d)	148. (b)	149. (d)	150. (c)
151. (d)	152. (b)	153. (a)	154. (a)	155. (a)	156. (d)
157. (a)	158. (b)	159. (b)	160. (b)	161. (c)	162. (d)
163. (b)	164. (b)	165. (d)	166. (a)	167. (a)	168. (a)
169. (b)	170. (d)	171. (c)	172. (d)	173. (c)	174. (c)
175. (d)	176. (b)	177. (c)	178. (d)	179. (d)	180. (d)
181. (d)	182. (c)	183. (c)	184. (b)	185. (c)	186. (b)
187. (d)	188. (b)	189. (c)	190. (b)	191. (c)	192. (d)
193. (c)	194. (d)	195. (a)	196. (a)	197. (c)	198. (a)

199. (d)	200. (a)	201. (c)	202. (c)	203. (b)	204. (b)
205. (a)	206. (d)	207. (a)	208. (d)	209. (a)	210. (c)
211. (a)	212. (b)	213. (c)	214. (d)	215. (d)	216. (c)
217. (c)	218. (d)	219. (b)	220. (a)	221. (a)	222. (d)
223. (c)	224. (b)	225. (a)	226. (a)	227. (d)	228. (a)
229. (d)	230. (d)	231. (b)	232. (c)	233. (b)	234. (a)
235. (c)	236. (c)	237. (d)	238. (a)	239. (b)	240. (c)
241. (c)	242. (b)	243. (b)	244. (d)	245. (c)	246. (a)
247. (b)	248. (c)	249. (b)	250. (b)	251. (d)	252. (b)
253. (c)	254. (c)	255. (c)	256. (c)	257. (c)	258. (d)
259. (d)	260. (c)	261. (a)	262. (c)	263. (c)	264. (d)
265. (d)	266. (a)	267. (b)	268. (b)	269. (c)	270. (d)
271. (d)	272. (a)	273. (c)	274. (c)	275. (d)	276. (a)
277. (a)	278. (b)	279. (a)	280. (c)	281. (d)	282. (c)
283. (c)	284. (c)	285. (b)	286. (c)	287. (a)	288. (b)
289. (b)	290. (a)	291. (d)	292. (d)	293. (c)	294. (d)
295. (d)	296. (d)	297. (b)	298. (d)	299. (b)	300. (a)
301. (d)	302. (c)	303. (c)	304. (c)	305. (c)	306. (d)
307. (c)	308. (c)	309. (a)	310. (a)	311. (d)	312. (d)
313. (d)	314. (c)	315. (c)	316. (a)	317. (d)	318. (a)
319. (a)	320. (a)	321. (a)	322. (b)	323. (c)	324. (b)
325. (a)	326. (c)	327. (d)	328. (b)	329. (d)	330. (c)
331. (c)	332. (c)	333. (d)	334. (b)	335. (a)	336. (c)
337. (a)	338. (a)	339. (a)	340. (d)	341. (a)	342. (c)
343. (c)	344. (c)	345. (b)	346. (b)	347. (d)	348. (d)
349. (b)	350. (d)	351. (c)	352. (a)	353. (c)	354. (b)
355. (d)	356. (a)	357. (c)	358. (c)	359. (c)	360. (b)
361. (d)	362. (b)	363. (b)	364. (c)	365. (d)	366. (c)
367. (d)	368. (c)	369. (d)	370. (a)	371. (d)	372. (a)
373. (b)	374. (a)	375. (a)	376. (c)	377. (c)	378. (d)
379. (b)	380. (c)	381. (a)	382. (d)	383. (c)	384. (a)
385. (d)	386. (c)	387. (c)	388. (a)	389. (c)	390. (a)
391. (b)	392. (d)	393. (d)	394. (d)	395. (c)	396. (b)
397. (a)	398. (d)	399. (d)	400. (c)	401. (d)	402. (a)

403. (b)	404. (a)	405. (a)	406. (b)	407. (b)	408. (c)
409. (b)	410. (b)	411. (c)	412. (b)	413. (c)	414. (d)
415. (b)	416. (b)	417. (d)	418. (c)	419. (d)	420. (a)
421. (b)	422. (d)	423. (b)	424. (a)	425. (a)	426. (a)
427. (c)	428. (b)	429. (c)	430. (d)	431. (c)	432. (d)
433. (d)	434. (b)	435. (d)	436. (d)	437. (c)	438. (b)
439. (c)	440. (b)	441. (d)	442. (b)	443. (d)	444. (d)
445. (b)	446. (a)	447. (c)	448. (d)	449. (c)	450. (a)
451. (a)	452. (d)	453. (a)	454. (c)	455. (c)	456. (a)
457. (a)	458. (b)	459. (a)	460. (a)	461. (d)	462. (c)
463. (d)	464. (d)	465. (a)	466. (c)	467. (c)	468. (c)
469. (d)	470. (a)	471. (c)	472. (a)	473. (c)	474. (c)
475. (c)	476. (a)	477. (c)	478. (b)	479. (c)	480. (a)
481. (c)	482. (c)	483. (c)	484. (b)	485. (a)	486. (d)
487. (d)	488. (d)	489. (b)	490. (b)	491. (a)	492. (a)
493. (c)	494. (c)	495. (d)	496. (b)	497. (c)	498. (c)
499. (c)	500. (c)	501. (a)			

5

Communication and Theories of Social Change

1. The tendency to fill the gaps perceptually when a stimulus is incomplete is known as the
   (a) The Law of Proximity
   (b) The Law of Continuity
   (c) The Law of Good Figure
   (d) The Law of Pragnaz
2. According to Wilbur Schramm, which of the following functions is performed by the mass media?
   (a) Watchdogs (b) Policymakers
   (c) Teachers (d) All of the above.
3. The mass media cannot
   (a) effect deep-rooted changes in a short period.
   (b) widen the mental horizons of people.
   (c) change or shape tastes of the masses.
   (d) enforce social norms on the masses.
4. The laws of figure and ground and perceptual grouping partially explain the concepts of
   (a) Depth Perception
   (b) Size Perception
   (c) Form Perception
   (d) Shape Perception
5. Why radio has not been able to play a major role in the process of social change in India?
   (a) The reach of radio was very low during the pre-Independence era.
   (b) TV software proved better to provoke the forces of societal change.
   (c) It is an aural (audio) medium. It does not affect audiovisual senses but only the aural senses.
   (d) None of the above.
6. The fact that there are two different kinds of receptors in the retina for bright and dimlight, for chromatic and achromatic vision was first suggested by
   (a) Franklin (b) Von Kries
   (c) Young (d) Helmholtz
7. Daniel Lerner has stated that five futures define the growth or take-off of a society. Which one of the following is among those five factors?
   (a) Voting
   (b) Industrialistion
   (c) Higher per capita income
   (d) Literacy
8. Which of the following countries progressed in economic terms, but did not change her cultural values?
   (a) England (b) Canada
   (c) USA (d) India
9. "Yellow Spot" of the eye is otherwise known as
   (a) Fovea
   (b) Conjuction
   (c) Blind Spot
   (d) Suspensory Ligaments
10. The opinions of a large proportion of the masses are valuable in

(a) a participant society.
(b) a non-participant society.
(c) Both (b) and (c).
(d) None of the above.

11. Which one of the following points is a mismatch?
(a) Joseph Klapper—The Two-step Theory
(b) Ruttan and Hayami—The Innovation Model of Communication and Change.
(c) Kimi Oshima—Study of the Filipino Society
(d) Eisenstadt—Cultural Codes

12. The state of preparedness for a particular kind of response is known as
(a) Set (b) Effect
(c) Span (d) Focus

13. During 1964-75, the media informed and entertained the masses of India, however, they were required to
(a) improve the quality of their software so that the masses could cling to them for entertaining themselves.
(b) prepare the masses for socio-economic change.
(c) prepare the masses for achieving literacy levels at par with those of the West.
(d) increase their reach to penetrate the far flung areas.

14. Illusions are confused or misinterpreted perceptions where as the hallucinations are
(a) Organized Perceptions
(b) Disorganized Perceptions
(c) False Perceptions
(d) Wrong Perceptions

15. During the mid-nineties, the Net had proved the most effective agent of social change for those people who had
(a) purchased computers and LAN networks to enhance their efficiency.
(b) accepted IT as the dominant tool for earning their livelihood.
(c) started using it as a tool for information exchange and business development.
(d) All of the above.

16. Who stated, "Wrong England had come to India during the days of the British Raj"?
(a) Raja Ram Mohun Roy
(b) Jawarlal Nehru
(c) R.N. Tagore
(d) M.K. Gandhi

17. Muller-Lyer illusion is
(a) a universal illusion.
(b) a discriminatory illusion.
(c) an individual illusion.
(d) a personal illusion.

18. How did Gandhi start the process of cultural and economic change in India during the days of the British Raj?
(a) He identified alienation of the classes from the masses and set free the forces to dissociate the masses from this alienation.
(b) He used the policy of Satyagraha and peaceful resistance.
(c) He accentuated the process of alienation of the masses from the Western culture prevalent in India by using anti-ruler rhetoric.
(d) He censured the Western value system and promoted the supremacy of the Indian value system.

19. According to the Global Village concept of Marshall McLuhan?
(a) electronic (electric) technologies can maintain person-to-person relations.
(b) the Electronic Age would not be able to enlighten the masses.

(c) electronic (electric) technologies can help the masses unite to effect change.
(d) most of new technologies make people secluded and individualistic.

20. In the context of the Old Paradigm, take-off should be defined by
(a) a percentage increase in foreign exchange reserves.
(b) literacy and voting.
(c) movement towards rural areas from urban areas.
(d) All of the above.

21. According to P.C. Joshi, radio and TV were
(a) two-way communication means.
(b) one-way communication means.
(c) one-way as well as two-way communication means.
(d) None of the above.

22. Which one of the following is a term given to the processes that select certain inputs for inclusion in the focus of experience?
(a) Emotion (b) Sensation
(c) Affection (d) Attention

23. What was the effect of transition from a pre-industrial society to an industrial society in the Indian context?
(a) This transition adopted our basic cultural values and allowed the Western institutions to take deep roots in our country.
(b) This transition improved our economic system, which, in turn, helped us consolidate our own value system.
(c) This transition consolidated our cultural values because we arc resistant to change.
(d) This transition helped us mingle with the West and get benefit from their commercial and trade operations.

24. Which are the well-known examples of the transformations and elaborations of sensory input that occur in the process of perceiving the world?
(a) Illusions (b) Attention
(c) Hallucinations (d) Sensations

25. During the days of the British Raj, the colonial forces effected cultural change in India. During the modern era, the communication revolution is also changing our culture and value system. What is the difference between these two kinds of change?
(a) During the rule of the British, .ange was effected perforce, but today, we are voluntarily using communication technologies and gadgets to effect cultural change.
(b) The communication techniques and gadgets of the period of the British Raj were primitive and their reach was low, but the new communication revolution has affected all the masses of our country.
(c) The colonial change forces were Western, but the new communication forces are a mix of Eastern and Western ideologies.
(d) Change was accepted during the days of the British Raj, but it is not being accepted today.

26. Who has first pointed out that the 'Whole' is more than the sum total of its parts?
(a) Kurt Koffka (b) Kohler
(c) Wertheimer (d) Kurt Lewin

27. Which of the following is not a phase of the diffusion process propounded by Everett M. Rogers?
(a) Awareness (b) Cogitation
(c) Trial (d) Evaluation

28. According to Jan Servaes, the most important hindrances to development are not the

(a) shortage of capital but the absence of management.
(b) shortage of capital or management, but must be sought in the present international system.
(c) shortage of capital or management but the internal problems of a country that are different from the problems of capital or management.
(d) None of the above.

29. Which one of the following is an increase in the activity to extract information from the environment as a result of experience or practice with the stimulation coming from it?
(a) Perceptual Learning
(b) Plasticity of Perception
(c) Convergence
(d) Divergence

30. Which of the following models emphasises on the strengthening of democratic processes and institutions and redistribution of power?
(a) The Alternative Paradigm
(b) The Ruttan-Hayami model
(c) The Old Model of Schramm
(d) The Participatory Model.

31. The first implementation exercise of the Package Programme Model was initiated in
(a) India (the IADP)
(b) Mexico (Puebla project)
(c) the Phillippines (Masagana)
(d) None of the above.

32. Which one of the following is formed whenever a marked difference occurs in the brightness or colour of the background?
(a) Shapes (b) Sizes
(c) Sets (d) Contours

33. Which one of the following is not a primary goal of development communication?
(a) It acts as a socialising agent, it aims to maintain some established values of the society.
(b) It acts as a transformation agent, it aims to enhance the quality of life.
(c) Both (a) and (b).
(d) It acts as a revolution agent, it effects revolutions in various countries.

33. In the parlance of the Dependency Model, who were the Dependistas?
(a) The researchers who criticised the Modernisation Paradigm and later, proposed the Dependency Paradigm.
(b) The countries that depended exclusively on the Alternative Paradigm, but were not from Latin America.
(c) The researchers who studied the relations between centre and Periphery nations and used economic variables to study Latin American countries.
(d) The countries that belonged to Latin America, but were a part of the Periphery.

34. A normal individual may experience hallucinations after taking drugs like
(a) Second (b) Pethedine
(c) Heroin (d) Morphine

35. What is Media Imperialism?
(a) The ownership, structure, and distribution of the media of a country are the pressures from the media interests of another country (or countries) and the affected country is not able to reciprocate in equal terms.
(b) The effects of the media that are prevalent in the affected country and have been created or perpetuated by the Imperialist powers.

(c) The influences and media interests of the government of a country affect her masses.
(d) None of the above.

36. The tendency to see the immobility of objects when he moves about is called
(a) Shape Constancy
(b) Depth Constancy
(c) Location Constancy
(d) Size Constancy

37. According to the concepts given by Denis Mcquail, the effects of technology
(a) are mediated through a relevant institution and as such, are unlikely to have a direct impact on cultural practices.
(b) and cultural change are not associated in any way—direct or indirect.
(c) has a direct impact on culture.
(d) None of the above.

38. Internationalisation of the media has led to
(a) homogenisation of cultures.
(b) chaos within the culture of a society due to the attacks on its values.
(c) polarisation of cultures.
(d) None of the above.

39. In which year Radio's National Channel was inaugurated?
(a) 1988 (b) 1990
(c) 1972 (d) 1983

40. The process of mass communication is not
(a) Anonymous
(b) Asymmetrical
(c) Effected on a large scale
(d) Personal

41. The Particularly Model is not concerned with
(a) making the communication creeper centric.
(b) disseminating the messages among a society under a linear transmission relationship.
(c) information exchange.
(d) learning what is the people's capacity to understand the action to be taken to liberate themselves.

42. The Asian Model of communication is
(a) Direct
(b) Explicit
(c) Implicit and indirect
(d) Dependent upon the situation

43. The structuralist view of the Dependency Paradigm is based on the
(a) ideology and content of the media.
(b) tenets of the Alternative Paradigm.
(c) premises of the Dominant Paradigm.
(d) research efforts of Schramm and Lerner.

44. A contour is the boundary between
(a) two similar figures.
(b) two dissimilar figures.
(c) a figure and its ground.
(d) a figure and another figure's ground.

45. Which of the following is not a key issue to be addressed and resolved in the nations of the Third World?
(a) Unemployment
(b) Illiteracy
(c) Poverty
(d) Maintenance of traditional folk culture

46. Different cultures have different
(a) power equations.
(b) modes of decay.
(c) identities and features.
(d) None of the above.

47. An object that has been constituted perceptually as a permanent and stable thing continues to be perceived as such, regardless of illumination, position,

distance, etc. This kind of stability of the environment experienced by human beings is termed as

(a) Size Constancy
(b) Shape Constancy
(c) Depth Constancy
(d) Perceptual Constancy

48. A dominated society
(a) loses its internal cohesion and values due to the influences of the dominant society.
(b) remains homogeneous and coherent even as the dominant society continues to make efforts to make it heterogeneous.
(c) adopts the values of a dominant society without undergoing agonies of change.
(d) None of the above.

49. A red ball looks red in broad daylight as well as in dark night. This is due to
(a) Size Constancy
(b) Colour Constancy
(c) Light Constancy
(d) Brightness Constancy

50. There is no Asian Model of development per se. However, Inayatullah had started using the term in the seventies anticipating that such a model could emerge in the future. The growth of which one of the following nations can be considered or discussed under the concept of Asian Development Model?
(a) Pakistan (b) Afghanistan
(c) South Korea (d) Nepal

51. The sender asks the receiver what is to be sent to him (the receiver). He also takes care of the aspirations of the receiver while he designs and transmits the message. This is the chief guiding tenet of the
(a) Old Paradigm.
(b) Dependency Paradigm.
(c) Participatory Model.
(d) Multiplicity Paradigm.

52. According to Schramm, the mass media can help in the development of a developing country through three modes. Which one of the following modes did he not propound?
(a) The mass media as tools of entertainment.
(b) The mass media as tools of decision making.
(c) The mass media as teachers.
(d) The mass media as watchdogs.

53. Which principle/law of organization in perception states that there is a tendency to organize stimuli to make a balanced or symmetrical figure that includes all parts?
(a) Law of Proximity
(b) Law of Pragnaz
(c) Law of Similarity
(d) Law of Symmetry

54. Indian society is
(a) a non-participant society and has never changed its status quo.
(b) slowly evolving into a participant society, though several non-participant societies coexist in its complex societal milieu.
(c) a fully participant society today, but was a non-participant society (in the old millenium).
(d) a fully participant society today (in the new millenium).

55. During the days of the British rule, the colonial rulers tried to change our culture through their administrative policies and procedures. During the present era, the same task is being performed (in India) by
(a) the mass media, through a blitzkrieg that draws its cultural sap from the Western value system.

(b) the components of the societies themselves, given that they also seek change of culture and values.
(c) international organisations like the UNO, WTO, ECOSOC, and the like.
(d) the MNCs and leading corporate firms.

56. An illusion is not a trick or misperception. It is a/an
(a) Emotion (b) Attention
(c) Sensation (d) Perception

57. Which of the following is not a critical view of the Dependency Paradigm?
(a) from a political angle.
(b) It is characterised by Western capitalistic expansion and domination.
(c) It is an erroneous evaluation of the production.
(d) None of the above.

58. The sender asks the receiver what is to be while he designs and transmits the message. This is the chief guiding tenet of the
(a) Multiplicity Paradigm.
(b) Participatory Model.
(c) Old Paradigm.
(d) Dependency Paradigm.

59. Who among the following is not a researcher in the field of development communication?
(a) Everett M. Rogers
(b) Nora C. Quebral
(c) Keith Davis
(d) F. Rosario Braid

60. Which of the following is not a glaring feature of mass culture?
(a) Non-technical character
(b) Homogenised
(c) Non-commercial
(d) Non-elite nature

61. "The whole (perception) is more than the sum of its parts (Sensory inputs)". This statement was given by
(a) Functionalists
(b) Psychoanalysts
(c) Behaviourists
(d) Gestalt Psychologists

62. The Dominant Paradigm is a
(a) non-deterministic view of media technology and messages.
(b) supporter of rejection of value neutrality.
(c) linear transmission model of effects.
(d) None of the above.

63. According to Denis McQuail, the media have been perceived as gatekeepers. What is the meaning of this statement?
(a) The media reflect the event of the society and world, though they distort such events during communication exercises.
(b) The media point out the way and make sense of what is otherwise fragmentary.
(c) The media could cut the masses from reality by giving false views of the world through fantasy or propaganda.
(d) The media select some views for the special attention of the masses, but close off some other views so that these views do not reach the masses.

64. Harris has likened social change to a
(a) long endless chain.
(b) net having several nodes, all of them having equal importance.
(c) web having many closed relations, but with strands of unequal weights.
(d) None of the above.

65. Critics argue that TV, as a communication medium, has failed to play a significant role in the development process. Why is that so?

(a) In India, TV was regulated by the state from 1959 up to 1990 and hence, it could not contribute to development.
(b) The audio-visual media are invariably unable to develop a society in social, economic, and moral terms.
(c) TV has effected moral development but not economic development.
(d) TV is chiefly an entertainment tool. It does not effect development of a society because of its commercial features.

66. What is the focus area of development communication?
(a) It is related to the study of the mass media that are dedicated to entertainment.
(b) It is concerned with the role of information and communication is social and economic development of an individual, society and nation.
(c) It is chiefly concerned with the role of communication in political development of a country.
(d) It deals with the mass media of developing countries.

67. In the context of the Dependency Paradigm, a Periphery nation is
(a) Mexico
(b) Japan
(c) The UK
(d) None of the above.

68. Who, among the following, is not a researcher in the field of development communication?
(a) Nora Quebral
(b) Keith Davis
(c) F. Rosario Braid
(d) Everette M. Rogers

69. In the context of the Modernisation Paradigm, what is demonstration?
(a) The developing nation learns from the mistakes committed by the developed nations and avoids repeating them.
(b) The developing nation tries to complete the task of development in less time than it took the developed nations.
(c) The developing nation tries to adopt more advanced techniques to catch up with the developed nations.
(d) None of the above.

70. Attention is the term given to the processes that select certain inputs for inclusion in the focus of
(a) Unconsiousness
(b) Experience
(c) Sensation
(d) Consciousness

71. Efforts were made to find out how mass communication would effect social change in our country. The first attempt was made in this context through the
(a) use of colour TV transmission (1982).
(b) introduction of an Internet gateway through the VSNL (1995).
(c) SITE (1975).
(d) Kheda Communication Project (1975-90).

72. The most fundamental process in form perception is the recognition of
(a) a figure without ground.
(b) the contour of a figure.
(c) a figure on a ground.
(d) a picture without background.

73. In the context of the Participative model, what is Access?
(a) The use of the media for public service.
(b) A higher level of public involvement in communication systems.
(c) The reach of radio and TV in developing nations.
(d) None of the above.

74. The events, we perceive clearly, are at the
(a) Focus (b) Side
(c) Margin (d) Centre

75. The Western mode of communication is
(a) Indirect
(b) Implicit
(c) Explicit and direct
(d) None of the above.

76. The mechanism of reflex action is called
(a) Reflex Path (b) Reflexology
(c) Reflexon (d) Reflex Arc

77. According to the researchers in the field of social change, Western individuals are
(a) inclined to act according to the particular situations they face.
(b) we-oriented (submerged in groups).
(c) I-oriented (individualistic).
(d) neither we-oriented nor I-oriented.

78. In the context of the Dependency Paradigm, a centre nation is
(a) India (b) Ethiopia
(c) Brazil (d) USA

79. Closure is a basic principle of
(a) Depth Perception
(b) Phiphenomenon
(c) Perceptual defence
(d) Perceptual Organization

80. According to Rosengren's model of relations between culture and society, autonomy is achieved when
(a) development and communication influence each other.
(b) development and communication do not influence each other.
(c) development influences communication but communication does not affect development.
(d) development does not influence communication but communication affects development.

81. Personal factors in perception are otherwise known as
(a) social factors in perception.
(b) cultural factors in perception.
(c) functional factors in perception.
(d) motivational factors in perception.

82. Which one of the following statements is false?
(a) The paradigms are not theories because they do not give explanations of various phenomenon.
(b) Inayatullah proposed the Asian Model during the early sixties.
(c) Schramm and Eisenstadt had done a lot of research on the Old Paradigm.
(d) McLuhan stated, "Medium is the message".

83. The gap between cornea and lens is filled with
(a) Vitreous Humour
(b) Amino Acid
(c) Aqueous Humour
(d) Unknown Fluid

84. Which one of the following statements is false?
(a) My Swaraj is to keep intact the genius of our civilisation—D.P. Mukherjee
(b) Our approach to cultural issues is fragmented—P.C. Joshi
(c) My life is my message—M.K. Gandhi
(d) None of the above.

85. The image of an object falling on the blind spot of the eye
(a) is not clear.
(b) will be visible.
(c) will not be visible.
(d) automatically vanishes.

86. In the context of social change in India, TV has done well to
(a) give an upper hand to traditional and folk media vis-à-vis the Western media.

(b) effect political change from time to time.
(c) retain the old values of culture of our masses.
(d) All of the above.

87. The gap between cornea and lens is known as
(a) Inner Chamber
(b) Secular Chamber
(c) Posterior Chamber
(d) Anterior Chamber

88. In the context of change in India, the advent of TV has not been able to
(a) alter or modify the views of the masses on specific issues.
(b) entertain the masses.
(c) educate the masses to make them fully literate.
(d) inform the masses about various socio-political issues.

89. The innermost layer of the eye is called
(a) Fovea (b) Blind Spot
(c) Retina (d) Cornea

90. Four approaches have been defined by researchers for relating communication to development. These are
(a) Empathy (Lerner), Diffusion (Rogers), Magic Multiplier (Schramm), Model of Relations (Rosengren).
(b) Diffusion (Rogers), Magic Multiplier (Schramm), Model of Relations (Rosengren), Cultural Codes (Eisenstadt).
(c) Empathy (Lerner), Diffusion (Rogers), Cultural Codes (Eisenstadt), Magic Multiplier (Schramm).
(d) None of the above.

91. The point at which the optic nerve gets out of the retina is called the
(a) Fovea (b) Light Spot
(c) Yellow Spot (d) Blind Spot

92. An author has stated that cultural colonialism causing annihilation of the national identity is much worse than erstwhile political colonialism: in most cases, the former has persisted even though direct political colonialism has ended. In the light of this statement, how can we check cultural colonialism in our country?
(a) We should not talk about cultural colonialism now. We have accepted their culture and they have accepted ours. The new cultural milieu would be different from our old traditional culture, but it would certainly be based on some of our deep-rooted values. Change is inevitable; this change would lead to a new global culture in the times to come.
(b) The Western media can be told to move out of the country and even punished, if they do not follow our commands. In their place, we should allow our traditional media and art forms to operate and prosper. That is the only solution.
(c) It cannot be checked. In the wake of the advent of a free market system, the West would certainly change our traditional culture.
(d) This is a temporary phase. Our masses would, sooner or later, return to their aeons-old traditional culture and then, retain it forever.

93. A person who has no cones at the fovea
(a) is not able to see yellow colour at all.
(b) is deprived of black and white vision.
(c) is a colour blind.
(d) is very often a colour blind.

94. According to the revised concept of the diffusion process, the steps in this process are
(a) awareness-evaluation-trial rationalisation.

(b) knowledge-persuasion-decision-confirmation.
(c) awareness-interest-evaluation-trial-adoption.
(d) None of the above.

95. Coal looks black even in very bright sunlight, while snow continues to look white even at night. This is due to
(a) Shape Constancy
(b) Colour Reflection
(c) Colour Constancy
(d) Constancy of Brightness

96. If social science is not culture oriented, it becomes
(a) biased towards a few concepts.
(b) biased against a few concepts.
(c) value-free or value-neutral.
(d) None of the above.

97. As the eyes become adapted to dark at one particular point, red colours begin to darken and the green and blues become brighter. This change is known as
(a) Purkinje Effect
(b) Perceptual Constancy
(c) Duplicity Theory of Colour Vision
(d) Herring's Theory of Colour Vision

98. In which year did John Stuart Mill wrote his essay On Liberty?
(a) 1857 (b) 1859
(c) 1865 (d) 1868

99. In which year was the Universal Declaration of Human Rights approved by the UN?
(a) 1948 (b) 1945
(c) 1953 (d) 1957

100. Meaningful sensation is otherwise known as
(a) Sensation (b) Attention
(c) Perception (d) Emotion

101. Who do you think give us a sound basis for press freedom?
(a) Plato (b) Machiavelli
(c) Milton (d) None of these

102. Who opposed the freedom of speech and expression?
(a) Mill (b) Milton
(c) Hegel (d) None of these

103. Size judgement is based on
(a) Clarity of Object
(b) Retinal Image
(c) Distance Information
(d) Object Size

104. Which article of the Indian Constitution provides the provisions relating to freedom of speech and expression?
(a) 14 (b) 18
(c) 19(1) (d) 36

105. "Perceived Size" approaches "physical size" when
(a) information is minimum.
(b) object is old.
(c) depth and distance cues are available.
(d) object is small.

106. Several researchers have insisted that India re-adopt the old traditional media and folk art forms to retain her cultural identity. How can that be possible, given that the Western media and software are ruling the TV and cinema worlds?
(a) Sprinkle traditional folk art software in the Western media to attract the attention of the masses.
(b) Promote traditional media channels so that only traditional folk art forms are highlighted through them.
(c) Ask the western media to give support to our folk art forms.
(d) Shut out the Western media and software from India.

107. Which one of the following happens to be an important factor in selectivity of attention?
(a) Interest (b) Attitude
(c) Concentration (d) Boredom

108. The "Hutchins Commission" gave its report in connection to the press of which country?
(a) UK (b) India
(c) South Africa (d) USA

109. An incorrect interpretation of the stimulus input is called
(a) Perception (b) Attention
(c) Hallucination (d) Illusion

110. In which country was the setting up of a voluntary press council recommended by the First Royal Commission?
(a) Britain (b) Sri Lanka
(c) USA (d) India

111. Each receptor requires some minimum level of energy to excite it. That minimum energy is called
(a) Absolute Threshold
(b) Boundary Threshold
(c) Contour Threshold
(d) Minimum Threshold

112. In which year was the voluntary press council established in Britain?
(a) 1945 (b) 1946
(c) 1953 (d) 1954

113. Monocular Cues are those which can operate when
(a) only one eye is looking.
(b) only one eye is invalid.
(c) two eyes are looking.
(d) both eyes are invalid.

114. Constitution Amendment Bill requires the support of how many members of the Lok Sabha actually present and voting?
(a) One-fourth (b) One-third
(c) One-half (d) Two-third

115. Under which rule, can a member raise any issue which he thinks is of public interest?
(a) Rule 385 (b) Rule 382
(c) Rule 377 (d) Rule 365

116. Which one of the following is a stimulus variable in the determination of attending?
(a) Attitude (b) Size
(c) Aptitude (d) Interest

117. Motion which enables a member to draw the attention of the government to development of public importance is
(a) Adjournment Motion
(b) Call Attention Motion
(c) No-confidence Motion
(d) None of the above.

118. The perception of the whiteness of the snow even though the night dark can be explained on the basis of
(a) Dark Adaptation
(b) Perceptual Defence
(c) Purkinje Effect
(d) Brightness Constancy

119. Which is not the quality of a science technology reporter?
(a) A narrow network of acquaintance among the scientists and technologiets of the region.
(b) An analytical mind that will not accept anything at face value.
(c) A perceptive mind that thrives on a keen awareness.
(d) An inherent scientific temper.

120. Perception of "Figure and Ground" results from
(a) trial and error.
(b) the structure of nervous system.

(c) experience.
(d) sensation pattern.

121. Which is not the style used in sports writing?
(a) Discovering new angle
(b) Writing lengthy articles
(c) Professional approach
(d) All of the above.

122. An one-eyed person would lose precision in the perception of
(a) Colour (b) Depth
(c) Height (d) Weight

123. In 1961, India's first school television service was commissioned at
(a) Delhi (b) Madras
(c) Bombay (d) Calcutta

124. The perceptual principle of 'proximity' states that
(a) the closer a stimulus is the more likely it is to be attended.
(b) stimuli coming from equal distance are perceived as part of the same figure
(c) when stimuli are close together they tend to be grouped.
(d) the nearer an object is the more likely it is to be perceived.

125. A science reporter can do justice to any write-up by
(a) adopting a lucid style of writing.
(b) referring to one's personal glossary of science.
(c) verifying its facts.
(d) All of the above.

126. Even though parallel, the rails appear to be meeting at a distance. This is a bright illustration of
(a) Visual Illusion
(b) Aerial Perspective
(c) Linear Perspective
(d) Distance Perception

127. India made its first Satellite Instructional Television Experiment (SITE) in
(a) 1972-73 (b) 1975-76
(c) 1980-81 (d) 1978-79

128. In a normal waking state, if an individual gets certain sensation with particular stimulus which is not available to others, this person is said to have
(a) a phiphenomenon.
(b) an illusion.
(c) a hallucination.
(d) a sensation.

129. 'Doordarshan-India' the International Channel is in operation from
(a) 1993 (b) 1995
(c) 1997 (d) None of these.

130. Figure and Ground perception results from
(a) Sensation Pattern
(b) Attention Pattern
(c) Emotional Pattern
(d) Perception Pattern

131. 'Prasar Bharati' the autonomous Broadcasting Corporation of India was set up on?
(a) 15th October 1992
(b) 26th December 1995
(c) 23rd November 1997
(d) None of the above.

132. In which year was the Universal Declaration of Human Rights approved by the UN?
(a) 1948 (b) 1933
(c) 1927 (d) 1946

133. Peculiarities of the language used in sports writing are
(a) war references like 'kill' are avoided.
(b) sports jargon itself finds mention only on a low key.

(c) report is written for general reader.
(d) All of the above.

134. We perceive a square as a square in whatever position it is held. This constancy in perception relates to
(a) Depth (b) Shape
(c) Weight (d) Size

135. In which year Registrar of Newspapers for India came into being?
(a) 1942 (b) 1947
(c) 1952 (d) 1956

136. A small stationary spot of light in a completely dark room will appear to move if a person fixates on it for sometime. This movement is known as
(a) Phiphenomenon
(b) Autokinetic Effect
(c) Real Motion Perception
(d) Retinal Image

137. According to McQuail, the Dominant Paradigm
(a) takes a liberalist pluralist ideal of the society.
(b) is a linear transmission model of effect.
(c) has a functionalist perspective.
(d) All of the above.

138. A gradient is a continuous change
(a) with highest stimulating agent.
(b) with lowest stimulating agent.
(c) without abrupt transitions.
(d) with abrupt transitions.

139. Which of the following statements is true?
(a) Dominant Paradigm favours the liberal norms of society.
(b) Dominant Paradigm is effective in many parts of the world.
(c) Dominant Paradigm is a model of research to know the position of market.
(d) None of the above.

140. Who founded Brahmo Samaj?
(a) Raja Ram Mohan Roy
(b) Iswar Chandra Vidyasagar
(c) Acharya J.B. Kriplani
(d) Srichand Kriplani

141. Who amongst the following was influenced by Darwin's theories of organic evolution in his theory of social change?
(a) Spencer (b) Marx
(c) Comte (d) Spengler

142. Friend of India was established by
(a) Thomas Ferm and J.P. Coupleson
(b) Edison and Barnaby
(c) William Corey and John Clark
(d) William Morrison and J. Marconi

143. Who was the first scholar to conduct a detailed study into the actual process of social change?
(a) Spencer (b) Alvin Toffler
(c) Comte (d) Durkheim

144. Who introduced the concept of noise in his communication model?
(a) Lasswell
(b) Osgood
(c) Gerbner
(d) Shannon and Weaver

145. Who amongst the following is asseciated with the critical theory in Frankfurt school?
(a) Theoder Adorno
(b) Walter Benjamin
(c) Max Horkheimer
(d) All of the above.

146. First Indian company to raise money in global markets with GDR issues is
(a) Reliance (b) Hindujas
(c) ONGC (d) Infosys

147. The Dependency theory was proposed by
(a) Ball-Rokeach
(b) Melvin DeFleur

(c) Both (a) and (b) both
(d) None of the above.

148. Whenever an object appears to maintain its shape despite marked changes in the retinal image, it is known as
(a) Shape Constancy
(b) Height Constancy
(c) Size Constancy
(d) Depth Constancy

149. Which of the following is not among the communication levels, defined by Dance and Larson, at which human communication can take place?
(a) Multiyadic communication
(b) Group communication
(c) Dyadic communication
(d) Intrapersonal communication

150. According to which theory of the mass media, thought not under the direct control of the state and the Seeling Closses, must do their bidding?
(a) Authoritarian Theory
(b) Soviet Media Theory
(c) Liberation Theory
(d) None of the above

151. Selective exposure and selective perception are two concepts of which theory?
(a) Individual Difference Theory
(b) Personal Influence Theory
(c) Bullet Theory
(d) None of the above.

152. Soldiers dressed in colours of uniform that merge with the background is called
(a) Brightness Constancy
(b) Camaouflage
(c) Colour Matching
(d) Colour Constancy

153. Which theory is derived from the studies of Saussure and Peirce?
(a) Hegemony Theory
(b) Political Economic Media Theory
(c) Mass Society Theory
(d) Culture and Semiotic Theory

154. When there is a deliberate confusion of figure and ground and it is difficult to organise form and distinguish objects from one another, it is called
(a) Colour Constancy
(b) Brightness Constancy
(c) Camaouflage
(d) Phiphenomenon

155. Which theories derived strength from Marxist ideology?
(a) Social Responsibility Theory
(b) Mass Society Theory
(c) Political Economic Media Theory
(d) Both (a) and (b).

156. According to which theory of media "the media area means of mental production of the ideology"?
(a) Authoritarian Theory
(b) Libertarian Theory
(c) Soviet Media Theory
(d) Social Responsibility Theory

157. According to which theory of media, "The media are a means of mental production of the ideology"?
(a) Libertarian theory
(b) Authoritarian theory
(c) Soviet Media theory
(d) Social Responsibility theory

158. Stimuli that make the lowest interruptions in contour also tend to be grouped together. The tendency to organize the fragmentary stimuli into a familiar pattern is called the principle of
(a) Continuation (b) Pragnaz
(c) Proximity (d) Similarity

159. Which theory is derived from Lenin's application of Marx and Engel's dictum in the German Ideology?

(a) Democratization theory
(b) Libertarian theory
(c) Development Communication theory
(d) Soviet Media theory

160. "Why do things look the way they do"? This question was asked by the Gestalt Psychologist.
(a) Kurt Lewin (b) K. Koffka
(c) W.G. Kohler (d) M. Wertheimer

161. Which theory is based on the need for local and community participation in media and news production?
(a) Democratization theory
(b) Authoritarian theory
(c) Development theory
(d) Social Responsibility theory

162. The second stage consisted of a series of "Relations" published in the forms of
(a) Coranto (b) Bhaskar
(c) The Diurnals (d) Relation

163. When was the media dependency theory originally proposed?
(a) In 1960 (b) In 1970
(c) In 1976 (d) In 1986

164. Who was the man who led the way to modern editorship?
(a) James bond (b) Diccan
(c) James Perry (d) Henry

165. Who among the following persisted in improving modernization model of development using the mass media?
(a) Lucian Pye
(b) Wilbur Schramm
(c) Daniel Lerner
(d) All of the above.

166. Who opened the telegraph office at Achen in Holland?
(a) Reuter
(b) Peter
(c) Coillion Cowper
(d) John Abraham

167. A media audience would be a participative community if we consider communication to be a
(a) merchandise.
(b) means for production.
(c) social good.
(d) None of the above.

168. What created the pressure on world within journalism?
(a) Reading (b) Dictation
(c) The Telephone (d) Telegraph

169. 'Media audience' is 'the masses' that need to be indoctrinated if communication is the means for
(a) social service.
(b) merchnandise.
(c) propaganda.
(d) None of the above.

170. Tell the name of the inventor, who in the year of 1940 developed the first version of the rotary press?
(a) John Milton (b) Shakespeare
(c) Richard Benson (d) Richard Hoe

171. Who define an audience as a 'conventionalized crowd'?
(a) Philosphers (b) Psychologists
(c) Statisticians (d) Sociologists

172. Which principle of perceptual organization makes our perceived world of form more complete than the sensory stimulation that is presented?
(a) The Law of Closure
(b) The Law of Proximity
(c) The Law of Pragnaz
(d) The Law of Similarity

173. The author of *Communication and Social Development* in India is
(a) B. Kuppuswamy
(b) Keshav Mukherjee
(c) Prof. B.C. Roy
(d) Uma Narula

174. The device which is used in perceptual experiments for the very brief presentation of stimuli is known as
(a) Polygraph
(b) Aesthesiometer
(c) Psychogalvanometer
(d) Tachistoscope

175. By whom was the cultivation theory developed?
(a) George Gerbner (b) John Donne
(c) John Milton (d) Harold Lasswell

176. Which theory of media effect was given the Joseph Kalpper?
(a) Norwsis Theory
(b) Incidental Effect Theory
(c) Uses Theory
(d) Limited Effect Theory

177. Who is the author of *The Play Theory of Mass Communication*?
(a) George Gerbner
(b) William Stephenson
(c) W.L. Rivers
(d) Horace Newcomb

178. Interpersonal Communication is
(a) Contemplation
(b) Meditation
(c) Individual reflection
(d) All of the above

179. Western theories of the mass media were first propounded by
(a) Denis McQuail
(b) Abraham Maslow
(c) Albert Bandura
(d) Fred Siebert

180. Initial stage of interpersonal communication is called
(a) The intimate stage
(b) The personal stage
(c) The phatic stage
(d) None of the above

181. Which theory of media is founded on the fundamental right of an individual to freedom of expression?
(a) Social Responsibility Theory
(b) Soviet Media Theory
(c) Free Press Theory
(d) None of the above.

182. Retinal disparity is the difference in the images falling on
(a) the blindspois of the two eyes.
(b) the corneas of the two eyes.
(c) the retinas of the two eyes.
(d) the foveas of the two eyes.

183. Which of the following theory can be said to have been derived from the Hutchins Report?
(a) Social Responsibility Theory
(b) Free Press Theory
(c) Liberation Theory
(d) Soviet Media Theory.

184. The powerful mass media is
(a) Radio (b) Newspaper
(c) Cinema (d) Television

185. Cultivation Analysis is a project associated with
(a) Denis McQuail
(b) George Gerbner
(c) Cees Hamelink
(d) James Halloran

186. The brain comparator is a system which compares information about muscle movements with movements of the
(a) After Image
(b) Retinal Image
(c) Fovea Image
(d) Image of the Blind Spot

187. The two-step flow theory was propounded by
(a) E. Katz and P. Lazarsfeld
(b) Osgood and Schramm

(c) Walter Lippman
(d) Daniel Lerner

188. Code of self-regulation in advertising was formulated in
(a) 1984 (b) 1986
(c) 1980 (d) 1983

189. The word 'homophily' is used in
(a) group communication
(b) public communication
(c) inter-personal communication
(d) intra-personal communication

190. All the television channels are owned by one particular company except one, which is that
(a) Gemini TV (b) Kairali TV
(c) Sun TV (d) SuryaTV

191. If a stationary spot is perceived as moving when its frame or background moves, it is known as
(a) Induced Movement
(b) Hallucination
(c) Autokinetic Effect
(d) Apparent Movement

192. Directive messages will have the element of
(a) Acceptance (b) Discipline
(c) Socialisation (d) Command

193. Press Trust of India was founded in
(a) 1949 (b) 1952
(c) 1942 (d) 1947

194. If you are in a motionless train in a platform and the train next to you starts to move, you may feel that you are moving too. This is an example of
(a) Apparent Movement
(b) Induced Movement
(c) Illusion
(d) Phiphenomenon

195. The number of essentials in the communicative process of George Gerbner is
(a) Four (b) Six
(c) Eight (d) Ten

196. Largest News Agency of India is
(a) PTI (b) IANS
(c) UNI (d) ANI

197. Who has defined perceptual learning "as an increase in the ability to extract information from the environment as a result of experience or practice within the stimulation coming from it"?
(a) Carter (1949)
(b) McGinnis (1948)
(c) Goodman (1947)
(d) Eleanox Gibson (1969)

198. Write the correct sequence of news factors identified by Galtung and Ruge
(a) Amplitude, Unambiguity, Familiarity, Frequency
(b) Unambiguity, Familliarity, Frequency, Amplitude
(c) Frequency, Threshold, Unambiguity, Meaningfulness
(d) Familiarity, Frequency, Unambiguity, Amplitude

199. UNI for Univarta and PTI
(a) Varta (b) PTI-Hindi
(c) PTI Varta (d) Bhasha

200. We, the common people, cannot distinguish the calls of birds easily. But an ornithologist can do it easily. This is an example of
(a) Perceptual Learning
(b) Identification
(c) Attending
(d) Motivational Perception

201. Identify the correct sequence of operation factors of news values which are
(a) Selection, Distortion, Replication and Version
(b) Version, Selection, Replication and Distortion

(c) Distortion, Replication, Version and Selection
(d) Selection, Replication, Version and Distortion

202. Urdu News Service was started for the first time in India by
(a) UNI (b) ANI
(c) PTI (d) IRNA

203. The nativists says that brain organization is determined by the genetic codes and therefore is
(a) Innate (b) Acquired
(c) Haphazard (d) Learned

204. Identify the correct order of four great reactions to the process of modernisation
(a) Counter-modernisation, Hyper-modernisation, De-modernisation, Post-modernisation
(b) Hyper-modernisation, De-modernisation, Post-modernisation, Counter-modernisation
(c) De-modernisation, Post-modernisation, Counter-modernisation, Hyper-modernisation
(d) Post-modernistaion, Counter-modernisation, Hyper-modernisation, De-modernisation

205. The oldest feature Agency in India is
(a) Star Feature Agency
(b) Indian News and Feature Alliance
(c) National Press Agency
(d) Indian Press Agency

206. Which theory of illusion reveals that the illusion figures have emotional significance that produces perceptual distortion?
(a) Perspective Theory
(b) Good Figure Theory
(c) Empathy Theory
(d) Eye-Movement Theory

207. The evolutionary universals of development were identified by
(a) John L. Woods
(b) Walt Rostow
(c) Wilbur Schramm
(d) Talcott Parsons

208. The headquarters of Press Information Bureau are located at
(a) Bangalore (b) Chennai
(c) New Delhi (d) Mumbai

209. Which theory of illusion supposes that certain features of illusion figures disturb eye movements?
(a) Good Figure Theory
(b) Eye-Movement Theory
(c) Perspective Theory
(d) Confusion Theory

210. The co-orientation approach in communication is popularly known as:
(a) Kite model
(b) Elite model
(c) Balance model
(d) Community model

211. The Advertising Agencies Association of India came into existence in
(a) 1945 (b) 1950
(c) 1935 (d) 1940

212. The tendency to perceive gaps as filled in is called
(a) Similarity (b) Proximity
(c) Good Figure (d) Closure

213. Karl Deutsch is associated with the concept of
(a) empathy
(b) social mobilisation
(c) protestant ethics
(d) N-Ach

214. NFDC headquarters are located at
(a) Bangalore (b) Chennai
(c) New Delhi (d) Mumbai

215. A doctor attends to the telephone even if he is asleep. This is an example of

(a) Distraction
(b) Habitual Attention
(c) Voluntary Attention
(d) Involuntary Attention

216. The developmental model proposed by Nair and White is
(a) knowledge sharing
(b) training and visit
(c) another development
(d) conscientisation

217. India's first museum of radio and television is located at
(a) Kolkata (b) Bangalore
(c) New Delhi (d) Mumbai

218. Perception is the knowledge of an object, that is
(a) "There" and "How"
(b) "Which" and "How"
(c) "Here" and "There"
(d) "Here" and "How"

219. Leon Festinger advanced the idea of
(a) meaning paradigm
(b) psychodynamic strategy
(c) cognitive dissonance
(d) knowledge model

220. Ideas are
(a) Sensory Processes
(b) Symbolic Processes
(c) Receptive Processes
(d) Effective Processes

221. Below the eyebrows, the eye balls are set in the cavity. These cavities are called
(a) Eyebrows (b) Eye Holes
(c) Sockets (d) Eye Balls

222. Programmes that do not offer easy solutions to social issues will create
(a) Cultural space (b) Public debate
(c) Fantasy (d) Dissonance

223. Which process can be defined as a substitute, that can arouse a selective response and that can be recalled if it ceases to be present?
(a) Attending Process
(b) Receptive Process
(c) Sensory Process
(d) Symbolic Process

224. The pupil is a circular hole formed by a set of muscles called the
(a) Optic Nerve (b) Fovea
(c) Iris (d) Ciliary Muscle

225. Newcomb's ABX model is an extension of
(a) cultivation theory
(b) socialisation theory
(c) balance theory
(d) pleasure theory

226. The mere segregation of a part of the stimulus-field is the
(a) Complex act of attention
(b) Simplest act of perception
(c) Complex act of perception
(d) Complex act of sensation

227. George Gerbner used a measuring procedure called
(a) Cultivation scale
(b) Cultivation profile
(c) Cultivation meter
(d) Cultivation differential

228. The part that is segregated from the stimulusfield appears to have a form or shape and it is called a/an
(a) Illusion (b) Figure
(c) Art (d) Ground

229. The problem-solving model of development communication was suggested by
(a) Vimal Dissanayake
(b) Shirley White
(c) R.G. Havelock
(d) Cees Hamelink

230. The third and innermost layer of the eye is
(a) Retina (b) Cornea
(c) Optic Nerve (d) Lens

231. The theory of symbolic interactionism emphasises on
(a) language and meanings
(b) symbols and signs
(c) human behaviour
(d) conventions and beliefs

232. The cones function in
(a) Light Dark (b) Bright Light
(c) Dim Light (d) Dark

233. Festinger proposed
(a) Cognitive dissonance theory
(b) Reader-response theory
(c) Symbolic convergence theory
(d) Structural theory

234. Cones are receptors for
(a) Both Black and White
(b) Colour Vision
(c) Black Vision Only Vision
(d) White Vision Only

235. Selectivity theories emphasize on
(a) Message (b) Source
(c) Channel (d) Entropy

236. The colour vision is otherwise known as
(a) Chromatic Vision
(b) Black and White Vision
(c) Achromatic Vision
(d) Dark Vision

237. The school of thought which advocated media manipulation of images and symbols to protect the interests of the dominant class is
(a) Frankfurt School
(b) Chicago School
(c) Toronto School
(d) Glasgow School

238. Achromatic Vision refers to
(a) Colour Vision
(b) Black and White Vision
(c) Colourless Vision
(d) White Vision

239. The assumption that individuals create meanings, have intentions and make real choices is
(a) Ariology theory
(b) Actional theory
(c) Nonactional theory
(d) Quotology

240. Which established theory of vision depicts that receptors of colour vision are different from the receptors of colourless vision?
(a) Duplicity Theory
(b) Ladd-Franklin Theory
(c) Young-Helmholtz Theory
(d) Herring Theory

241. Find out the correct sequence of Daniel Lerner's indicators of modernization
(a) Urbanization-Mass media exposure-Literacy-Political participation
(b) Urbanization-Political participation-Mass media exposure-Literacy
(c) Urbanization-Literacy-Political participation-Mass media exposure
(d) Urbanization-Literacy-Mass media exposure-Political participation

242. Gestalt Psychologists placed the structural factors in perceptual organization under three catagories and these are
(a) external, central and reinforcing.
(b) internal, suggestive and stimulative.
(c) internal, reinforcing and exceptional.
(d) internal, effective and motivating.

243. Identify the correct sequence of stages in diffusion of innovations model:
(a) Knowledge-Confirmation-Persuasion-Decision

(b) Knowledge-Decision-Confirmation-Persuasion
(c) Knowledge-Persuasion-Decision-Confirmation
(d) Knowledge-Persuasion-Confirmation-Decision

244. Good Figure has two principles and these are
(a) Continuity and Closure
(b) Similarity and Closure
(c) Similarity and Proximity
(d) Continuity and Proximity

245. Identify the correct set of normative theories as formulated by Siebert.
(a) Authoritarian, Libertarian, Soviet media, Social responsibility.
(b) Authoritarian, Individual difference, Social responsibility, Soviet media.
(c) Social responsibility, Development media, Authoritarian, Libertarian.
(d) Authoritarian, Democratic participant, Development media, Libertarian.

246. The principle of "Continuity" is otherwise known as
(a) The Principle of Closure
(b) The Principle of Nearness
(c) The Principle of Approximation
(d) The Principle of Direction

247. Symbols associated with strong emotions and possess the power to stimulate large scale mass action are known as
(a) master symbols
(b) multiple symbols
(c) single symbol
(d) special symbols

248. "We perceive things as we are." This statement emphasises upon
(a) organizational factors in perception.
(b) voluntary attention.
(c) functional factors in perception.
(d) involuntary attention.

249. Under the functionalist paradigm, the news function is denoted as
(a) correlation (b) mobilisation
(c) propaganda (d) surveillance

250. The ability to read other people's thoughts is called
(a) Psychokinesis
(b) Clairvoyance
(c) Prerecognition
(d) Telepathy

251. Which of the following is from the critical school of thought?
(a) Diffusion of innovations
(b) Cultivation analysis
(c) Cultural imperialism
(d) Uses and gratifications

252. From the following, which one, according to you, will demand immediate attention?
(a) A song
(b) Temperature of the room
(c) A detective story
(d) A police siren

253. Who among the following theorists was the first to identify women as primary agents of social change?
(a) David McClelland
(b) Everett Rogers
(c) Everett Hagen
(d) Talcott Parsons

254. Who conducted a pioneering experiment to show that "Value" has a considerable effect on perception?
(a) Postman
(b) Carter
(c) Bruner and Goodman
(d) Dember

255. 'Multiplicity in one world' is the concept advocated by

(a) Jan Servaes
(b) Bella Mody
(c) J.L. Woods
(d) Diaz-Bordenave

256. The fact that the moon looks larger near the horizon than high in the sky is called the
(a) Ponzo Illusion
(b) Moon Illusion
(c) Muller Lyer Illusion
(d) Jastrow Illusion

257. The perception of the actual physical movement of objects in the world is termed as
(a) Autokinetic Effect
(b) Real Motion Perception
(c) Apparent Motion Perception
(d) Phiphenomenon

Directions: Questions 258 to 262 are of multiple statements type. Chose the correct answer from the codes given below the statements.

258. Who were the great apologizes of the theory of liberation
1. John Stuart Mill
2. John Milton
3. John William

Codes:

(a) 1 and 3 (b) 1, 2 and 3
(c) 1 and 3 (d) 2 and 3

259. Chose who amongst the following do/ does not accept evolutionary theory of social change. Select your answer from the codes given below:
1. Spencer 2. Spengler
3. Marx 4. Comte
5. Pareto 6. Sorokin
7. Toynbee 8. Hobhouse

Codes:

(a) 3 only (b) 1, 2, 3 and 8
(c) 2, 5, 6 and 8 (d) 2, 5, 7 and 8

260. Arrange the following forms of ownership of newspaper according to their circulation in ascending order
1. Firms 2. Associates
3. Trust 4. Government

Codes:

(a) 2, 1, 4, 3 (b) 4, 1, 3, 2
(c) 3, 1, 2, 4 (d) 2, 1, 3, 4

261. Which of the following statements are true?
1. The mass society theory is also called grand theory.
2. Magic bullet theory is also called Hypodermic Needle theory.
3. Limited effect theory is also known as attitude change theory.
4. Social diffusion theory is also known as Diffusion of Innovation theory.

Codes:

(a) 2 and 3 (b) 3 and 4
(c) 1 and 3 (d) 2 and 4

262. Which of the following statements are true?
1. Social change is a universal phenomenon.
2. Social change occurs as an essential law.
3. Speed of social change is not uniform.
4. Social change involve change in community.

Codes:

(a) 1 and 3 (b) 2 and 4
(c) 1, 2 and 3 (d) 1, 2, 3 and 4

Directions: Questions 263 to 270 are of Matching type. Match List-I with List-II and select the correct answer using the codes given below the lists.

263. **List-I**
(A) Modernisation Paradigm
(B) Alternative Paradigm

(C) Dominant Paradigm
(D) Participatory Model

List-II

1. Qualitative methodology
2. Qualitative research and variable analysis
3. Democratisation and participation of receivers at all the levels
4. Use of western influences to effect changes in the social milieu of the underdeveloped/developing nations.

Codes:	A	B	C	D
(a)	3	4	2	1
(b)	2	1	3	4
(c)	4	1	2	3
(d)	1	2	4	3

264. List-I
(A) Modernisation paradigm
(B) Alternative paradigm
(C) Dominant paradigm
(D) Participatory model

List-II

1. Qualitative methodology
2. Qualitative research and variable analysis
3. Democratisation and participation of receivers at all the levels
4. Use of western influences to effect changes in the social milieu.

Codes:	A	B	C	D
(a)	3	2	1	4
(b)	4	1	2	3
(c)	1	2	3	4
(d)	2	3	4	1

265. List-I — List-II

(A) Social Darwinism — 1. Darwin
(B) Survival of fittest — 2. Spencer
(C) Changes due to social clashes — 3. Durkheim
(D) Critique of Comte's sociological approach — 4. Marx

Codes:	A	B	C	D
(a)	1	2	3	4
(b)	4	3	2	1
(c)	3	4	1	2
(d)	2	1	4	3

266. List-I (Social Change Theories) — List-II (Thinkers)

(A) Evolutionary theory — 1. Spencer
(B) Cyclic Theory — 2. Pareto
(C) Social change is a process in which better informed would assist the less informed — 3. Schramm

Codes:	A	B	C
(a)	3	1	2
(b)	1	2	3
(c)	1	3	2
(d)	2	3	1

267. List-I (Theories)
(A) The agenda setting theory
(B) Dependency theory
(C) Reinforcement theory
(D) Attitude change theory

List-II (Thinkers)

1. Joseph Klapper
2. A.G. Frank
3. Donald Shaw
4. Hovland

Codes:	A	B	C	D
(a)	4	2	1	2
(b)	3	2	1	4
(c)	1	2	3	4
(d)	2	3	4	1

268. List-I (Theories) — List-II (Thinkers)

(A) Cultural theories — 1. Davis
(B) Cultivation analysis — 2. Gerbner
(C) Frankfurt school — 3. Adorno
(D) Symbolic interaction — 4. Faules

Codes:	A	B	C	D
(a)	2	3	4	1
(b)	1	2	3	4
(c)	3	4	1	2
(d)	4	3	2	1

269.

List-I (Concepts)	List-II (Authors)
(A) Global village	1. Herbert Schiller
(B) Cultural Imperialism	2. Marshall McLuhan
(C) Many voices one world	3. Cees Hamelink
(D) Cultural Autonomy	4. Sean MacBride

Codes:	A	B	C	D
(a)	3	4	1	2
(b)	1	3	4	2
(c)	2	1	4	3
(d)	2	4	1	3

270.

List-I (Authors)	List-II (Concepts)
(A) M.K. Gandhi	1. Ideological constraints of development
(B) L.R. Beltran	2. Safety first principle
(C) J. Scott	3. Idea of justice
(D) Amartya Sen	4. Trusteeship of society

Codes:	A	B	C	D
(a)	1	2	4	3
(b)	2	1	4	3
(c)	4	1	2	3
(d)	3	4	1	2

Directions: Questions 271 to 289 consist of two statements, one labelled as 'Assertion' (A) and the other labelled as 'Reason' (R). You are to examine these two statements carefully and decide the Assertion (A) and the Reason (R) are individually true and if so, whether the Reason is a correct explanation of the Assertion. Select your answer to these questions using the codes given below:

(a) Both (A) and (R) are true and (R) is the correct explanation of (A).
(b) Both (A) and (R) are true but (R) is not the correct explanation of (A).
(c) (A) is true but (R) is false.
(d) (A) is false but (R) is true.

271. **Assertion (A):** During the recent times, the capitalist system has become self-centered and secluded.

Reason (R): Growing clout of developing nations that were hitherto dominated makes the system self centered.

272. **Assertion (A):** The productive and administrative structures of the media also function on the basis of a general policy set by the society.

Reason (R): Every society is transformed by the messages created and disseminated by those media that thrive in it.

273. **Assertion (A):** The electric (or electronics) technologies do not ensure the formation of person-to-person relations.

Reason (R): Electric (or electronics) technologies are so complex that they do not ensure efficient person-to-person contacts

274. **Assertion (A):** The new communication revolution is being accepted with zeal in the new millennium.

Reason (R): The technologies and gadgets offered by this revolution have been able to fascinate the masses.

275. **Assertion (A):** GNP is not an adequate measure of development.

Reason (R): GNP is only an average figure and does not give a clear picture of the distribution of the national income. Further, it is an economic indicator and not a social one.

276. **Assertion (A):** TV has failed to become an instrument of social change in india.

Reason (R): TV has been nothing but an entertainment media in our country.

277. **Assertion (A):** Development communication is not a tool but a product.

Reason (R): Development communication is a goal-oriented concept.

278. **Assertion (A):** The Dominant Paradigm is a linear transmission of effects.

Reason (R): In the Dominant Paradigm, the message is transmitted as a signal from a source to a destination. Noise and interference can distort this message.

279. **Assertion (A):** The Asian societies are we-oriented.

Reason (R): The Western media influence have led to this we-orientation of the Asian societies.

280. **Assertion (A):** The mass media do not play major roles in the campaign of development through communication.

Reason (R): The unidirectional communication models were less effective, but bi-directional models tend to make the initial message more effective.

281. **Assertion (A):** The communication task involves rights and obligations.

Reason (R): The media must communicate within a framework of social and judicial responsibility because they provide a public service.

282. **Assertion (A):** The social responsibility theory goes beyond the libertarian theory

Reason (R): It lays more stress on the responsibility of the press towards society and not on the freedom of the press.

283. **Assertion (A):** The model of research in the field of mass communication is known as dominant paradigm.

Reason (R): This model is still taught and applied.

284. **Assertion (A):** Marx approaches the evolutionary theory of social change.

Reason (R): Marx saw a series of successive changes from primitive hunting to modern industrialism.

285. **Assertion (A):** Pareto says that the social change is brought about by the struggles between groups for political power.

Reason (R): According to Pareto, there are alternating periods of harsh rule by a vigorous and newly triumphant elite and mild, humanitarian rule by a declining elite.

286. **Assertion (A):** Creativity is an innate ability.

Reason (R): Creativity can be developed.

287. **Assertion (A):** The process of social learning depends upon indirect experiences and formal learning.

Reason (R): Most of social learning is based on imitation or successful behaviours depicted in media.

288. **Assertion (A):** The two-step flow theory of communication has been proved wrong.

Reason (R): In a developing society information has to cross not one but many barriers.

289. **Assertion (A):** Mass media have wider sets of responsibilities and obligations in a developing society.

Reason (R): When the public service broadcasting is supported by commercial interests.

ANSWERS

1. (d)	2. (d)	3. (a)	4. (c)	5. (c)	6. (b)
7. (b)	8. (a)	9. (a)	10. (a)	11. (a)	12. (a)
13. (b)	14. (c)	15. (c)	16. (d)	17. (a)	18. (a)
19. (a)	20. (b)	21. (b)	22. (d)	23. (a)	24. (a)
25. (a)	26. (a)	27. (b)	28. (b)	29. (a)	30. (d)
31. (a)	32. (d)	33. (c)	34. (c)	35. (c)	36. (c)
37. (a)	38. (a)	39. (a)	40. (a)	41. (b)	42. (d)
43. (c)	44. (c)	45. (a)	46. (d)	47. (d)	48. (c)
49. (c)	50. (a)	51. (c)	52. (c)	53. (d)	54. (a)
55. (b)	56. (d)	57. (a)	58. (b)	59. (b)	60. (c)
61. (d)	62. (c)	63. (d)	64. (c)	65. (d)	66. (b)
67. (a)	68. (b)	69. (c)	70. (d)	71. (c)	72. (c)
73. (a)	74. (a)	75. (c)	76. (d)	77. (b)	78. (d)
79. (d)	80. (b)	81. (c)	82. (b)	83. (c)	84. (a)
85. (c)	86. (b)	87. (d)	88. (c)	89. (c)	90. (a)
91. (d)	92. (a)	93. (c)	94. (b)	95. (d)	96. (c)
97. (a)	98. (b)	99. (a)	100. (c)	101. (b)	102. (c)
103. (c)	104. (c)	105. (c)	106. (d)	107. (a)	108. (d)
109. (d)	110. (a)	111. (a)	112. (c)	113. (a)	114. (d)
115. (c)	116. (b)	117. (b)	118. (d)	119. (a)	120. (d)
121. (b)	122. (b)	123. (a)	124. (c)	125. (d)	126. (a)
127. (b)	128. (c)	129. (b)	130. (a)	131. (c)	132. (a)
133. (d)	134. (b)	135. (d)	136. (b)	137. (d)	138. (c)
139. (b)	140. (a)	141. (a)	142. (c)	143. (b)	144. (d)
145. (d)	146. (a)	147. (c)	148. (a)	149. (b)	150. (a)
151. (a)	152. (b)	153. (d)	154. (c)	155. (d)	156. (c)
157. (c)	158. (a)	159. (d)	160. (d)	161. (d)	162. (a)
163. (c)	164. (c)	165. (d)	166. (a)	167. (c)	168. (d)
169. (c)	170. (d)	171. (d)	172. (a)	173. (a)	174. (d)
175. (a)	176. (d)	177. (b)	178. (d)	179. (d)	180. (c)
181. (c)	182. (c)	183. (a)	184. (c)	185. (b)	186. (b)
187. (a)	188. (d)	189. (c)	190. (b)	191. (a)	192. (d)
193. (d)	194. (b)	195. (d)	196. (a)	197. (d)	198. (c)

199. (d)	200. (a)	201. (a)	202. (a)	203. (a)	204. (a)
205. (b)	206. (c)	207. (d)	208. (d)	209. (b)	210. (a)
211. (a)	212. (d)	213. (b)	214. (d)	215. (b)	216. (c)
217. (d)	218. (d)	219. (c)	220. (b)	221. (c)	222. (d)
223. (d)	224. (c)	225. (c)	226. (b)	227. (d)	228. (b)
229. (c)	230. (a)	231. (b)	232. (b)	233. (a)	234. (b)
235. (b)	236. (a)	237. (a)	238. (c)	239. (b)	240. (a)
241. (d)	242. (a)	243. (c)	244. (a)	245. (a)	246. (d)
247. (a)	248. (c)	249. (b)	250. (d)	251. (c)	252. (d)
253. (c)	254. (c)	255. (a)	256. (b)	257. (b)	258. (c)
259. (c)	260. (c)	261. (d)	262. (d)	263. (c)	264. (b)
265. (d)	266. (b)	267. (b)	268. (b)	269. (c)	270. (c)
271. (d)	272. (c)	273. (d)	274. (a)	275. (a)	276. (a)
277. (d)	278. (a)	279. (c)	280. (b)	281. (a)	282. (a)
283. (a)	284. (a)	285. (b)	286. (d)	287. (b)	288. (d)
289. (a)					

6

Research Methods and Process

1. A variable that is correlated with the independent variable and thus can be responsible for the effect in question is known as
   (a) Controlled Variable
   (b) Confounded Variable
   (c) Independent Variable
   (d) Dependent Variable

2. Which one of the following statements is false?
   (a) The number of TV sets to which, the SITE software was beamed was 2,330.
   (b) The SITE project was commenced on August 1, 1975.
   (c) The satellite used of the SITE project was ATS-6.
   (d) The number of states covered by the SITE was 6.

3. Usually people's interaction with media is
   (a) Inactive (b) Inquisitions
   (c) Homogeneous (d) All of the above

4. In the census method of data collection, we collect data from
   (a) a sample of the population.
   (b) some people at random and then, form all the people by using a non-random sampling method.
   (c) every unit of the population.
   (d) None of the above.

5. According to the researchers and the studies conducted by the IIMC, radio lost ground to TV. What would be the reason of decline in the number of radio audience?
   (a) Radio announcers and disk jockeys were not as smart TV announcers and video jockeys.
   (b) TV sets were cheap whereas radio sets were not so cheap.
   (c) TV, as an audio-visual medium was able to impinge upon the audio-visual sense of the audiences whereas radio was only an aural medium.
   (d) The government was keen to promote TV as the official mass communication mode during the early eighties.

6. A controlled variable is a characteristic of the subjects or of the environment that is kept constant across all levels of
   (a) the confounded variable
   (b) the extraneous variable
   (c) the independent variable
   (d) the dependent variable

7. A sample must not be
   (a) adequate for the purpose of study/research.
   (b) having the same nature as that of the universe.
   (c) representative of the population.
   (d) None of these.

8. Which was the golden age of journalism according to writers and owners of newspapers in England?

(a) The 1650's and 1505's
(b) The 1000's and 1990's
(c) The 1850's and 1840's
(d) The 1755's and 1690's

9. Media research is a part of
(a) marketing research.
(b) evaluative advertising research.
(c) strategic advertising research.
(d) None of the above.

10. What is canalising?
(a) The message can succeed if it slightly modifies the attitudes values, and objectives of the targeted audiences.
(b) The message can succeed if it is sent through popular media vehicles.
(c) The message can succeed if it drastically changes the attitudes, values, and objectives of the targeted receivers.
(d) None of the above.

11. Which element promoted the industrialization of wireless telegraphy?
(a) The First World War
(b) Post Independence
(c) The Second World War
(d) None of the above

12. In the parlance of communication research in India, TV started making an impact on the mass audience during the
(a) early seventies (b) early eighties
(c) late eighties (d) late nineties

13. Indian State Broadcasting Service (ISBS), the government run broadcasting company was set up under the ministry of
(a) CPWD
(b) Public Health and Engineering Department
(c) The Department of Industries and Labour
(d) Ministry of Information and Broad-casting

14. In the Galvanic Skin Response test,
(a) longer the quantify of current, less is the intensity of reaction of the respondent.
(b) young children all swayed by romantic movies.
(c) longer the quantity of current, more is the intensity of reaction of the respondent.
(d) the reaction of the respondent is not at all related to current flow.

15. A design which counterbalances the practice and fatigue effects during the experimental period is called
(a) Single group design
(b) Double group design
(c) Counterbalancing design
(d) ABAB design

16. The three objectives of the SITE were
(a) academics, communication, and enlightenment.
(b) enlightenment, entertainment, and academics.
(c) communication, education, and information.
(d) entertainment, education and information.

17. While performing a chi-square hypothesis test, what happens when expected frequencies in several cells are too small?
(a) The values of χ^2 would be overestimated.
(b) The null hypothesis is more likely to be rejected than it should be.
(c) Both (a) and (b).
(d) The degrees of freedom are reduced.

18. The establishment year of the 'Audit Bureau of Circulation' was
(a) 1930 (b) 1948
(c) 1945 (d) 1939

19. When violence and sex are coupled in a programme or movie, they can create a ________ feeling in the mind of the adolescent.
(a) powerful but negative
(b) sarcastic
(c) predator-prey
(d) pleasant and positive

20. Readership surveys was first conducted by
(a) *The Hindu* (b) *Reader's Digest*
(c) *Times of India* (d) All of the above

21. Which of the following is a measure of central tendency?
(a) Mode
(b) Medium
(c) Geometric Mean
(d) All of the above.

22. The British Government in India set up the 'Central Bureau of Public Information' in
(a) 1932 (b) 1930
(c) 1942 (d) 1923

23. Why are conclusive research and exploratory research a part of a cyclic process?
(a) Exploratory research follows conclusive research.
(b) Most market researchers prefer to undertake conclusive research and exploratory research in a cyclic order.
(c) The results of conclusive research generate new ideas, which become the inputs for exploratory research. Hence, the process is cyclic in nature.
(d) All of the above.

24. Thc 'Public Society of India' was set up in the year of
(a) 1939 (b) 1942
(c) 1923 (d) 1926

25. While performing a two-tailed test for the difference between means, with a null hypothesis of $\mu_1 = \mu_2$, the hypothesised differences between the two population means would be
(a) Infinity (b) Positive
(c) Negative (d) Zero

26. Who among the following set up the "Pubic Society of India"?
(a) N.W. Ayer (b) I.S. Taylor
(c) D.J. Keyner (d) None of the above

27. Testing at the begnining of the creative process mostly includes
(a) qualitative research.
(b) statistiscal methods and formulae.
(c) quntitative research.
(d) None of the above.

28. When was the first Indian Readership Survey's conducted?
(a) 1996 (b) 1993
(c) 1992 (d) 1995

29. In the parlance of copy testing, which one of the following is not a principle of PACT?
(a) Demonstrates radiability and validity.
(b) Avoids multiple measurements.
(c) Based on a model of human response to communications.
(d) Takes into account basic considerations of smaple definition.

30. Which of the following conditions give characterization to primary groups?
(a) Small size of group
(b) Lasting nature of the bond
(c) A close physical proximity
(d) All of the above

31. In aided recall methods, the respondent or test subjects is shown
(a) a number of ads and told to identify the ad that has impressed him the most.

(b) a picture of the ad but not the name of the sponsor of the ad or brand name.
(c) the complete ad and asked whether he can recall the products of competitors that correspond to the ad shown to him.
(d) None of the above.

32. Which group is characterized a less close relationship between members?
(a) Peer group (b) Reference group
(c) Primary group (d) All of the above

33. Which of the following statements is not correct?
(a) A weighted mean should be used when it is necessary to take the importance of each value into account.
(b) Some data sets do not have means.
(c) Calculation of mean is affected by extreme data value.
(d) All the above are correct.

34. The influence of a group in the attitude of an individual is generally treated in terms of the concept of
(a) Reference group (b) Peer group
(c) Primary group (d) None of the above

35. In Before-After testing, the advertising researcher
(a) defines the goals of the advertising message before the execution of the ad campaign.
(b) uses different test subjects in the 'before' and 'after' stages of the test.
(c) uses low-cost tests during the 'before' stage and high-cost tests during the 'after' stage.
(d) defines the goals of the advertising message after the execution of the ad campaign.

36. Where is the National Library of India located?
(a) Delhi (b) Kolkata
(c) Mumbai (d) Hyderabad

37. If some persons are shown TV advertisements in the office of an advertising agency and told to give comments on the products featured in those advertisements, what type of research is this?
(a) Laboratory experiment
(b) After only design
(c) Field experiment
(d) None of the above.

38. If one null hypothesis is H_0: u = 90 and the alternative hypothesis is H_1: H < 90, it is appropriate to use a
(a) right-tailed test (b) chi-square test
(c) two-tailed test (d) left-tailed test

39. The variable that is manipulated by the "E" (Experimenter) is called
(a) Confounded Variable
(b) Extraneous Variable
(c) Dependent Variable
(d) Independent Variable

40. Participants of concept tests bring data about the competing products and advertisements and thus, affect the test in an adverse manner, i.e. to add bias to the ongoing test. This phenomenon is also called
(a) audience data bias
(b) illicit data seepage
(c) competitors' bias
(d) competitive test

41. Every thing which surrounds the units of inheritence is known as
(a) Situation (b) Environment
(c) Fact (d) Event

42. Which one of the following is a correct relationship?
(a) Median = (Mean + Mode)/3
(b) Mean = 2 Median – 3 Mode

(c) Mode = 3 Median – 2 Mean
(d) Mean = 2 (Median – Mode)

43. Which of the following is not true about geometric mean?
(a) It is mathematically tractable and need for rearranging the data does not arise.
(b) It gives more weightage to small numbers as exampled to large data.
(c) It is less complicated and useful only for small distribution.
(d) It is less affected by changes in extreme values.

44. Testing at the beginning of the creative process mostly includes
(a) statistical methods and formulae.
(b) quantitative research.
(c) qualitative research.
(d) None of these.

45. If a group of data has only one mode and its value is less than that of the mean, it can be concluded that the graph of the distribution is
(a) skewed to the left
(b) skewed to the right
(c) symmetrical
(d) None of the above.

46. Motivation research tries to analyse
(a) why consumers buy specific products and/or services.
(b) what is the geographic and demographic profile of a targeted market niche.
(c) how consumers buy or shun particular products.
(d) All of the above.

47. An experiment has been aptly described as a
(a) question put to psychologists.
(b) question put to nature Stimuli.
(c) question put to self.
(d) question put to.

48. In the context of mass media effects, what is priming?
(a) TV and radio act as primers to perpetuate the tendency to watch crime movies in theatres.
(b) When people are exposed to some events through the mass media, their thoughts lead to the generation of sementically related ideas and action tendencies after some time.
(c) People associate the events watched, read, or heard in the media to their own needs.
(d) People tend to associate themselves with cinema stars who have a macho image.

49. Who can be given the credit of being the pioneer of media effects research in the USA?
(a) The Payne Fund Studies (1929-32)
(b) Edgar Dale (Circa 1930)
(c) Woodrow Wilson (1917)
(d) William Randolph Hearst (1898)

50. If an advertising researcher collects data from a research firm such as AC Neilsen, the IMRB or ORG, this data would be deemed
(a) collated data
(b) primary data
(c) secondary data
(d) raw data and facts

51. Anything that can take on a number of values is called a
(a) Variable (b) Stimulus
(c) Fact (d) Situation

52. Which of the following examples amply demonstrates the efficiency of the limited effects model (under the gamut of media effects studies)?

(a) I would buy Surf Excel if it is offered to me through a scheme of freebies at my residence.
(b) I would not buy Surf Excel if a salesman offers it to me at my home. However, I would buy it if ads appear on TV to promote it.
(c) I would not buy Surf Excel if it is advertised on TV, but might buy it when the sales girl at the counter of her shop offers it to me.
(d) None of the above.

53. In a test of differences between proportions, two samples are taken. In the first sample, a sample size of 100 shows 25 successes. In the second sample, a sample size of 80 shows 25 successes. What would be the value of B in this case?
(a) $\frac{30}{100} \times \frac{25}{80}$ (b) $\frac{30}{100} + \frac{25}{80}$
(c) $\frac{30}{180} + \frac{25}{180}$ (d) $\frac{30 + 25}{180}$

54. The formula for calculating mode is as follows:

$$Z = L_1 + \frac{f_1 - f_0}{(f_1 - f_0) + (f_2 - f_0)}$$

In this formula, f_2 represents the
(a) frequency of the modal class.
(b) frequency of the class that precedes the modal class.
(c) lower limit of the modal class.
(d) frequency of the class that succeeds the modal class.

55. A samples must not be
(a) adequate for the purpose of study/research.
(b) having the same nature as that of the universe.
(c) representative of the population.
(d) None of these.

56. What is the Safety Valve Theory?
(a) Exposure to pornographic software is likely to suppress or satisfy the urge of a targeted person to commit sex crimes.
(b) A person who watches pornographic material would certainly commit sex crimes later.
(d) Pornographic material disseminated through the media is a good source for educating the youth about the acts of sex.
(d) None of the above.

57. In 1913, C.G. Jung has established his own school which was popularly known as
(a) Analytical Psychology
(b) Child Psychology
(c) Psychoanalysis
(d) Individual Psychology

58. After watching a horror movie in a theatre, in the mind of a viewer
(a) the feelings of fear precedes the feeling of joy and euphoria.
(b) mixed feelings of joy and fear are experienced.
(c) the feeling of joy and euphoria never comes because he is always fearful.
(d) the feeling of joy and euphoria precedes fear.

59. An experiment is set up to confirm or refute some
(a) Events (b) Enquiry
(c) Questions (d) Hypotheses

60. In which of the following cases would mode be the most useful indicator of central tendency?
(a) Every value in a data set occurs only once.
(b) Every observation in a data set has the same value.

(c) All values in a data set can occur 100 times each.
(d) All but three values in a data set occur once, three values occur 100 times each.

61. If a group of data has only one mode and its value is less than that of the mean, it can be concluded that the graph of the distribution is
(a) skewed to the right.
(b) symmetrical.
(c) skewed to the left.
(d) None of these.

62. Which of the following is not the strength of media effects research?
(a) It helps media organisations alter the software according to the needs of the targeted audiences.
(b) It can help researchers and their sponsors learn the relatives of media effects at very low cost.
(c) It can help the state take necessary actions to control the effects of the media.
(d) It can determine the harmful effects of the media on the youth.

63. A German Psychologist, H. Ebbinghaus, had done pioneering experiments on
(a) Memory (b) Perception
(c) Emotion (d) Learning

64. The latest audiences to be studied by the proponents of media research are
(a) broadcast audience (TV)
(b) print media audience
(c) broadcast audience (radio)
(d) None of the above.

65. Through the chi-square test, we can judge whether two characteristics of a population are
(a) able to effect the chief characteristics of a population.
(b) related to each other, or are independent of each other.
(c) related to a third characteristic.
(d) None of the above.

66. Clinical psychology deals with the practical aspect of
(a) Child Psychology
(b) Abnormal Psychology
(c) Experimental Psychology
(d) Comparative Psychology

67. In the parlance of the chi-square test, the number of degrees of freedom is given by the formula
(a) Rows + Columns
(b) (Rows + 1) (Columns)
(c) (Rows) (Columns)
(d) (Rows – 1) (Columns)

68. Quota sampling is a type of
(a) random sampling
(b) startified sampling
(c) judgement sampling
(d) None of the above.

69. The technique of regulating various variables in an expriment is called
(a) Experimental control
(b) Controlled variable
(c) Independent variable
(d) Dependent variable

70. Which of the following distributions has a pair of degrees of freedom?
(a) chi-square (b) Poisson
(c) Normal (d) None of these

71. Psychologists with the biological perspective try to relate behaviour to functions of
(a) Unconscious (b) Subconscious
(c) Mind (d) Body

72. The Central Limit Theorem informs us that

(a) sampling distribution of the mean is not affected due to variations in the sample size.
(b) sampling distribution of the mean approaches normal as the sample size increases.
(c) sampling distribution of the mean approaches normal as the smaple size decreases.
(d) None of the above.

73. A little girl Leny pushed Bapula, her brother, off his tricycle. She learned to behave this way because the behaviour paid off in the past. In other words, she learned to act aggressively in certain situations because she was rewarded for such behaviour in the past. With which perspective, a psychologist can study this type of problem?
(a) Cognitive Perspective
(b) Developmental Perspective
(c) Biological Pespective
(d) Behavioural Perspective

74. A chief limitation of Quartile Deviation (QD) is that
(a) it is a fine measurement of dispersion.
(b) it ignores 50 per cent of extreme items.
(c) it is not affected by extreme items.
(d) None of the above.

75. The perspective which is concerned with characteristic changes that occur in people as they mature is known as
(a) Humanistic Perspective
(b) Cognitive Perspective
(c) Developmental Perspective
(d) Biological Perspective

76. The formula for calculating Harmonic Mean (HM) is
(a) $H = \frac{N}{\Sigma(1/x)}$
(b) H = S(x) (N)/2
(c) H = N/X
(d) None of the above.

77. A person's sense of self is emphasized by
(a) Humanistic Perspective
(b) Cognitive Perspective
(c) Psychoanalytic Perspective
(d) Developmental Perspective

78. The data of the Audit Bureau of Circulation is a type of
(a) primary data
(b) secondary data
(c) unimportant data
(d) depends upon the user

79. A key psychodynamic idea is that when unconscious impulses are unacceptable or when they make us anxious; to reduce anxiety, we use
(a) Super Ego
(b) Frustration
(c) Defense Mechanisms
(d) Instincts

80. According to Robert Cialdini, if you are not sure how to behave, you would seek guidance of those who are around you. This principle is called
(a) The Principle of Authority
(b) The Principle of Social Proof
(c) The Principle of Liking
(d) The Principle of Reciprocity

81. The distinction between a clinical psychologist and a psychiatrist is that
(a) a clinical psychologist holds a special degree in psychology and a psychitrist holds a Ph.D. degree in psychology.
(b) a clinical psychologist holds an M.A. degree in psychology and a psychiatrist holds Ph.D. degree in psychology.

(c) a clinical psychologist normally holds a Ph.D. or M.A. degree or Psy.D (Doctor in Psychology) and a psychiatrist holds an MD degree.

(d) a clinical psychologist holds a Ph.D. degree in psychology and a psychiatrist holds both Psy.D. degree and Ph.D. degree.

82. The Coefficient of Skewness (J) is givn by

(a) $J = \frac{\text{Mean} - \text{Mode}}{\sigma}$

(b) $J = \frac{(\text{Mean})\,(\text{Mode})}{\sigma}$

(c) $J = \frac{\text{Mean} + \text{Mode}}{\sigma}$

(d) None of the above.

83. The subject "Psychology" was formally recognised in Germany in the year

(a) 1879 (b) 1789
(c) 1968 (d) 1668

84. The media creates news out of an insipid innocuous event. This statement can be easily associated with the

(a) Persuasion Triangle.
(b) Agenda Setting Theory.
(c) Principle of Reciprocity (under media persuasion).
(d) tendency of Illusion of Personal Invulnerability.

85. To study Abnormal Psychology means, to study mainly the nature of

(a) Subconscious Mind
(b) Abnormal Mind
(c) Conscious Mind
(d) Unconscious Mind

86. Who can be given the credit of being the pioneer of media effects research in the USA?

(a) Edgar Dale (Circa 1930)
(b) Woodrow Wilson (1917)
(c) William Randolph Hearst (1898)
(d) The Payne Fund Studies (1929-32)

87. Which one of the following was a disaster movie?

(a) *Silence of the Lambs*
(b) *Chicago*
(c) *The Rock*
(d) *The Towering Inferno*

88. What does the term NC-17 mean?

(a) No child below the age of 17 years is allowed to watch this movie.
(b) A child of 17 years of age can watch a movie with 'U' certification.
(c) A movie with 'A' certification can be watched by a child of 17 years of age.
(d) No female below the age of 17 years is allowed to watch this movie.

89. The unit of sociology is the "Group", whereas the unit of psychology is the

(a) Institution (b) Animal
(c) Individual (d) Stimulus

90. Which of the following is a technique of personal interview?

(a) In-Home interviews
(b) Mall-Intercept interviews
(c) Computer-Assisted interviews
(d) All of the above.

91. The branch of psychology which deals with the study of animal behaviour is known as

(a) Differential Psychology
(b) Comparative Psychology
(c) Social Psychology
(d) Abnormal Psychology

92. In the parlance of study of kurtosis, a flat-topped curve is called a

(a) Platykurtic curve
(b) Leptokurtic curve
(c) Mesokurtic curve
(d) None of the above.

93. In which of the following cases, would mode be the most useful indicator of central tendency?
   (a) Every observation in a data set has the same value.
   (b) All values in a data set can occur 100 times each.
   (c) Every value in a data set occurs only once.
   (d) All but three values in a data set occur once, three values occur 100 times each.

94. In a normal distribution
   (a) Mean = Median = Mode
   (b) Mean < Median < Mode
   (c) Mean > Median > Mode
   (d) None of the above.

95. For the first time, the word 'Psychology' was used by
   (a) William James (b) E.B. Titchener
   (c) C.G. Jung (d) Rudolf Goeckle

96. Copy-testing techniques are a part of
   (a) target audience analysis
   (b) message research
   (c) evaluation of advertising effectiveness (post-test techniques)
   (d) media research

97. The literal meaning of "Psychology" is
   (a) Science of Consciousness
   (b) Science of Temperament
   (c) Science of Behaviour
   (d) Science of Soul

98. Why has competitive analysis become an essential activity in marketing research nowadays?
   (a) It helps the firm find out what are ad spend patterns of competitors.
   (b) It helps the firm position its advertising message vis-à-vis those of its competitors so that it could get the maximum mileage from its own ad campaigns.
   (c) It helps the firm learn about new products and services that the competitors plan to launch in the future.
   (d) It helps the firm analyse the prices of competitors and eventually, it gives a competitive price tag to its own product.

99. Rudolf Goekle used the word "Psychology" for the first time in
   (a) 1905 AD (b) 1590 AD
   (c) 1950 AD (d) 1095 AD

100. Which of the following is not a limitation of the census method for collecting data?
   (a) It is costly.
   (b) It is time consuming.
   (c) It is not so reliable as a data collection tool.
   (d) None of the above.

101. Psychology as the "Science of Mind" was defined by
   (a) Functionalists
   (b) Ancient Greek Philosophers
   (c) Psychoanalysis
   (d) Behaviourists

102. Research that helps a manager arrive at a logical decision is called
   (a) Conclusive Research
   (b) Casual Research
   (c) Exploratory Research
   (d) Descriptive Research

103. Scientific Psychology came into existence during
   (a) 20th century (b) 17th century
   (c) 19th century (d) 15th century

104. Which of the following is an example of a parameter?
   (a) η (b) μ
   (c) $\bar{x}$ (d) None of these

105. J.B. Watson defined "Psychology" as the science

(a) Behaviour (b) Mind
(c) Soul (d) Experience

106. If an experimental variable is such that exposure to it can be determined in an objective manner on an ex post facto basis, the ex post facto design becomes a/an
(a) Latin square design.
(b) after only with control group design.
(c) continuous diary panel design.
(d) four-group six-study design.

107. Woodworm's approach to define psychology is
(a) Dynamic (b) Constant
(c) Simple (d) Fluctuating

108. What is the formula for calculating the Semi Inter Quartile Range?
(a) $\frac{Q_3 - Q_1}{Q_3 + Q_1}$ (b) $(Q_3)\ (Q_1)$
(c) $\frac{Q_3 - Q_1}{2}$ (d) None of these.

109. Who defined psychology as the science of immediate experience with consciousness being the main subject matter?
(a) E.B. Titchener
(b) Wilhelm Wundt
(c) Sigmund Freud
(d) Both (a) and (b)

110. It is better to pre-test an ad in the selected sample of customers because
(a) the ad can be modified to suit needs of the targeted customers.
(b) the efficiency of the ad can be determined that way.
(c) Both (a) and (b).
(d) the researcher can get in-depth data about the sample population.

111. Any systematically organised body of verified knowledge about a certain class of facts and events is known as
(a) Fact (b) Theory
(c) Experiment (d) Science

112. A chief limitation of Mean Deviation (MD) is that
(a) it ignores plus and minus signs.
(b) it is based on measurement and not on estimation.
(c) it is not affected by extreme items.
(d) None of the above.

113. Psychology is
(a) a Biological Science
(b) a Social Science
(c) a Natural Science
(d) Both Natural and Social Science

114. The mass medium is the hypodermic needle and the message is a fluid. Which model makes this assumption?
(a) The Magic Bullet Model
(b) The Cause and Effect Model
(c) The Limited Effects Model
(d) None of the above.

115. Behaviouristic School was established by
(a) I.P. Pavlov (b) William James
(c) W. Kohler (d) J.B. Watson

116. The following is the correct formula for calculating the Coefficient of Variation.
(a) $CV = \frac{\sigma}{\overline{X}} \times 100$
(b) $CV = \frac{\overline{X}}{\sigma} \times 100$
(c) $CV = (\sigma)\ (\overline{X}) \times 100$
(d) $CV = \frac{\sigma}{\overline{X}}$

117. The most effective method of studying psychology is
(a) Introspection Method
(b) Clinical Method
(c) Experimental Method
(d) Observation Method

118. People think that they would never be swayed by the pressure of the brainstorming techniques of the media, but they also assume that the same techniques would certainly work on other people. This is called
(a) Illusion of Personal Invulnerability
(b) International Persuasion of the Media
(c) Illusory Placebo Effect
(d) None of the above.

119. Anything which evokes a response in the Organism is called
(a) Thing (b) Stimulus
(c) Incidence (d) Situation

120. A people meter is a tool used to measure
(a) the viewing habits of TV and cattle audiences.
(b) the listening habits of radio audiences.
(c) the reading habits of newspaper audiences.
(d) None of the above.

121. The researcher asks the following question from the test subject: Which ad would help you buy shaving cream of your choice?
(a) The ad shown to you in a newspaper
(b) A radio ad jingle
(c) The ad shown to you on TV
(d) The ad shown to you in amen's magazine

122. In order to calculate average speed, we should calculate
(a) harmonic mean
(b) weighted harmonic mean
(c) arithmetic mean
(d) any one of these can be used

123. That, which cannot be observed by another person, is called
(a) Activity (b) Experience
(c) Event (d) Action

124. What is intentional persuasion of the media?
(a) The media intentionally send some messages to motivate the targeted audiences to take certain actions.
(b) The media motivate the audiences to dissuade them from shifting to other (competing) media.
(c) The media are intentionally made cost-effective to attract large audiences.
(d) The media send many messages that inadvertently affect targeted audiences.

125. The first psychological laboratory was established in Leipzig by Wilhelm Wundt in the year
(a) 1879 (b) 1897
(c) 1789 (d) 1899

126. The formula for calculating the standard deviation of the distribution of sample means is given by
(a) $\sigma_{\bar{x}_1-\bar{x}_2} = \left(\sigma_1^2 + \sigma_2^2\right)^2$
(b) $\sigma_{\bar{x}_1-\bar{x}_2} = \sqrt{\dfrac{\sigma_1^2}{x_1} + \dfrac{\sigma_2^2}{x_2}}$
(c) $\sigma_{\bar{x}_1-\bar{x}_2} = (\sigma_1 + \sigma_2)^2$
(d) $\sigma_{\bar{x}_1-\bar{x}_2} = \dfrac{(x_1)^2 + (x_2)^2}{\sigma_1 + \sigma_2}$

127. "S-R" concept was first established by
(a) William James
(b) I.P. Pavlov
(c) J.B. Watson
(d) Wilhelm Wundt

128. Secondary data are
(a) easily converted into useful data.
(b) always inefficient.
(c) much better than primary data, even if they all stale.
(d) cheap and easy to get.

129. When customers are studied as a purchasing group or market segment, this type of research is termed

(a) Motivation Research
(b) Target Audience Analysis
(c) Marketing Research
(d) Market Research

130. We can calculate the mean of any data set, if we have its frequency distribution. This statement is
(a) true.
(b) false.
(c) insufficient information to predict.
(d) irrelevant to the concept of mean.

131. A systematic study of facts according to a reliable and correct method of study is called a
(a) Scientific Study
(b) Methodology
(c) Biological Study
(d) Social Technique

132. Who wrote *Mass Media and National Development*?
(a) Wilbur Schramm
(b) Gutenberg
(c) Val Gielgud
(d) Daniel Lerner

133. Which of the following is not a limitation of the census method for collecting data?
(a) It is not so reliable as a data collection tool
(b) It is time consuming
(c) It is costly
(d) None of these is a limitation of the census method

134. In which year was the Non-Aligned News Agencies Pool formally launched?
(a) 1971 (b) 1973
(c) 1975 (d) 1976

135. The occurrence of "O" in "S-O-R" concept is responsible in regulating the behaviour of the organism and making psychological activity
(a) Fixed (b) Complex
(c) Puzzled (d) Dynamic

136. In which year was the BBC World Service started in India?
(a) 1991 (b) 1992
(c) 1993 (d) 1995

137. Which of the following is not a measure of central tendency?
(a) Medium
(b) Geometric Mean
(c) Mode
(d) All the above are the measures of central tendency

138. In which year was the Asian Television Network started?
(a) 1995 (b) 1993
(c) 1991 (d) 1990

139. After E.B. Titchener's definition, which relationship, to serve the very purpose of Psychology, was lost?
(a) "S-P-R" (b) Cause-Effect
(c) "S-O-R" (d) "S-R"

140. *The Republic* is written by
(a) Rousseau (b) Machiavelli
(c) Marx (d) Plato

141. The study of the interaction of heredity and environment is made by
(a) Comparative Psychologists
(b) Educational Psychologists
(c) Physiological Psychologists
(d) Child Psychologists

142. Who wrote *Areopagitica*?
(a) Hegel (b) Plato
(c) John Milton (d) Mill

143. In recent years, physiological psychology is getting attached to the developing science of
(a) Psychology (b) Sociology
(c) Anthropology (d) Physiology

144. In which year did BBC become a public corporation?
(a) 1925 (b) 1927
(c) 1929 (d) 1932

145. Introspective Method is otherwise known as
(a) Objective Observation
(b) Survey Method
(c) Self-Observation Technique
(d) Subjective Observation

146. In order to be a good writer one should not be
(a) modest in approach
(b) using complex words
(c) focussed
(d) to the point

147. Field Observation is always
(a) Complex (b) Very Simple
(c) Objective (d) Subjective

148. Impact, Timeliness, Conflict and Prominence are
(a) basis of good news story.
(b) qualities to be adopted by a writer.
(c) criteria on which the editors insist upon.
(d) None of the above.

149. In which year did the IPDC commenced its work?
(a) 1982 (b) 1984
(c) 1986 (d) 1988

150. Regulating the "Relevant Variable" is called
(a) Antihypothesis
(b) Hypothesis
(c) Constant Error
(d) Experimental Control

151. What is meant by the 'middle'?
(a) The middle paragraph of the article.
(b) It means middle of the page.
(c) The middle pages of the newspapers.
(d) Small and light article printed in the middle of the editorial page.

152. When more than one independent variable work in an experimental situation, it is called
(a) Variable Crisis
(b) Situational Crisis
(c) Interaction
(d) Multisituational Effect

153. Which is not the weapon in the armoury of an argumentative editorial writer?
(a) Refuting the opponent's view.
(b) Not playing on the emotions of the people.
(c) Blowing one's trumptet.
(d) All of the above.

154. It is not possible or even desirable to rule out the differential effects of all relevant variables by means of experimental control. In such instances, psychologists employ controlled conditions by mathematical methods. This is called
(a) Physiological Control
(b) Experimental Control
(c) Psychological Control
(d) Statistical Control

155. In which year did the All-India Newspaper Editors' Conference formulated a code of ethics?
(a) 1962 (b) 1968
(c) 1970 (d) 1971

156. Gestalt School was founded by
(a) Kurt Koffka (1886-1941)
(b) Kurt Lewin (1890-1947)
(c) Max Wertheimer (1880-1943)
(d) Wolfgang Kohler (1887-1937)

157. Who wrote the book *The Press and America*?
(a) Laurence Greene (b) Richard Nixon
(c) Joseph Pulitzer (d) Edwin Emery

158. The theory of evolution was propounded by

(a) Sir Charles Darwin (1809-82)
(b) John Deway (1859-1952)
(c) William James (1842-1910)
(d) Kurt Lewin (1890-1947)

159. The article can be rejected if
(a) the article does not have a focus.
(b) the information lacks facts to make the argument credible.
(c) the language is not good.
(d) All of the above.

160. E.B. Titchener (1867-1927) defined "Psychology" as the science of
(a) Experience
(b) Behaviour
(c) Soul
(d) Conscious Experience

161. Who introduced licensing of the Press in 1823?
(a) John Adams
(b) Lord Amherst
(c) Lord Auckland
(d) Warran Hastings

162. If an experimental variable is such that exposure to it can be determined in an objective manner or an ex-post facto basis, the ex-post facto design becomes a/an
(a) four-group six-study design.
(b) after only with control group design.
(c) continuous diary panel design.
(d) Latin square design.

163. In which country did the concept of Ombudsman originate?
(a) Sweden (b) Finland
(c) UK (d) USA

164. Who has constructed the first intelligence test as a psychologist and made important contributions to our understading of the thought process?
(a) Alfred Binet
(b) William James
(c) J.B. Watson
(d) William McDougall

165. In which country was the concept of Ombudsman first adopted?
(a) Denmark (b) India
(c) Sweden (d) USA

166. The mass medium is the gun and the message is a fluid. Which model makes this assumption?
(a) The Cause and Effect Model
(b) The Limited Effects Model
(c) The Hypodermic Needle Model
(d) None of these

167. When was the Press Council of India set up?
(a) September 8, 1961
(b) August 4, 1963
(c) July 4, 1966
(d) June 4, 1968

168. Which law deals with the least noticeable differences in different stimuli?
(a) Weber-Fechner Law
(b) Binet Law
(c) Gestalt Law
(d) Watson's Law

169. Who reintroduced licensing in 1857?
(a) Lord Bentick (b) Lord Hardinge
(c) Lord Canning (d) Lord Dalhousie

170. "The coefficient of correlation explains the percentage of the total variation of the dependent variable." This statement is
(a) Partially true
(b) Insufficient information to predict
(c) True
(d) False

171. $\frac{Q_3 - Q_1}{2}$ is a formula for calculating
(a) semi-interquartile range
(b) harmonic mean
(c) median
(d) arithmetic mean

172. Wilhelm Wundt setup the first psychological laboratory in 1879 at the University of
(a) Toronto (b) L.N.M.G.
(c) Leipzig (d) Queens

173. *Audience Analysis* is written by
(a) Denis McQuail
(b) Mary Kelly
(c) Vilfredo Pareto
(d) JW Carey

174. A statistical measure based upon the entire population is called parameter while measure based upon a sample is known as
(a) Inference (b) Statistic
(c) Sample parameter (d) None of these

175. In the process of systematic sampling how many unit/units is/are selected at random from the population?
(a) One (b) Three
(c) Five (d) Seven

176. Generalized conclusion on the basis of a sample is technically known as
(a) parameter inference.
(b) statistical inference of external validity of the research.
(c) data analysis and interpretation.
(d) All of the above.

177. In statistics, the portion which is chosen from a given population, is known as
(a) Mode (b) Population
(c) Sample (d) None of these.

178. A researcher selects only 10 members as a sample from the total population of 5000 and considers it good because
(a) he was guided by his supervisor.
(b) the populations was homogeneous.
(c) he was a good researcher.
(d) All of these.

179. Which of the following relationship is correct in a normal distribution?
(a) Median > Mean > Mode
(b) Median = $\frac{\text{Mean}+\text{Mode}}{2}$
(c) Mean = Median = Mode
(d) Mean > Median > Mode

180. A researcher divides his population into certain groups and fixes the size of the sample from each group. It is called
(a) Stratified sample (b) Quota sample
(c) Cluster sample (d) All of the above

181. Which of the following is not a technique of collection of primary data?
(a) Personal Interview
(b) Sampling
(c) Observation
(d) Questionnaire.

182. Experimentation is a formal process through which we gather and analyse the necessary information to understand
(a) Behaviour (b) Mind
(c) Events (d) Facts

183. Which of the following is not true about the idea generation process?
(a) In this process the top brass cannot help.
(b) In this process, the marketing executive can give new ideas.
(c) This process starts with search for now product ideas.
(d) In this process R&D staff can also give new ideas.

184. Experiments vary along a continuum from true experiments at one end to
(a) clinical studies at the other end.
(b) artificial studies at the other end.
(c) correlational or observational studies at the other end.
(d) situational studies at the other end.

185. Using of all elements in the population and taking lottery to select the desired number of elements from theft totality is
(a) Stratified Random Sampling
(b) Cluster Sampling
(c) Simple Random Sampling
(d) None of the above

186. Any variable that has not been controlled and that also varies systematically with the levels of the independent variables is known as
(a) Confounded Variable
(b) Extraneous Variable
(c) Dependent Variable
(d) Controlled Variable

187. Multi-stage sampling is also called as
(a) Purposive sampling
(b) Quota sampling
(c) Stratified sampling
(d) Cluster sampling

188. Which variable is regarded as the characteristic of a subject that is observed and measured by an "E" (Experimenter)?
(a) Extraneous Variable
(b) Confounded Variable
(c) Independent Variable
(d) Dependent Variable

189. Which sampling involves picking up of cases that are judged to be 'typical' of the population?
(a) Accidental sampling
(b) Quota sampling
(c) Purposive sampling
(d) Cluster sampling

190. The advantage of interviewing over questionnaire is
(a) it yields a better sample of the population.
(b) the method can be used with illiterates.
(c) it possesses great flexibility.
(d) All of the above.

191. A group which does not receive treatment in an experiment is called
(a) Comparing group
(b) Extra group
(c) Control group
(d) Situational group

192. In 1992, the survey 'the perception of viewers on the socio-cultural impact of cable and satellite television' was conducted by
(a) The Indian Institute of Mass Communication
(b) *Hindustan Times*
(c) *India Today*
(d) *The Hindu*

193. The tests which rate or measure observed reactions to actual life situations are called
(a) Controlled tests
(b) Group tests
(c) Situational tests
(d) Behaviour tests

194. Non-parametric tests are the statistical tests that measure the variable at
(a) probability level (b) ratio level
(c) interval level (d) nominal level

195. The number of respondents who actually participate in a research project is described as
(a) actual subjects (b) real sample
(c) net incidence (d) filtered public

196. Science is invariably characterised by
(a) its hypothesis (b) its factors
(c) its methodology (d) its theory

197. Research samples which are similar in their characteristics are identified as
(a) Similar samples
(b) Matched samples
(c) Model samples
(d) Comparison samples

198. In the analysis of communication language, words and sentences are known as
(a) Paradigms (b) Syntagms
(c) Metaphors (d) Conventions

199. An experiment that is done to discover a relationship is called
(a) Exploratory type of experiment
(b) Reflectory type of experiment
(c) Confirmatory type of experiment
(d) Situational type of experiment

200. In media research, the premise that the simplest method is the most preferable, is termed as
(a) Parsimony (b) Grassrooting
(c) Level Field (d) Smooth Search

201. An error created by an unknwon factor in media research is described as:
(a) Error apprehension
(b) Error disturbance
(c) Error variance
(d) Non-objective factor

202. The supposition which is based on the results of previous observations is known as
(a) Control (b) Hypothesis
(c) Design (d) Factor

203. The square of standard deviation is called
(a) Sample Variation
(b) Standard Variance
(c) Sample error
(d) Estimation error

204. The statistical test developed by R.A. Fisher is
(a) Anova (b) Chi-square test
(c) Z-test (d) Sign test

205. The first step in exploratory research is to conduct
(a) a literature survey
(b) an experience survey
(c) a string of case studies
(d) a sample survey

206. The father of 'Experimental Psychology' is
(a) E.B. Titchener (b) C.G. Jung
(c) Wilhelm Wundt (d) Sigmund Freud

207. In reception analysis, findings are not easily
(a) Replicable (b) Convertible
(c) Differentiate (d) Identifiable

208. In factor analysis, a factor is a
(a) Construct (b) Bias
(c) Variable (d) Scale

209. Which approach emphasises the role of instinctual processes and their modification in the course of interaction with the society?
(a) Wholistic Approach
(b) Stimulus-Response-Behaviouristic Approach
(c) Dynamic and Psychoanalytic Approach
(d) Cognitive Approach

210. The unquantifiable information about media is labelled as
(a) soft data (b) spot data
(c) qualitative data (d) descriptive data

211. A reader who has close emotional bonds with a medium and reads it regularly is described as
(a) main reader (b) major reader
(c) star reader (d) primary reader

212. An inductive method is normally used in
(a) statistical tests
(b) content analysis
(c) path analysis
(d) exploratory research

213. Sigmund Freud is regarded as the father of

(a) Behaviourism
(b) Stricturalism
(c) Gestalt Psychology
(d) Psychoanalysis

214. An important principle of ethnographic research is
(a) applicability
(b) holism
(c) discovery
(d) levels of measurement

215. Defining a variable in a manner that permits to be measured is described as
(a) measurement
(b) treatment
(c) operationalisation
(d) analysis

216. One-tailed test is a statistical test based on the presumption that the hypothesis in question is
(a) asymmetrical (b) linear
(c) non-linear (d) directional

217. Existentialism tries to reach modern man, offer him help in terms of clarifying his values, work out a meaningful and purposive existence. Psychologists who shaped this are
(a) Erickson and Sullivan
(b) Piaget, Bruner and Witkin
(c) Rollo May, R.D. Laing and Erick Fromm
(d) G.W. Allport, R.B. Catell and H.J. Eysenk

218. The consistency of a result or of a measure at different points in time is known as
(a) Snowball (b) Multistage
(c) Simulation (d) Stability

219. The use of scientific research methods in Journalism is known as
(a) Armchair Journalism
(b) Analytical Journalism
(c) Precision Journalism
(d) Sting Journalism

220. Identify the correct sequence of research in content analysis
(a) Data analysis-Subject categories-Unit of analysis-Coding.
(b) Unit of analysis-Subject categories-Coding-Data analysis.
(c) Unit of analysis-Subject categories-Data analysis-Coding.
(d) Unit of analysis-Data analysis-Coding-Subject categories.

221. The formal statement under which observations have to be made is called
(a) Experimental Situation
(b) Expenmental Design
(c) Experimental Control
(d) Experimental Hypothesis

222. Identify the correct order of research elements from the following:
(a) Variable-Construct-Concept-Hypothesis.
(b) Hypothesis-Variable-Concept-Construct.
(c) Concept-Construct-Variable-Hypothesis.
(d) Construct-Hypothesis-Concept-Variable.

223. The standard deviation of the sampling distribution of means is called
(a) Standard error
(b) Standard variance
(c) Standard distance
(d) Standard deficiency

224. Which type of experimentation is often known as "hypothesis testing experimentaion"?
(a) Confirmatory experiments
(b) Modern psychological experiments

(c) Exploratory experiments
(d) Situational experiments

225. A combination of document analysis, observation and interviews are applied usefully in
(a) Survey research
(b) Field experiment
(c) Case study
(d) Content analysis

226. Testing the clarity of a tool or instrument for collecting information is known as
(a) Pilot-test (b) Pre-test
(c) Post-test (d) Summative-test

227. A provisional theory to explain observed facts is known as
(a) Event (b) Hypothesis
(c) Theory (d) Construct

228. Administrative research is mainly aimed at
(a) dispute resolution.
(b) development of institution and policy implementation.
(c) searching for useful inputs from other sources.
(d) launching organizations.

Directions: Question 229 is of multiple statements type. Choose the correct answer from the codes given below the statements.

229. A feature writer must have
1. The ability to collect, categorise and analyse facts
2. A weak command on the language
3. A lucid style of presenting his thoughts

Codes:
(a) 1 only (b) 2 only
(c) 2 and 3 (d) 1 and 2

Directions: Questions 230 to 236 are of matching type. Match List-I with List-II and select the answer using codes given below the lists.

230. **List-I**
(A) Media research
(B) Marketing
(C) Data of the RNI
(D) Market Research

List-II
1. Primary data
2. Study of customers as a segment
3. A kind of material data
4. Study of broadcast audience

Codes:	A	B	C	D
(a)	2	4	2	4
(b)	3	1	1	3
(c)	4	3	3	2
(d)	1	2	4	1

231. **List-I**
(A) Media research
(B) Marketing
(C) Data of the RNI
(D) Market Research

List-II
1. Primary data
2. Study of customers as a segment
3. A kind of material data
4. Study of broadcast audience

Codes:	A	B	C	D
(a)	3	4	1	2
(b)	4	3	1	2
(c)	1	2	3	4
(d)	2	3	4	1

232. **List-I**
(A) Arithmetic mean
(B) Geometric mean
(C) Harmonic mean
(D) Median

List-II
1. $\frac{\Sigma f(n)}{n}$ 2. $\sqrt[n]{x_1, x_2, x_3, \ldots}$
3. $\frac{n}{\Sigma(1/n)}$ 4. $\frac{(n+1)}{2}$ th item

Codes:	A	B	C	D
(a)	3	4	1	2
(b)	1	2	3	4
(c)	4	3	1	2
(d)	2	3	4	1

233. **List-I (Statistical Tests)**

(A) The 't' test
(B) Chi-square
(C) ANOVA
(D) Factor analysis

List-II (Descriptions)

1. Similarities of difference between two or more frequency distribution
2. Comparison between means
3. Uses principal component analysis
4. Uses F statistic

Codes:	A	B	C	D
(a)	1	3	2	4
(b)	3	2	4	1
(c)	2	1	4	3
(d)	4	3	1	2

234. **List-I (Concepts in Research)** **List-II (Types of Research or Procedures)**

List-I	List-II
(A) Text	1. Quota Sampling
(B) Unit of Analysis	2. Survey Research
(C) Matrix	3. Historical Research
(D) Schedule	4. Content Analysis

Codes:	A	B	C	D
(a)	3	4	2	1
(b)	4	1	3	2
(c)	1	2	4	3
(d)	2	3	1	4

235. **List-I (Concepts in Research)** **List-II (When applied)**

List-I	List-II
(A) Pilot-test	1. After programme is completed
(B) Pre-test	2. Programme when in making
(C) Post-test	3. Schedule/ Questionnaire (Instruments)
(D) Process-test	4. Programme in a restricted context

Codes:	A	B	C	D
(a)	3	4	1	2
(b)	4	2	3	1
(c)	4	3	1	2
(d)	3	1	4	2

236. **List-I** **List-II**

List-I	List-II
(A) T test	1. Prediction
(B) X^2 test	2. Comparison of means of two groups
(C) Correlation	3. Observed Vs. expected frequencies
(D) Multiple regression	4. Covariance

Codes:	A	B	C	D
(a)	3	2	1	4
(b)	2	3	4	1
(c)	1	4	3	2
(d)	4	1	2	3

Directions: Questions 237 to 245 consist of two statements, one labelled as 'Assertion' (A) and the other labelled as 'Reason' (R). You are to examine these two statements carefully and decide if the Assertion (A) and the Reason (R) are individually true and if so, whether the Reason is a correct explanation of the Assertion. Select your answers to these questions using the codes given below.

(a) Both (A) and (R) are true and (R) is the correct explanation of (A).
(b) Both (A) and (R) are true but (R) is not the correct explanation of (A).
(c) (A) is true but (R) is false.
(d) (A) is false but (R) is true.

237. **Assertion (A):** Pasquale lays stress on the ethical political facet of the problem.

Reason (R): He states that in future, the demand for related research would increase.

238. **Assertion (A):** Motivation research is a part of consumer research.

Reason (R): Motivation research tries to find out the motives of purchase of the prospective customers.

239. **Assertion (A):** Content of Indian media is determined by the needs of the audiences.

Reason (R): Media research helps to determine the information needs of the people.

240. **Assertion (A):** Random sample is representative of the universe.

Reason (R): Random sample has the units of the universe who are opinion leaders.

241. **Assertion (A):** Normally the relationship between an independent variable and a dependent variable is considered linear.

Reason (R): The dependent variable impacts the independent variable to produce infinite results.

242. **Assertion (A):** Research in media history in India is imprecise and shabby.

Reason (R): Because Indians depend too much on oral history.

243. **Assertion (A):** Designing an effective survey study involve a series of challenging decisions. The sample of people surveyed influences the kind of responses one obtains and generalization of those responses. The strategy used to reach survey respondents also influences both response rate and responses as well as the ways in which survey questions are worded and ordered.

Reason (R): Researchers adopting the survey method must establish clear goals and administer these techniques carefully if they are to generate valid data.

244. **Assertion (A):** Concurrent validity in research is closely related to predictive validity.

Reason (R): The measuring instrument is not checked against any present criterion in concurrent validity.

245. **Assertion (A):** SITE was a hardware success, a software failure.

Reason (R): Because the contents were produced without the inputs from social scientists.

ANSWERS

1. (b)	2. (a)	3. (d)	4. (c)	5. (d)	6. (c)
7. (d)	8. (b)	9. (c)	10. (a)	11. (a)	12. (b)
13. (c)	14. (c)	15. (c)	16. (d)	17. (c)	18. (b)
19. (c)	20. (d)	21. (d)	22. (d)	23. (c)	24. (d)
25. (b)	26. (b)	27. (a)	28. (d)	29. (b)	30. (d)
31. (b)	32. (a)	33. (b)	34. (a)	35. (a)	36. (b)
37. (a)	38. (d)	39. (d)	40. (d)	41. (b)	42. (c)
43. (c)	44. (c)	45. (b)	46. (a)	47. (a)	48. (b)

49. (d)	50. (c)	51. (a)	52. (b)	53. (d)	54. (d)
55. (d)	56. (a)	57. (a)	58. (a)	59. (d)	60. (d)
61. (a)	62. (b)	63. (a)	64. (d)	65. (b)	66. (b)
67. (d)	68. (c)	69. (a)	70. (d)	71. (d)	72. (b)
73. (d)	74. (b)	75. (c)	76. (a)	77. (a)	78. (d)
79. (c)	80. (b)	81. (c)	82. (a)	83. (a)	84. (b)
85. (d)	86. (c)	87. (d)	88. (a)	89. (c)	90. (d)
91. (b)	92. (a)	93. (d)	94. (a)	95. (d)	96. (b)
97. (d)	98. (b)	99. (b)	100. (c)	101. (b)	102. (a)
103. (c)	104. (b)	105. (a)	106. (b)	107. (a)	108. (c)
109. (d)	110. (c)	111. (d)	112. (a)	113. (b)	114. (a)
115. (d)	116. (a)	117. (c)	118. (a)	119. (b)	120. (a)
121. (a)	122. (b)	123. (b)	124. (a)	125. (a)	126. (b)
127. (c)	128. (d)	129. (d)	130. (b)	131. (a)	132. (a)
133. (a)	134. (d)	135. (d)	136. (a)	137. (d)	138. (c)
139. (b)	140. (d)	141. (d)	142. (c)	143. (c)	144. (b)
145. (c)	146. (b)	147. (c)	148. (c)	149. (a)	150. (d)
151. (d)	152. (c)	153. (b)	154. (d)	155. (b)	156. (c)
157. (d)	158. (a)	159. (d)	160. (d)	161. (a)	162. (b)
163. (a)	164. (a)	165. (a)	166. (c)	167. (c)	168. (a)
169. (c)	170. (d)	171. (a)	172. (c)	173. (a)	174. (b)
175. (a)	176. (b)	177. (c)	178. (b)	179. (c)	180. (c)
181. (b)	182. (a)	183. (a)	184. (c)	185. (c)	186. (a)
187. (d)	188. (d)	189. (c)	190. (d)	191. (c)	192. (c)
193. (d)	194. (d)	195. (c)	196. (c)	197. (a)	198. (b)
199. (a)	200. (a)	201. (c)	202. (b)	203. (b)	204. (b)
205. (a)	206. (c)	207. (a)	208. (c)	209. (c)	210. (a)
211. (d)	212. (b)	213. (d)	214. (c)	215. (d)	216. (d)
217. (c)	218. (d)	219. (c)	220. (b)	221. (b)	222. (c)
223. (a)	224. (a)	225. (a)	226. (b)	227. (b)	228. (a)
229. (d)	230. (c)	231. (b)	232. (b)	233. (a)	234. (a)
235. (c)	236. (b)	237. (a)	238. (a)	239. (b)	240. (c)
241. (c)	242. (b)	243. (b)	244. (c)	245. (d)	

7

International Communication

1. The Advertising Agencies Association of India was founded in
   (a) 1950 (b) 1954
   (c) 1945 (d) 1940
2. The mass media are educators and propagandists. Which theory of the Press supports this ideology?
   (a) Authoritarianism
   (b) Libertarian
   (c) Social Responsibility
   (d) Communist
3. What was founded by a group of newspapers in 1961 to provide competition to PTI?
   (a) DPA (b) NANA
   (c) UNI (d) AFP
4. At present, the French Press is
   (a) highly centralised
   (b) highly decentralised
   (c) partially controlled by the state
   (d) None of the above.
5. What was established in India in the later half of 19th century?
   (a) PTI (b) UNI
   (c) Anglo Indian Press (d) None of these
6. The 1948, the United Nations Conference on Freedom of Information was held in
   (a) Davos (b) Geneva
   (c) New York (d) Paris
7. Which of the following is a purely Indian Ad Agency?
   (a) Thomson (b) O and M
   (c) Lintas (d) Mudra
8. The World Association of Press Councils (WAPC) was founded by the Press Councils of
   (a) Australia and New Zealand
   (b) Nepal and Sri Lanka
   (c) Turkey and United Kingdom
   (d) All of the above
9. Who founded the Indian Languages Newspaper Association?
   (a) Bal Gangadhar Tilak
   (b) Mahatma Gandhi
   (c) Mamman Mother
   (d) Amrit Lal Seth
10. The tabloid, *The Sun*, is published from
    (a) Paris (b) Rome
    (c) Los Angeles (d) London
11. Press Trust of India was founded in
    (a) 1949 (b) 1952
    (c) 1942 (d) 1947
12. In which year did BBC become a public corporations?
    (a) 1925 (b) 1926
    (c) 1929 (d) 1933
13. When was Samachar created?
    (a) In 1975 (b) In 1977
    (c) In 1979 (d) In 1981
14. Largest News Agency of India is
    (a) PTI (b) IANS
    (c) UNI (d) AFP

15. Which of the following was not a focus area of the WAPC?
    (a) Development of an international code of ethics.
    (b) The right to privacy.
    (c) Development of wire services in NAM nations.
    (d) Legal eastrictions on the Press.

16. Urdu News Service was started for the first time in India by
    (a) UNI (b) ANI
    (c) PTI (d) IRNA

17. During the nineteenth century, most of the newspapers of Britain were owned by
    (a) foreign firms of the West but not belonging to Britain.
    (b) the government.
    (c) families.
    (d) private shareholders.

18. The oldest feature Agency in India is
    (a) Star Feature Agency
    (b) Indian News and Feature Alliance
    (c) National Press Agency
    (d) Indian Press Agency

19. The international news agencies have been accused of
    (a) spreading information at a pace that is much faster than the pace at which it can be assimilated.
    (b) homogenising the culture of the nation in which they operate.
    (c) supporting the development issues of the LDCs.
    (d) spreading altered facts about the targeted developing nations.

20. In operant conditioning procedure, the role of reinforcement is
    (a) negligible.
    (b) not necessary.
    (c) strikingly significant.
    (d) very insignificant.

21. How Joseph Pulitzer changed the Press scenario of the USA?
    (a) He published *New York Sun* and sold it at the rate of one penny a paper; that was done in 1833.
    (b) He bought *New York Journal* and used gloss to sell his publication; that was done in the year 1895.
    (c) He gave gossip, sensational news, scandulous news and features of human interest in *New York World*; this was done beginning from the year 1883.
    (d) None of the above.

22. Skinner (1935) distinguished two classes of responses. These are
    (a) Permanent and Temporary
    (b) Formal and Informal
    (c) Positive and Negative
    (d) Respondents and Operants

23. No newspaper appeared in the British Colonies of America until?
    (a) 1704 (b) 1712
    (c) 1727 (d) 1733

24. What is the full form of CANA?
    (a) Caribbean News Agency
    (b) Cambodian News Alliance
    (c) Canadian News Agency
    (d) None of the above.

25. The first daily newspaper was started by
    (a) Benjamin Browne
    (b) Benjamin Jowne
    (c) Benjamin Jownfield
    (d) Benjamin Crown

26. The AFP belongs to which country?
    (a) France (b) Mexico
    (c) The Netherlands (d) Belgium

27. The Covenant of Human Rights was an International Bill of Rights dealing with all human rights, including the right of

(a) making an application in the International Court of Justice for getting a grievance addressed (in the context of freedom of information).
(b) freedom of fair hearing.
(c) freedom of information.
(d) None of the above.

28. Bryce edited
(a) *Asiatic Minority* (b) *Asian Chronicle*
(c) *Asiatic Mirror* (d) *Asia Minor*

29. When we discuss the issue of freedom of the Press, we generally refer to the freedom of the Press from the
(a) control of various governments under which the Press institutions of countries operate.
(b) control of the non-profit organisations that have become powerful due to the rising concern for society.
(c) rules delineated in the UN Conferences that are defined from time to time.
(d) None of the above.

30. According to Skinnerian Operant Conditioning Theory, a negative reinforcement is
(a) a withdrawing or removal of a positive reinforcer.
(b) an instinctive drift.
(c) nothing but punishment.
(d) a biofeedback.

31. Akahata, a newspaper of Japan, has a tilt towards the
(a) authoritarian system that supports the rule of communist parties.
(b) free market system.
(c) capitalist ideology.
(d) communist ideology.

32. In the early 18th century, who presented all the preconditions for the rapid growth of a newspaper growth?
(a) English colonies
(b) Indian colonies
(c) American colonies
(d) African colonies

33. What was the view of the NAM about news?
(a) It is a developmental process
(b) It is not needed in the South
(c) It is distorted by the South
(d) It is essentially a stooge of the North.

34. When a new era in American Journalism was begun?
(a) Dec. 10, 1890 (b) Sep. 3, 1833
(c) Sep. 5, 1950 (d) None of these

35. How was the report of the Sean MacBride Commission received by its critics ?
(a) It had some rational ideas, but it was an opinion of the members of commission and not a consensus.
(b) It was effective and implemented too.
(c) It was received well by the Press of the West.
(d) It failed miserably.

36. Aversion is one of the conditioning procedures used in
(a) Psychoanalytic Therapy
(b) Non-directive Therapy
(c) Chemotherapy
(d) Behaviour Therapy

37. The Vividh Bharati service of the AIR was started in
(a) December 1950 (b) June 1957
(c) October 1957 (d) April 1958

38. The current broadcasting policy is based on
(a) The AIR code of 1968
(b) The AIR code of 1970
(c) The AIR code of 1969
(d) None of the above

39. Media amalgamations in Australia and other advanced nations have led to the creation of a few rich media empires. What should be the Indian stand on this?
(a) Amalgamations could be the necessity of the new era, but new empires must take care of the needs of the masses, especially the burning issue of cultural homogenisation.
(b) The governments should not allow large firms to take over small firms in the parlance of media operations in their countries, especially in India.
(c) Let the media firms unite to form large business empires.
(d) This is a bad trend. Powerful rich people would exploit the masses through the media.

40. The world communication year (1983) was sponsored by
(a) UNESCO (b) UNICEF
(c) European Union (d) United Nations

41. The Freedom of Information Centre was set up in 1958 in
(a) San Francisco, California
(b) Austin, Texas
(c) Missouri, Columbia
(d) Santiago, Chile

42. The continuous reinforcement schedule is generally used
(a) in the middle period of training.
(b) in both last and first part of training.
(c) in the last part of training.
(d) in early stages of training.

43. Why did Soviet Union oppose the Draft Convention on Freedom of Information?
(a) She feared that the content of the Draft might be altered.
(b) She wanted the West to follow these norms first.
(c) She did not positively set forth such obligations.
(d) None of the above.

44. In real life, reinforcement of every response (CRF) is
(a) not necessary.
(b) of the nature of an exception rather than the rule.
(c) impossible.
(d) necessary.

45. Who is better known as "Baghdad Pete"?
(a) Christiane Amanpour
(b) Peter Arnett
(c) Robert Hutchins
(d) Daniel Pearl

46. Respondents are elicited and operants are not elicited but they are
(a) Permanent Responses
(b) Temporary Responses
(c) Emitted Spontaneously
(d) Emitted Voluntarily

47. Springer Press was formed in
(a) Germany (b) Austria
(c) Canada (d) Italy

48. The Third International Conference of the WAPC was organised in
(a) March 1995 (b) March 1992
(c) December 1991 (d) October 1992

49. The Freedom of Information Act (2003) does not allow the public to
(a) get information as a facsimile copy of a document.
(b) get information on microfiches.
(c) get information from the Public Information Officer.
(d) get information regarding the records of deliberations of the council of ministers.

50. Current positive reinforcement requires the individual to imagine performing a

particular task or behaviour followed by a

(a) Neutral Consequence
(b) Negative Consequence
(c) Zero Consequence
(d) Positive Consequence

51. Which news agency was providing news to the Indian newspapers during the pre-Independence era?
(a) Reuters (b) The IRNA
(c) The AFP (d) The CANA

52. As a rule, variable ratio schedule (VR) arrangements sustain
(a) zero responding.
(b) 90% of responding.
(c) low rates of responding.
(d) high rates of responding.

53. Neue Zurcher Zeitung is a daily newspaper of
(a) Switzerland (b) Austria
(c) Belgium (d) Germany

54. Under conditions of variable ratio schedule, the only sensible way to obtain more reinforcements is through emitting
(a) 90% responses.
(b) 50% responses.
(c) greater number of responses.
(d) less number of responses.

55. What is the concept of Mass Press?
(a) Publish newspapers to keep the newspaper cost at the lowest ebb.
(b) Publish newspapers to attract large audiences by keeping the newspaper cost low but giving wholesome entertainment.
(c) Publish newspapers to get large reading audiences.
(d) None of the above.

56. What is the total number of bulletins put out by the News Service Division of AIR from the various radio stations every day?
(a) 284 (b) 200
(c) 65 (d) 131

57. Who set up the Free Press of India (FPI)?
(a) Bal Gangadhar Tilak; 1932
(b) B.V. Karanth; 1948
(c) James Augustus Hickey; 1948
(d) S. Sadanand; 1930s

58. Who is the head of the News Services Division?
(a) Director General
(b) Managing Director
(c) Editor-in-charge
(d) Directional officer

59. The NANAP was the outcome of the deliberations among the
(a) ASEAN nations
(b) NAM nations
(c) NATO nations
(d) SAARC nations

60. In which schedule of reinforcement, the delay intervals vary as per a previously decided plan?
(a) Fixed Interval Schedule
(b) Variable Interval Schedule
(c) Fixed Ratio Schedule
(d) Variable Ratio Schedule

61. When was the First Press Regulation Act (having an element of censorship) passed in India?
(a) In 1790 (b) In 1792
(c) In 1795 (d) In 1799

62. Which news script is the combination of sound bite and stand up?
(a) Voice over (b) Supers
(c) Package (d) Talking Heads

63. What was the name of the report of the MacBride Commission?

(a) *Many Voices, One Mode*
(b) *International Communication Report*
(c) *The NWICIO*
(d) *Many Voices, One World*

64. The idea of creating a news agency pool for the member nations of the NAM came up during the
(a) NAM Summit in 1961 at Belgrade.
(b) NAM Summit in 1973 at Algiers.
(c) NAM Summit in 1983 at New Delhi.
(d) NAM Summit in 1992 at Jakarta.

65. The expression "Contingencies of reinforcement" occurs frequently in
(a) Trial and Error Learning Literature
(b) Latent Learning Literature
(c) Operant Conditioning Literature
(d) Classical Conditioning Literature

66. How many Articles of the Convention of Freedom of Information were adopted by the Third Committee of the General Assembly?
(a) Three (b) Four
(c) Five (d) Six

67. Who illucidates the contiguity theory of reinforcement in the most pronounced and consistent manner?
(a) J.B. Watson (b) McDougall
(c) Guthrie (d) C. Hull

68. The journalist community, through various institutions and conventions, strived to get the right to
(a) print without reprisal or duress.
(b) distribute information without any interference of the government.
(c) get information.
(d) All of the above.

69. In comparison with drive-reduction or need-reduction interpretation, stimulus intensity reduction theory has an added advantage in that
(a) it has some mathematical derivations which are conducive for learning theorists.
(b) all learning theories can be explained through this.
(c) it offers a unified account of primary and learned drives as also of primary and conditioned reinforcement.
(d) it is very precise and placed importance on Trial and Error Learning.

70. The Press of Hungary
(a) has become free and is aligning itself with the NWIO.
(b) is still undemocratic.
(c) is being controlled by the state.
(d) None of the above.

71. Who preferred to call Classical Conditioning" by the name of "Sign Learning"?
(a) Mowrer (b) L.P. Pavlov
(c) J.B. Watson (d) Miller

72. Which of the following is not one of McNelly's Four Positions that explain the developmental role of mass communication?
(a) The Pragmatic Position
(b) The Freedom of Information Position
(c) The Null Position
(d) The Cautious Position.

73. Which type of learning tells us what to do with the world and applies to what is commonly called habit formation?
(a) Trial and Error Learning
(b) Classical Conditioning
(c) Insightful Learning
(d) Instrumental Learning

74. The world's first Press Council was set up by
(a) the USA in 1920
(b) Sweden in 1916

(c) India in 1956
(d) the UK in 1931

75. Who propounded the expectancy theory of learning?
(a) C. Hull (b) I.P. Pavlov
(c) Guthrie (d) Tolman

76. The COMSAT was established by the US Congress in the year
(a) 1973 (b) 1971
(c) 1968 (d) 1963

77. Who said that any act is a movement but not vice versa?
(a) W. Kohler (b) E.L. Thorndike
(c) J.B. Watson (d) Guthrie

78. The underdeveloped nations of the world opposed the Convention on International Transmission of News because
(a) they opined that the activities of the correspondents of developed nations might harm their prestige.
(b) they feared that their correspondents might not get news from the West.
(c) they feared that there might be an information boom in their countries.
(d) All of the above.

79. Guthrie believed that conditioning should take place
(a) after a single trial.
(b) after ten trials.
(c) after two trials.
(d) after three trials.

80. In the parlance of the philosophy of the libertarians, what is negative freedom?
(a) The freedom to remain neutral to the event covered.
(b) The freedom to disseminate news or information at a global level.
(c) The freedom to act autonomously.
(d) The freedom to achieve some good.

81. According to Guthrie, forgetting is not a matter of decay of old impressions and associations but
(a) a result of generalizations of stimuli.
(b) a result of discrimination.
(c) a result of inhibition of old connections by new ones.
(d) a result of disinhibitions of old connections.

82. Should the government become a publisher?
(a) Yes! Only if the private Press of a country is irresponsible and unfair towards the masses.
(b) Yes! It must keep the flow of Press information under its control.
(c) No! In a democratic system, the free market forces should work and not the state (to disseminate news and views).
(d) None of the above.

83. The great learning theorist, Clark Hull was influenced by the moderate wing of
(a) Behaviouristic Orientation
(b) Psychoanalytic Literature
(c) Logical Positivism and by conventionalism
(d) Gestalt Psychology

84. The second oldest Press Council was set up in
(a) South Africa (b) the USA
(c) Switzerland (d) West Germany

85. Who defined "Need" as a state of the organism in which a deviation of the organism from the optimum of biological conditions necessary for survival takes place?
(a) E.L. Thorndike (b) I.P. Pavlov
(c) Clark H. Hull (d) McDougall

86. What is the basic tenet of the Null Position of John T. McNelly?

(a) Mass communication takes place when information flows from the mass media to the opinion leaders and from them, to the general public.
(b) Mass communication effects national development.
(c) Mass communication helps in bringing stability in the developing nations.
(d) Mass communication has little or no role in national development.

87. Which of the following is not one of Mcneily's Four Positions that explain the developmental role of mass communication?
(a) The Pragmatic Position
(b) The Freedom of Information Position
(c) The Cautious Position
(d) The Null Position

88. The AFP was carved out of the
(a) The CANA
(b) The NANAP
(c) Havas news agency
(d) Associated Press

89. In continuous reinforcement schedule (CRF), every appropriate response
(a) is sometimes reinforced.
(b) is an instinctive drift.
(c) is reinforced.
(d) is not reinforced.

90. When did the Chinese government start reducing the number of privately owned newspapers in the country?
(a) In 1950 (b) In 1951
(c) In 1959 (d) In 1960

91. Who defined stimulus (S) in terms of physical energy such as mechanical pressure, sound, light, etc.?
(a) W. Kohler (b) E.L. Thorndike
(c) Clark Hull (d) E.C. Tolman

92. The process of economic harassment of the Press in Romania was started by
(a) the Soviet Armistice Commission
(b) the officials of Komsomol
(c) Nicolai Ceausescu
(d) None of the above.

93. In which schedule of reinforcement, appropriate movements are reinforced after varying number of responses?
(a) Variable Ratio Schedule
(b) Variable Interval Schedule
(c) Fixed Ratio Schedule
(d) Fixed Interval Schedule

94. The act passed to overcome certain difficulties in respect of fixation of the rate of wages is
(a) Newspaper Act, 1908
(b) Press Act, 1951
(c) Newspaper Act, 1956
(d) Working Journalists Act, 1958

95. The molar approach deals with the organism as a whole, the molecular approach
(a) has nothing to do with the organism.
(b) deals with the detailed, fine and exact elements of action of the nervous system.
(c) deals with responses.
(d) deals with parts.

96. According to Section 2 of the Contempt of Court Act, 1971, how many kinds of contempt are there?
(a) One (b) Two
(c) Three (d) Four

97. The hypothetico-deductive system in geometry was developed by
(a) C. Hull (b) E.C. Tolman
(c) Pieri (d) I.P. Pavlov

98. Who stated that democracy extends the sphere of individual freedom and socialism restricts it?
(a) Alexis de Tocqueville
(b) Sean MacBride

(c) Ralph D. Barney
(d) Elihu Katz

99. Whenever behaviour is correlated to specific eliciting stimuli, it is
(a) Stimulant Behaviour
(b) Static Behaviour
(c) Respondent Behaviour
(d) Operant Behaviour

100. Who authenticates a declaration filed by a publisher?
(a) Press Council of India
(b) I&B Minister
(c) Press Registrar
(d) Magistrate

101. Whenever behaviour is not correlated to any specific eliciting stimuli, it is
(a) Static Behaviour
(b) Modified Behaviour
(c) Respondent Behaviour
(d) Operant Behaviour

102. The Purpose of the Official Secrets Act, 1923 is to
(a) maintain the security of the state against leakage of secret documents.
(b) help journalists to keep secrets.
(c) help journalists to unearth secrets.
(d) Both (a) and (b).

103. A very useful principle of learning is that a new response is strengthened by
(a) Biofeedback
(b) Discriminative Stimulus
(c) Punishment
(d) Reinforcement

104. Spying on Indian defence-related matter is punishable by
(a) fine up to 14000 rupees
(b) life imprisonment
(c) jail term up to 14 years
(d) death sentence

105. According to Skinnerian theory, the "S" type of conditioning applies to
(a) Operant Behaviour
(b) Respondent Behaviour
(c) Modified Behaviour
(d) Stimulant Behaviour

106. *Deccan Herald* is a regional newspaper published from
(a) Hyderabad (b) Bangalore
(c) Mumbai (d) Kerala

107. The sign-gestalt expectation represents a combination of
(a) Perception and Motivation
(b) Intelligence and Learning
(c) Perception and Learning
(d) Intelligence and Perception

108. The largest number of English newspapers are published from
(a) Delhi (b) Hyderabad
(c) Chennai (d) Mumbai

109. Who stated that appetites and aversions are "states of agitation"?
(a) W. Kohler (b) Clark Hull
(c) E.L. Thorndike (d) E.C. Tolman

110. Which is the first Marathi daily to be published from Bombay after Independence?
(a) *Bombay Durpan*
(b) *Maharashtra Times*
(c) *Lokmat*
(d) *Loksatta*

111. Who said that the ultimate goal of aversion is the state of physiological quiescence to be reached when the disturbing stimulus ceases to act upon the organism?
(a) E.C. Tolman (b) Clark Hull
(c) E.L. Thorndike (d) W. Kohler

112. What is the total number of bulletins put out by the News Service Division of AIR

from the various radio stations every day?

(a) 284 (b) 200
(c) 165 (d) 131

113. According to E.C. Tolman, there are two aversions: fright and pugnacity. Fright is avoidance of injury and pugnacity is avoidance of

(a) Motivation (b) Interference
(c) Perception (d) Affiliation

114. In which news story does the news-caster begins and then introduces the reporter who speaks from the location?

(a) Package (b) Voice Over
(c) Stand-up (d) Sound Bite

115. "Equivalence Belief is a connection between a positively cathected type of disturbance object and a type of what may be called

(a) a motivating object.
(b) a goal-oriented object.
(c) an interfering object.
(d) a subdisturbance object.

116. Who is the head of the News Services Division of All India Radio?

(a) Directional officer
(b) Editor-in-charge
(c) Managing Director
(d) Director General

117. Who revealed that "Field expectancy" takes place when one organism is repeatedly and successfully presented with a certain environmental set-up?

(a) I.P. Pavlov (b) E.L. Thorndike
(c) C.L. Hull (d) E.C. Tolman

118. Who selects the 'leads' and the 'breaks' for a news bulletin?

(a) News Editor
(b) Director-General
(c) Joint Directors
(d) Additional Director General

119. Dollard and Miller related Thorndike's spread of effect to the

(a) principle of preparedness.
(b) gradient of reinforcement.
(c) biological constraints.
(d) None of the above.

120. Which is not the rule of television?

(a) Brevity
(b) Passive Voice
(c) Clarity
(d) None of the above.

121. Miller and Dollard are more concerned with

(a) physiological and social factors in learning.
(b) personal factors in learning.
(c) biological factor in learning.
(d) social factor in learning.

122. The Indian state with the largest share of circulation of English newspapers is

(a) Bihar
(b) Madhya Pradesh
(c) Uttar Pradesh
(d) Maharashtra

123. Mowrer's sign learning comes close to Guthrie's contiguity and his 'solution learning' corresponds to

(a) Skinner's instrumental learning.
(b) Thorndike's trial and error learning.
(c) Pavlov's classical conditioning.
(d) Kohler's insightful learning.

124. Which news script is the combination of sound bite and stand up?

(a) Talking Heads (b) Supers
(c) Package (d) Voice Over

125. Mowrer's two-factor theory takes into consideration the fact that

(a) the organism learns to make a response to a specific stimulus
(b) learning is purposive and goal-oriented

(c) some conditioning do not require reward and some do
(d) every conditioning requires reinforcement

126. Names or bits of information superimposed on the TV screen is called
(a) Sound bite (b) Voice Over
(c) Stand-up (d) Supers

127. When learning in one situation influences learning in another situation, there is evidence of
(a) Premise of Equipotentiality
(b) Transfer of Training
(c) Avoidance Learning
(d) Learned Helplessness

128. In which news script is the news-caster followed by the expert interviewed on the subject?
(a) Package (b) Sound bite
(c) Voice over (d) Stand-up

129. If learning in situation "A" may favourably influence learning in situation "B", then we have
(a) Zero Transfer
(b) Bilateral Transfer
(c) Positive Transfer
(d) Neutral Transfer

130. The TV channel National Geographic, is owned by
(a) Star TV Group
(b) BBC
(c) Tea Touner Group
(d) NDTV India

131. If learning in situation "A" has a detrimental effect on learning in situation "B", then we have
(a) Neutral Transfer (b) Negative transfer
(c) Positive Transfer (d) Zero Transfer

132. What is meant by MS?
(a) Mid Script (b) Medium Size
(c) Mid Shot (d) Mid Slot

133. Mediation occurs when one member of an associated pair is linked to the other by means of
(a) generalization.
(b) secondary reinforcement.
(c) a reinforcement.
(d) an intervening element.

134. Which is the element that make news?
(a) Timeliness
(b) Proximity
(c) Human Interest
(d) All of the above

135. Zero transfer is otherwise known as
(a) Negative Transfer
(b) Bilateral Transfer
(c) Neutral Transfer
(d) Positive Transfer

136. In which year did the U.S. Congress passe a law requiring most passengerships to have radio equipment and operators?
(a) 1905 (b) 1910
(c) 1912 (d) None of these

137. Negative transfer of training is otherwise known as
(a) Zero Transfer
(b) Bilateral Transfer
(c) Neutral Transfer
(d) Habit Interference

138. In which year United States began regular television broadcasting?
(a) 1930 (b) 1939
(c) 1941 (d) 1945

139. "If you do not like milk, you may not like all milk products like cheese butter, ghee and curd". This is due to
(a) Transfer of Training
(b) Generalization Gradient

(c) Avoidance Learning
(d) Biological Constraints

140. In which year German Radio started Programme in Indian languages?
(a) 1940 (b) 1941
(c) 1942 (d) 1943

141. Who told, "Although Classical Conditioning is a laboratory procedure, it is easy to find real world examples"?
(a) Kimble and Germazy (1980)
(b) McGeoch (1942)
(c) C.B. Osgood (1957)
(d) B.J. Underwood (1983)

142. Which of the following is correctly matched?
(a) AFP - department for making rules
(b) CANA - A newspaper in US
(c) ASIASAT-1 - A satellite
(d) Reuters - A satellite channel

143. According to Hull, a systematic behaviour or learning theory can be possible by happy amalgamation of the technique of conditioning and the
(a) Law of Frequency (b) Law of Recency
(c) Law of Effect (d) Law of Exercise

144. Freedom Information Act was passed in Britain in
(a) April 1997
(b) March 1998
(c) November 2000
(d) January 2003

145. The methods of verbal learning are important because
(a) they minimise the effect of punishment.
(b) punishment has no effect on learning.
(c) the use of standard methods for learning makes comparisons of results possible.
(d) rewards are not necessary here.

146. Which of the following is known as Auntie?
(a) SONY (b) BBC
(c) MTV (d) CVO

147. Positive transfer of training is possible with
(a) Similar tasks (b) Verbal tasks
(c) Dissimilar tasks (d) Motor tasks

148. New World Information and Communication Order (NWICO) which has been mentioned in ten clauses of information principles of professional ethics in journalism (UNESCO) lays stress on
(a) the need to set up news agencies like NANAP and CANA.
(b) respect for the people of underprivileged classes of West.
(c) the need for decolonisation and democratisation of information and communication.
(d) None of the above.

149. Punishment is effective only when it weakens
(a) Positive Response
(b) Negative Response
(c) Undesirable Response
(d) Desirable Response

150. 'Liberation Theory' is also called as
(a) Communist Media Theory
(b) Free Press Theory
(c) Authoritarian Theory
(d) Social Responsibility Theory

151. Which one of the following psychologists is not associated with the theories of learning?
(a) Thorndike (b) Guthrie
(c) C. Hull (d) Sullivan

152. Soviet Media Theory is another name for
(a) Communist Media Theory
(b) Democrat-Participant Media Theory
(c) Social Responsibility Theory
(d) Development Communication Theory

153. In which method, the entire list is once exposed to "S" and then he is asked to anticipate each item in the list before it is exposed on the memory drum?
(a) Relearning and Saving
(b) Anticipation Method
(c) Recall
(d) Recognition

154. The Non-aligned News Agencies Pool (NANAP) came into existence in
(a) 1962 (b) 1970
(c) 1976 (d) 1979

155. When did the Chinese government start reducing the number of privately owned newspapers in the country?
(a) In 1951 (b) In 1953
(c) In 1960 (d) In 1949

156. In which of the following languages NANAP news is not exchanged?
(a) Chinese (b) Arabic
(c) French (d) English

157. Learning to make new responses to identical or similar stimuli results in a
(a) Zero Transfer
(b) Neutral Transfer
(c) Negative Transfer
(d) Positive Transfer

158. Janet Cooke was awarded ______ for a story that was later found to be fabricated.
(a) Noble Prize
(b) Bharat Ratna
(c) Pulitzer Prize
(d) Gandhi Peace Prize

159. Both positive and negative transfers arelargely the result of
(a) coordination of responses in the first and the second task.
(b) both similarity and dissimilarity of responses in the first and the second task.
(c) similarity of responses in the first and the second task.
(d) dissimilarity of responses in the first and the second task.

160. Which one of the following is not among the ideal purposes of International broadcasting according to UNESCO?
(a) To present regional co-operation.
(b) To present the best culture and ideals of the broadcasting country.
(c) To promote international understanding.
(d) To present world news objectively.

161. The greater the similarity between the stimuli of the first task and the second task
(a) the minimum the extent of transfer.
(b) no transfer occurs.
(c) the less the extent of transfer.
(d) the greater the extent of transfer.

162. First Indian company to raise money in global market with a GDR issue is
(a) L&T (b) Reliance
(c) Infosys (d) ONGC

163. A high positive transfer results when stimuli are similar and responses are
(a) Not Identical (b) Identical
(c) Equipotential (d) Haphazard

164. Indian agencies are part of
(a) UNI (b) NANAP
(c) ANA (d) None of these

165. It is possible to maximize a positive transfer from a classroom situation to real life situation by making formal education more realistic or closely connected with
(a) Temporary Problems
(b) Easy Problems
(c) Real-life Problems
(d) Imaginary Problems

166. The first newspaper was printed on April 24, 1704. It was called
(a) *Boston Express*
(b) *Boston Newsletter*
(c) *Boston Times*
(d) *American Times*

167. In programmed learning, the importance is placed on
(a) Classical Conditioning
(b) Operant Conditioning
(c) Trial and error Learning
(d) Latent Learning

168. The editor and publisher of the Boston Newsletter was
(a) Wright Brothers
(b) Postmaster John Campbell
(c) Daniel P. Hutton
(d) Franklin Brothers

169. In our daily life, any kind of looking for things which occur without any reference to our behaviour may illustrate the application of
(a) Fixed Ratio
(b) Variable Interval Schedule
(c) Fixed interval Schedule
(d) Variable Ratio Schedule

170. In which year was the first news agency founded?
(a) 1833 (b) 1835
(c) 1840 (d) 1842

171. Who has first devised a machine for teaching in 1920?
(a) D.O. Hebb (b) H.F. Harlow
(c) M.R.F. Maier (d) S.L. Pressey

172. In which year was founded the United Press Association?
(a) 1907 (b) 1908
(c) 1909 (d) 1910

173. In the system of programmed learning, the learner becomes
(a) a neutral age in acquiring the acquisition.
(b) instrumental in acquiring the acquisition.
(c) an active agent in acquiring the acquisition.
(d) a passive agent in acquiring the acquisition.

174. In which year INS decided to merge with United Press International?
(a) 1960 (b) 1959
(c) 1958 (d) 1956

175. Programmed learning
(a) is not helpful in classroom situation.
(b) is not helpful for teachers.
(c) is not helpful for teaching.
(d) is not helpful in the socialization of the child.

176. Which news agency is a post war successor to the Agence Havas?
(a) Reuters
(b) Agence France-Presse
(c) Associated Press
(d) TASS

177. Lewin's field theory gives more importance to behaviour and motivation and less to
(a) Drive (b) Incentive
(c) Intelligence (d) Experience

178. According to Hullian Theory, under the pressure of needs and drives, the organism undertakes
(a) learning by hindsight.
(b) transfer of training.
(c) adaptive actions.
(d) learning by foresight.

179. In 1946, the World Service of _____ was created.
(a) Associated Press (b) AFP
(c) Reuters (d) UPI

180. Kurt Lewin regards the environment of the individual as his
(a) Instinctive Drift (b) Life-Space
(c) Foresight (d) Autoshaping

181. In which year was the Non-aligned News Agencies Pool formally launched?
(a) 1979 (b) 1978
(c) 1976 (d) 1975

182. Guthrie's theory of learning is known as the learning by
(a) Representation (b) Interpretation
(c) Response (d) Substitution

183. In which year did the IPDC commenced its work?
(a) 1982 (b) 1983
(c) 1984 (d) 1986

184. The new items which are added to the original list in recognition method are known as
(a) Distractors (b) Gradients
(c) Respondents (d) Stimulants

185. Most human habits are reinforced in a
(a) Partial Manner
(b) Particular Time Span
(c) Variable Fashion
(d) Constant Fashion

186. The Hutchins Report led to the
(a) Press subsidies
(b) Establishment of Press Council
(c) Anti-monopoly legislation
(d) All of the above

187. Who said that the event that is drive reducing is satisfying?
(a) E.L. Thorndike (b) Clark H. Hull
(c) E.C. Tolman (d) R.S. Woodworm

188. Which news agency was founded in U.S.A. in 1907?
(a) UPI (b) AFP
(c) AP (d) Reuters

189. Materials like food for hungry animals or water for thirsty animals are called
(a) Intermittent Reinforcers
(b) Fixed Reinforcers
(c) Secondary Reinforcers
(d) Primary Reinforcers

190. Which country is the largest film producer in the world?
(a) UK (b) China
(c) USA (d) India

191. When a thing acquires some characteristics of a reinfoconsistent association with rcer because of its consistent association with the primary reinforcement, we call it a/an
(a) Fixed Reinforcer
(b) Intermittent Reinforcer
(c) Secondary Reinforcer
(d) Primary Reinforcer

192. Which is the best example of group of the computers?
(a) Internet
(b) FoxPro
(c) DTP
(d) None of the above

193. In one experiment, the chimpanzees were taught to insert poker chips in a vending machine in order to obtain grapes. When this was done, they were made to pull, with all their strength, an iron bar attached to a similar machine to obtain poker chips. The chimpanzees learned it too, because they were allowed to cash those chips for grapes afterwards. Here the token chips had only a/an
(a) Special Reinforcing Value
(b) Secondary Reinforcing Value
(c) Primary Reinforcing Value
(d) Extra Reinforcing Value

194. AP (Associated Press) is the news agency of which country?

(a) Japan (b) Britain
(c) USA (d) France

195. Partial Reinforcement is often called
(a) Span of Reinforcement
(b) Reinforcement Schedule
(c) Intermittent Reinforcement
(d) Schedules of Reinforcement

196. In which year was the Universal Declaration of Human Rights approved by the UN?
(a) 1947 (b) 1948
(c) 1949 (d) 1957

197. Reinforcing a given response only for sometime on trials is known as
(a) Reinforcement Schedule
(b) No Reinforcement
(c) Partial Reinforcement
(d) Continuous Reinforcement

198. The Hutchins Commission on freedom of the press was established by
(a) Robert Hutchins
(b) Franklin Roosevelt
(c) Henry Luce
(d) None of the above

199. Most human habits are resistent to extinction because these are reinforced
(a) every now and then.
(b) in a variable fashion.
(c) in a constant fashion.
(d) All the times.

200. When and where was the first American newspaper printed?
(a) In Boston on April 24, 1704
(b) In Los Angeles on March 1, 1721
(c) In Chicago an April 20,1725
(d) In New York on March 15, 1730

201. Which type of learning experiments show how the behaviour of animals can be controlled or shaped in a desired direction by making a careful use of reinforcement?
(a) Latent Learning
(b) Sign Learning
(c) Classical Conditioning
(d) Operant Conditioning

202. A newspaper that come out in New York on Sept. 18, 1851 was called
(a) *English Daily Times*
(b) *The New York Daily Times*
(c) *American Daily Times*
(d) *USA Today*

203. In Operant Conditioning, the strength of an operant response is usually measured in terms of the frequency of lev ressing
(a) as a whole.
(b) in a day.
(c) per unit of time.
(d) in every five minutes.

204. When was the first international film festival (IFFI) held in India?
(a) 1972 (b) 1963
(c) 1960 (d) 1952

205. The method we use in memorising poetry is called
(a) Distributed Learning
(b) Serial Memorisation
(c) Syntactic Memorisation
(d) Paired-associate Learning

206. Since when is the IFFI held annually?
(a) 1975 (b) 1983
(c) 1992 (d) 1997

207. Shifting from righthand driving in (in U.S.A.) to a lefthand driving (in India) is an illustration of
(a) positive transfer of training.
(b) neutral transfer of training.
(c) both neutral and positive transfer of training.
(d) negative transfer of training.

208. The Broadcasting Bill to check foreign channels was introduced in Parliament in

(a) May 1997 (b) June 1997
(c) July 1998 (d) August 1998

209. The replacement of one conditioned response by the establishment of an incompatible response to the same conditioned stimulus is known as
(a) Forward Conditioning
(b) Highorder conditioning
(c) Backward Conditioning
(d) Counter Conditioning

210. What is NWICO?
(a) New World Information and Civilian Order.
(b) New World Information and Communication Order.
(c) North West Information and Communication Order.
(d) None of the above.

211. Experimental literature revealed that experiments on latent learning were done by
(a) Pavlov and Watson
(b) Kohler and Wertheimer
(c) Tolman and Honzik
(d) Gibson and Harlow

212. Digital Audio Broadcasting (DAB) arose out of European project called
(a) Eureka-Eureka (b) Eureka-147
(c) Forbes-147 (d) Eureka Forbes

213. Working with monkeys, Harlow (1949) propounded that the general transfer effect from one situation to another may be accounted for by the concept of
(a) Latent learning
(b) Plateau
(c) "Learning how to learn" or "Learning Sets"
(d) Sign learning

214. Where is the secretariat of ITU?
(a) Geneva (b) London
(c) Washington (d) Hamburg

215. The remarkable feats of blind people are often matters of
(a) Perceptual Learning
(b) Latent Learning
(c) Operant Conditioning
(d) Classical Conditioning

216. Which one of the following agencies allocate frequencies for international boardcasting
(a) Worldwide Communications Commission
(b) International Telecommunications Union
(c) Global Telecommunications Union
(d) United Nations Telecommunications Union.

217. What has been called avoidance conditioning involves a combination of the features of
(a) perceptual learning and classical conditioning.
(b) insightful learning and operant conditioning.
(c) classical and instrumental conditioning.
(d) operant and trial and error learning.

218. Which one of the following is a mismatch?
(a) Deutsche Presse Agentur–Germany
(b) Kyodo–Japan
(c) Xinhua–China
(d) Associated Press–UK

219. Identify the correct pair
(a) Many Voices, One World–MacBride Commission Report
(b) Good Times, Bad Times–Edward T. Hall
(c) Understanding Media–Harold Evans
(d) The Silent Language–Marshall McLuhan

220. Experiments on "Latent Learning" reveal that learning can occur

(a) without response.
(b) without stimulus.
(c) without reinforcement.
(d) with reinforcement.

221. The debate on the new international information order was initiated by
(a) UNESCO (b) ILO
(c) ASEAN (d) SAARC

222. When complete learning has taken place, the best way of responding to a situation becomes
(a) Haphazard (b) Unnecessary
(c) Temporary (d) Permanent

223. "ANN" stands for
(a) Association of National Newspapers
(b) Agency for Nonconventional News
(c) Asian Network of News
(d) Asian News Network

224. The first psychological research concerned with associative learning was conducted by E.L. Thorndike on
(a) Chimpanzees (b) Animals
(c) Cats (d) Human beings

225. In the United Kingdom, audience research for television is conducted by
(a) ITCA (b) BARB
(c) AG B Research (d) ABC

226. The theory of E.L. Thorndike reveals that the most characteristic form of learning in both lower animals and men is
(a) Insightful Learning
(b) Trial and Error Learning
(c) Instrumental Conditioning
(d) Classical Conditioning

227. The concept of telephone newspapers originated in
(a) Japan
(b) The United States
(c) Hungary
(d) France

228. A boy who is learning to ride a bicycle will have to discard many wrong movements until he learns how to ride it perfectly. The principle underlying this process of learning is called
(a) Classical Conditioning
(b) Instrumental Conditioning
(c) Trial and Error
(d) Insight

229. Among the following national dailies which is not published from the UK?
(a) Daily Express
(b) Daily Telegraph
(c) The Times
(d) Daily Chronicle

230. A principle in Thorndike's theory reveals that the strength of the bond decreases proportionately with the non-use of a particular bond or a connection over a period of time. What is the name of this principle?
(a) Law of Disuse
(b) Law of Frequency
(c) Law of Effect
(d) Law of Recency

231. Convergent media buying is related to
(a) Television (b) Internet
(c) Radio (d) Outdoor

232. "Negative Reinforcement" and "Punishment" are
(a) similar to some extent.
(b) similar depending on the situation.
(c) similar terms.
(d) dissimilar terms.

233. The International Telecommunication Union (ITU) has its headquarters at
(a) Berlin (b) Geneva
(c) Paris (d) New York

234. Negative reinforcement involves the termination of a pleasant situation while punishment involves causing an

unpleasant condition in an attempt to eliminate
(a) Undesirable Behaviour
(b) Any Stimulus
(c) Any Response
(d) Desirable Behaviour

235. The country that has the highest density of newspaper readership is
(a) Sweden
(b) Japan
(c) the United States of America
(d) Norway

236. If a child refuses to carry or touch dishes for the fear of breaking them and getting punished, then it is called
(a) Aversive Training
(b) Effective Reaction
(c) Escape Training
(d) Avoidance Conditioning

237. The establishment of the Hutchins Commission was prompted by
(a) James Reston
(b) Joseph Pulitzer
(c) Catherine Graham
(d) Henry Luce

238. The term SER is usually explained as
(a) Successive Approximation
(b) Retroactive Inhibition
(c) Habit Strength
(d) Effective Reaction

239. The first television channel to adopt the all-news radio format is
(a) BBC (b) CNN
(c) ABC (d) CBS

240. Imprinting is a special form of learning in which a specific stimulus-response connection is established at
(a) Critical periods (b) Adulthood
(c) Childhood (d) Early childhood

241. Which of the following sequence is the correct order of history of the publication of newspaper?
(a) *The Times* (Britain), *Le Figaro* (France), *The New York Sun* (US), *The Sydney Morning Herald* (Australia)
(b) *The Times* (Britain), *Le Figaro* (France), *The Sydney Morning Herald* (Australia), *The New York Sun* (US)
(c) *The Sydney Morning Herald* (Australia), *Le Figaro* (France), *The Times* (Britain), *The New York Sun* (US)
(d) *The New York Sun* (US), *The Times* (Britain), *Le Figaro* (France), *The Sydney Morning Herald* (Australia)

242. Global electronic media are collectively described as
(a) mediascape (b) media monopoly
(c) media culture (d) media iceberg

243. The first psychologist to term one type of rigid learning as imprinting was
(a) B.F. Skinner (b) G.A. Kimble
(c) Konrad Lorenz (d) Clark L. Hull

244. The technological process through which the same content can be distributed in several channels
(a) Informatization
(b) Superhighway
(c) Convergence
(d) Divergence

245. "A psychologist applied a technique which was found very much effective in case of the not-so-young children who used to wet their beds every night. These children were made to sleep on especially-designed cots which emitted mild shock as soon as they tried to wet the bed. This gradually led to the unlearning of this habit".
This technique is popularly known as

(a) Reward Expectancy
(b) Effective Reaction
(c) Successive Approximation
(d) Aversive Therapy

246. Find the correct sequence of news agencies that were started
(a) Reuters - IPS - AFP - AP
(b) IPS - AP - AFP - Reuters
(c) AP - Reuters - AFP - IPS
(d) AFP - AP - Reuters - IPS

247. Which procedure involves a rationale opposite to the one involved in systematic desensitization?
(a) Aversive Therapy
(b) Place Learning
(c) Flooding or Implosive Therapy
(d) Systematic Deconditioning

248. The campaign for a New World Information and Communication Order (NWICO) was the result of the movement carried out mainly by
(a) East European nations
(b) African countries
(c) Nordic countries
(d) Non-Aligned Nations

249. "Sometimes the patients who are phobic to rats or snakes are suddenly made to touch live snakes or rats (which are harmless) rather than asking them first imagine the objects of their phobias. This method includes on trial learning or unlearning." Which method is this?
(a) Flooding or Impulsive Therapy
(b) Imprinting
(c) Aversive Therapy
(d) Place Learning

250. The wire-based international news agencies were the first significant form of
(a) Continental media
(b) Regional media
(c) Global media
(d) Sub-regional media

251. Where is the permanent Secretariat of the SAARC?
(a) Kathmandu (b) New Delhi
(c) Islamabad (d) Colombo

252. The under-developed, newly independent countries forced to seek technological, training and other support from former Colonizers can be characterised as
(a) Dependency
(b) North-South relations
(c) South-South dependency
(d) Development

253. Sometimes mothers and teachers reward successively better pronunciation in their children's speech. This is an example of
(a) Language Acquisition
(b) Systematic Deconditioning
(c) Biofeedback
(d) Successive Approximation

254. Identify the correct chronological order of the news agencies.
(a) Havas – Reuters – Associated Press – United Press International.
(b) Reuters – United Press International – Havas – Associated Press.
(c) Associated Press – Havas – Reuters – United Press International.
(d) United Press International – Reuters – Associated Press – Havas.

Directions: Question 255 is of multiple statements type. Choose the correct answer from the codes given below the statements.

255. Which of the following is an element of the emerging online media grammar?
1. Hypertext 2. Websites
3. Typography
(a) 1 only (b) 2 only
(c) 1 and 2 (d) 2 and 3

Directions: Questions 256 to 261 are of matching type. Match List-I with List-II and select the correct answer using the codes given below the lists.

256.

List-I (News Agencies)	List-II (Headquarters)
(A) Kyodo	1. Paris
(B) DPA	2. Doha
(C) Al-Jazeera	3. Berlin
(D) AFP	4. Tokyo

Codes:	A	B	C	D
(a)	4	3	2	1
(b)	2	3	4	1
(c)	1	3	4	2
(d)	4	3	1	2

257.

List-I (Organisations)	List-II (Places)
(A) UNESCO	1. Singapore
(B) AMIC	2. Geneva
(C) ITU	3. Kuala Lumpur
(D) AIBD	4. Paris

Codes:	A	B	C	D
(a)	3	1	4	2
(b)	4	1	2	3
(c)	1	3	4	2
(d)	3	1	2	4

258.

List-I (TV Channels)	List-II (Headquarters)
(A) CNN	(1) Hongkong
(B) Al-jazira	(2) London
(C) STAR	(3) Atlanta
(D) BBC	(4) Doha

Codes:	A	B	C	D
(a)	1	2	3	4
(b)	4	3	2	1
(c)	3	4	1	2
(d)	3	4	2	1

259.

List I	List II
A. Indian Telegraph Act	1. 1933
B. Indian Wireless Act	2. 1957
C. Copyright Act	3. 1995

Codes:	A	B	C
(a)	1	2	3
(b)	1	3	2
(c)	3	1	2
(d)	2	1	3

260.

List-I (News agency)	List-II (Country)
(A) Kyoda	1. Indonesia
(B) DPA	2. Japan
(C) Xinhua	3. Germany
(D) Bernama	4. China

Codes:	A	B	C	D
(a)	4	2	1	3
(b)	1	3	2	4
(c)	3	1	2	4
(d)	2	3	4	1

261.

List-I (Countries)	List-II (Newspapers)
(A) France	1. Al-Ahram
(B) Pakistan	2. The Times
(C) Egypt	3. Le Monde
(D) England	4. The Dawn

Codes:	A	B	C	D
(a)	3	4	1	2
(b)	1	4	2	3
(c)	2	3	4	1
(d)	4	1	2	3

Directions: Questions 262 to 268 consist of two statements, one labelled as 'Assertion' (A) and the other labelled as 'Reason' (R). You are to examine these two statements carefully and decide if the Assertion (A) and the Reason (R) are individually true and if so, whether the

Reason is a correct explanation of the Assertion. Select your answer to these questions using the codes gives below:

(a) Both (A) and (R) are true and (R) is the correct explanation of (A).
(b) Both (A) and (R) are true but (R) is not the correct explanation of (A).
(c) (A) is true but (R) is false.
(d) (A) is false but (R) is true.

262. **Assertion (A):** The Asian societies are we oriented.

Reason (R): Asian societies are influenced by Western media.

263. **Assertion (A):** The liberal and pluralist norms of the society were threatened in a communist nation.

Reason (R): The media of the totalitarian system were altered to make them the tools for stifling democratic values.

264. **Assertion (A):** Convergence of technologies has reduced the digital divide.

Reason (R): Technologies are value loaded.

265. **Assertion (A):** Internet is a medium of confidential communication between members of a group.

Reason (R): On Internet any message can be accessed by anyone else.

266. **Assertion (A):** In the near future newspapers will disappear.

Reason (R): The rate of growth of television and Internet is very high.

267. **Assertion (A):** There is a rapidly extending global communication infrastructure, as well as a network of interconnected ownership and management of communication business. Under current conditions, the internationalization of politics and of trade and commerce supports and is stimulated by communication globalization.

Reason (R): The effect of such changes may not be experienced directly in respect of culture and have a weak effect on international political and economic relations.

268. **Assertion (A):** The "Law" of the suppression of radical potential, will act as a brake on innovation to protect the social or corporate status quo.

Reason (R): The institutionalization of all technologies has led to the suppression of any radical tendency and there is no particular reason to suppose that this will be different with the latest inventions.

ANSWERS

1. (c)	2. (a)	3. (c)	4. (b)	5. (c)	6. (b)
7. (d)	8. (d)	9. (d)	10. (d)	11. (d)	12. (b)
13. (a)	14. (a)	15. (c)	16. (a)	17. (c)	18. (b)
19. (d)	20. (c)	21. (c)	22. (d)	23. (a)	24. (a)
25. (b)	26. (a)	27. (c)	28. (c)	29. (a)	30. (a)
31. (d)	32. (c)	33. (a)	34. (a)	35. (a)	36. (d)
37. (c)	38. (d)	39. (a)	40. (d)	41. (c)	42. (d)
43. (c)	44. (b)	45. (b)	46. (c)	47. (a)	48. (d)

49. (d)	50. (d)	51. (a)	52. (d)	53. (a)	54. (c)
55. (b)	56. (a)	57. (d)	58. (a)	59. (b)	60. (b)
61. (d)	62. (c)	63. (d)	64. (b)	65. (a)	66. (c)
67. (c)	68. (d)	69. (c)	70. (a)	71. (a)	72. (b)
73. (d)	74. (b)	75. (d)	76. (d)	77. (d)	78. (a)
79. (a)	80. (c)	81. (c)	82. (a)	83. (c)	84. (c)
85. (c)	86. (d)	87. (b)	88. (c)	89. (c)	90. (b)
91. (c)	92. (a)	93. (a)	94. (d)	95. (b)	96. (b)
97. (c)	98. (a)	99. (c)	100. (d)	101. (d)	102. (a)
103. (d)	104. (c)	105. (b)	106. (b)	107. (a)	108. (a)
109. (d)	110. (d)	111. (a)	112. (a)	113. (b)	114. (c)
115. (d)	116. (d)	117. (d)	118. (a)	119. (b)	120. (b)
121. (d)	122. (d)	123. (a)	124. (c)	125. (c)	126. (d)
127. (b)	128. (b)	129. (c)	130. (a)	131. (b)	132. (c)
133. (d)	134. (d)	135. (c)	136. (b)	137. (d)	138. (c)
139. (a)	140. (a)	141. (a)	142. (c)	143. (c)	144. (c)
145. (c)	146. (b)	147. (a)	148. (c)	149. (c)	150. (a)
151. (d)	152. (a)	153. (b)	154. (c)	155. (b)	156. (a)
157. (c)	158. (c)	159. (c)	160. (a)	161. (d)	162. (b)
163. (b)	164. (b)	165. (c)	166. (b)	167. (b)	168. (b)
169. (b)	170. (b)	171. (d)	172. (a)	173. (c)	174. (c)
175. (d)	176. (b)	177. (d)	178. (c)	179. (a)	180. (b)
181. (c)	182. (d)	183. (a)	184. (a)	185. (c)	186. (d)
187. (b)	188. (a)	189. (d)	190. (d)	191. (c)	192. (d)
193. (b)	194. (c)	195. (c)	196. (b)	197. (c)	198. (c)
199. (b)	200. (a)	201. (d)	202. (b)	203. (c)	204. (d)
205. (b)	206. (a)	207. (d)	208. (a)	209. (d)	210. (b)
211. (c)	212. (b)	213. (c)	214. (a)	215. (a)	216. (b)
217. (c)	218. (d)	219. (c)	220. (c)	221. (a)	222. (d)
223. (d)	224. (b)	225. (b)	226. (b)	227. (d)	228. (c)
229. (d)	230. (a)	231. (b)	232. (d)	233. (b)	234. (a)

235. (b)	236. (d)	237. (d)	238. (d)	239. (d)	240. (a)
241. (b)	242. (c)	243. (c)	244. (c)	245. (d)	246. (d)
247. (c)	248. (d)	249. (a)	250. (c)	251. (a)	252. (a)
253. (d)	254. (a)	255. (a)	256. (a)	257. (b)	258. (c)
259. (c)	260. (d)	261. (a)	262. (c)	263. (a)	264. (b)
265. (c)	266. (d)	267. (c)	268. (a)		

8

Radio, TV and Video

1. The pitch of footpath was taken to the TV studio by Ron Popeil. Now, it has been taken to
   (a) Internet websites
   (b) home theatre systems
   (c) DVD players
   (d) cinema theatres
2. Currently, people meters have been installed in
   (a) all the major and minor cities of India.
   (b) twenty cities of India.
   (c) only four metropolitan cities of India.
   (d) None of these.
3. Which of the following organisations is using TV pitch to sell products and services of various kinds?
   (a) Lintas
   (b) Asian Sky Shop
   (c) Ogilvy and Mather
   (d) Mudra Videotec
4. The number of guests handled by a radio presenter should normally not exceed
   (a) One (b) Two
   (c) Three (d) Four
5. Why the CAS could not succeed in Mumbai and Delhi?
   (a) There was a confusion among the masses about which set-top box to choose—digital or analogue.
   (b) The cost of package plus the cost of the set-top box was too high for an ordinary TV viewer.
   (c) The government did not implement the CAS simultaneously in the urban areas of India.
   (d) The digital technology of the CAS was not avant-garde.
6. What is a sound bite?
   (a) It is a quotation used on radio or TV to express an idea.
   (b) It is a digital audio signal that identifies a TV or radio station.
   (c) It is the audio command given by the TV/radio producer to the TV newscaster.
   (d) It is the first line of a TV announcer when he faces the camera in a line programme.
7. Which of the following is not a standard RS-232C signal?
   (a) VDR (b) DSR
   (c) CTS (d) RTS
8. What was the famous byline of Ron Popeil during the course of a pitch?
   (a) Buy one and get another one free of cost.
   (b) Aha! Here I come, friends.
   (c) Hello friends, we will come back.
   (d) You can have a lot many things at low costs.
9. According to George Gerbner,
   (a) people are addicted to TV because they find it more convenient than cinema.

(b) TV is not able to blur the traditional distinctions of people's view of thier world.
(c) TV blends people's realities into the cultural mainstream.
(d) All of the above.

10. While covering a disaster event like earthquake, the TV cameraman should
(a) use the background to show the damage done due to the disaster, but he should include the TV journo upto his chest in the coverage.
(b) concentrate only on the scene of the damage, and he should exclude the TV journo from the picture.
(c) take the medium shot of the TV journo and exclude the background.
(d) None of the above.

11. In August 2009, the total number of people meters installed in India was (nearly)
(a) 2,100 (b) 3,900
(c) 6,000 (d) 4,000

12. The process of identifying the useless audio or video signal and cutting it form the tape is called
(a) Tape Splicing
(b) Video Editing
(c) Tape Deselection
(d) Chop off

13. If you have to record the interview in a windy area, you should use a
(a) microphone with mounting stand.
(b) microphone without a wind filter.
(c) microphone with a wind filter.
(d) None of the above.

14. If you want to make an engineering presentation that would include video clips, you should use
(a) MS-Excel
(b) MS-Powerpoint
(c) Adobe Photoshop
(d) Adobe Director

15. Who developed the world wide web?
(a) Tim-Berners-Lee; 1992
(b) Steve Paul Jobs; 1990
(c) Michael Dell; 1997
(d) Henry William Gates; 1995

16. Which of the following is not an application of CATV?
(a) Cellular telephone operations
(b) Internet connection
(c) VOD
(d) FTA channels

17. An advantage of PM6.5 over MS Word is that
(a) page make-up is possible in PM6.5 but not in MS-Word.
(b) pages of PM6.5 remain frozen and hence, the text and tables are not disturbed.
(c) editing can be done at a quicker pace in PM6.5 but not in MS-Word.
(d) All of the above.

18. A high speed communication equipment typically would not be needed for
(a) supporting communication between nodes in a LAN.
(b) transferring large volume of data.
(c) E-mail.
(d) All of the above.

19. CATV started its marathon run during the
(a) 1940s (in the USA)
(b) 1960s (in Europe)
(c) 1980s (in the USA)
(d) 1990s (in Asia)

20. Currently, CATV is facing tough competition (in Europe and the USA) from
(a) the DTH (b) the CAS
(c) dish antennae (d) All of these.

21. Long shot takes the view of a subject
    (a) from his head to his waist.
    (b) from his head to his knees.
    (c) from his head to his feet.
    (d) None of the above.

22. Which of the following is not an advantage of DTH?
    (a) Some TV channels can be blocked so that children may not have access to them.
    (b) The viewer can select as many channels as he wishes.
    (c) Signals are clear because they are digital.
    (d) The initial installation costs as well as operational costs are very low.

23. Which of the following files can be edited with the help of software?
    (a) Exe (b) MP3
    (c) Wave (d) All of the above

24. In MS-Front Page 2000, if you wish to see the HTML code of a programme created by you, the icon would that be clicked is
    (a) Preview Tab
    (b) Reports View Tab
    (c) Normal View Tab
    (d) None of the above.

25. What is the sleeper effect put forth by Rao?
    (a) The nature of the media effects the audiences.
    (b) The effects of a message vary according to the prestige attached to the source.
    (c) People tend to believe in the messages given by the state organs.
    (d) A person would usually believe the information that he gets from a source in which, he has faith.

26. Which of the following ISO level is more closely related to the physical communications facilities?
    (a) Data link (b) Network
    (c) Session (d) Application

27. What is the modus operandi of TAM?
    (a) It adds up the number of households connected to C&S systems and thus, calculates the reach of a TV station through this figure.
    (b) It measures the number of households connected to CATV.
    (c) It uses the measurement of the frequency of viewing of a channel in a panel home.
    (d) None of the above.

28. If the radio announcer puts a finger on her throat (in a horizontal fashion) she wants to tell the operator
    (a) cut my voice
    (b) go off air
    (c) start my microphone
    (d) None of the above.

29. By 2010, people meters were installed in
    (a) all the major and minor cities of India.
    (b) Mumbai and Chennai only.
    (c) Sixteen top cities of India.
    (d) None of the above.

30. Radio and TV are the examples of
    (a) human communication
    (b) group communication
    (c) mediated communication
    (d) interpersonal communication

31. Which of the following is not a field in the Ethernet message packet?
    (a) Pin-code (b) Address
    (c) Type (d) Data

32. Which one of the following is not a net hierarchy?

(a) Soc-social interactions
(b) Dat-digital data
(c) Sci-science
(d) News-news

33. An example of WAN is
(a) a network operating within a city.
(b) two PCs connected to a server.
(c) a network in a large organisation within a building.
(d) Internet.

34. Assuming that for a given network layer implementation, connection establishment overhead is 100 bytes and disconnection overhead is 28 bytes. What would be the minimum size of a packet the transport layer needs to keep up, if it wishes to implement a datagram service above the network layer and needs to keep its overhead to a maximum of 12.5%. (Ignore transport layer overhead.)
(a) 1152 bytes (b) 6024 bytes
(c) 512 bytes (d) 768 bytes

35. If you want to record the message of a person on the footpath (for radio), you should use a/an
(a) hyper-cardioid microphone.
(b) cardioid microphone.
(c) omni-directional microphone.
(d) Any one of the above.

36. Radio affects the mind of the _____ whereas TV affects the minds of the _____.
(a) group; individual
(b) society; country
(c) public; masses
(d) individual; group

37. If a PA system is to be installed for addressing an audience of 500 persons, the minimum audio power of such a system would be
(a) 50 watts (b) 100 watts
(c) 400 watts (d) 500 watts

38. The network topology that supports bidirectional links between each possible node is
(a) Mesh (b) Tree
(c) Star (d) Ring

39. We buy products from the Asian Sky Shop because
(a) TV pitch works on our minds.
(b) selling gimmicks are powerful enough to draw us towards a purchase decision.
(c) the footpath pitch works on our minds.
(d) None of the above.

40. Why radio is deemed a passive media?
(a) People actively take part in media like Internet and give it full attention, but they listen to radio while they complete their daily chores.
(b) People watch TV commentaries with keen interest, but do not listen to radio commentaries with keen interest.
(c) Radio is an aural media and hence, it is passive.
(d) People have small radio sets but large TV sets and that is why, they are not actively involved in the listening process (in radio listening).

41. On a CD-ROM, the minimum length of a pit or land between two pits is
(a) 1.2 micro-metre
(b) 0.9 micro-metre
(c) 0.6 micro-metre
(d) 0.3 micro-metre

42. In a broad sense, a railway track is an example of
(a) Full-duplex (b) Simplex
(c) Half-duplex (d) All of these

43. A TV producer is not supposed to
    (a) edit and rewrite the sitcom script.
    (b) prepare the final VTR for the purpose of broadcasting.
    (c) oversee the editing process.
    (d) be present during the recording of a sitcom.

44. It would not be recommended to use a digital CAS if the number of subscribers of a cable TV operator is
    (a) 18,00,000 or less
    (b) 5,00,000 or less
    (c) 2,00,000 or less
    (d) 1,00,000 or less

45. The frequency range at which the land coaxial cables will be used is
    (a) 10^3 to 10^4 Hz (b) 10^{14} to 10^{15} Hz
    (c) 10^6 to 10^8 Hz (d) 10^{10} to 10^{11} Hz

46. Radio is the theatre of the ________ and TV is the theatre of the ________.
    (a) mind; home
    (b) society; home
    (c) soul; consciousness
    (d) individual; group

47. The DTH system would not work without a
    (a) telephone line
    (b) conventional linear antenna
    (c) CATV connection
    (d) smart card

48. Protocols are
    (a) physical communication channels used for transferring data.
    (b) agreements on how communications components and DTE's are to communicate.
    (c) logical communication channels used for transferring data.
    (d) None of the above.

49. Which of the following is not a peripheral of the computer?
    (a) Web camera (b) Laser printer
    (c) SDRAM (d) Scanner

50. Which of the following is not an advantage of DTH?
    (a) The initial installation costs as well as operational costs are very low.
    (b) Some TV channels can be blocked so that children may not have access to them.
    (c) The viewer can select as many channels as he wishes.
    (d) Signals are clear because they are digital.

51. Which of the following is an example of sitcom (situation comedy)?
    (a) Shakalaka Boom Boom
    (b) Sarabhai vs. Sarabhai
    (c) Kahin Kissi Roz
    (d) Kyon Hota Hai Pyar

52. Baud means
    (a) the number of bytes transmitted per unit time.
    (b) the rate at which the signal changes.
    (c) the number of bits transmitted per unit time.
    (d) None of the above.

53. The medium shot of the camera is up to the
    (a) feet of the subject
    (b) knees of the subject
    (c) waist of the subject
    (d) None of the above

54. What is treatment?
    (a) It is the removal of the unwanted footage from the outdoor shoot, and it is normally done on the tape.
    (b) It is the long shot taken with the help of a mounted camera.
    (c) It is the screen play of a sitcom.
    (d) It is the draft script of a researcher that contains the list of main camera

shots and the flow of the programme that the team would follow during the actual shoot.

55. In August 2003, there were _____ CATV households in rural India.
(a) 15 million (b) 21 million
(c) 20 million (d) 30 million

56. Who invented the Dial-O-Matic?
(a) Peter Beiler (b) Ad Valent
(c) Sam Popeil (d) Ron Popeil

57. An italicised paragraph is
(a) not used in books and magazines.
(b) easy to read if its type size is high.
(c) always easy to read.
(d) difficult to read.

58. Pick the incorrect statements.
(a) Peer to peer protocol provides equal status to all sites on the channel.
(b) TDM is a primary/secondary non-priority system.
(c) Priority, non-priority types come under master/slave protocol.
(d) Both (b) and (c).

59. Which channel was given the first DTH license in India?
(a) Aaj Tak
(b) Zee
(c) NDTV 24 × 7
(d) AOL Time Warner

60. What is the combined effect of the commands del#?
(a) Delete and leave one space
(b) Add one #
(c) Add one # and one comma
(d) Delete and leave two spaces

61. Pick the incorrect statements in error retransmission used in continuous ARQ method.
(a) Selective repeat involves complex login than Go-back-N.
(b) Go-back-N method requires more storage at the receiving site.
(c) Go-back-N has better line utilization.
(d) Both (a) and (b).

62. What is the difference between a hypertext link and a hypermedia link?
(a) A hypertext link can be created on the Net but a hypermedia link cannot be.
(b) A hypermedia link can be created on the Net but a hypertext link cannot be.
(c) A hypertext link connects two different texts, but a hypermedia link is used to connect two different pages that may have multimedia files.
(d) None of the above.

63. A level shot is
(a) a bird's eye view of the scene.
(b) a worm's eye view of the scene.
(c) above the head of the subject.
(d) in the line of the eyes of the subject.

64. A daily record covering all periodical publications providing such information is called
(a) Journal (b) Periodical
(c) Magazine (d) None of these

65. In the process of distribution, in the parlance of ad insertion, which of the following process takes place?
(a) The digital video software copies the video from the master video library and distributes it over the cable operator's data network to headends, where it is stored in video servers for future play.
(b) The analogue base video is digitised and comprised in real tome with the keep of standard MPEG-2 hardware.
(c) Video is stored on a disc-base video library.
(d) The video cassettes DATs are sent to the office/studio of the cable operator.

66. Pick the systems that can be used in both priority and non-priority modes.
    (a) TDM
    (b) carrier sense systems
    (c) token passing
    (d) Both (b) and (c)
67. The payload bandwidth in the case of Video on Demand (VOD) is
    (a) 45 bytes (b) 48 bytes
    (c) 53 bytes (d) 55 bytes
68. What does the term DIG mean?
    (a) the TV signal is free to air
    (b) the TV signal is direct
    (c) the TV signal is digital
    (d) All of the above.
69. DD Bharati's specification sheet mentions a value –4.0033 V. What does the value signify?
    (a) Polarisation (b) Crypt
    (c) EEC (d) S/R
70. When the TV announcer explains the event even as the VTR rolls to broadcast the event, the action of the TV announcer is called
    (a) Audio Back-up (b) Line Audio
    (c) Line Cover (d) Voice Over
71. Adaptive or dynamic directory used in packet routing changes
    (a) with each user session.
    (b) within each user session.
    (c) at system generation time only.
    (d) Both (a) and (b).
72. What is time shifting in the parlance of TV operations?
    (a) The viewer records a TV programme and watches it at a later time or date.
    (b) The viewer records more than one programme at a given time.
    (c) The viewer can watch a TV programme through the VOD facility.
    (d) None of the above.
73. The last stage in the process of digital ad insertion (on TV programme) is
    (a) Verification (b) Distribution
    (c) Scheduling (d) Insertion
74. The method of network routing where every possible path between transmitting and receiving DTE is used is called
    (a) Packet Flooding
    (b) Random Routing
    (c) Message Switching
    (d) Directory Routing
75. What is zapping in the parlance of TV operations?
    (a) The viewer/recorder records programmes of one channel and excludes all other channels.
    (b) The viewer/recorder switches off the VCR/Digital recorder when the ads are being broadcast on TV, but he records the movie when it is broadcast. Thus, he skips ads during the recording.
    (c) The viewer/recorder records the broadcast for some period, say three hours.
    (d) None of the above.
76. Who invented the Dialomatic?
    (a) Ad Valent (b) Peter Beiler
    (c) Ron Popeil (d) Sam Popeil
77. All the channels of DD switched to the digital transmission mode from
    (a) November 2003
    (b) April 2003
    (c) December 2003
    (d) January 2004
78. What is channel surfing?
    (a) Locking unwanted channels, as is the case in CAS and DTH operations.
    (b) Briefly stopping at a TV channel and then, moving on to next one.

(c) Excluding some channels from the programme (through the remote).
(d) All of the above.

79. The command *Stet* means
(a) move flush top (by 0.5 inch).
(b) delete all.
(c) let it remain as such.
(d) move flush left.

80. In order to send and receive good video conferencing signals, the data transfer speed should be at least
(a) 56 KPPS (b) 128 KBPS
(c) 384 KBPS (d) None of these

81. How would you add a semicolon after the worn communicate?
(a) Punctuation (b) Separater
(c) Character (d) None of these

82. In PM6.5, what would be the effect of the command Ctrl+Shift+K?
(a) Convert the highlighted text into upper case.
(b) Convert the highlighted text into bold face.
(c) Convert the highlighted text into italics.
(d) None of the above.

83. Which of the following would take minimum attention of a person while he is at work?
(a) A book
(b) A song on radio
(c) A sitcom on TV
(d) A newspaper

84. Which of the following is not an advantage of the digital set-top box?
(a) Open-system hardware is used in it.
(b) It cannot be upgraded.
(c) Its audio quality is better than that of an analogue set-top box.
(d) It can be used to receive more than 400 video channels.

85. The number of cross point needed for 10 lines in a cross point switch which is full duplex in nature and there are no self-connection is
(a) 90 (b) 50
(c) 45 (d) 100

86. In the case of a video disc, the average track pitch is
(a) 1.0 micro-metre
(b) 1.3 micro-metre
(c) 1.6 micro-metre
(d) 2.5 micro-metre

87. Press Trust of India was found(ı
(a) 1947 (b) 1949
(c) 1951 (d) 1953

88. The Non-Aligned News Agencies Pool (NANAP) came into existence in
(a) 1982 (b) 1980
(c) 1976 (d) 1969

89. In which of the following languages NANAP news is not exchanged?
(a) Chinese (b) Arabic
(c) English (d) French

90. A terminal multiplexer has six 1200 bps terminals and 'n' 30p bps terminals connected to it, the outgoing line is 9600 bps. What is the maximum value of n?
(a) 28 (b) 8
(c) 16 (d) 4

91. If you use the transpose command on the word phrase 'Be that', what would be the result?
(a) Be/that (b) That be
(c) Be it that (d) Be that

92. Which of the following is not a type of crypt?
(a) MGRD (b) VGRD
(c) SSU (d) NTL

93. In PM6.5, the command to move a phrase in the centre of the page is

(a) Alt+Shift+C (b) Alt+Shift+K
(c) Ctrl+Shift+C (d) Alt+Shift+C

94. In PM6.5, the command to make a phrase bold faced is
(a) Alt+Shift+K (b) Alt+Shift+B
(c) Alt+Shift+C (d) Ctrl+Shift+B

95. The symbol *lc* is used to convert
(a) an upper-case letter into a lower-case letter.
(b) any letter into an italicised letter.
(c) a boldletter into an italicised letter.
(d) a lower-case letter into a bold-faced letter.

96. BSC is a
(a) character-oriented protocol.
(b) bit-oriented protocol.
(c) half-duplex protocol.
(d) Both (a) and (c).

97. Which of the following is not a secondary storage device?
(a) CD-ROM (b) Magnetic Tape
(c) Floppy diskette (d) DAT

98. When was the television service at the Delhi Kendra inaugurated?
(a) Nov. 25, 1958 (b) Aug. 15, 1959
(c) Sep. 15, 1959 (d) Sept. 20, 1960

99. In how many states was the SITE (Satellite Instructional Television Experiment) programmes launched?
(a) 4 (b) 6
(c) 8 (d) 9

100. When was the first English newspaper, *Bengal Gazette* published?
(a) 1755 A.D. (b) 1760 A.D.
(c) 1770 A.D. (d) 1780 A.D

101. Microphone is a hi-fi instrument. Here 'fi' means
(a) final (b) financial
(c) finish (d) fidelity

102. Which of these is a characteristic of radio?
(a) A mass medium
(b) An intimate medium
(c) A medium of sound
(d) All of the above

103. ______ is the supreme medium to express yesterday, today, and tomorrow with its own unique language.
(a) Newspaper (b) Television
(c) Radio (d) Cinema

104. A daily record of experiences and observations is called a
(a) journal
(b) periodical
(c) magazine
(d) None of the above

105. The difference between a multiplexer and a statistical multiplexer is
(a) statistical multiplexers need buffers while multiplexers do not need buffers.
(b) multiplexers use the X.25 protocol, while statistical multiplexers use the ALOHA protocol.
(c) multiplexers use TDM (time division multiplexing), while statistical multiplexer uses FDM (frequency division multiplexing).
(d) multiplexers often waste the output link capacity, while statistical multiplexers optimize its use.

106. Which is the bi-monthly media journal of Press Institute of India?
(a) *RIND Survey* (b) *Vidura*
(c) *Data India* (d) *Depth News*

107. Who is known as the father of Indian language journalism?
(a) Swami Vivekananda
(b) V.D. Savarkar

(c) Bhupendra Nath Dutta
(d) Raja Ram Mohan Roy

108. In which year was Press Institute of India founded?
(a) 1964 (b) 1963
(c) 1960 (d) 1952

109. The Advertising Agencies Association of India was established in
(a) 1945 (b) 1955
(c) 1962 (d) 1970

110. If the data rate of ring is 20 Mbps, signal propagation sneed is 200 m/s, then the number of bits that can be plaped on the channel of jig 200 km is
(a) 1,000 bits (b) 2000 bits
(c) 20,000 bits (d) None of these

111. The Indian Newspaper Society was founded in
(a) 1939 (b) 1940
(c) 1947 (d) 1955

112. The Sangam age is considered to be a landmark in the history of
(a) Eastern India
(b) Southern India
(c) Western India
(d) Northern India

113. Which of these is not a characteristic of TV?
(a) A mobile medium
(b) A living room medium
(c) A medium of immediacy
(d) A democratic medium

114. Which theory says that for sustained growth the investment should be spread in a balanced manner over a number of sectors, the demand for the products of which is interlinked?
(a) Siage theory
(b) Unbalanced growth theory
(c) Dualism theory
(d) Balanced growth theory

115. How many main news agencies are there in India?
(a) One (b) Two
(c) Three (d) Four

116. Large and highly diverse groups that represent the broad cross-section of the society form the ________ audience.
(a) general
(b) specialised
(c) elite
(d) None of the above.

117. ICI (interface control information) is
(a) a combination of service data unit (SDU) and protocol control information (PCI).
(b) a temporary parameter passed between N and N — I layers to involve service functions between two layers.
(c) used to transfer user data from layer to layer.
(d) used to exchange information by peer entities at different sites on the network to instruct an entity to perform a service function.

118. Which of the Indian agency was a subsidiary of the Reuters?
(a) UNI (b) PTI
(c) API (d) None of these.

119. In which year did PTI launch UNIVARTA, its Hindi wing?
(a) 1982 (b) 1983
(c) 1984 (d) 1985

120. Which news agency was founded in USA in 1907?
(a) AFP (b) UPI
(c) Reuters (d) AP

121. Which agency introduced the world's first Urdu news service in May 1992?
(a) PTI
(b) UNI

(c) Both (a) and (b)
(d) None of the above.

122. The method of communication in which transmission takes place in both directions, but only in one direction at a time, is called
(a) Full duplex
(b) Half duplex
(c) Simplex
(d) Four wire circuit

123. The Hindi wing started by PTI is called
(a) Samachar Bharati
(b) UNIVARTA
(c) Hindustan Samachar
(d) PTI Bhasha

124. FM stand for (technically)
(a) Fast movement
(b) Frequency Modulation
(c) Factual Methods
(d) Friendly Matters

125. The first practical demonstration of colour television was made by
(a) J.L. Baird
(b) Fank Gray
(c) E.H. Armstrong
(d) George Valensi

126. In the case of a video disc, the average track pitch is
(a) 3.9 micro-metre (b) 1.0 micro-metre
(c) 2.5 micro-metre (d) 1.6 micro-metre

127. Who amongst the following was not associated in any way with the invention of television?
(a) J.L. Baird
(b) Dr. Frank Conard
(c) A.A. Campbell
(d) David Sarnoff

128. General manager is the chief operating officer of the TV station. He is responsible for
(a) selection and broadcasting of news.
(b) the selection and broadcasting of any item.
(c) the financial needs of the programmes.
(d) the overall operation of the station.

129. The Conditional Access System (CAS) allows the viewers to
(a) interact with TV channel through set top boxes.
(b) cut down cost of television viewing.
(c) select TV channels of their choice.
(d) None of the above.

130. In which news script is the news caster followed by the expert interviewed on the subject?
(a) Package (b) Voice over
(c) Stand-up (d) Sound bite

131. Error detection at the data link level is achieved by
(a) hamming codes.
(b) equalization.
(c) bit stuffing.
(d) cyclic redundancy codes.

132. Which news script is the combination of sound bite and stand up?
(a) Supers (b) Voice over
(c) Talking Heads (d) Package

133. Names or bits of information superimposed on the TV screen is called
(a) Voice over (b) Supers
(c) Stand-up (d) Sound bite

134. Who selects the 'leads' and the 'breaks' for a news bulletin?
(a) Joint Directors
(b) Additional Director General
(c) Director-General
(d) News Editor

135. Which is not the rule of television?
(a) Passive Voice
(b) Clarity

(c) Brevity
(d) None of the above

136. In August 2003, there were ______ C&S households in urban India.
(a) 25 million (b) 40 million
(c) 27 million (d) 18 million

137. To keep only the essential parts in the picture is called
(a) editing
(b) edging
(c) cropping
(d) None of the above

138. AIR launched Frequency Modulation (FM) channel launched in Bombay on
(a) September 27, 1995
(b) November 27, 1994
(c) August 15, 1994
(d) August 15, 1993

139. A bromide paper is used in
(a) Laser Printing
(b) Camera
(c) Photography
(d) None of the above

140. Which of these is characteristic of radio?
(a) A mass medium
(c) A medium of sound
(b) An intimate medium
(d) All of the above.

141. Start and stop bits are used in serial communication for
(a) synchronization.
(b) slowing down the communication.
(c) error detection.
(d) error correction.

142. In which year the Supreme Court declared that 'the airwaves are the public property'?
(a) 1991 (b) 1992
(c) 1995 (d) 1998

143. The cable TV had its origin in
(a) Canada (b) Japan
(c) South America (d) North America

144. The new name of Radio Ceylon is
(a) MLBC (b) DLBC
(c) KLBC (d) SLBC

145. The first Director General of All India Radio was
(a) AS. Bokhari (b) Lionel Fielden
(c) Charles Barnes (d) B.V. Keskar

146. "TRP" is an index of
(a) Viewership
(b) Teledensity
(c) Information dissemination
(d) Segmentation

147. Unmodulated signal coming from a transmitter is known as
(a) Primary Signal (b) Carrier Signal
(c) Baseband Signal (d) None of these

148. A succession of pictures put together to create a unified effect is
(a) Montage (b) Mortise
(c) Measure (d) Make-ready

149. Identify the correct pair
(a) Zoom-in-Microphone
(b) Back light-Camera
(c) Tripod-Lenses
(d) Track-in-editing

150. Improvement in audio quality by altering the frequency feature is done through
(a) erasing (b) correcting
(c) equalisation (d) wiping

151. The French term 'mise-en-scene' means:
(a) Control scene (b) orderly scene
(c) scene by scene (d) Placed in scene

152. The television gross rating points are determined by the formula of
(a) Cover × Cost
(b) Cost × Frequency
(c) Cover × Frequency
(d) Frequency × Cost

153. Editing a sequence of shots in which the subject jerks from one position to another position is described as
(a) rough cut (b) move up
(c) jump cut (d) leveller

154. Manchester code is a
(a) bi-polar code.
(b) polar code.
(c) non-return to zero code.
(d) Both (b) and (c).

155. The other name for vision mixer is
(a) scrambler (b) integrator
(c) switcher (d) router

156. Switches to preset the zoom of a camera in a studio are called
(a) switch box (b)` cable box
(c) central box (d) shot box

157. Communication audit is an examination of internal and external methods of communication employed in
(a) media organisations
(b) public opinion
(c) event management
(d) advertising agencies

158. A tape or film that leads to the beginning of a broadcast is called
(a) initiator (b) leader
(c) mover (d) starter

159. Identify the correct sequence
(a) Morse code - A.M. Radio - F.M. Radio - World Space Radio
(b) A.M. Radio - F.M.Radio - Morse code - World Space Radio
(c) World Space Radio - A.M. Radio - F.M.Radio - Morse Code
(d) World Space Radio - Morse code - A.M. Radio - F.M. Radio

160. Which one of the following is not a net hierarchy?
(a) Dat-digital data
(b) Soc-social interactions
(c) Sci-science
(d) News-news

161. Car radio was invented by
(a) I-H SingandLiang Ling Tsan
(b) Richard Hoe and Johannes Gutenberg
(c) William Lear and Elumen Wavereng
(d) J. Nicephore Niepce

162. Non-broadcast television normally belongs to the category of
(a) Community Televison
(b) Instructional Television
(c) Domestic Televison
(d) Corporate in-house Television

163. The other name for a jingle is
(a) Ident (b) Back tune
(c) Prop up (d) Music clip

164. The insertion of a shot in a picture sequence is known as
(a) Cut in (b) Cut away
(c) Cut out (d) cut over

165. Location sound recorded while a footage is taken is described as
(a) Spot Sound
(b) Footage Sound
(c) Track Sound
(d) Natural Sound

166. Pick the correct statements.
(a) Non-switched leased line supports higher data volume and quality than switched lines.
(b) A switched circuit is a dial-up circuit that may encounter blockage (busy signal).
(c) Switched circuit provides faster response time.
(d) Both (a) and (b).

167. Pictures on the television screen are made up of
(a) Colours (b) Pixels
(c) Lines (d) Waves

168. The correct sequence of the width of the film negatives that were used for projection is
(a) 16mm-35mm-8mm-70mm cinemascope
(b) Cinemascope-8mm-16mm-35mm-70 mm
(c) 8mm-16mm-35mm-70mm-cinemascope
(d) 8 mm - 16 mm - 35 mm - cinemascope - 70 mm

169. In the carrier sense network if the prevailing condition is a 'channel busy', then which of the following are correct?
(a) If the technique used is 1-persistent then the channel is continually sensed.
(b) If the technique used is non-persistent then it results in randomised wait and sense.
(c) If the method used is non-persistent then continuous sensing results.
(d) Both (a) and (b).

170. The size of the camera lens opening is measured in terms of
(a) F-stops (b) Light codes
(c) Hertz (d) Neutral density

171. The interlaced lines for NTSC colour standard number
(a) 475 (b) 500
(c) 525 (d) 550

172. Modifying a video signal to be received only by the intended receiver is referred to as
(a) Selective focus (b) Scrambling
(c) Scooping (d) Comet-tailing

173. Short phrases of music used as punctuation devices in television broadcasting are called
(a) Stylised music (b) Prompters
(c) Stingers (d) Sound bites

174. The correct sequence of the four key concepts of digital media is:
(a) Multimedia, interactivity, automation and ethereal quality
(b) Ethereal quality, interactivity, automation and multimedia
(c) Automation, ethereal quality, interactivity and multimedia
(d) Interactivity, ethereal quality, multimedia and automation

175. Which of the following pairs includes synonymous expressions?
(a) NOISE, Interference
(b) Misspelling, Fuzzy picture
(c) Broken radioset, dead battery
(d) Newspaper in a mud puddle, a magazine not delivered.

176. Burner is a device to convert digital signals to
(a) analog signal disc
(b) broadband carrier
(c) optical laser disc
(d) video switcher

177. The first colour-corrected film print returned to the editor from the laboratory for verification is known as
(a) first print (b) correction print
(c) collect print (d) answer print

178. Which of the following are non-polling system?
(a) Xon/Xoff
(b) TDMA
(c) Continuous ARQ
(d) Both (a) and (b)

179. What indicates the size of the aperture opening on a camera?
(a) Auto Focus (b) F-stop
(c) Shutter (d) Viewfinder

180. The illusion of spatial distance in a two dimensional medium is referred to as
(a) balance
(b) linear perspective

(c) phase
(d) pitch

181. Sounds that have a complementary effect on the visual are considered as
(a) parallel sound (b) contact sound
(c) support sound (d) patch sound

182. How many characters per sec (1 bits + 1 parity) can be transmitted oven a 2400 bps line if the transfer is synchronous (start and istop bit)?
(a) 240 (b) 250
(c) 275 (d) 300

183. The volume of information that can be transmitted through a communications medium or link is referred to as
(a) memory (b) power
(c) bandwidth (d) amplitude

184. Cel is the base material to draw individual:
(a) animation frames
(b) infographics
(c) colour combinations
(d) characters

185. Short and rapid variations in the speed of the reproducer will create an audio distortion known as
(a) Mechanical noise
(b) Equipment distortion
(c) Conclusion
(d) Flutter

186. The comprehensive sequence of lines that contain the field of lines creating a video picture is identified as
(a) record mode
(b) resolution
(c) raster
(d) safe action area

187. In broadcast language, verbs are
(a) short and active
(b) long and passive
(c) long and active
(d) short and passive

188. A model of a final film product is known as
(a) Rough cut (b) Release print
(c) Archival print (d) Censored print

189. A specially designed oscilloscope used to graphically display a video signal:
(a) Vu Meter
(b) Viewfinder
(c) Studio Monitor
(d) Waveform Monitor

190. A brief and compact proposal outlining a television programme production
(a) Focus (b) Treatment
(c) Talent (d) Splice

191. The degree of clarity in a picture is called as:
(a) Resolution (b) Registration
(c) Shading (d) Sweetening

192. Which one of the following networks uses dynamic or adaptive routing?
(a) SNA (IBM System Network Architecture)
(b) TYMNET
(c) ARPANET
(d) None of the above

193. Identify the shot that is not frequently used in Television.
(a) Close-up
(b) Extreme close-up
(c) Long shot
(d) Mid shot

194. The signals through fibre-optics are transmitted by
(a) Light wave (b) Electric wave
(c) Sound wave (d) Magnetic wave

195. The correct sequence of production of visual programme follows
(a) Dailies–Fine cut–Rough cut–Final cut.
(b) Rough cut–Dailies–Fine cut–Final cut.
(c) Final cut–Dailies–Fine cut–Rough cut.
(d) Dailies–Rough cut–Fine cut–Final cut.

196. What cannot dictate the content every minute on news channels?
(a) Planned approach
(b) Marketing constraints
(c) Unplanned approach
(d) Rural areas

197. Which of the following has become a winning formula for the ratings game?
(a) Programming for rural areas
(b) Programming with upper class factor
(c) Marketing programming
(d) Cricket programming

198. News gathering genre that is most expensive across all news channels is
(a) Cricket coverage
(b) Urban news coverage
(c) Rural news coverage
(d) General news coverage

199. Ambient light is a
(a) natural light available to shoot.
(b) dim-night light available to shoot.
(c) back light placed behind the object.
(d) background light.

200. Photomatic means a series of
(a) photographs presented with a sound track.
(b) storyboard drawings.
(c) visuals in a video format.
(d) drawings replaced by a series of still photographs.

Directions: Questions 201 and 202 are of multiple statements type choose the correct answer from the codes given below the statements.

201. Which of these is false?
1. A development TV report should include a lot of field based footages.
2. 'Sustainable Development' means more industrialization
3. Television relies heavily on the words of a reporter than the visuals

Codes:
(a) 1 only (b) 2 only
(c) Both 1 and 3 (d) Both 2 and 3

202. Which of the following do the news channels cover?
1. Rural areas
2. Stories that may not get ratings
3. Unpopular events

Codes:
(a) 1 only (b) 2 only
(c) 1 and 2 only (d) 1 and 3 onlyxds

Directions: Question Nos. 203 and 204 are of matching type. Match List-I with List-II and select the correct answer using the codes given below the lists.

203. **List-I (Light)**
(A) Key light (B) Fill light
(C) Back light (D) Scoop

List-II (Function)
1. Lighting from a behind a subject
2. Provides soft light
3. Provides hard light
4. Illuminates shadow areas

Codes:	A	B	C	D
(a)	1	2	4	3
(b)	2	1	3	4
(c)	3	4	1	2
(d)	4	2	1	3

204. **List I**
A. Session layer
B. Transport layer
C. Application layer
D. MDI (Medium Dependent Interface)

List II
1. Connects DCE into physical channel.
2. Provides end to end accountability.

3. Provides organised means to exchange data between users, (like synchronization points.
4. Supports an end user process and performs required file transfer.

Codes:	A	B	C	D
(a)	4	3	2	1
(b)	4	3	2	1
(c)	3	4	2	1
(d)	3	2	4	1

Drections: Questions 205 to 213 consist of two statements, one labelled as 'Assertion' (A) and the other labelled as 'Reason' (R). You are to examine these two statements carefully and decide if the Assertion (A) and the Reason (R) are individually true and if so, whether the Reason is a correct explanation of the Assertion. Select your answer to these question using the codes given below:

205. **Assertion (A):** The editing process consumes a lot of time of the editor.

Reason (R): The DAT playback is done in real-time.

206. **Assertion (A):** Wipes are moving optical effects in which one scene pushes another scene off the screen.

Reason (R): In wipe one scene blends into another.

207. **Assertion (A):** Reverberation is the persistence of a sound generated after the sound stimulus has ceased.

Reason (R): Reverberation can be controlled through acoustic treatment.

208. **Assertion (A):** Piece-to-camera gives authenticity to news.

Reason (R): Piece-to-camera is a visual showing of the camera man on the spot of the news.

209. **Assertion (A):** Radio has emerged as a medium for the youth in India.

Reason (R): Radio receiver set is an inexpensive equipment.

210. **Assertion (A):** A story's duration in a newscast reflects its news-worthiness.

Reason (R): Time-value is important in broadcast news.

211. **Assertion (A):** Time is not an important factor in television news production.

Reason (R): Journalists cannot explain what the viewer watches and how much.

212. **Assertion (A):** Visual emphasis is directly related to the size of the subject in the shot. A close-up, by definition, excludes all other picture elements except the principal subject from the viewer's attention.

Reason (R): As the shot widens out to include more of the principal subject and less of the background area, the principal subject becomes physically reduced and shares the video space with other elements in the shot.

213. **Assertion (A):** A cut from one shot to another is similar to what our eyes do as they rapidly focus on various parts of our surroundings. The cut can also radically change time and place in the video space.

Reason (R): The cut is the most obvious transition because it occurs so slowly and the speed of a cut is not fixed like other transitional devices.

ANSWERS

1. (a)	2. (c)	3. (b)	4. (c)	5. (b)	6. (a)
7. (a)	8. (c)	9. (c)	10. (a)	11. (b)	12. (a)
13. (c)	14. (d)	15. (a)	16. (a)	17. (b)	18. (c)
19. (a)	20. (a)	21. (c)	22. (d)	23. (c)	24. (d)
25. (d)	26. (a)	27. (c)	28. (a)	29. (c)	30. (c)
31. (a)	32. (b)	33. (d)	34. (b)	35. (c)	36. (d)
37. (a)	38. (a)	39. (a)	40. (a)	41. (b)	42. (c)
43. (a)	44. (c)	45. (c)	46. (a)	47. (d)	48. (b)
49. (c)	50. (a)	51. (b)	52. (b)	53. (c)	54. (d)
55. (a)	56. (c)	57. (d)	58. (d)	59. (b)	60. (a)
61. (d)	62. (c)	63. (d)	64. (a)	65. (a)	66. (d)
67. (b)	68. (c)	69. (a)	70. (d)	71. (b)	72. (a)
73. (a)	74. (a)	75. (b)	76. (d)	77. (d)	78. (b)
79. (c)	80. (c)	81. (c)	82. (a)	83. (a)	84. (b)
85. (c)	86. (c)	87. (a)	88. (c)	89. (a)	90. (b)
91. (b)	92. (c)	93. (c)	94. (d)	95. (a)	96. (d)
97. (d)	98. (c)	99. (b)	100. (d)	101. (d)	102. (d)
103. (d)	104. (a)	105. (a)	106. (b)	107. (d)	108. (b)
109. (a)	110. (c)	111. (a)	112. (b)	113. (a)	114. (d)
115. (b)	116. (a)	117. (b)	118. (c)	119. (a)	120. (b)
121. (b)	122. (b)	123. (d)	124. (b)	125. (a)	126. (d)
127. (b)	128. (d)	129. (c)	130. (d)	131. (d)	132. (d)
133. (b)	134. (d)	135. (a)	136. (c)	137. (c)	138. (d)
139. (c)	140. (d)	141. (a)	142. (c)	143. (d)	144. (d)
145. (a)	146. (a)	147. (c)	148. (a)	149. (b)	150. (c)
151. (c)	152. (c)	153. (c)	154. (d)	155. (c)	156. (d)
157. (a)	158. (b)	159. (a)	160. (a)	161. (c)	162. (d)
163. (d)	164. (b)	165. (d)	166. (d)	167. (b)	168. (b)
169. (d)	170. (a)	171. (c)	172. (b)	173. (c)	174. (a)
175. (a)	176. (a)	177. (d)	178. (d)	179. (b)	180. (b)

181. (a)	182. (d)	183. (c)	184. (a)	185. (d)	186. (c)
187. (a)	188. (b)	189. (d)	190. (b)	191. (a)	192. (c)
193. (b)	194. (a)	195. (d)	196. (b)	197. (d)	198. (a)
199. (a)	200. (a)	201. (d)	202. (c)	203. (c)	204. (d)
205. (b)	206. (c)	207. (a)	208. (a)	209. (b)	210. (b)
211. (d)	212. (c)	213. (c)			

9

Marketing and Promotion

1. What is the basic objective of market segmentation?
   (a) To define clearly such market niches that have similar characteristics and features.
   (b) To divide the market into a few geographical sections so that logistics operations could be facilitated.
   (c) To identify target market niches.
   (d) All the above are true.
2. The societal marketing perspective is different from the marketing perspective in the sense that
   (a) the former also addresses the needs of the society while the latter addresses the needs of the market.
   (b) the former is slightly amorphous due to its broad approach while the latter is specific due to its focus on the targeted markets.
   (c) the former concentrates on the product while the latter concentrates on the market.
   (d) None of the above.
3. The last stage of a PLC is
   (a) Introduction (b) Growth
   (c) Maturity (d) Decline
4. What is space marketing?
   (a) It is the pre-purchase research activity carried out by a prospective customer.
   (b) It is the promotional effort of the firm through which, it buys space in newspapers, and inserts its ad supplements in the newspapers to reach the readers of such newspapers.
   (c) It is the set of those bargaining tools that a buyer uses to get the best deal from the seller.
   (d) It is a tendency of the buyer to purchase the cheapest brand available in the market.
5. Which of the following is an example of demand?
   (a) Ice-cream (b) Cadillac
   (c) Salt (d) Bread
6. If the price of which of the following products were increased, its demand would remain inelastic?
   (a) Apparel (b) Gold
   (c) Computer (d) Petrol
7. In the process of new product development, the commercialisation step would follow
   (a) screening and evaluation of ideas.
   (b) generation of new product ideas.
   (c) test marketing.
   (d) business analysis.
8. Singha beer is packed in an aluminium can, which is a
   (a) secondary package
   (b) label
   (c) primary package
   (d) tertiary package

9. If a firm is in shiping business and buys an IT firm, what is this kind of expansion called?
   (a) Horizontal
   (b) Vertical
   (c) Both (a) and (b)
   (d) Neither (a) nor (b)
10. A marketing executive wants to clinch a deal. He visits the client's office but finds that the latter is too busy to talk. He should
    (a) talk to the assistant/secretary of the client and get another appointment.
    (b) leave immediately because anger has taken the batter of him.
    (c) wait outside at the reception.
    (d) go back and come in the next day.
11. Marketing is the creation of standards of living. That is because
    (a) customers are motivated to work hard and buy new products and services and in so doing, they increase the pace of economic growth of their city, region, or country.
    (b) the government does not impose any restrictions on marketers due to the presence of a free market system and so, the standards of living of the masses improve.
    (c) marketers force consumers to buy new products/services.
    (d) sellers do not persuade the customers to buy their products but customers themselves beat their paths to the offices/showrooms of sellers.
12. According to Maslow's theory of needs hierarchy,
    (a) there is no pattern of satisfaction of needs of an individual.
    (b) needs and wants are one and the same thing.
    (c) higher order needs would be satisified first.
    (d) lower order needs would be satisfied first.
13. Which of the following is not a part of content factors in the context of tourism marketing mix?
    (a) Bank
    (b) Airport-hotel transfers
    (c) Park
    (d) Museum
14. Who takes purchase decisions in the case of a teenaged boy?
    (a) The parents in consultation with the boy
    (b) The boy himself
    (c) His mother
    (d) None of the above.
15. Which of the following is not a technique of demand forecasting?
    (a) Correlation Analysis
    (b) Chi-Square Analysis
    (c) Delphi Technique
    (d) Direct Derivation
16. What is word-of-mouth publicity?
    (a) A sales girl gives a beautiful registration form to a prospective tourist in the office of a travel agency.
    (b) The satisfied customer tells his friends and kith and kin about the services of the airline.
    (c) A disgruntled sea traveller informs his boss that the airline he had used last Friday is lously.
    (d) None of the above.
17. Airline seats are a perishable product. That is because
    (a) the aircraft cannot travel safely over high seas.
    (b) the seats of an aircraft cannot be sold through the Net.

(c) the accountant cannot account for the expenses of vacant seats once the aircraft is airborne.
(d) once the aricraft is airborne, the vacant seats mean a loss to the airline.

18. What is the idea of making the Maharaja an Arab or a Britisher in the advertisements of Air India?
(a) The airline must keep the Maharaja in live spirits and that is why, such types of advertisements are issued.
(b) The airline management wants do attract the attention of customers through funny sketches.
(c) The airline management wants the airline to identify with each and every country to which its aircrafts are flown.
(d) None of the above.

19. In the production concept, the emphasis is on producing
(a) large volumes of goods without giving any consideration to quality.
(b) such goods and services that do not harm the ecology and environment.
(c) high-quality goods.
(d) the product with the best possible features.

20. A wholesaler, in the parlance of tourism industry is the
(a) travel agency (b) resort owner
(c) airline (d) tour operator

21. How can a firm be more creative while marketing its products to prospective passengers?
(a) A new scheme to give you more discount! Join this scheme and avail discounts.
(b) You are a gem! Please use our product.
(c) We are raising our prices w.e.f. April 2012.
(d) We are pleased to offer discounts (varying from 10-20 per cent) on all the brands.

22. Which of the following is not a function of advertising?
(a) Understanding the buying capacity of the customer.
(b) Reminding the customer for a repeat purchase.
(c) Persuading the customer.
(d) Informing the customer.

23. Some consumers are laggards; they buy the product when everyone else has purchased it. How can we motivate them to buy the product?
(a) Everyone has bought it, why don't you?
(b) Come on! You are the pioneers.
(c) You should give us an opportunity to serve you!
(d) You are prudent enough to judge and make rational, cool decisions.

24. If a retailer tells a customer that his child would get a chocolate free of cost, if he buys 5 kg of rice, this activity of the retailer would fall under the gamut of
(a) Advertising (b) Marketing
(c) Sales promotion (d) Personal selling

25. Which of the following is an example of anit-congnitive advertising?
(a) A firm advertising with the USP—*You did the right thing by buying ABC Brand.*
(b) A firm advertising with the USP—*Heavy discounts in 3N/4D Packages to Shimla.*
(c) A firm advertising with the USP—*The Best Deal on Wheels.*
(d) None of the above.

26. The rate of a Goa-Mumbai night (sleeper) coach is ₹ 800 per person. The competitor

reduces the price to ₹ 750 per person. The firm should

(a) give better services on route but keep the rate as such.
(b) have a fight with the competitor regarding the issue of price cut.
(c) promote the coach as the best one on the route.
(d) reduce the cost as the least one on the route.

27. Every package tour becomes a success due to the coordination among and team spirit of the members of various travel agncies, hotel and resort owners. What would be the best strategy to build such a team?
(a) Sort out deties in isolation.
(b) Discuss problems across the table or through e-mail and find concrete solutions.
(c) Let aggreived persons in the team form cliques.
(d) Clearly define the commission rates in advance.

28. Which newspaper or magazine would be used by a deluxe hotel to issue its advertisements?
(a) A magazine with an ethnic touch.
(b) A local language magazine.
(c) A national level magazine.
(d) A local newspaper.

29. If a firm advertises its own products in a magazine, this would be a/an
(a) direct advertising effort
(b) indirect advertising effort
(c) Both (a) and (b)
(d) Neither (a) nor (b)

30. Who amongst the following is not a part of the distribution channel?
(a) Packaging firm (b) Wholesaler
(c) Retailer (d) Shipper

31. A fussy passenger aboard an aircraft demands beer even after the dinner is over. The airhostess should
(a) give him one can of beer and state, "No more beer, please".
(b) give him one can of beer and state, "Sir, the inflight kitchen would be closed now. Thank you!".
(c) tell him politely that stocks of beer have run out.
(d) stop him.

32. A skeptic buyer is one who
(a) carefully weighs the cost and pros and cons of the product being offered.
(b) has a negative image about the seller.
(c) is keen to return the product if it does not work properly.
(d) makes impulsive purchases.

33. Self-motivation would be developed among the hotel staff if
(a) they are treated nicely in the hotel by the guests.
(b) the premises of the hotel are fully air conditioned.
(c) they are given weekly off days to take rest.
(d) their seniors motivate them to work harder and take care.

34. When a war is on, the FMCG firm suffers. How can it try to increase the number of its customers?
(a) This is a moment of distress and grief, but let us continue our work
(b) Everything would be normal pretty soon.
(c) Do not buy the produts of ABC firm.
(d) None of the above.

35. During a lean period, a firm should
(a) decrease the price of its products
(b) keep the price at the same level
(c) increase the price of its products
(d) None of these.

36. A positive personality can be developed by
    (a) reading good text, attending personality development programmes and thinking about problems in a positive manner.
    (b) reading books.
    (c) watching others and judging how they handle their problems.
    (d) attending conferences.

37. How is a brand name different from a brand mark?
    (a) A brand name can be uttered but a brand mark cannot be.
    (b) A brand name is visible but a brand mark is not.
    (c) A brand name is recognised by the targeted customer but a brand mark is not.
    (d) The brand name has legal protection but a brand mark does not.

38. Which of the following is not a component of marketing plan?
    (a) Situation analysis
    (b) Marketing objectives
    (c) Marketing budget
    (d) None of the above.

39. Shailaja thinks that a sofa set would cost ₹ 20,100. To her delight, she finds that the price of the sofa set in the retail showroom is ₹ 20,000. This is a strategy of
    (a) target profit pricing
    (b) going rate pricing
    (c) cost plus pricing
    (d) perceived value pricing

40. Who are the targets of a tourist spot that is located at great heights?
    (a) Business tycoons
    (b) Adventure tourists
    (c) Children
    (d) Women

41. The final marketing mix should be decided according to
    (a) limitations imposed by the promotion mix and product mix.
    (b) results of market research surveys. and interviews of prospective clients.
    (c) the commands of the top brass.
    (d) needs of the marketing manager.

42. The IT industry is basically
    (a) attraction-based
    (b) product-based
    (c) service-based
    (d) None of the above

43. What is the USP of a fashion designer's apparels?
    (a) Brand (b) Elegance
    (c) Both (a) and (b) (d) Utility

44. How should a travel agency handle a fussy customer who is keen to go on an individual tour but is willing to pay only the price of a Group Inclusive Tour (GIT)?
    (a) A GIT would help you and other group members enjoy the tour.
    (b) If you are planning for an individual tour and not a GIT, you would end up paying more.
    (c) If you are looking for privacy, spend more.
    (d) If you are egocentric, do not go through a GIT.

45. A firm is keen to promote its tourist resort that is located close to a sea beach. It should
    (a) attract customers from far and wide by giving heavy off-season discount.
    (b) use print media advertisements in national-level newspapers.
    (c) use individual campaigns to target such families of the area.
    (d) promote heavily through Internet.

46. Under the concept of operant conditioning
    (a) outcome is independent of what the learner does.
    (b) change is chiefly in the frequency of response.
    (c) change is chiefly in the effectiveness of the stimulus.
    (d) None of the above.

47. A satisifed customer is likely to
    (a) recommend to his friends that the tourist spot may not be visited due to high costs involved in the tour.
    visit the tourist spot time and again.
    talk to the travel agent that he would like to go to a tourist spot that is different from the one he had visited earlier.
    (d) at least try to go to that tourist spot once again.

48. What is semantic generation?
    (a) It is a process of establishing meanings for words that essentially do not have meanings.
    (b) It refers to the fact that the continuous use of word can make it less meaningful.
    (c) It is a process of recalling those meanings that are hidden in the long-term memory of an individual.
    (d) None of the above.

49. In the concept of megamarketing,
    (a) lawyers, PR executives, and officials of the firm are actively involved to manipulate six 'Ps'.
    (b) investment costs are low.
    (c) only four 'Ps' of marketing are used.
    (d) None of the above.

50. The principle of simplicity states that
    (a) people have a tendency to organize their perceptions into simple patterns.
    (b) proximate objects are easy to organize in the mind of the targeted person.
    (c) people tend to forget less known brands.
    (d) the context is more important than closure.

51. Advertising has been criticized because
    (a) it generates the demand not needed by consumers.
    (b) it is high-profile and glossy and therefore, it enthralls to win customers.
    (c) it motivates consumers to try new products.
    (d) All of the above.

52. In the parlance of the communication process
    (a) feedback should be not sent by the receiver as the sender must make efforts to recieve it.
    (b) feedback is important from the viewpoint of the receiver.
    (c) barriers are likely to change the message for the benefit of the sender.
    (d) fax transmissions are able to send clear messages across the continents.

53. Kotler has defined two more P's of marketing. These are
    (a) Product Strategy and Power
    (b) Power and Place
    (c) Power and Political Influence
    (d) Political Influence and Place

54. Why does a hotel provide shampoo and hair conditioner (in pouches) in the rooms?
    (a) The customer may be too busy to carry such things with him.
    (b) Bathrooms do not look nice without these sundry items.
    (c) The hosekeeping staff must do something; so, it places these items in the bathroom.
    (d) It has already charged the price of the same from the guest.

55. Which of the following is not a basis for the demographic segmentation of a market?
   (a) Nationality (b) User Status
   (c) Age (d) Income

56. Which of the following is not a part of the communication mix?
   (a) Group Discussion
   (b) Sales Promotion
   (c) PR
   (d) Publicity

57. According to David Ogilvy, firms should
   (a) use direct sales method to build the image of the brand.
   (b) use advertising and sales promotion in equal proportions.
   (c) depend more upon sales promotion than upon sales advertising.
   (d) depend more upon advertising than upon sales promotion.

58. Which of the following is not a motivational factor for an air hostess?
   (a) Support of the crew
   (b) Adequate training and competence level
   (c) Overnight duty
   (d) Good salary.

59. Which one of the following is a product rational motive?
   (a) Recommendations
   (b) Prestige
   (c) Suitability
   (d) Imitation.

60. During the post-purchase phase, the maximum effectiveness is that of
   (a) publicity
   (b) advertising
   (c) sales promotion
   (d) personal selling

61. The marketing mix variables are the ones over which a manager
   (a) has control, but he takes decisions according to the trends of external factors, needs of customers, and competitive forces.
   (b) does not have any control.
   (c) has control and he can take decisions by using various communications of such variables.
   (d) None of the above.

62. What is the chief message to be given to a laggard?
   (a) You are in the majority.
   (b) You are a respected person of the society.
   (c) You are an adventurous individaul.
   (d) Come out of your old shell.

63. In the parlance of the PLC, what is rapid penetration?
   (a) Keep the price and promotion expenditure very low.
   (b) Keep the price low but spend more on promotion.
   (c) Keep the price high and spend more on promotion.
   (d) None of the above.

64. In the parlance of public opinion, the issue that creates a public opinion is set by
   (a) contesting interest groups.
   (b) neutral people.
   (c) immediate interest groups.
   (d) None of the above.

65. Which of the following is not an example of POP material?
   (a) Product accessories, which may not necessarily be fitted, into or on to the product, at the retail shop.
   (b) Brochures and catalogues at the retail shop.

(c) Placards showing the product at the retail shop.
(d) Coupons available at the retail shop.

66. What is cognitive dissonance?
(a) A feeling of resentment that is always present in the mind of the consumer (towards the products that he shuns).
(b) The exhilarating experience in the mind of the customer while purchasing a product of his choice.
(c) Post-purchase dissatisfaction that creeps into the mind of the consumer after he buys the product.
(d) None of the above.

67. Which of the following statements is false?
(a) Propaganda helps the masses realize the vitality of the core issue.
(b) Propaganda can be done by misrepresenting facts and supplying wrong sets of information.
(c) Propaganda affects people in a large city, area, state, nation, or the world.
(d) A device used in one propaganda campaign may not be useful in another.

68. In the case of industrial goods, the
(a) advertising and personel selling budgets would have equal allocations.
(b) advertising budget would be less.
(c) personel selling budget would be less.
(d) None of the above.

69. Drive is a
(a) strong internal urge that forges an action or a set of actions.
(b) feeling that motivates person to hold on to some beliefs.
(c) strong inner verge that dissuades a person from taking a positive action.
(d) All of the above.

70. Retention depends upon
(a) clarity of the message
(b) values
(c) time gap
(d) All of the above

71. The features of the product have some advantages, which deliver some benefits to the customer. This concept is better known as the
(a) FAB (b) SR
(c) AIDA (d) DAGMAR

72. A person in the age group of 6-12 years is not likely to buy
(a) sports cars
(b) The Harry Potter series
(c) chocolates
(d) Maggi noodles

73. Advertising and PR are very effective at raising the awareness levels but not nearly as effective as when it comes to actually moving the consumer towards making a purchase. This relates to
(a) The websites of the Internet
(b) Conference
(c) Personal selling
(d) Sales Promotion

74. Public Relations aims to build a favourable opinion. This can be achieved by
(a) increasing production.
(b) advertising.
(c) giving eloquent speeches.
(d) genuine action and honest communication.

75. Public Relations is described as a planned activity. This is because it involves
(a) budgeting
(b) evaluation of public opinion
(c) reaching the targeted audience
(d) All of the above

76. Ethical concepts change with
   (a) situation
   (b) time
   (c) place
   (d) All of the above

77. Public Relations Communication should be based on
   (a) full information
   (b) truth
   (c) knowledge
   (d) All of the above

78. What influences the attitudes?
   (a) Appeals through communication
   (b) Value symbols
   (c) Events
   (d) All of the above

79. Which is not the primary function of PR?
   (a) Advisory and counselling role.
   (b) Information gathering and monitoring trends.
   (c) Analysing the prevailing issues and opportunities.
   (d) None of the above.

80. The Film Enquiry Committe in 1951 recommended the creation of a
   (a) a film institute for training
   (b) film export corporation
   (c) film finance corporation
   (d) All of the above

81. In which year was the Film Federation of India formed?
   (a) 1953 (b) 1952
   (c) 1951 (d) 1950

82. The messages for different publics of the same organizations have to be framed differently because
   (a) they deserve different levels of treatment.
   (b) it is better that they remain distant from each other.
   (c) their capacity to understand differs.
   (d) their interests and information needs are different.

83. When was the first International Film Festival held in India?
   (a) 1952 (b) 1953
   (c) 1954 (d) 1955

84. When only computer data can be exchanged among multiple locations, it is called
   (a) video graphic conference
   (b) video conferencing
   (c) computer conferencing
   (d) audio conferencing

85. In a system where in addition to audio and computer data still graphics like drawings, maps, etc. can also be exchanged is called
   (a) audio conferencing
   (b) video conferencing
   (c) computer conferencing
   (d) audio graphic conferencing

86. When the participants can actually talk to one another as if in a face-to-face situation is called
   (a) audio graphic conferencing
   (b) computer conferencing
   (c) video conferencing
   (d) audio conferencing

87. The first Indian attempt at colour in the country came in 1937 which was that film?
   (a) *Jhansi Ki Rani* (b) *Shakuntala*
   (c) *Kisan Kanya* (d) *Alam Ara*

88. When was the Film and Television Institute of India set-up in Pune?
   (a) 1963 (b) 1962
   (c) 1961 (d) 1960

89. In which year was the Children's Film Society established in India?

(a) 1950 (b) 1955
(c) 1965 (d) 1970

90. The highest form of teleconferencing in which a two-way exchange of moving pictures is possible is called
(a) audio conferencing
(b) audio graphic conferencing
(c) video conferencing
(d) computer conferencing

91. The word 'stringer' is used for
(a) proof reader
(b) part-time reporter
(c) reporter
(d) writer

92. The phrase newspaper 'goes to sleep' means
(a) take some rest.
(b) stops printing because of less number of readers.
(c) goes for printing.
(d) None of the above.

93. Which of the following enforce people to search and ask for a product or service?
(a) Motive of being a detective
(b) Buying motive
(c) Consuming motive
(d) None of the above.

94. Which of the following is not correctly matched?
(a) Tissue Overlay: Usually a thin transparent paper placed over artwork for protection uses for making colour breaks and other printer instructions.
(b) Transfer Tape: A peel and stick tape used in business forms.
(c) Transparency: A positive photographic slide on film allowing light to pass through.
(d) Must: A fantastic story.

95. What do you understand by GRPs?
(a) Number of advertising insertions in one campaign.
(b) Number of points earned by an advertising campaign.
(c) Number of readers reading an advertising.
(d) Any one of these.

96. Public Relations Communication should be based on
(a) knowledge
(b) full information
(c) truth
(d) All of the above

97. Which one of the following is not a core product?
(a) Toothpaste
(b) Salt
(c) Santro Xing
(d) Medical treatment.

98. First modern 'advertising agency was started by
(a) James Hicky
(b) D.J. Keymer
(c) N.W. Ayer
(d) J. Walter Thompson

99. When did the discounts in advertising begin to be offered?
(a) Mid of eighteenth century
(b) Beginning of nineteenth century
(c) Mid of nineteenth century
(d) End of nineteenth century

100. When did the 'Calcutta Advertising Agency' start operating?
(a) 1909 (b) 1904
(c) 1897 (d) 1892

101. The 'Advertising Agencies Association of India' was established in
(a) 1939 (b) 1940
(c) 1942 (d) 1945

102. Advertising agency with highest Gross Income in India is
(a) Hindustan Thompson Associate Ltd.
(b) Ogilvy and Mother Ltd.
(c) Mudra Communication Ltd.
(d) None of the above

103. 'Development' advertising is the form of
(a) Public Service Advertising
(b) Product Advertising
(c) Classified Advertising
(d) Institutional Advertising

104. Which of the following is the tool for Public Relation?
(a) Welfare activities
(b) Brouchers
(c) Press Conferences
(d) All of the above

105. The large display of the 'achievements' of the State Government is a type of advertising
(a) Industrial (b) Classified
(c) Institutional (d) Public service

106. In which type of advertising, description is precise and technical?
(a) Corporate (b) Industrial
(c) Classified (d) Service

107. The 'Publicity Society of India' was set up in the year of
(a) 1926 (b) 1932
(c) 1923 (d) 1939

108. Public Relations Communications should be based on
(a) knowledge
(b) full Information
(c) truth
(d) All of the above

109. Public Relations aims to build a favourbale opinion. This can be achieved by
(a) genuine action and honest communication.
(b) advertising.
(c) giving eloquent speeches.
(d) increasing production.

110. Public relations is described as a planned activity. This is because it involves
(a) budgeting
(b) evaluation of public opinion
(c) reaching the targeted audience
(d) All of the above

111. SEBI stands for
(a) Software Export of India.
(b) Securities and Exchange Board of India.
(c) Services Evaluation Board of India.
(d) South East Broadcast Incorporated.

112. Who differentiated between 'hot and cold' messages?
(a) Wilbur Schramm
(b) Val Gielgud
(c) Marshall McLuhan
(d) Raymond Williams

113. Which is the primary function of PR?
(a) Advisory and counselling role.
(b) Information gathering and monitoring trends.
(c) Analysing the predicting issue and opportunities.
(d) All of the above.

114. What was the major effect of the mushroom growth of cable and satellite television advertising?
(a) They got many awards.
(b) They earned huge profits.
(c) They popularised India.
(d) None of the above.

115. *Hamara Desh* was India's first
(a) Hindi Newspaper
(b) Advertising campaign
(c) Radio Station
(d) Wall Newspaper

116. Public Relations Society of India observes national PR day on:
(a) April 21 (b) March 21
(c) April 20 (d) March 20

117. The most successful product by direct mail advertising is
(a) *India Today* (b) *The Week*
(c) *Reader's Digest* (d) *Frontline*

118. What is a bleed advertisement?
(a) Colours are allowed to blend into one another.
(b) An emotion-based ad.
(c) An ad that runs to the edge of a page.
(d) An ad requesting for donations.

119. How is newspaper space sold for display ads?
(a) By column-centimetre.
(b) By the number of words.
(c) By the size of the ad in square centimetres.
(d) By the number of illustrations in the ad.

120. Which language newspapers have a major share of advertising revenue?
(a) English (b) Hindi
(c) Urdu (d) Bengali

121. To draw out the consumer's minds, emotions and sense in the 'AIDA Model', the letter I refers to
(a) Interest (b) Influence
(c) Insurance (d) Intelligence

122. Advertising education is organised by CAM (Communication, Advertising and Marketing) in
(a) Germany
(b) France
(c) the United States
(d) the United Kingdom

123. The number of readers who recall seeing an advertisement is termed as
(a) Recall score
(b) Memory score
(c) Identification score
(d) Noting score

124. A rate which does not offer discount for advertisers is known as
(a) Hard rate
(b) Unsubsidised rate
(c) Market rate
(d) Flat rate

125. Which is not the technique of Tost Testing' of advertisement?
(a) Strategy measures
(b) Folder test
(c) Area Test
(d) Econometrics

126. Milking a brand means reducing promotional activity to improve
(a) Profitability (b) Reach
(c) Access (d) Frequency

127. Response decay is the rate of decline in response to
(a) an advertisement
(b) an editorial
(c) a news story
(d) a letter to the editor

128. Social advertising relates to the advertising of
(a) Social leaders
(b) Socially relevant ideas
(c) Socialisation
(d) Social acceptability

129. In mass media, space selling means
(a) Allocation of space to different departments of the media organisation in its office.
(b) Buying and selling space for the building of a media organisation.
(c) Selling time units for radio and TV and print space in print media.
(d) Marketing parking lots for satellites in the space.

130. Canvassing for a cause of an individual or an organisation amongst decision makers is termed as
(a) Lobbying (b) Public relations
(c) Crusading (d) Image building

131. An opinion statement about an organisation or a product is known as
(a) Dirty copy (b) Spoof
(c) Spam (d) Puffery

132. Expression of Public opinion in mass media is generally referred to as
(a) mass effect
(b) mass culture
(c) Vox Populi
(d) massing opinions

133. The percentage-of-sales approach to advertising budgets ties budgeting to:
(a) last year's sales
(b) anticipated sales of the year
(c) next year's forecast sales
(d) competitors'sales

134. According to the British Institute of Public Relations, the fourth stage in any Public Relations campaign is of
(a) Media selection (b) Exploration
(c) Evaluation (d) Publication

135. The research unit of the advertising agency, 'the Hindustan Thompson Associates' is
(a) NRS (b) IMRB
(c) ORG (d) MARG

136. The sequence of mental states through which a buyer passes in purchasing and using a product is
(a) Action-Reaction-Awareness - Interest - Desire
(b) Desire - Interest - Awareness - Action -Reaction
(c) Awareness - Interest - Desire-Action - Reaction
(d) Interest - Awareness - Desire - Action - Reaction

137. Advertising aimed at consumer promotions where a specific offer is made is known as
(a) scheme advertising
(b) promotional advertising
(c) selective advertising
(d) focus advertising

138. Impact impression is the degree of consumer reaction to
(a) a product
(b) a service
(c) an advertisement
(d) an in-house offer

139. The period when commercials are to be broadcast is identified as
(a) prime time (b) break time
(c) time channel (d) time message

140. A commercial message affects viewers' receptivity through
(a) churning of products
(b) felt emotions
(c) controversy
(d) highest ratings

141. When the colours in an advertisement are out of line, they are described as
(a) out of border
(b) out of justification
(c) out of relief
(d) out of register

142. A computerised media optimisation programme is called
(a) meteor
(b) media plan
(c) efficiency strategy
(d) operational research

143. The act of forgetting the source and remembering the message is known as
(a) Hearing effect
(b) Demonstration effect
(c) Visual effect
(d) Sleeper effect

144. Theatre test is conducted to check the effects of a
(a) Campaign (b) Service
(c) Advertisement (d) PR

145. A set of characteristics that make a brand unique in the market place
(a) Segmentation (b) Imaging
(c) Brand equity (d) Stereotyping

146. Transformational advertising influences
(a) Feelings (b) Perceptions
(c) Learning process (d) Attitudes

147. One of seven major types of appeals in most of the advertisements is
(a) Environment
(b) Fear
(c) Irrationality
(d) Submissiveness

148. An effective PR programme requires coordination of all efforts towards
(a) Policymaking (b) Defined goals
(c) Budgeting (d) Planning

149. Specific requirements of the client in an ad campaign are called
(a) Preferences (b) Must haves
(c) Definites (d) Mandatories

150. What are GRP's?
(a) Group rating points
(b) General rating points
(c) Gross rating points
(d) Generated rating points

151. Spin doctors help to
(a) Maximise favourable publicity
(b) Maximise unfavourable publicity
(c) Minimise favourable publicity
(d) Ensure fair coverage

152. The concept of monochromic behaviour is related to
(a) advertising (b) public relations
(c) television (d) internet

153. Presentation of a POP advertisement is known as
(a) layout (b) dummy
(c) thumbnail (d) display stand

154. PR-mix is a blend of
(a) population mix
(b) promotion mix
(c) propaganda mix
(d) external media mix

Directions: Question 155 is of multiple statements type. Choose the correct answer from the codes given below the statements.

155. To guide their efforts the PR professionals should not
1. make a choice of tools
2. ensure receptivity
3. carelessly position his messages
4. communicate dishonestly
(a) 1 and 2
(b) 2 and 3
(c) 3 and 4
(d) 1, 3 and 4

Directions: Questions 156 to 158 are of matching type. Match List-I with List-II and select the correct answer using the codes given below the lists.

156. **List-I (Terms)** / **List-II (Media)**

List-I (Terms)	List-II (Media)
(A) Icons	1. Television
(B) NLE	2. Newspapers
(C) Blogs	3. Computer
(D) Banner	4. Internet

Codes:	A	B	C	D
(a)	3	1	4	2
(b)	1	4	2	3
(c)	1	3	4	2
(d)	2	4	1	3

157.

List-I (Persons)	List-II (Fields)
(A) Lional Fielden	1. Radio
(B) Noam Chomsky	2. Advertising

(C) David Ogilvy — 3. Public Relations

(D) Ivy Lee — 4. Media Criticism

Codes:	A	B	C	D
(a)	2	4	1	3
(b)	3	1	4	2
(c)	4	3	2	1
(d)	1	4	2	3

158. **List-I (Model)** — **List-II (Proponent)**

(A) Hierarchy of effects — 1. George Gerbner

(B) Audience-centred social marketing — 2. Janice Radway

(C) Mean World Index — 3. Rice and Atkin

(D) Feminist reception studies — 4. Brenda Dervin

Codes:	A	B	C	D
(a)	3	4	1	2
(b)	4	1	2	3
(c)	1	2	3	4
(d)	2	3	4	1

Directions: Questions 159 to 172 consist of two statements, one labelled as 'Assertion' (A) and the other labelled as 'Reason' (R). You are to examine these two statements carefully and decide if the Assertion (A) and the Reason (R) are individually true and if so, whether the Reason is a correct explanation of the Assertion. Select your answers to these questions using the codes given below:

(a) Both (A) and (R) are true and (R) is the correct explanation of (A).

(b) Both (A) and (R) are true but (R) is not the correct explanation of (A).

(c) (A) is true but (R) is false.

(d) (A) is false but (R) is true.

159. **Assertion (A):** We can create the need for those products which are not required for human race.

Reason (R): Unrequired things are easy to adopt.

160. **Assertion (A):** Advertisement of wholesalers are normally image building exercise.

Reason (R): A wholesaler has to create an image in the market that would draw retailers to his fold.

161. **Assertion (A):** Advertising is any paid form of non-personal presentation and promotion of ideas, goods or services by an identified sponsor.

Reason (R): Public service advertising are devised to answer a public need.

162. **Assertion (A):** Public relations is an essential function of management.

Reason (R): Public relations helps to raise the motivational levels of the employees.

163. **Assertion (A):** Surrogate advertising is a legitimate practice.

Reason (R): Surrogate Advertising provides information about the products.

164. **Assertion (A):** The dominating trend in the contemporary media is that the brand manager decides what should appear and how, instead of professional in the media.

Reason (R): This reflects the global trend in media management.

165. **Assertion (A):** The line of distinction between advertising and public relations is vanishing.

Reason (R): Corporate impact is the cause of the trend.

166. **Assertion (A):** In a consumer society, happiness is defined as a pleasure through spending.

Reason (R): Because TV commercials sell products of various types and brands.

167. **Assertion (A):** Communications service is the role most frequently associated with

public relations. It includes the inward communication of information about the company and its activities to all publics of interest to the company. The communications may be given by any appropriate media.

Reason (R): It is broader than mere issuance of press releases as it encompasses the total process of projecting the corporate image using news media, corporate citizenship and by the use of other tools of external communication.

168. **Assertion (A):** The audio control console is a central co-ordination point for all audio signals in a television programme. It is at the audio console where all sound sources including microphones, tapes, records, sound tracks and film and videotape, are regulated, mixed and sent out to the stations transmitter or to a videotape recorder.

Reason (R): Each individual sound source must be controllable by the audio engineer for a proper audio level. Consequently, each sound source which enters the audio board must be regulated by its own separate control.

169. **Assertion (A):** Copy testing is a message building methodology that is used when an advertisement is conceived or it is in its initial stages of development prior to ad making.

Reason (R): The tests are designed to solicit responses to the main message of ad as well as the format in which that message is being presented.

170. **Assertion (A):** The experimental filmmakers, whether favouring rhythmical abstraction or surrealistic projections of inner reality, approach the cinema with conceptions which alienate it from nature.

Reason (R): They are ignoring the spirit of modern printing and literature and preferring creativity that inhibit camera exploration of reality.

171. **Assertion (A):** Public Relations is a deliberate, planned and sustained effort.

Reason (R): It is a predetermined and long process.

172. **Assertion (A):** The profession of Public Relations in India has not made much head-way despite best efforts by a good number of dedicated professionals.

Reason (R): Lack of industrial and corporate interest in media relations is mainly responsible for the dismal situation.

ANSWERS

1. (a)	2. (a)	3. (d)	4. (b)	5. (b)	6. (d)
7. (c)	8. (c)	9. (a)	10. (a)	11. (a)	12. (d)
13. (b)	14. (a)	15. (b)	16. (d)	17. (d)	18. (c)
19. (a)	20. (d)	21. (a)	22. (a)	23. (d)	24. (a)
25. (a)	26. (a)	27. (b)	28. (c)	29. (a)	30. (a)
31. (b)	32. (a)	33. (d)	34. (a)	35. (a)	36. (a)
37. (a)	38. (d)	39. (d)	40. (b)	41. (b)	42. (c)
43. (c)	44. (a)	45. (b)	46. (b)	47. (d)	48. (a)

49. (a)	50. (a)	51. (a)	52. (b)	53. (c)	54. (a)
55. (b)	56. (a)	57. (d)	58. (c)	59. (c)	60. (b)
61. (a)	62. (d)	63. (b)	64. (a)	65. (a)	66. (c)
67. (a)	68. (b)	69. (a)	70. (d)	71. (a)	72. (a)
73. (a)	74. (d)	75. (d)	76. (d)	77. (d)	78. (d)
79. (d)	80. (d)	81. (c)	82. (d)	83. (a)	84. (c)
85. (d)	86. (c)	87. (c)	88. (d)	89. (b)	90. (c)
91. (b)	92. (c)	93. (b)	94. (d)	95. (a)	96. (d)
97. (c)	98. (c)	99. (c)	100. (a)	101. (d)	102. (a)
103. (a)	104. (d)	105. (c)	106. (c)	107. (a)	108. (d)
109. (a)	110. (d)	111. (b)	112. (c)	113. (d)	114. (b)
115. (d)	116. (a)	117. (c)	118. (c)	119. (a)	120. (a)
121. (a)	122. (d)	123. (a)	124. (d)	125. (d)	126. (a)
127. (a)	128. (b)	129. (c)	130. (a)	131. (b)	132. (c)
133. (a)	134. (a)	135. (b)	136. (c)	137. (b)	138. (c)
139. (b)	140. (b)	141. (d)	142. (b)	143. (d)	144. (c)
145. (b)	146. (a)	147. (b)	148. (d)	149. (d)	150. (c)
151. (a)	152. (a)	153. (d)	154. (b)	155. (c)	156. (a)
157. (d)	158. (a)	159. (c)	160. (b)	161. (b)	162. (c)
163. (c)	164. (c)	165. (a)	166. (c)	167. (d)	168. (b)
169. (a)	170. (c)	171. (c)	172. (a)		

10

Writing Techniques and Production Methods

1. The term "300 DPI" means that there are
   (a) 300 dots in one square inch.
   (c) 9000 dots in one square inch.
   (b) 900 dots in one square inch.
   (d) 90000 dots in one square inch.
2. The DPI is equal to
   (a) the LPI
   (b) twice the LPI
   (c) three times as the LPI
   (d) four times the LPI
3. In PB binding,
   (a) forms are stitched without the use of glue.
   (b) glue may or may not be used.
   (c) forms are joined with the help of glue.
   (d) None of the above.
4. Authors quite often opine that it is difficult to write the first paragraph (or the first few paragraphs) of a story. How would you overcome this problem, if you are told to write a short story?
   (a) I will start from the last few paragraphs of the short story.
   (b) I will write the first paragraph, then some paragraphs in the middle of the story, and finally its end. Later, I will fill the gaps between these paragraphs and pages of the story.
   (c) I will write the first few lines, then the first paragraph, and then, the subsequent paragraphs.
   (d) I will organise the story first, write its basic structure, and then write according to this very structure.
5. Screen resolution, in the case of a TV or a computer monitor, is always in
   (a) cm^2 (b) pixels
   (c) DPI (d) LPI
6. A dual-tone photograph shall have
   (a) one colour (b) two colours
   (c) three colours (d) four colours
7. What does the term EPS mean?
   (a) Encapsulated Post Script
   (b) Encapsulated Partial Script
   (c) Entry of Post Script
   (d) Extra Passive Script
8. The first stage of layout is also called
   (a) thumbnail sketch
   (b) rough layout
   (c) tight layout
   (d) comprehensive layout
9. The second stage of layout is also called
   (a) rough layout (b) tight layout
   (c) dummy art (d) finished layout
10. How many words would be written for an area of 21 picas × 269 picas if a point size of 2 point leading with devanagari type is used?
    (a) 1350 (b) 2160
    (c) 2260 (d) 2960
11. The typesetter has to set 3040 words in point type 18 pica line length, with 2

point leading. What would be the depth of the galley in picas?

(a) 248 picas (b) 340 picas
(c) 348 picas (d) 440 picas

12. When printing on an offset machine is done from a plain surface, the process is called
(a) photo offset (b) planography
(c) litho offset (d) rotogravure

13. Which of the following is an advantage of Pre-sensitised (PS) plates?
(a) Efficient and automatic
(b) Time saving
(c) Clean
(d) All of the above.

14. When did the UNI begin its operations?
(a) March 21, 1961
(b) June 20, 1962
(c) July 10, 1963
(d) September 15, 1963

15. The National Photo Service of the UNI has been started in collaboration with
(a) the NANAP (b) the AFP
(c) the AP (d) Reuters

16. The first Chairman of NANAP was
(a) Egypt (b) Yugoslavia
(c) Indonesia (d) India

17. What is the manual density of print for getting the CRCs of a book?
(a) 300 DPI
(b) 600 DPI
(c) 1200 DPI
(d) None of the above.

18. Which of the following statements would be apt for writing short stories for children in the age groups of 6-12 years?
(a) It is better to write career-oriented and nature-oriented text for them.
(b) The technicality of a machine can be converted into the story to arouse their interest.
(c) Serious crime stories would enthrall them beyond compare.
(d) Politics would be an ideal subject.

19. A book for children in the age group of 6-8 years should have
(a) more photographs and less text.
(b) text and photographs in equal proportions.
(c) more text and less photographs.
(d) None of the above.

20. If an artist is not keen to draw the art work with his hands, he had better use
(a) Director 8
(b) Microsoft PowerPoint
(c) A digital tablet with a handhold panel
(d) CorelDraw 10

21. A student of class XII should preferably read books and magazines dedicated to
(a) crime syndicate and mafia gangs.
(b) cine magazines and sex.
(c) natural beauty and tourist spots of the world.
(d) career building.

22. How can a freelancer help a newspaper organization?
(a) By giving sensational news that the news editor does not want to collect through his own men.
(b) By providing news about the area where he is located.
(c) By working on behalf of a regular correspondent who is sick or on leave.
(d) All of the above.

23. Which of the following is an example of yellow journalism?
(a) Somashukla Sinha Walunjkar gives a two-star rating to a movie that has been reviewed by another newspaper.
(b) A film reporter writes "Rekha finds Akshay delicious".

(c) A film *Jine do* (on TV) describes how the Muhurat shot of a new movie was taken.

(d) Bhavna Somaiya reaches out at a movie that is poorly made (in her film review).

24. In the term CMYK, the term K refers to the colour

(a) Yellow (b) Black
(c) Magenta (d) Red

25. Which newspaper did a pioneering job in the field of development reporting?

(a) *Hindustan Times* (b) *The Hindu*
(c) *The Statesman* (d) *Bengal Gazette*

26. Which of the following topics would not be covered by a development journalist?

(a) Coverage of news of the business
(b) Construction of dams
(c) Water management
(d) Protection of environment

27. Which of the following is an example of investigative journalism?

(a) An interview with Rahul Gandhi while he is on a tour to Amethi.
(b) An interview of the CBI chief about the Radia tapes scandal.
(c) The reporting about Commanwealth Games.
(d) The Tehelka expose.

28. Syndicates are the firms that produce a programme or help

(a) creating news networks
(b) in making advertisement
(c) in local station placement
(d) None of the above.

29. If a photograph is being printed in six colours, the other two colours besides CMYK are

(a) grey and gold (b) gold and cyan
(c) yellow and gold (d) black and grey

30. What is a print dummy?

(a) A book sans all the diagrams and colour photographs.
(b) A dummy book without any printed pages.
(c) A dummy book with all printed pages.
(d) A book that has been sent to the binding section for the purpose of lamination.

31. A disadvantage of a trigger is that

(a) he may be less accountable than the regular staff of the newspaper.
(b) he may prove costly to the newspaper that may give him an assignment.
(c) In the parlance of radio and TV production, an input editor takes the stories and an executive puts them out for the purpose of broadcasting.
(d) he may be less experienced than the regular staff of the newspaper and he may not be able to use his knowledge about the beat he usually covers.

32. A person reviewing a book should

(a) give impartial comments on the content, style, and presentation of the book.
(b) read only a few chapters of the book.
(c) get in touch with the author to ask questions related to the content.
(d) not review the book, if he does not like its author's style.

33. Foreign letter, words, phrases, and symbols (printed in a book) are always

(a) in bold face.
(b) underlined.
(c) printed according to the policy of the editor.
(d) in italics.

34. Why is there a need to promote development journalism in India?

(a) The new breed of development journalist has been created because of our new media policies. Like all other journalists, development journalists are also in vogue.

(b) India is a poor country; it ought to be developed at a quick pace and for that purpose, development journalists are needed.

(c) India is a developing country; in order to hasten the pace of her development on the right track, development journalists are required to collect the news and disseminate the same in all parts of the country.

(d) None of the above.

35. Serif fonts are preferred in book publishing because

(a) such fonts connect one letter to the next one and hence, it is easy to read the text at high speeds.

(b) such fonts look beautiful when printed and book publishers prefer them due to this very reason.

(c) such fonts are always in bold face.

(d) None of the above.

36. Yellow journalism

(a) is an essential prerequisite for succeeding in commercial terms in the mass media scenario of today.

(b) does not spoil the society.

(c) helps the publisher or journal mint millions.

(d) All of the above.

37. If an investigative journo has to focus on society during the course of his assignment, his area of operation would certainly not include

(a) the disadvantaged groups of society.

(b) ecology and environment.

(c) judicial institutions of the state.

(d) political parties and machinations of these.

38. The PTI was founded on

(a) August 27, 1947

(b) February 1, 1948

(c) August 18, 1948

(d) July 12, 1949

39. Why is cropping done?

(a) To add blank space around a human figure.

(b) To enlarge a photograph so that print area could be covered.

(c) To make the size of the photograph proportionate by trimming its parts.

(d) None of the above.

40. A bold face text would be ideal for printing the

(a) text

(b) heading

(c) Both (a) and (b)

(d) None of the above

41. The NANAP does not exchange news in this language.

(a) English (b) Spanish

(c) Arabic (d) Hindi

42. Small magazine publishers publish their magazines by taking out the

(a) output on the system.

(b) CRCs of the final proofs.

(c) butter paper printouts of the final proofs.

(d) None of the above.

43. If an TJ focuses on the state, his area of operation would certainly not include

(a) Judiciary

(b) IT

(c) financial health of PSUs

(d) individuals and operations of them

44. What is Blueline?

(a) A blue line on the back cover of a magazine to show that it is dedicated to medical or veterinary sciences.

(b) A horizontal blue line in the middle of a page.
(c) A blue photographic proof used to check layout and position of all image elements.
(d) None of the above.

45. What is Burn?
(a) Exposing a printing plate to a high-intensity light, or placing an image on a printing plate by light.
(b) Too much exposure of a negative to light.
(c) Bringing of the image of negative to a positive.
(d) None of the above.

46. While writing a long novel
(a) the plot is of least importance.
(b) the font and type size must help the reader read at a quick pace.
(c) the illustrations are not at all important (in the text).
(d) Both (b) and (c).

47. A skid is a
(a) pallet used for pile of cut sheets.
(b) kind of gripper used to handle sheets in the press.
(c) where paper sheets are kept.
(d) None of the above.

48. A columnist is not gaudy to write
(a) a column on the political bickerings between two (political) parties.
(b) an editorial regarding economic development of the country.
(c) an issue of development and society transformation.
(d) a column on a sports events.

49. Legibility is reduced in such fonts that have
(a) extremely tweak strokes
(b) normal type faces
(c) a type size of 10-12 points
(d) None of the above.

50. A quality control matter used to measure the density of printing ink is called
(a) density gauge (b) crome gauge
(c) colour meter (d) densitometer

51. What is Imprint?
(a) Adding copy to a previously printed page.
(b) Printing six colours on a page.
(c) Printing only black colour on a page.
(d) Printing a page for the first time.

52. The magenta colour, in the parlance of printing technology, is also called
(a) process red (b) crimson
(c) red (d) brick red

53. Fog Index is a measure of the
(a) degree of complexity of an article.
(b) measure of abstraction and complexity of words.
(c) number of words in a paragraph.
(d) None of the above.

54. Recto is always the
(a) first page of a book.
(b) last page of a book.
(c) left-hand page of a book.
(d) right-hand page of a book.

55. Plate gap is the area on the sheet of paper where
(a) printing is done.
(b) the grippers hold it and pass it through the press.
(c) glue is applied.
(d) paper is trimmed.

56. What is the definition of wove paper?
(a) A paper whose weight is more than 80 gsm.
(b) A paper having horizontally aligned cellulose grains.
(c) a paper having a uniform unlined surface with a smooth finish.
(d) All of the above.

57. If a book has been made in an octavo, the number of pages per form is
(a) 8 (b) 16
(c) 24 (d) 32

58. The part of the lower case letter that exclude ascenders and descenders is called
(a) Overlay (b) Gutter
(c) Y-column (d) X-height

59. Which of the following is a Hindi font?
(a) Ravan (b) Bookman
(c) Baskerville (d) Helvetica

60. What is a skyline?
(a) A banner head running above a plate.
(b) A blank portion below the PS plate.
(c) A plate that has been used many times and ought to be discarded.
(d) A blank plate.

61. The spine of a book is its
(a) binding edge where the forms are joined.
(b) title page.
(c) hard bound cover.
(d) first page.

62. Which one of the following statements is true?
(a) The n-dash is smaller in length than the m-dash.
(b) Dope is private information that is added to news, and it contains gossip too.
(c) A clean copy is the one that needs to be corrected.
(d) A galley is the final proof of a book.

63. One inch is equal to
(a) 2 picas (b) 5 picas
(c) 6 picas (d) 8 picas

64. A photograph of 18 cm × 22 cm is to be reduced to 15 cm width. What will be its length?
(a) 18.3 cm (b) 19.5 cm
(c) 20.3 cm (d) 25.5 cm

65. In a quarto book, the form is
(a) folded once (b) folded twice
(d) never folded (c) folded thrice

66. Which one of the following is a warm colour?
(a) Red-Orange (b) Blue-violet
(c) Blue (d) Green

67. The paper coated on one side is called
(a) chromo art paper
(b) low gloss paper
(c) matt finished paper
(d) None of the above.

68. A justified paragraph of text is aligned
(a) on both the sides
(b) in the centre
(c) to the right
(d) to the left

69. Who is the sacred cow?
(a) A subtext or person who always gets favourable news treatments in a newspaper.
(b) A politician who is quite often censured by a newspaper (in its editorials).
(c) The chief editor of a newspaper.
(d) None of the above.

70. The third stage of layout is also called
(a) Art copy (b) CRC
(c) final copy (d) galley copy

71. It is better to print a mono-colour hand out on a/an
(a) mini offset press
(b) offset press
(c) laser printer
(d) None of the above.

72. *Mirat-ul-Akbar* belonged to
(a) Maulana Abul Kalam Azad
(b) Syed Abdulla Brelvi
(c) Raja Ram Mohan Roy
(d) Aurobindo Ghose

73. Bennett, Coleman & Co. Ltd. publishes which newspaper?
(a) *The Tribune*
(b) *The Hindu*
(c) *The Hindustan Times*
(d) *The Times of India*

74. In which newspaper did Gandhi wrote "I have taken up journalism not for its sake, but merely as an aid to what I have conceived to be my mission in life".
(a) *The Madras Standard*
(b) *Bangalee*
(c) *Bombay Chronicle*
(d) *Young India*

75. Who is a Router?
(a) A person who prints a sample copy for checking the impression.
(b) A person who mounts the engraving ethed type or image plated by cutting it to size and filling holes in it so that the same could be used in the printing press.
(c) A person who cuts away metal from the non-printing part of the plate to prevent it from touching the inking hollers during printing.
(d) None of the above.

76. Who was the owner of *The Hindu*?
(a) Surendranath Banerjee
(b) Kasturi Ranga Iyengar
(c) Motilal Ghosh
(d) Mahatma Gandhi

77. In which year Indian State Broadcasting Service was set up?
(a) 1952 (b) 1948
(c) 1937 (d) 1930

78. Commercials were introduced on All India Radio in
(a) 1958 (b) 1967
(c) 1972 (d) None of these

79. The first news bulletin went on air from Bombay station in
(a) Oct. 1936 (b) July 1927
(c) July 1923 (d) April 1919

80. Where is the Headquarters of Akashvani's National Channel?
(a) Parliament Street, New Delhi
(b) Jawaharlal Nehru Stadium, New Delhi
(c) Indraprashta Bhavan, New Delhi
(d) None of the above.

81. The reference to a story that should go in a single column at the top of a page is known as
(a) Top (b) Turn
(c) Slug (d) Trim

82. Embargo is
(a) a theory of market research.
(b) a deadline for the release of a story.
(c) a news agency.
(d) a trend in the pattern of social change.

83. Which of the following is not correctly, matched?
(a) HO - Hold for release
(b) Run - A reporter's beat
(c) Ears - Sound box
(d) Rush - An instruction

84. Which of the following comprises the place of filling, less than half a dozen words of text, the signature of the sender, and the time at which it was sent?
(a) Feature (b) Flash
(c) Filler (d) File

85. Which of the following is an organisation that sells articles and features on behalf of a writer?
(a) Scoop (b) Slug
(c) Syndicate (d) None of these.

86. Which of the following is not correctly matched?

(a) Space-out: Instruction to printer to put more space between parts of set matter
(b) Silhouette Halftone: A term used for an outline halftone
(c) Substrate: Essence of an article
(d) Skid: A pallet used for a pile of cut sheets

87. Which of the following is not correctly matched?
(a) Step-and-repeat: A procedure for placing some image on plates in multiple places
(b) Stock: The material (paper) to be printed
(c) Stone: Paper weight
(d) Stamping: Term for foil stamping

88. Which of the following is not correctly matched?
(a) Flash: A rarely used message of a few words describing a momentous event
(b) Follow-up: Further developments in a story
(c) HO: Hold for Release
(d) Embargo: Cover page of a newspaper

89. Which of the following is not correctly matched?
(a) Under-run: Production of fewer copies than ordered
(b) Editorial: Front page article written by editor
(c) Printing two or three up: Printing multiple copies of the same image on the same sheet
(d) Type Book: A book showing various families of type, which a press uses in printing

90. Which of the following is not correctly matched?
(a) Obit: An announcement of a death
(b) Overnight: A story filed by a reporter or turned out by a rewrite man for the first edition of an afternoon newspaper of the following day.
(c) Run: News on line
(d) Name Plate: Paper's name given on top of front page

91. Which of the following is not correctly matched?
(a) With the Grain: Folding or feeding paper into the press or folder parallel to the grain of the paper
(b) Work and Tumble: Printing one side of a sheet and turning it over from the gripper to the tail
(c) Recto: Left-hand page of an open book
(d) Wire-o-Binding: A method of wire binding book along the binding edge

92. Which of the following is not correctly matched?
(a) Split Fountain: Putting more than one ink in a printing fountain to achieve special colour affects
(b) Spine: The binding edge of a book or publication
(c) Tints: Dust of sand used in printing
(d) Specifications: A precise description of print order

93. Which of the following is not correctly matched?
(a) Watermark: A distinctive design created in paper at the time of manufacture than can be easily seen by holding the paper up to a light
(b) Washup: Removing printing ink form a press, washing the rollers and blanket. Certain ink colours require multiple washups to avoid ink and chemical contamination
(c) Rush: Crowd of journalists in a media firm
(d) Waste: A term for planned spoilage

94. Which of the following is not correctly matched?
   (a) PM's: Special news
   (b) Filler: Small items used to fill out columns where needed
   (c) Feature: A story of interest beyond and more than the news
   (d) File: The act of despatching copy to or from a news centre

95. Which of the following is not correctly matched?
   (a) Must: When this term is used on a copy, it indicates that the story must be used
   (b) Musthead: A statement, usually on the editorial page, giving information about the newspaper's ownership, place of publication, etc. Some times confused with the nameplate
   (c) Morgue: A news library, also known as reference section
   (d) None of the above.

96. Which of the following is not correctly matched?
   (a) Shoulder: Usually for the top line of a headline that is set in smaller type on one side (left) while the rest of the headline is set usual
   (b) Stringer: A correspondent of a newspaper who is not on the regular payroll.
   (c) Run: News online
   (d) Slug: Each story has a name, which is called a slug. The slug must be included with each page number. A story on Sachin Tendulkar may be slugged as Sachin-1, Sachin-2, and so on until the last page is marked Sachin-last.

97. An article can be rejected if
   (a) it does not have a focus.
   (b) the information lacks facts to make the argument credible.
   (c) the language is not good.
   (d) All of the above.

98. Which of the following is not correctly matched?
   (a) Spread: An elaborate layout
   (b) Lebel: Outlines on cover page
   (c) Spoilage: Planned paper waste for all printing operation
   (d) Spot Varnish: Varnish used to highlight a specific part of the printed sheet

99. Which of the following is not correctly matched?
   (a) Trim Marks: Similar to crop or register marks
   (b) Trim Size: The final size of one printed image after the last trim is made
   (c) Trapping: The ability to print one ink over the other
   (d) Stone: Ink used in printing

100. Which of the following is not correctly matched?
   (a) Web Press: The name of a type of presses that print form rolls of paper
   (b) Wire O: A bindery trade name for mechanical binding using double loops of wire through a hole
   (c) Tints: Dust of sand used in printing
   (d) Web: A roll of printing paper

101. Which composing method is also called as cold type setting?
   (a) Phototype setting
   (b) Hand setting
   (c) Machine setting
   (d) None of the above.

102. Which of the following is not correctly matched?
   (a) Stone: The platform or table on which, the printer makes the page
   (b) Stripping: The positioning of film on a flat to platemaking

(c) Substance Weight: A term of basis weight when referring to bond papers
(d) Beat: A cover story

103. Which of the following is not correctly matched?
(a) Text Paper: Grades of uncoated paper with textured surfaces
(b) Tints: A shade of a single color or combined colors
(c) Substrate: Any surface on which printing is done
(d) Lead: Headline

104. Which of the following is not correctly matched?
(a) Vignette Halftone: A halftone whose background gradually fades to white
(b) UV Coating: Squid laminate bonded and cured with ultraviolet light
(c) Lints: Dust of sand used in printing
(d) Varnish: A clear liquid applied to printed surfaces for looks and protection

105. Import of newsprint including glazed newsprint was put under Open General Licence (OGL) in
(a) 2000 (b) 1998
(c) 1997 (d) 1995

106. In order to be a good writer one should not be
(a) focussed
(b) using complex words
(c) to the point
(d) modest in approach

107. Impact, Timeliness, Conflict and Prominence are
(a) basis of a good news story
(b) qualities to be adopted by a writer
(c) criteria on which the editors insist upon
(d) None of the above

108. The art of printing originated from
(a) Germany (b) China
(c) USA (d) UK

109. Who installed the first steam printing press?
(a) John Donne (b) John Walter I
(c) John Milton (d) John Walter II

110. Where was the mechanical and organizational basis laid for the popular newspaper of the twentieth century?
(a) Africa and England
(b) China and South Africa
(c) America and Europe
(d) England and Europe

111. Peculiarities of writing style that the court reporter usually has to adopt are
(a) the defendant must never be addressed as the guilty one.
(b) no need to note down every word that is uttered.
(c) major decisions, points of issue and comments need to be recorded in one's notes.
(d) All of the above.

112. In which century the metal type printing machine in Mainz was made?
(a) Fifteenth century
(b) Sixteenth century
(c) Seventeenth century
(d) Eighteenth century

113. Which is most important department in newspapers?
(a) Press (b) Administration
(c) Editorial (d) Advertisements

114. Yellow Journalism started with
(a) Rupert Murdoch
(b) Joseph Pulitzer
(c) B.G. Horniman
(d) Winston Churchill

115. What is meant by cropping?
(a) Editing a news item
(b) Adjusting box items

(c) Cutting the size of the photo
(d) Reducing the columns

116. What is the limit of Foreign Direct Investment (FDI) in non-news and non-current affairs publications, mainly technical and medical journals?
(a) Seventy-four per cent
(b) Fifty-one per cent
(c) Thirty-three per cent
(d) Twenty-six per cent

117. In a newspaper office, the work takes place in the following order
(a) Reporting, Editing, Printing, Page Make Up
(b) Reporting, Editing, Page Make Up, Printing
(c) Page Make Up, Printing, Reporting, Editing
(d) Editing, Reporting, Page Make Up, Printing

118. What must the editorials that criticise, include in order to be balanced?
(a) Warnings
(b) Helpful suggestions
(c) Humour
(d) Persuasion

119. A reader advertisement is set in
(a) news style (b) editorial style
(c) feature style (d) column style

120. In gravure printing, the image to be printed is transferred to a
(a) zinc plate (b) butter sheet
(c) carbon tissue (d) plastic disc

121. The message under a message that is implicitly conveyed by media is referred to as
(a) Subtext (b) Hidden Text
(c) Masked Text (d) Subline Text

122. The retail selling price of print media is called
(a) Retail Price (b) Subscription
(c) Hawker Price (d) Cover Price

123. The new media technology's database facility is described as
(a) Digital Soup
(b) Digital Domain
(c) Digital Kitchen
(d) Digital Arrow

124. In letterpress printing, line length and column widths are measured in terms of
(a) Inches (b) Ems
(c) Centimeters (d) Characters

125. Patches of white space due to uneven typesetting are called
(a) Rivers (b) Run-ins
(c) Canals (d) Skyspace

126. The computer language for formatting documents to transmit through the world wide web is
(a) HTML (b) binary
(c) assembly (d) linux

127. The printing of a negative film on a negative film stock will result in
(a) reverse film
(b) back-to-back film
(c) film positive
(d) double negative

128. Identify the correct order of the basic elements of media as studied in most media courses
(a) Technology, reception, production, context, text
(b) Reception, production, technology, context, text
(c) Text, production, context, reception, technology
(d) Production, technology, text, context, reception

129. Proofs of a full-colour advertisement printed in one colour at a time are called:

(a) monochrome proofs
(b) single colour proofs
(c) progressive proofs
(d) testing proofs

130. Reader advertisement is set in
(a) the news style
(b) the editorial style
(c) the feature style
(d) the letter style

131. Identify the correct chronological sequence of invention of following printing processes
(a) relief printing, intaglio, offset, rotary
(b) offset, rotary, intaglio, relief printing
(c) relief printing, intaglio, rotary, offset
(d) intaglio, relief printing, rotary, offset

132. Fog Index refers to
(a) Framing (b) Readability
(c) Visibility (d) Availability

133. Participatory content creation is known as
(a) Precision journalism
(b) Citizen journalism
(c) Turncoat journalism
(d) Envelope journalism

134. The style of news writing in which the identification of the source is not immediately revealed
(a) Summary lead (b) Question lead
(c) Blind lead (d) Satirie lead

135. Identify the correct sequence of evolution of printing press
(a) Rotary - Cylinder - Treddle - Offset
(b) Cylinder - Rotary - Offset - Treddle
(c) Treddle - Cylinder - Rotary - Offset
(d) Rotary - Treddle - Offset - Cylinder

136. The items that indicate inside content in a newspaper are called
(a) Ears (b) Ear Panels
(c) Flags (d) Teasers

137. Fulcrum is the optic centre for designing a newspaper's
(a) front page (b) editorial page
(c) sports page (d) inside pages

138. The offset printing plate is made of
(a) Aluminium (b) Copper
(c) Rubber (d) Steel

Directions: Questions 139 to 140 are of multiple statements type. Choose the correct answer from the codes given below the statements.

139. What should be avoided while conducting an interview?
1. Sticking to your subjects
2. Be understanding
3. Do interrupt until the interviewee has relaxed
4. Don't show that you know about the information the interviewee gives you

(a) 3 only
(b) 1 and 4
(c) Both 3 and 4
(d) None of the above.

140. Verify the compatibility of the statements to each other
1. Retreat by government has made new communications cartels possible.
2. New technology has contributed to the media freedom.
3. The Indian Press is heavily subsidised and hence, cannot criticise the Governments.

(a) 1 only (b) 2 only
(c) 1 and 2 (d) 1, 2 and 3

Directions: Questions 141 to 143 are of Matching type. Match List-I with List-II and select the correct answer using the codes given below the lists.

141.

List-I	List-II
(A) Wire service	1. A news agency
(B) Short	2. A filler

(C) PM's — 3. Afternoon paper

(D) Leader — 4. Editorial

Codes:	A	B	C	D
(a)	4	1	2	3
(b)	3	4	1	2
(c)	1	2	3	4
(d)	2	3	4	1

142. **List-I**

(A) Lower Case
(B) Stick
(C) Run Over
(D) Take

List-II

1. A page of the copy
2. Size of nearly two inches
3. Jump
4. Small letters

Codes:	A	B	C	D
(a)	1	2	3	4
(b)	3	4	1	2
(c)	2	3	4	1
(d)	4	2	3	1

143.

List-I	List-II
(A) Chennai	1. Manorama
(B) Pune	2. ACJ
(C) Kottayam	3. IIMC
(D) New Delhi	4. Symbiosis

Codes:	A	B	C	D
(a)	3	2	1	4
(b)	2	4	1	3
(c)	4	1	2	3
(d)	2	3	1	4

Directions: Questions 144 to 147 consist of two statements, one labelled as 'Assertion' (A) and the other labelled as 'Reason' (R). You are to examine these two statements carefully and decide if the Assertion (A) and the Reason (R) are individually true and if so, whether the Reason is a correct explanation of the Assertion. Select your answers to these question using the codes given below:

(a) Both (A) and (R) are true and (R) is the correct explanation of (A)
(b) Both (A) and and (R) are true but (R) is not the correct explanation
(c) (A) is true, but (R) is false
(d) (A) is false, but (R) is true

144. **Assertion (A):** Non-linear editing technology has expanded the scope of creating special effects.

Reason (R): Special effects always enhance the aesthetic quality of the programme.

145. **Assertion (A):** In print media, round-up leads have become popular these days.

Reason (R): The reader wants encapsuled text for a quick glance.

146. **Assertion (A):** New technology is the only driving force behind the media boom in India.

Reason (R): Media contents are produced to meet the market-imputed needs.

147. **Assertion (A):** Post-modernist trends are blatantly visible in the content and design of Indian newspapers.

Reason (R): Because of impact and competition from the medium of television.

ANSWERS

1. (d)	2. (b)	3. (c)	4. (d)	5. (b)	6. (b)
7. (a)	8. (a)	9. (a)	10. (b)	11. (c)	12. (b)
13. (d)	14. (a)	15. (b)	16. (d)	17. (a)	18. (a)
19. (a)	20. (c)	21. (d)	22. (c)	23. (b)	24. (b)
25. (a)	26. (a)	27. (d)	28. (c)	29. (a)	30. (c)
31. (a)	32. (a)	33. (d)	34. (c)	35. (a)	36. (c)
37. (c)	38. (a)	39. (c)	40. (b)	41. (d)	42. (c)
43. (d)	44. (c)	45. (a)	46. (d)	47. (a)	48. (b)
49. (a)	50. (d)	51. (a)	52. (a)	53. (b)	54. (d)
55. (b)	56. (c)	57. (b)	58. (d)	59. (a)	60. (a)
61. (a)	62. (a)	63. (c)	64. (a)	65. (b)	66. (a)
67. (a)	68. (a)	69. (a)	70. (a)	71. (a)	72. (c)
73. (d)	74. (d)	75. (c)	76. (b)	77. (d)	78. (b)
79. (b)	80. (a)	81. (a)	82. (b)	83. (c)	84. (b)
85. (c)	86. (c)	87. (c)	88. (d)	89. (b)	90. (c)
91. (c)	92. (c)	93. (c)	94. (a)	95. (b)	96. (c)
97. (d)	98. (b)	99. (d)	100. (c)	101. (a)	102. (d)
103. (d)	104. (c)	105. (d)	106. (b)	107. (c)	108. (b)
109. (d)	110. (c)	111. (d)	112. (a)	113. (c)	114. (b)
115. (c)	116. (a)	117. (a)	118. (b)	119. (b)	120. (c)
121. (a)	122. (d)	123. (b)	124. (d)	125. (a)	126. (a)
127. (d)	128. (c)	129. (a)	130. (b)	131. (a)	132. (b)
133. (b)	134. (c)	135. (b)	136. (d)	137. (d)	138. (a)
139. (c)	140. (c)	141. (c)	142. (d)	143. (b)	144. (c)
145. (a)	146. (d)	147. (a)			

Previous Year Papers

DECEMBER 2012 (PAPER – II)

Note: This paper contains fifty (50) objective type questions of two (2) marks each. All questions are compulsory.

1. Mass communication gets filtered by
   (a) audience (b) media
   (c) gatekeepers (d) encoders
2. New India was established by
   (a) S. Sadanand
   (b) Mrs. Annie Besant
   (c) B.G. Horniman
   (d) Phiroze Shah Mehta
3. New media have facilitated the type of communication which is
   (a) abstract (b) conceptual
   (c) public (d) interactive
4. *The Times of India* has launched its edition in the month of February, 2012 from
   (a) Gangtok
   (b) Amritsar
   (c) Thiruvananthapuram
   (d) Panaji
5. For some feminist critics, mass media are used to portray women as belonging to
   (a) aristocratic culture
   (b) sentimental culture
   (c) rustic culture
   (d) middle brow culture
6. Which of the following is the latest development in the field of television set production?
   (a) LCD sets (b) LED sets
   (c) Smart sets (d) HDTV sets
7. *Searchlight* was a newspaper published from
   (a) Bihar (b) Assam
   (c) Punjab (d) Uttarakhand
8. In Britain, the Press Council was replaced by
   (a) the Royal Press Commission
   (b) the MediaComplaints Commission
   (c) the News Council
   (d) the Media Ombudsman
9. The National news agency of Indonesia is
   (a) Kyodo (b) Novosti
   (c) Garuda (d) Antara
10. The Second Press Commission of India recommended the establishment of
    (a) Press Council of India
    (b) National Media Training Institute
    (c) Newspaper Development Corporation
    (d) Media Competition Commission
11. The word 'journalist' is derived from
    (a) Journalography (b) Diurnalis
    (c) Diurna (d) Journology
12. Trans personal communication is
    (a) conversing with relatives
    (b) conversing with spirits and ancestors
    (c) conversing with the divine
    (d) conversing with the sages
13. 'Deep throat' was the source of information for the reporters investigating

(a) the Watergate scandal
(b) the Irangate scandal
(c) the Profumo-Christine Keeler scandal
(d) the Mundhra scandal

14. The first amendment to Article 19(1)(a) of the Indian Constitution was mainly aimed to include ______ as a cause for reasonable restriction.
(a) Public order
(b) Censorship
(c) Newspaper registration
(d) Licensing printing press

15. The post-industrial society is identified with
(a) traditional media
(b) print media
(c) visual media
(d) new media

16. Development, for some modernization theorists, is
(a) evolution (b) differentiation
(c) discrimination (d) affirmation

17. Modern mass media have made, by providing diverse choices, their audiences
(a) homogeneous (b) massive
(c) fragmented (d) integrated

18. A newspaper can infringe others' copyright provided it is in
(a) business interest
(b) protection of privacy
(c) corporate domain
(d) fair dealing

19. In public information model of public relations, importance is given to
(a) impact (b) reception
(c) truth (d) fair deal

20. Scientific research in mass communication demands the demonstration of
(a) Continuity (b) Permanence
(c) Transitivity (d) Co-variation

21. A specific communication task to be accomplished with a specific target audience during a specific period of time is termed
(a) advertising campaign
(b) advertising objective
(c) advertising criterion
(d) advertising evaluation

22. Which form of advertising is heavily used to introduce a new product?
(a) Persuasive advertising
(b) Reminder advertising
(c) Inferential advertising
(d) Informative advertising

23. In offset printing, the plate image is transferred to
(a) rubber blanket
(b) paper sheets
(c) paper maché plate
(d) plastic foils

24. Monopoly of cultural products at the global level has led to
(a) political hegemony
(b) economic colonization
(c) social domination
(d) information imperialism

25. The writers for media have adopted the narrative technique of
(a) convolution
(b) deconstruction
(c) story telling
(d) over-dramatization

26. **Assertion (A):** Mass media in India now suffer from celebrity syndrome.

Reason (R): Inter-media competition has compelled them to opt for it to survive in the field.

Codes:
(a) Both (A) and (R) are true.
(b) Both (A) and (R) are true, but (R) is not the correct explanation of (A).

(c) (A) is true, but (R) is false.
(d) (A) is false, but (R) is true.

27. **Assertion (A):** The idea of controlling social media through legislation in India is controversial.

    Reason (R): The third sector has opposed the proposal because it has found the social media effective for reacting the educated sections of the society.

    Codes:
    (a) Both (A) and (R) are true.
    (b) Both (A) and (R) are true, but (R) is not the correct explanation of (A).
    (c) (A) is true, but (R) is false.
    (d) (A) is false, but (R) is true.

28. **Assertion (A):** Media cannot set any agenda for national debates.

    Reason (R): Media audience select contents of their choice.

    Codes:
    (a) Both (A) and (R) are true.
    (b) Both (A) and (R) are true, but (R) is not the correct explanation of (A).
    (c) (A) is true, but (R) is false.
    (d) (A) is false, but (R) is true.

29. **Assertion (A):** Media manufactured culture is transient and keep on changing.

    Reason (R): Mediated culture is vulgar and does not have any artistic value.

    Codes:
    (a) Both (A) and (R) are true.
    (b) Both (A) and (R) are true, but (R) is not the correct explanation of (A).
    (c) (A) is true, but (R) is false.
    (d) (A) is false, but (R) is true.

30. **Assertion (A):** Indian media have national development as a high priority area for coverage.

    Reason (R): India is an emerging economic power and has to compete with China in the global market.

    Codes:
    (a) Both (A) and (R) are true.
    (b) Both (A) and (R) are true, but (R) is not the correct explanation of (A).
    (c) (A) is true, but (R) is false.
    (d) (A) is false, but (R) is true.

31. **Assertion (A):** Historical research in mass communication is more than chronological.

    Reason (R): It is more event oriented including social, political and economic developments to provide a holistic interpretation than a statement of dates and facts.

    Codes:
    (a) Both (A) and (R) are true.
    (b) Both (A) and (R) are true, but (R) is not the correct explanation of (A).
    (c) (A) is true, but (R) is false.
    (d) (A) is false, but (R) is true.

32. **Assertion (A):** Sting journalism has infused fear among the corrupt power wielders.

    Reason (R): Sting journalism often invades the privacy of the individuals.

    Codes:
    (a) Both (A) and (R) are true.
    (b) Both (A) and (R) are true, but (R) is not the correct explanation of (A).
    (c) (A) is true, but (R) is false.
    (d) (A) is false, but (R) is true.

33. **Assertion (A):** Feminist discourse in media has lost its importance and relevance.

    Reason (R): Women celebrities have replaced the larger issues concerning women.

    Codes:
    (a) Both (A) and (R) are true.
    (b) Both (A) and (R) are true, but (R) is not the correct explanation of (A).
    (c) (A) is true, but (R) is false.
    (d) (A) is false, but (R) is true.

34. **Assertion (A):** The post modernist approach has affected both visual and textual communication in recent times.

    Reason (R): Because the architecture of media contents is technology-driven.

    Codes:

    (a) Both (A) and (R) are true.
    (b) Both (A) and (R) are true, but (R) is not the correct explanation of (A).
    (c) (A) is true, but (R) is false.
    (d) (A) is false, but (R) is true.

35. **Assertion (A):** Inter-personal communication has more credibility than mediated communication in extension.

    Reason (R): Farmers do not have access to media and media contents are highly deceptive in nature.

    Codes:

    (a) Both (A) and (R) are true.
    (b) Both (A) and (R) are true, but (R) is not the correct explanation of (A).
    (c) (A) is true, but (R) is false.
    (d) (A) is false, but (R) is true.

36. Identify the correct sequence of the following newspapers on the basis of their origin.

    (a) *Bombay Darpan, Bombay Samachar, Bombay Courier, Bengal Gazette.*
    (b) *Bengal Gazette, Bombay Courier, Bombay Samachar, Bombay Darpan.*
    (c) *Bombay Samachar, Bombay Courier, Bombay Darpan, Bengal Gazette.*
    (d) *Bombay Courier, Bombay Samachar, Bombay Darpan, Bengal Gazette.*

37. Identify the correct sequence of the following in term of authorship of theories.

    (a) Walter Lippmann, Daniel Boorstin, Noam Chomski, Daniel Bell.
    (b) Daniel Bell, Walter Lippmann, Daniel Boorstin, Noam Chomski.
    (c) Noam Chomski, Daniel Bell, Walter Lippmann, Daniel Boorstin.
    (d) Daniel Boorstin, Noam Chomski, Daniel Bell, Walter Lippmann.

38. Identify the correct chronological sequence of the following theories:

    (a) Information theory, Public opinion theory, Magic bullet theory, Selectivity theory.
    (b) Public opinion theory, Magic bullet theory, Selectivity theory, Information theory.
    (c) Magic bullet theory, Public opinion theory, Information theory, Selectivity theory.
    (d) Selectivity theory, Information theory, Public opinion theory, Magic bullet theory.

39. Identify the correct sequence of the Ministers of Information and Broadcasting in India.

    (a) Indira Gandhi, B.V. Keskar, Vallabh Bhai Patel, Nandini Satapathy.
    (b) Nandini Satapathy, B.V. Keskar, Vallabh Bhai Patel, Indira Gandhi.
    (c) B.V. Keskar, Vallabh Bhai Pate, Indira Gandhi, Nandini Satapathy.
    (d) Vallabh Bhai Pate, B.V. Keskar, Indira Gandhi, Nandini Satapathy.

40. Identify the correct chronological sequence of the following editors:

    (a) Robert Knight, Frank Moraes, V.K. Narasimhan, Vinod Mehta.
    (b) V.K. Narasimhan, Vinod Mehta, Frank Moraes, Robert Knight.
    (c) Frank Moraes, V.K. Narasimhan, Robert Knight, Vinod Mehta.
    (d) Vinod Mehta, Robert Knight, Frank Moraes, V.K. Narasimhan.

41. Match the List-I with List-II:

List-I (Theory)	List-II (Theorists)
a. Balance Theory	1. Two-step flow of Information
b. Congruity Theory	2. Charles Osgood
c. Elihu Katz	3. Diffusion of Innovation
d. Everett Rogers	4. Fritz Heider

Codes:	a	b	c	d
(a)	1	3	2	4
(b)	2	4	3	1
(c)	3	1	4	2
(d)	4	2	1	3

42. Match the List-I with List-II:

List-I (Films)	List-II (Directors)
a. Fire	1. Shakti Sama
b. Aradhana	2. Nandita Das
c. Wild Straberries	3. Deepa Meht
d. Firaaq	4. Ingmar Berg

Codes:	a	b	c	d
(a)	1	2	3	4
(b)	2	4	1	3
(c)	3	1	4	2
(d)	4	3	2	1

43. Match the List-I with List-II:

List-I (Terms)

a. Focus out b. Focus
c. Blimp d. Bloop

List-II (Explanation)

1. Camera cover to lessen the sound of a camera.
2. Tape to paste on a spliced film to reduce sound.
3. Editing device.
4. Camera operation to sharpen the image.

Codes:	a	b	c	d
(a)	1	2	3	4
(b)	4	3	2	1
(c)	3	4	1	2
(d)	2	1	4	3

44. Match List-I with List-II:

List-I (Software)

a. Director b. Protool
c. Quark express d. Dreamweaver

List-II (Purpose to use)

1. To create web
2. To edit sound
3. To create animation/multimedia film
4. To layout the page

Codes:	a	b	c	d
(a)	1	3	2	4
(b)	3	2	4	1
(c)	4	1	3	2
(d)	2	4	1	3

45. Match List-I with List-II:

List-I

a. Circulation war
b. Check book Journalism
c. Paid news
d. Column

List-II

1. Pothen Joseph
2. Money to Journalists
3. Money to Source
4. Joseph Pulitzer

Codes:	a	b	c	d
(a)	4	3	2	1
(b)	3	2	1	3
(c)	2	4	3	1
(d)	1	2	3	4

Read the following passage and answer question Nos. 46-50.

The matter of adaptation of literary or theatrical works to the Cinema has been taken for granted by most early filmmakers including —not the least among them—Sergei Eisenstein. The Lessons With Eisenstein, as recorded by one of his students, Vladimir Nizhny, are, in fact, lessons in film adaptation.... Reading Lessons with Eisenstein gives the impression that filmmaking is adaptation. Were not some of our most memorable film experiences derived from novels, plays, Broadway shows? So, what is the problem? The author is dead—or nearly so. Texts are open—or can be opened. Plagiarism is an empty concept.

Adaptation has been an issue in both classic and post-classic—that is, pre-mid-1960s and post-mid-1960s—film theory. But whereas classical theory dealt with the transfer of a work from one set of codes to another set, recent film theory of adaptation offers but variations on the theme of authorship. For, to paraphrase Robin Wood, if you have a masterpiece, sooner or later the presence of the master will be felt. This is why film adaptation remains an important issue today in as much as auteurism endures.

One could, of course, allude here to the observation of McLuhan that any new medium absorbs the products of earlier media. That is what film did with regard to literary and theatrical works. And we can see the same phenomenon occurring today with television. This new comer, indeed, absorbs everything; journalism, education, religion, entertainment, sports, arts, business—all. But McLuhan has not done much more, in this respect, than to help us to take note of a rather obvious phenomenon. This phenomenon creates problems for the filmmaker. The latter shows that a screening of his or her film on the TV network has important implications regarding the very perception of the film—let alone necessary market implications. While making film, a filmmaker may have to keep in mind that his or her film may eventually be shown on TV and this may mean disaster to the complex sound track, to image composition where the values of colour and masses may be neutralized, and, above all, to framing. It is not a purists matter of the work being unaltered, faithfully reproduced. It is a matter of life or death: there are film segments that just won't go on the small screen.

Similarly, the adaptation of a literary or theatrical work to film can be a matter of life or death for the work concerned. As Andrey Tarkovsky has noticed:

Some works have a wholeness, and are endowed with a precise and original literary image, characters are drawn in unfathomable depths, the composition has an extraordinary capacity for enchantment, and the book is indivisible; through the pages comes the astonishing, unique personality of the author; books like that are master pieces, and only someone who is actually indifferent both to fine prose and to the Cinema can conceive the urge to screen them. It is all the more important to emphasize this point now, when the time has come for literature to be separated, once and for all, from cinema.

46. What did the Lessons with Eisenstein talk about?
   (a) Lessons of adaptation of literary works to cinema
   (b) Eisenstein's life
   (c) About cinema making
   (d) About what Eisenstein taught his students

47. What is the difference between the classical theory and recent film theory on adaptation?
   (a) The difference in authorship of the adapted film.
   (b) The variations on film themes.
   (c) The classical one talks about the original while the recent one talks about the new theme.
   (d) Classical theories talk about changes of codes, whereas the recent theories talk of variations of authorship of themes.

48. What is the opinion of McLuhan on adaptation?
    (a) A new work of art is created through adaptation.
    (b) The new medium takes in the past works of art and absorbs.
    (c) All art works are absorbed by television.
    (d) All works of art are destroyed by emerging media.
49. Identify the areas of negative influence that television may have on an adapted film?
    (a) The director's business
    (b) The story, character and dialogue
    (c) The sound track, colour and framing
    (d) The screening of a film in TV
50. What is the suggestion of Tarkovsky to solve the problem of 'life and death for a film'?
    (a) Showing a film in television to be made compulsory.
    (b) Adaptation from literature is a must for films.
    (c) Separate the author from the film.
    (d) Separate literature from Cinema completely.

ANSWERS

1. (c)	2. (b)	3. (d)	4. (c)
5. (b)	6. (c)	7. (a)	8. (b)
9. (d)	10. (c)	11. (b)	12. (b)
13. (a)	14. (a)	15. (d)	16. (b)
17. (c)	18. (d)	19. (c)	20. (d)
21. (b)	22. (d)	23. (a)	24. (d)
25. (c)	26. (b)	27. (a)	28. (d)
29. (c)	30. (d)	31. (a)	32. (a)
33. (b)	34. (a)	35. (c)	36. (b)
37. (a)	38. (b)	39. (d)	40. (a)
41. (d)	42. (c)	43. (c)	44. (b)
45. (a)	46. (a)	47. (d)	48. (b)
49. (c)	50. (d)		

DECEMBER 2012 (PAPER – III)

Note: This paper contains seventy five (75) objective type questions of two (2) marks each. All questions are compulsory.

1. Mass media, according to, Lazarsfeld and Merton, reinforce
   (a) public image
   (b) religious participation
   (c) social norms
   (d) economic ideas
2. The universal model of communication will have
   (a) six components
   (b) five components
   (c) four components
   (d) three components
3. E.M. Rogers, in his theoretical advocacy of diffusion of innovation, introduced the concept of
   (a) developmental symbolism
   (b) technocracy
   (c) cosmopoliteness
   (d) social interactionism
4. When media companies are owned by non-media business houses, it is called
   (a) Chain ownership
   (b) Joint Stock ownership
   (c) Conglomerate media ownership
   (d) Business ownership
5. George Gerbner while propounding the cultivation theory emphasized on the concepts of: Heavy viewers, light viewers and mainstreaming, the last one being.....
   (a) Resonance
   (b) Cognitive association

(c) Affectivity
(d) Priming

6. Majid Tehranian has spoken of development becoming a/an
(a) philosophy
(b) idea
(c) ism
(d) concentric concept

7. For Woolfson, individual consciousness, permeated by social communication is
(a) socio-ideological
(b) politico-creative
(c) psycho-persuasive
(d) ideo-cultural

8. The news media's primary responsibility to its audience is to provide truthful and accurate information in support of
(a) anti-establishment movements
(b) understanding news values that influence media decisions
(c) Advertising campaigns for establishing brand names
(d) Governmental policies of revenue generation

9. The Westley and McLean Model of communication identifies ______ role of the receiver.
(a) the advocacy
(b) the environmental
(c) the gatekeeper
(d) the behavioural

10. When media audience derive different meanings from the same text, the message is considered
(a) polysemic (b) denotative
(c) connotative (d) contrived

11. When media consumers search for knowledge as a motive, the need becomes
(a) biased (b) selective
(c) affective (d) cognitive

12. Stuart Hall asserted that the media created
(a) 'Virtual imagery'
(b) 'Societal contact'
(c) 'Preferred readings'
(d) 'Perception fluctuation'

13. In societal corporation, the Government and society collaborate through
(a) symmetrical communication
(b) asymmetrical communication
(c) individual communication
(d) corporate communication

14. The communication channels are kept open by
(a) removing regulations
(b) proactive access
(c) Phatic function
(d) Emotive function

15. Metanyms are power conveyors of
(a) Myth (b) Morality
(c) Creativity (d) Reality

16. The first International Convention related to Copyright was held at
(a) Berne (b) London
(c) Geneva (d) Rome

17. The Indian Constitution's provision for the Right to Freedom of Speech and Expression is notionally drawn from
(a) Bill of Rights
(b) Soviet Constitution
(c) Magna Carta
(d) Universal Declaration of Human Rights

18. In the cases of defamation, the term 'Manipulation' means
(a) Rumour
(b) Propaganda
(c) Abuse
(d) Allegation of fact

19. The applicability of Article 14 of the Indian Constitution was invoked by the

Supreme Court in the case involving the newspaper:
(a) Sakal
(b) Aajkal
(c) The Hindustan Times
(d) The Times of India

20. The Second Press Commission of India recommended the removal of Section 5 of
(a) the Press Council Act, 1978
(b) the Official Secrets Act, 1923
(c) the Contempt of Courts Act, 1971
(d) the Press and Registration of Books Act, 1867

21. In research, language and argumentation are expected to objectivise:
(a) human experiences
(b) creativity
(c) idealism
(d) institutional norms

22. The positivist paradigm, adopted by researchers in Mass Communication, makes a liberal use of
(a) descriptions
(b) fictional narratives
(c) aesthetics
(d) quantifications

23. A distinction between administrative and critical communication research was first drawn by
(a) Harold Lasswell
(b) Walter Lippmann
(c) Paul Lazarsfeld
(d) Elihu Katz

24. Human simulations for research are identified as
(a) role play
(b) experimentation
(c) operation
(d) games

25. The fitness of good test of applying chi-square to find out the association between two variables demands a minimum sample of
(a) 20 (b) 30
(c) 40 (d) 50

26. Fiske and Hartley have identified the concept of
(a) community radio
(b) bardic television
(c) delinquent media
(d) juvenile media

27. The metaphor of a wired universe interlinked by a network of computers was popularised by
(a) Al Gore
(b) Wilbur Schramm
(c) Jacobson
(d) George Gerbner

28. ________ can be called as presentational media.
(a) Magazines
(b) Newspapers
(c) Teletext
(d) Body language

29. The Arabic television channel Al-Jazeera has its headquarters at
(a) Cairo (b) Tunis
(c) Doha (d) Muscat

30. Motilal Ghosh was associated with
(a) Anand Bazaar Patrika
(b) Amrit Bazaar Patrika
(c) Jana Shakti
(d) Ganashakti

31. The Mail, published from the erstwhile city of Madras (now Chennai) was
(a) an eveninger
(b) a morning newspaper
(c) a weekly newspaper
(d) a bi-weekly newspaper

32. The Amit Mitra Committee was to prepare a report on

(a) national broadcast policy
(b) programme quality of AIR
(c) broadcast code of ethics
(d) radio recruitment policy

33. Narratology generally deals with two major elements; one is Suzyet, i.e. structure, the other being
(a) Character (b) Author
(c) Fabula (d) Climax

34. Editing in newspapers means the removal of ________ in writing.
(a) articles (b) fog
(c) atmosphere (d) treatment

35. The largest advertising agency of the world is
(a) J. Walter Thompson
(b) Saatehi and Saatehi
(c) David Ogilvy Inc.
(d) MacConn-Erikson Worldwide

36. According to a survey, advertisements published by women's magazines were ________ women.
(a) conferring status to
(b) commoditizing
(c) promoting employment of
(d) ethicising

37. An economy dependent upon selling and purchasing goods and services besides advertising to create a climate of purchases is supposed to promote:
(a) brand names
(b) sale society
(c) consumer culture
(d) advertising environment

38. ________ is the basis of public relations, advocated by the English Philosopher, Jeremy Bentham.
(a) Internationalism
(b) Religious morality
(c) Utilitarianism
(d) Stakeholder benefit

39. The systems theory of public relations is described as a set of united
(a) pressure groups
(b) subsystems
(c) employee systems
(d) production systems

40. Identification and analysis of situation, problem and offering solution to achieve organisational objectives will come under
(a) diplomacy
(b) Crisis management
(c) Strategic communication
(d) Community relations

41. Corporate public relations de: with
(a) the whole organisation
(b) goods and services
(c) profits and payments
(d) publicity and propaganda

42. The making of a film based on a novel is called adaptation, whereas a novel based on a film is called
(a) Adoption (b) Novelization
(c) Spinoff (d) Telecine

43. The mathematical ratio between the vertical and the horizontal measurements of a film/video is referred to as
(a) Frame ratio (b) Format ratio
(c) Size ratio (d) Aspect ratio

44. A Jump Cut is an editing technique that is employed
(a) at the end of a shot
(b) in between two scenes
(c) within a scene
(d) in between two sequences

45. Setting the best colour and density for the printing of each shot in film is known as
(a) colour setting
(b) colour temperature
(c) colour combination
(d) colour timing

46. Separation of a programme signal from the carrier wave is
    (a) Modulation
    (b) Demodulation
    (c) Co-modulation
    (d) Clear modulation

47. The down-the-line interview is conducted
    (a) face-to-face
    (b) with panellists
    (c) when the interviewer is at studio and the interviewee at another centre
    (d) in a large crowd

48. The commercial broadcasting wing of AIR, Vividh Bharati, was started as a counter to
    (a) Voice of America
    (b) BBC
    (c) Radio Ceylon
    (d) Radio Moscow

49. Extra programmes to make the already exiting radio programmes more attractive and interesting are well-known as
    (a) add-ons (b) infusions
    (c) go-buttons (d) frills

50. What is an F-stop?
    (a) Measurement of the flow of electricity
    (b) The size of the opening of a diaphragm
    (c) Measurement of the light temperature
    (d) The valve that stops the movement of a Camera mounted on a tripod

51. **Assertion (A):** The social media have become a global craze in recent times.

    Reason (R): Social media cut across the barriers of age, sex, culture and status.
    (a) Both (A) and (R) are true.
    (b) Both (A) and (R) are true, but (R) is not the correct explanation of (A).
    (c) (A) is true, but (R) is false.
    (d) (A) is false, but (R) is true.

52. **Assertion (A):** Corporate ownership of media is beneficial for audiences in the rural hinterland.

    Reason (R): Market-driven media will not bother much about their social responsibility as they concentrate more on returns than anything else.
    (a) Both (A) and (R) are true.
    (b) Both (A) and (R) are true, but (R) is not the correct explanation of (A).
    (c) (A) is true, (R) is false.
    (d) (A) is false, but (R) is true.

53. **Assertion (A):** The printing technology of massive production will soon be replaced by customised printing, possibly at home.

    Reason (R): The new technology of communication has already affected the exiting technology through colour Xeroxing.
    (a) Both (A) and (R) are true.
    (b) Both (A) and (R) are true, but (R) is not the correct explanation of (a).
    (c) (A) is true, but (R) is false.
    (d) (A) is false, but (R) is true.

54. **Assertion (A):** Educational broadcasting in India demands complete overhauling in terms of contents and presentation to reach larger audience.

    Reason (R): The private sector participation in educational broadcasting has necessitated the need for life-long learning.
    (a) Both (A) and (R) are true.
    (b) Both (A) and (R) are true, but (R) is not the correct explanation of (a).
    (c) (A) is true, but (R) is false.
    (d) (A) is false, but (R) is true.

55. **Assertion (A):** It is difficult to use folk media for the development of scientific temperament among masses in rural India.

Reason (R): Folk media depend upon religious discourses to reach out to the masses with moralistic overtones.

(a) Both (A) and (R) are true.
(b) Both (A) and (R) are true, but (R) is not the correct explanation of (A).
(c) (A) is true, but (R) is false.
(d) (A) is false, but (R) is true.

56. **Assertion (A):** New media has a negative impact on the writing skills of the new generation.

Reason (R): New media has altered the art of writing.

(a) Both (A) and (R) are true.
(b) Both (A) and (R) are true, but (R) is not the correct explanation for (A).
(c) (A) is true, (R) is false.
(d) (A) is false, but (R) is true.

57. **Assertion (A):** The Public Relations exercises seldom save a company in crises.

Reason (R): Public Relations exercises are dubious in nature.

(a) Both (A) and (R) are true.
(b) Both (A) and (R) are true, but (R) is not the correct explanation of (A).
(c) (A) is true, but (R) is false.
(d) (A) is false, but (R) is true.

58. **Assertion (A):** Radio is making a comeback as people listen to radio more these days.

Reason (R): Only those who drive cars listen to radio.

(a) Both (A) and (R) are true.
(b) Both (A) and (R) are true, but (R) is not the correct explanation of (A).
(c) (A) is true, but (R) is false.
(d) (A) is false, but (R) is true.

59. **Assertion (A):** The editors have lost out to the commercial influence within the newspapers.

Reason (R): Existence of "newswhole" is the reason for that.

(a) Both (A) and (R) are true.
(b) Both (A) and (R) are true, but (R) is not the correct explanation of (A).
(c) (A) is true, but (R) is false.
(d) (A) is false, but (R) is true.

60. **Assertion (A):** There is a decline in the popularity of the old media as new media penetrates the society.

Reason (R): Because the ownership of new media is not centered on one person or one organization.

(a) Both (A) and (R) are true.
(b) Both (A) and (R) are true, but (R) is not the correct explanation of (A).
(c) (A) is true, but (R) is false.
(d) (A) is false, but (R) is true.

61. Match List-I with List-II:

List-I (Concepts)	**List-II (Similar Concepts)**
a. Dailies	1. T-numbers
b. F-stops	2. Clapper board
c. Cinemascope	3. Rushes
d. Slate	4. Vitascope

Codes:	**a**	**b**	**c**	**d**
(a)	2	4	1	3
(b)	3	1	4	2
(c)	1	2	3	4
(d)	4	3	2	1

62. Match List-I with List-II:

List-I	**List-II**
a. Salman Khan	1. Dus ka Dum
b. Sunidhi Chauhan	2. Bade Achhe Lagte Hain
c. Sakshi Tanwar	3. Indian Idol
d. Archana Puran Singh	4. Comedy Circus

Codes:	**a**	**b**	**c**	**d**
(a)	4	2	3	1
(b)	1	3	2	4

(c)	3	1	4	2
(d)	2	4	1	3

63. Match List-I with List-II:

List-I (Films)	List-II (Heroine)
a. Aradhana	1. Rekha
b. Pyasa	2. Rani Mukherjee
c. Umrao-Jan	3. Sharmila Tagore
d. Black	4. Waheeda Rehman

Codes:	a	b	c	d
(a)	3	4	1	2
(b)	1	2	3	4
(c)	2	1	4	3
(d)	4	3	2	1

64. Match List-I with List-II:

List-I	List-II
a. Daskathia	1. Kerala
b. Koodiyattam	2. Odisha
c. Raslila	3. Maharashtra
d. Keertana	4. Manipur

Codes:	a	b	c	d
(a)	1	2	3	4
(b)	4	2	1	3
(c)	2	1	4	3
(d)	3	4	1	2

65. Match List-I with the List-II:

List-I	List-II
a. Mathrubhoomi	1. Odisha
b. Dinamalar	2. Kerala
c. Sadhana	3. Tamil Nadu
d. Dharitri	4. Gujarat

Codes:	a	b	c	d
(a)	3	2	4	1
(b)	4	1	2	3
(c)	2	3	4	1
(d)	1	4	3	2

66. Match List-I with the List-II:

List-I (Films)	List-II (Directors)
a. The Birds	1. Robert Flaharty
b. Nanook of the North	2. Satyajit Ray
c. The Days and Nights in Forest	3. Alfred Hitchcock
d. October	4. S.M. Eisenstein

Codes:	a	b	c	d
(a)	4	3	1	2
(b)	2	4	3	1
(c)	1	2	4	3
(d)	3	1	2	4

67. The correct sequence of the stages in the developmental idea campaigns is
(a) Distribution, penetration, participation, legitimacy, identification
(b) Identification, legitimacy, participation, penetration, distribution
(c) Identification, participation, penetration, legitimacy, distribution
(d) Participation, penetration, legitimacy, identification, distribution

68. Find out the correct chronological sequence of following news agencies:
(a) Free Press of India, United Press of India, Press Trust of India, Press News Bureau
(b) United Press of India, Press News Bureau, Press Trust of India, Free Press of India
(c) Press News Bureau, Free Press of India, United Press of India, Press Trust of India
(d) Free Press of India, Press News Bureau, United Press of India, Press Trust of India

69. Identify the correct chronological order of the following books:
(a) Mass Media and National Development; The Political Economy of Growth; Communication for Development: One World, Multiple Cultures; The Internet Galaxy

(b) The Internet Galaxy; Communication for Development: One World; Multiple Cultures; The Political Economy of Growth; Mass Media and National Development
(c) Communication for Development; One World, Multiple Cultures; The Internet Galaxy; Mass Media and National Development; The Political Economy of Growth
(d) The Political Economy of Growth; Communication for Development; One World; Multiple Cultures; The Internet Galaxy; The Mass Media and National Development

70. Which is the correct order of the following newspaper houses in India in terms of circulation and revenue?
(a) Dainik Bhaskar, The Hindustan Times, Jagran, The Times of India
(b) The Times of India, Jagran, The Hindustan Times, Dainik Bhaskar
(c) The Hindustan Times, The Times of India, Dainik Bhaskar, Jagran
(d) Jagran, Dainik Bhaskar, The Hindustan Times, The Times of India

Read the following passage and answer question nos. 71 to 75:

The Swiss Linguist Ferdinand de Saussure is the founder of semiology, and the American philosopher Charles Sanders Peirce is the founder of semiotics—both sciences are involved with how to interpret signs. In recent years, in part to make life simpler for ourselves, we have taken to using the term semiotics to stand for both methods of analysing signs. But what is a sign? I will explain Saussure's theories first and then deal with Peirce's. For Saussure, the important thing to remember about signs is that they are made up of sounds and images, what he called signifiers, and the concepts these sounds and images bring to mind, what he called signifiers, and the concepts these sounds and images bring to mind, what he called signified.... Words are signs, but so are many other things, such as facial expressions, body language, clothes, haircuts—you name it. To a semiotician, everything can be taken for a sign....

Saussure said there was something very important to remember about signs: The relation between signifier and signified is based on CONVENTION, IS ARBITARRY. The word tree and the large stemmed plant for which the word tree stands is not natural but historical, tied to conventions and choices that people made. He distinguished symbols from signs by saying that symbols, which he saw as a subcategory of signs are not completely arbitrary.... What is important to remember is that symbols have enormous significance in our lives and play an important role in our thinking and behaviour.

Peirce had a different system. He believed there were three different kinds of signs : icons, indexes, and symbols. Icons signify by resemblance, indexes signify on the basis of convention.

71. What do the semiotics and semiology mean?
(a) Both mean analysing of signs.
(b) Semiotics is theory and semiology is the interpretation of that theory.
(c) Semiotics studies signs while semiology creates models.
(d) Semiotics studies signs while semiology studies symbols.

72. Signifier means:
(a) meaning
(b) concepts
(c) signs and symbols that one sees around
(d) a collection of signs and symbol

73. Facial expressions, hair cuts and body languages are known as
(a) Signs (b) Meaning
(c) Semiotics (d) Semiology

74. The connection between the signifiers and signified is
(a) logical (b) arbitrary
(c) calculations (d) theory oriented

75. The symbol, according to Peirce is based on
(a) Customs (b) Deductions
(c) Formula (d) Relativism

ANSWERS

1. (c)	2. (b)	3. (c)	4. (c)
5. (a)	6. (c)	7. (a)	8. (b)
9. (d)	10. (a)	11. (d)	12. (c)
13. (a)	14. (c)	15. (d)	16. (a)
17. (a)	18. (d)	19. (d)	20. (b)
21. (a)	22. (d)	23. (c)	24. (d)
25. (d)	26. (b)	27. (a)	28. (d)
29. (c)	30. (b)	31. (a)	32. (a)
33. (c)	34. (b)	35. (d)	36. (b)
37. (c)	38. (c)	39. (b)	40. (c)
41. (a)	42. (b)	43. (d)	44. (c)
45. (d)	46. (b)	47. (c)	48. (c)
49. (d)	50. (b)	51. (a)	52. (d)
53. (c)	54. (c)	55. (a)	56. (b)
57. (c)	58. (c)	59. (a)	60. (b)
61. (b)	62. (b)	63. (a)	64. (c)
65. (c)	66. (d)	67. (b)	68. (c)
69. (a)	70. (b)	71. (a)	72. (c)
73. (a)	74. (b)	75. (a)	

JUNE 2012 (PAPER – II)

Note: This paper contains fifty (50) objective type questions of two (2) marks each. All the questions are compulsory.

1. The Shannon and Weaver model of communication is:
(a) Modular (b) Circular
(c) Linear (d) Non-linear

2. The medium that has the widest reach in India is:
(a) Print (b) Radio
(c) Television (d) Internet

3. The Surgeon-General's report focussed on the impact of television violence on
(a) youth (b) women
(c) children (d) ethnic minorities

4. The 'Limited effects' model of mass communication was a counter to
(a) ABX model
(b) Circular model
(c) Diffusion model
(d) Hypodermic needle model

5. The issue of monopoly press was debated extensively during the Prime Ministership of
(a) Jawaharlal Nehru
(b) Indira Gandhi
(c) I.K. Gujral
(d) H.D. Deve Gowda

6. The code of ethics drawn in 1978 was a form of self-censorship by
(a) the Indian Languages Newspaper Association
(b) the Advertising Standards Council of India.
(c) The All-India Newspaper Editors' Conference
(d) The Editors' Guild

7. A licence in copyright matters creates in the license

(a) public right (b) personal right
(c) proprietory right (d) statutory right

8. The distinction of being the editor of two major English newspapers, The Times of India and the Statesman was held by
(a) Robert Knight
(b) James Bryce
(c) Peter Reed
(d) Rudyard Kipling

9. The community radio concept is identified with
(a) broadcasting (b) narrowcasting
(c) personal casting (d) podcasting

10. One of the major recommendations of the First Press Commission of India was introduction of
(a) Price-page schedule
(b) Right to Information Act
(c) Press freedom as a constitutional guarantee
(d) Codification of journalistic privileges

11. The communication theory of developmental communication emphasized
(a) top-down communication
(b) mechanistic communication
(c) epistemological approach
(d) extensive demonstrations

12. A strategy that is integrated into communication for development is
(a) religious lecture
(b) social marketing
(c) propaganda
(d) rural publicity

13. The middle range theory of communication was advocated by
(a) John Fiske (b) Robert Merton
(c) Karl Marx (d) M.S. Archer

14. F.R. Leavis stressed on ___ of media text.
(a) practical criticism
(b) inter-relatedness
(c) transience
(d) commercial elements

15. A universal generalisation is the main feature of _____ explanation.
(a) purposive (b) accidental
(c) inductive (d) deductive

16. The Likert scale is used to find out _____ of items selected.
(a) the argumentative structure
(b) the meaning
(c) the objectives
(d) the discriminative power

17. In the two-way symmetric model of public relations, the model of communication used is
(a) person-to-person
(b) group-to-group
(c) person-to-group
(d) group-to-person

18. The single-sheet advertisements printed on one-side are known as
(a) brochures (b) fliers
(c) leaflets (d) posters

19. Multi-tasking in journalism is due to
(a) media globalisation
(b) economic liberalisation
(c) social integration
(d) technology convergence

20. After determining its advertising objectives, a company has to set ____ for each product.
(a) advertising strategies
(b) advertising budget
(c) advertising format
(d) advertisement positioning

21. Which of the following is the combination of sound bite and stand up?
(a) Package (b) Talking heads
(c) Voice-over (d) Supers

22. The social network medium that has gone for global IPO recently is
(a) Facebook (b) Twitter
(c) Orkut (d) Youtube

23. The soviet media theory had its roots in
(a) Italian Fascist philosophy
(b) Free enterprise approach of the west
(c) German ideology
(d) Japanese imperialist edicts

24. The readability tests, Fog Index and Reading. Ease score, were first employed by
(a) newspapers
(b) syndicates
(c) television networks
(d) news agencies

25. The television news writing these days includes
(a) hyperboles
(b) non-sequiturs
(c) gender-neutral words
(d) uncommon abbreviations

26. **Assertion (A):** Small and Medium newspapers in India will have bleak future with the corporatisation of mass media.

Reason (R): The Union Government has not declared media business as an industry and it is responsible for their bleak future.
(a) Both (A) and (R) are true.
(b) Both (A) and (R) are true, but (R) is not the correct explanation of (A).
(c) (A) is true, but (R) is false.
(d) (A) is false, but (R) is true.

27. **Assertion (A):** The print media in India are registering increase in circulation unlike the developed countries.

Reason (R): Increased literacy and expanding market have contributed for consolidation of print media.
(a) Both (A) and (R) are true.
(b) Both (A) and (R) are true, but (R) is not the correct explanation of (A).
(c) (A) is true, but (R) is false.
(d) (A) is false, but (R) is true.

28. **Assertion (A):** The Right to Information has created hurdles for good governance in India.

Reason (R): The Right to Information has become a credible source of news for mass media for investigative journalism.
(a) Both (A) and (R) are true.
(b) Both (A) and (R) are true but (R) is not the correct explanation of (A).
(c) (A) is true, but (R) is false.
(d) (A) is false, but (R) is true.

29. **Assertion (A):** Social networking can make the Indian political class watchful and refrain from getting involved in misdeeds.

Reason (R): Social media have made the Arab spring possible and hence, the Indian political class is cautious.
(a) Both (A) and (R) are true.
(b) Both (A) and (R) are true, but (R) is not the correct explanation of (A).
(c) (A) is true, but (R) is false.
(d) (A) is false, but (R) is true.

30. **Assertion (A):** The Government has made legislations on corporate social responsibility for effective community relations.

Reason (R): The corporate giants must do their bit for national development.
(a) Both (A) and (R) are true.
(b) Both (A) and (R) are true, but (R) is not the correct explanation of (A).
(c) (A) is true, but (R) is false.
(d) (A) is false, but (R) is true.

31. **Assertion (A):** The Press Council of India must be converted into a media council is a matter of opinion.

Reason (R): Since the reach and access of electronic media have increased tremendously, there are issues to be considered involving all of them.
(a) Both (A) and (R) are true.
(b) Both (A) and (R) are true, but (R) is not the correct explanation of (A).
(c) (A) is true, but (R) is false.
(d) (A) is false, but (R) is true.

32. **Assertion (A):** The obsession of Indian print media with politics is a historical legacy.

Reason (R): Because many political leaders were associated with newspapers to advocate the cause of freedom before 1947.
(a) Both (A) and (R) are true.
(b) Both (A) and (R) are true, but (R) is not the correct explanation of (A).
(c) (A) is true, but (R) is false.
(d) (A) is false, but (R) is true.

33. **Assertion (A):** In times of global recession, paid news is a supplementary source of revenue for media houses in India.

Reason (R): Media houses in India have been experiencing increased production cost and staff wages in the last few years.
(a) Both (A) and (R) are true.
(b) Both (A) and (R) are true, but (R) is not the correct explanation of (A).
(c) (A) is true, but (R) is false.
(d) (A) is false, but (R) is true.

34. **Assertion (A):** Editing is a lost art in print journalism.

Reason (R): These days, language precision is not a qualification for recruitment by newspapers.
(a) Both (A) and (R) are true.
(b) Both (A) and (R) are true, but (R) is not the correct explanation of (A).
(c) (A) is true, but (R) is false.
(d) (A) is false, but (R) is true.

35. **Assertion (A):** The new international information and communication order is a dead horse in a unipolar world.

Reason (R): The developing countries do not opt for policy initiatives to strengthen the global efforts for a new international and communication order.
(a) Both (A) and (R) are true.
(b) Both (A) and (R) are true, but (R) is not the correct explanation of (A).
(c) (A) is true, but (R) is false.
(d) (A) is false, but (R) is true.

36. Identify the chronological sequence of the following communication theorists.
(a) Harold Lasswell, Shannon and Weaver, Theodore Newcomb, Elisabeth Noelle Neuman.
(b) Shannon and Weaver, Theodore Newcomb, Elisabeth Noelle Newman, Harold Lasswell.
(c) Theodore Newcomb, Elisabeth Noelle Newman, Harold Lasswell, Shannon and Weaver.
(d) Shannon and Weaver, Theodore Newcomb, Elisabeth Noelle Newman, Harold Lasswell.

37. Identify the proper sequence of the films given below in terms of their historicity.
(a) Swayamvaram, Coolie, Slumdog Millionaire, Pather Panchali
(b) Pather Panchali, Swayamvaram, Coolie, Slumdog Millionaire
(c) Coolie, Slumdog Millionaire, Swayamvaram, Pather Panchali
(d) Slumdog Millionaire, Coolie, Swayamvaram, Pather Panchali

38. Identify the sequence of the following developmental models chronologically:
(a) Diffusion of innovation, dependency, multiplicity, modernization
(b) Modernization, diffusion of innovation, dependency, multiplicity

(c) Multiplicity, modernization, diffusion of innovation, dependency
(d) Dependency, multiplicity, diffusion of innovation, modernization

39. Identify the correct sequence of following magazines in terms of their circulation.
(a) India Today, Sarita, Kangumum, Kumudam
(b) Sarita, Kumudum, Kungumum, India Today
(c) Kumudum, Kungumum, India Today, Sarita
(d) India Today, Kungumum, Kumudum, Sarita

40. Identify the correct sequence of the following laws of the press.
(a) Right to Information Act, Copyright Act, Official Secrets Act, Contempt of Courts Act
(b) Copyright Act, Official Secrets Act, Contempt of Courts Act, Right to Information Act
(c) Official Secrets Act, Copyright Act, Contempt of Courts Act, Right to Information Act
(d) Contempt of Courts Act, Copyright Act, Right to Information Act, Official Secrets Act

41. Match the List-I with List-II:

List-I	List-II
(a) Bob Wood	1. With malice to one and all
(b) Kuldeep Nayyar	2. Editor of Indian Express
(c) Khuswant Singh	3. Investigative Reporting
(d) Arun Shourie	4. Between the Lines

Codes:	(a)	(b)	(c)	(d)
(a)	(3)	(4)	(1)	(2)
(b)	(2)	(1)	(4)	(3)
(c)	(1)	(2)	(4)	(3)
(d)	(4)	(1)	(3)	(2)

42. Match the List-I with List-II.

List-I	List-II
(a) Banner	(1) Emergency
(b) Sedition	(2) Headlines
(c) Berliner	(3) Independence
(d) Swadesh Mitran	(4) Newspaper format

Codes:	(a)	(b)	(c)	(d)
(a)	(2)	(1)	(4)	(3)
(b)	(3)	(4)	(1)	(2)
(c)	(1)	(2)	(4)	(3)
(d)	(4)	(1)	(3)	(2)

43. Match the List-I with List-II.

List-I	List-II
(a) Shobha De	(1) Antagonist of Censorship
(b) Barkha Dutt	(2) Columnist
(c) Aswini Sarin	(3) T.V. Anchor
(d) K.A. Abbas	(4) Investigative reporting

Codes:	(a)	(b)	(c)	(d)
(a)	(1)	(4)	(3)	(2)
(b)	(2)	(3)	(4)	(1)
(c)	(3)	(2)	(1)	(4)
(d)	(4)	(1)	(2)	(3)

44. Match the List-I with List-II.

List-I	List-II
(a) Coffingate	(1) B.G. Verghese
(b) 2G Spectrum expose	(2) Gopikrishnan
(c) Television	(3) Tarun Tejpal
(d) MacBride Commission	(4) Pranav Roy

Codes:	(a)	(b)	(c)	(d)
(a)	(3)	(4)	(1)	(2)
(b)	(3)	(2)	(4)	(1)
(c)	(1)	(2)	(3)	(4)
(d)	(4)	(3)	(2)	(1)

45. Match the List-I with List-II:

List-I	List-II
(a) DAVP	(1) International news flow
(b) ABC	(2) Association
(c) INS	(3) Certification
(d) NWICO	(4) Publicity

Codes:	(a)	(b)	(c)	(d)
(a)	(2)	(3)	(4)	(3)
(b)	(1)	(2)	(3)	(4)
(c)	(4)	(3)	(2)	(1)
(d)	(3)	(4)	(1)	(2)

Read the following passage and answer question no. 46 to 50.

The term "ethnomethodology" was thought up by a distinguished sociologist, Harold Garfinkel. In an article titled "The origins of the term 'Ethnomethodology', Garfinkel explains how he thought up the name:

"Ethno" seemed to refer, somehow or other, to the availability to a member of commonsense knowledge of his society as commonsense knowledge of the 'whatever'. If it were ethno-botany, then it had to do somehow or other with his knowledge of and his grasp of what were for members adequate methods of dealing with botanical matters. Someone from another society, like an anthropologist in this case, world recognize the matters as botanical matters. The member would employ ethnobotany as adequate grounds of inference and action in the conduct of his own affairs in the company of others like him. It was that plain, and the notion of "ethnomethodology" or the term "ethnomethodology" was taken in this sense....

Thus ethnomethodology is interested in how people think and act in everyday life situations, in contrast to, for example, laboratory experiments or focus groups or other situations in which people recognize that they are, one way or another, being studied. 'Common sense' becomes a subject of inquiry, not just a 'given' that is neglected for other concerns.

These interests of ethnomethodologists have implications for advertising, in that advertisers want to know how people make sense of the world and how they react to 'Commonsense' appeals. Advertisers want to be able to 'reach' targeted segments of the population and to influence them, which means advertisers want to understand people's 'grounds for inference'. Thus, ethnomethodology has important implications when it comes to making commercials and print advertisements.

Ethnomethodologists assume that people have common understandings—which they don't always articulate—and this leads ethnomethodologists to examine how people reason and what's behind their everyday activities. It isn't easy to find these common understandings or to determine how people reason....

The question arises now. How can we use ethnomethodology in our research in communication and media analysis? Let me suggest a few answers to this question.

What ethnomethodology provides us, we must remember, is a way of studying the codes and unconscious belief systems that lie behind our utterances and everyday actions. We can adopt Ethnomethodological approaches to the media by asking the same questions. Ethnomethodologists ask—not about conversation ê but about dialogue in films and television shows, lyrics in songs, and similar phenomena.

There are differences between the analysis of dialogue in media and the analyses that ethnomethodologists make of real-world conversations in that dialogue in mass-mediated texts is created by writers. In a sense, therefore, when we do research on dialogue in a film or other mass-mediated text, we are dealing with a writer's perception of the world, but because writers create texts for large numbers of people, who presumably share their perceptions, we can assume that analyzing dialogue in mediated texts is not that different from analyzing dialogue in every day situations.

46. What is meant by ethnomethodology?
    (a) Special sociological research method.
    (b) Study of a particular group
    (c) Ways and methods applied to study the common-sense knowledge of a person about the society
    (d) Study of tribal culture
47. Why do the advertisers show interest in ethnomethodology?
    (a) To have good understanding about ethnic goups.
    (b) To know how people make sense of their surrounding and what influences their decision making.
    (c) To create a market
    (d) To make an ad copy
48. What do ethnomethodologists examine?
    (a) The activities of people
    (b) The articulations of people
    (c) The cultural rules of the society
    (d) The reasoning process of people and their activities
49. What are the units the ethnomethodologists study in films and TV shows?
    (a) Dialogues and lyrics
    (b) All sounds and music
    (c) The main conversations
    (d) The themes and sub-themes
50. Why do mediated text and everyday conversation are assumed to be the same?
    (a) There is no difference between the real life and television drama.
    (b) Mass media and reality shown in TV emanate from the same society
    (c) The perception of the writer about the world and the real life is considered to be the same
    (d) The perception of the people as assumed and shared by the writer and the reality are the same.

ANSWERS

1. (c)	2. (b)	3. (c)	4. (d)
5. (b)	6. (c)	7. (b)	8. (a)
9. (b)	10. (a)	11. (c)	12. (b)
13. (b)	14. (a)	15. (d)	16. (d)
17. (b)	18. (b)	19. (d)	20. (b)
21. (a)	22. (a)	23. (c)	24. (d)
25. (c)	26. (b)	27. (a)	28. (d)
29. (b)	30. (d)	31. (a)	32. (a)
33. (d)	34. (c)	35. (a)	36. (a)
37. (b)	38. (b)	39. (d)	40. (c)
41. (a)	42. (a)	43. (b)	44. (b)
45. (c)	46. (c)	47. (b)	48. (d)
49. (a)	50. (d)		

JUNE 2012 (PAPER – III)

Note: This paper contains seventy five (75) objective type questions of two (2) marks each. All questions are compulsory.

1. Denis McQuail identified the mass media function of
   (a) surveillance of environment
   (b) transmission of culture
   (c) non-formal education
   (d) promotion of democratic participation
2. The largest circulated English news magazine of India is
   (a) Outlook (b) The Week
   (c) India Today (d) The Frontline
3. Indian Express was originally published from

(a) Bombay (b) Calcutta
(c) Madras (d) Nagpur

4. Charles R. Wright was the first theorist who identified the media function of
(a) information (b) education
(c) interpretation (d) entertainment

5. 'Marattha' was the sister publication of
(a) Lok Satta
(b) Kesari
(c) Sakal
(d) Maharashtra Times

6. The British Broadcasting Corporation's main revenue source for a long time was
(a) Government subsidy
(b) Licence fee
(c) Public donations
(d) Sale of bonds

7. The Yuva Vani programme of All India Radio was introduced during the tenure of ______ as the Minister for Information and Broadcasting.
(a) B. Gopala Reddy
(b) Pramod Mahajan
(c) I.K. Gujral
(d) Indira Gandhi

8. Indian television channels are accused of promoting the stereotype of women being
(a) aggressive (b) affectionate
(c) submissive (d) critical

9. The functional analysis approach in communication is related to
(a) personal influence approach
(b) mass culture approach
(c) persuasive technology approach
(d) social systems approach

10. Who first described mass media as a culture industry?
(a) Stuart Hall
(b) Theodor Adorno
(c) Stuart Mill
(d) Jean Boudrillard

11. ______ is considered as a mechanical medium.
(a) Book (b) Newspaper
(c) Television (d) Puppetry

12. The main purpose of asymmetric two-way model of public relations is
(a) distortion of facts
(b) scientific persuasion
(c) personality promotion
(d) discourage competition

13. Central to the uses and gratifications approach in communication would be
(a) messages (b) channels
(c) audiences (d) encoders

14. In communication, redundancy has
(a) highest predictability
(b) lowest predictability
(c) balanced predictability
(d) imperfect predictability

15. The process school of communication leans heavily on
(a) linguistics (b) applied arts
(c) semiotics (d) social sciences

16. 'Enlightened self-interest' is the notion behind
(a) risk management
(b) event management
(c) corporate social responsibility
(d) publicity campaigns

17. The creative function of communication is important in
(a) encoding (b) feedback
(c) rituals (d) propaganda

18. According to Umberto Eco, aberrant decoding takes place in a
(a) tribal society
(b) farming society

(c) mass society
(d) convergent society

19. The deontological theory of Immanuel Kant prescribed categorical imperatives based on
(a) Public Opinion
(b) Moral Law
(c) Political Behaviour
(d) Personal Convenience

20. Gatefold can be mostly seen in
(a) magazines (b) newspapers
(c) books (d) posters

21. The Vidyalankar Committee was assigned to prepare a report on
(a) Press Information Bureau
(b) Functioning of AIR
(c) Central Publicity
(d) Information and Broadcasting Ministry

22. Section 95 of the Criminal Procedure Code permits a State Government the forfeiture of
(a) offending publication
(b) security deposit
(c) printing press
(d) journalistic accreditation

23. The legal doctrine of direct impact is applied in the cases involving limitation of
(a) Personal Freedom
(b) Newspaper Circulation
(c) Editorial Independence
(d) Taxation on Advertisements

24. The constitutional restriction on Article 19(1)(a) in the form of public order falls within the concentric circle of
(a) obscenity (b) law and order
(c) security of State (d) defamation

25. In a case of contempt of Parliament, R.K. Karanjia of the Blitz was ______ by the Speaker of Lok Sabha.
(a) admonished (b) imprisoned
(c) excluded (d) reprimanded

26. The protection of publication of proceedings of Parliament and State Legislature is guaranteed by Article ______ of the Indian Constitution.
(a) 105 (b) 194
(c) 361 A (d) 375

27. The multiplicity model of developmental communication was advocated by
(a) Jan Servaes (b) Lucien Pye
(c) Shirley White (d) Bella Mody

28. For Daniel Lerner, exposure to media would energise the process of ______ for development.
(a) sensitivity (b) anxiety
(c) sympathy (d) empathy

29. The advertising medium that has the advantage of high selectivity, immediacy and low cost is
(a) Newspaper (b) Direct Mail
(c) Radio (d) Online

30. Most correlational designs have the problem of manipulating
(a) conceptual definitions
(b) control variables
(c) independent variables
(d) dependent variables

31. The main problem of simulation in communication research is
(a) atmosphere (b) response
(c) validity (d) modelling

32. The panel study is sensitive to
(a) experimental mortality
(b) cost-effectiveness
(c) response classification
(d) instrumental criticality

33. The snowball sampling method is useful when the universe is small and

(a) scattered (b) specific
(c) general (d) concentrated

34. Discourse analysis considers all human communication as a
(a) content (b) starting point
(c) narrative (d) contemplation

35. The closed systems approach is reflected in ______ public relations.
(a) proactive (b) reactive
(c) reflective (d) selective

36. The mathematical centre is not the optic centre when we design the front page of a
(a) standard daily newspaper
(b) leaflet
(c) brochure
(d) booklet

37. A sentence used in communication is a ______ of words.
(a) paradigm (b) syntagm
(c) consequence (d) movement

38. The reference code often used for television recordings is known
(a) real time (b) clock time
(c) virtual time (d) clear time

39. When the frames of a TV commercial are shown to a select group of samples to get their opinion, it is called
(a) An Attitude test
(b) A Starch test
(c) A Bruzzone test
(d) A Persuasion test

40. What is a Spinoff?
(a) Is the second part of a film made earlier.
(b) Is a new TV serial created by taking elements from an earlier serial.
(c) Is the depiction of a serial murder that happened earlier.
(d) Is a merger of two earlier films.

41. Who identified that 'online gambling is a serious issue that has not been addressed under any law'?
(a) Asian Cyber Law Institute
(b) Indian Online Institute
(c) Asian Internet Association
(d) American Cyber Law Institute

42. Reuters has invested in the Indian news agency
(a) Press Trust of India
(b) Asia News International
(c) United News of India
(d) Indo-Asia News Agency

43. The news agency that has the largest number of foreign correspondents is
(a) United Press International
(b) Reuters
(c) Associated Press
(d) Agencè France Pressè

44. An editor, in order to maintain consistency in visual style in his newspaper, should
(a) use outlines in bold types
(b) use all cap headlines
(c) use fonts within one type family
(d) use italics for intros

45. A panel designed to absorb or reflect sound is identified as
(a) bouncer (b) level board
(c) battle (d) blimp

46. Simultaneous presentation of two contradictory visuals is called
(a) Counter point (b) Counter angle
(c) Counter bias (d) Counter view

47. Measuring the number of digital errors in a single signal is known as
(a) error rate
(b) distortion scale
(c) fader head
(d) single error code

48. A broadcast commercial produced for the purpose of demonstration is identified as
    (a) trial commercial
    (b) exhibition commercial
    (c) model spot
    (d) speculation spot

49. The Aristotalian dramatic structure that is generally adopted for feature flim has five phases. The four phases are exposition, rising action, climax and falling action. The fifth is
    (a) Ending
    (b) Resolution
    (c) Conclusion
    (d) Recommendation

50. In newspapers, news headlines should be written around a strong ______
    (a) Adjective (b) Adverb
    (c) Verb (d) Participle

51. **Assertion (A):** Confidentiality of news sources is difficult to maintain these days.

    Reason (R): Media persons have become part of the system for personal gains as well as politically ambitious in democratic societies.
    (a) Both (A) and (R) are true.
    (b) Both (A) and (R) are true, but (R) is not the correct explanation of (A).
    (c) (A) is true, but (R) is false.
    (d) (A) is false, but (R) is true.

52. **Assertion (A):** With exposure to global media, the organic model of development is lost sight of.

    Reason (R): Western values and consumerism have taken over the mindset of common people exposed to Western culture through media.
    (a) Both (A) and (R) are true.
    (b) Both (A) and (R) are true, but (R) is not the correct explanation of (A).
    (c) (A) is true, but (R) is false.
    (d) (A) is false, but (R) is true.

53. **Assertion (A):** Self-regulation by media in India is a Myth.

    Reason (R): Media tabloidization is a reality in India and there is no statutory code of ethics to control them.
    (a) Both (A) and (R) are true.
    (b) Both (A) and (R) are true, but (R) is not the correct explanation of (A).
    (c) (A) is true, but (R) is false.
    (d) (A) is false, but (R) is true.

54. **Assertion (A):** The tribe of eminent newspaper editors has vanished from India.

    Reason (R): The corporatisation of Indian press and the focus on profits have made it difficult for conscientious people to enter the profession.
    (a) Both (A) and (R) are true.
    (b) Both (A) and (R) are true, but (R) is not the correct explanation of (A).
    (c) (A) is true, but (R) is false.
    (d) (A) is false, but (R) is true.

55. **Assertion (A):** Proper and effective use of ICT can change the face of rural development in India.

    Reason (R): Projects like e-seva and Bhoomi were responsible for the success of rural initiatives as they provided e-literacy kits to kids in these States of Andhra Pradesh and Karnataka.
    (a) Both (A) and (R) are true.
    (b) Both (A) and (R) are true, but (R) is not the correct explanation of (A).
    (c) (A) is true, but (R) is false.
    (d) (A) is false, but (R) is true.

56. **Assertion (A):** The language newspaper in India is expanding exponentially whereas newspaper is on the decline in the Western countries.

    Reason (R): There is a large number of neo-literates in various States of India and they buy newspaper to read.

(a) Both (A) and (R) are true.
(b) Both (A) and (R) are true, but (R) is not the correct explanation of (A).
(c) (A) is true, but (R) is false.
(d) (A) is false, but (R) is true.

57. **Assertion (A):** The community radio stations are not yielding the kind of results that the protagonists had expected.

Reason (R): No feasibility study was done before establishing the community radio stations.

(a) Both (A) and (R) are true.
(b) Both (A) and (R) are true, but (R) is not the correct explanation of (A).
(c) (A) is true, but (R) is false.
(d) (A) is false, but (R) is true.

58. **Assertion (A):** The television in India does not cater to the needs of the common people.

Reason (R): All the television channels are owned by the rich and powerful persons.

(a) Both (A) and (R) are true.
(b) Both (A) and (R) are true, but (R) is not the correct explanation of (A).
(c) (A) is true, but (R) is false.
(d) (A) is false, but (R) is true.

59. **Assertion (A):** Communication Research is only confined to the elements of transmission model.

Reason (R): No fund is available to explore the new areas of communication.

(a) Both (A) and (R) are true.
(b) Both (A) and (R) are true, but (R) is not the correct explanation of (A).
(c) (A) is true, but (R) is false.
(d) (A) is false, but (R) is true.

60. Assertion (A): Every year a large number of new brands fail and thus die.

Reason (R): Brands survive only when they have functional value.

(a) Both (A) and (R) are true.
(b) Both (A) and (R) are true, but (R) is not the correct explanation of (A).
(c) (A) is true, but (R) is false.
(d) (A) is false, but (R) is true.

61. Find out the correct chronological sequence of following television networks of India:

(a) Star, Zee, Sony, Doordarshan
(b) Doordarshan, Star, Zee, Sony
(c) Sony, Zee, Doordarshan, Star
(d) Zee, Star, Doordarshan, Sony

62. Find out the correct chronological sequence of the following news agencies:

(a) Havas, Reuters, United Press International, Bloomberg
(b) Reuters, Havas, Bloomberg, United Press International
(c) Bloomberg, Havas, Reuters, United Press International
(d) United Press International, Reuters, Bloomberg, Havas

63. Identify the correct sequence of the following Chairpersons of the Press Council of India:

(a) Justice T.S. Rajagopala Iyengar, Justice P.B. Sawant, Justice G.N. Ray, Justice Markandeya Katju
(b) Justice P.B. Sawant, Justice G.N. Ray, Justice Markandeya Katju, Justice T.S. Rajagopala Iyengar
(c) Justice G.N. Ray, Justice Markandeya Katju, Justice T.S. Rajagopala Iyengar, Justice P.B. Sawant
(d) Justice Markandeya Katju, Justice T.S. Rajagopala Iyengar, Justice P.B. Sawant, Justice G.N. Ray

64. Find out the correct sequence of the stages identified in the information processing theory.

(a) Attention, comprehension, acceptance, retention, action

(b) Comprehension, acceptance, retention, attention, action
(c) Attention, acceptance, comprehension, retention, action
(d) Attention, action, comprehension, acceptance, retention

65. Match List-I with List-II:

List-I	List-II
(a) World this week	(1) R.K. Lakshman
(b) Over a cup of tea	(2) Karan Thapar
(c) Devil's Advocate	(3) Pothen Joseph
(d) You said it	(4) Pranav Roy

Codes:	(a)	(b)	(c)	(d)
(a)	(1)	(2)	(3)	(4)
(b)	(4)	(3)	(2)	(1)
(c)	(3)	(1)	(4)	(2)
(d)	(2)	(4)	(1)	(3)

66. Match List-I with List-II:

List-I (Personality)	List-II (Associated with)
(a) Edward Muybridge	(1) Cinematography
(b) Thomas Edison	(2) Recording of Animal Movements
(c) Louis Lumiere	(3) Cathiere Du Cinema
(d) Andre Bazin	(4) Kinetoscope

Codes:	(a)	(b)	(c)	(d)
(a)	(1)	(2)	(3)	(4)
(b)	(4)	(3)	(2)	(1)
(c)	(2)	(4)	(1)	(3)
(d)	(3)	(1)	(4)	(2)

67. Match List-I with List-II:

List-I (Film)
(a) Kashmir Ki Kali
(b) Welcome to Sajjanpur
(c) Singham
(d) Aarakshan

List-II (Hero)
(1) Amitabh Bachchan
(2) Shammi Kapoor
(3) Sreyash Talpade
(4) Ajay Devgan

Codes:	(a)	(b)	(c)	(d)
(a)	(4)	(2)	(1)	(3)
(b)	(1)	(4)	(3)	(2)
(c)	(3)	(1)	(2)	(4)
(d)	(2)	(3)	(4)	(1)

68. Match List-I with List-II:

List-I (Terms)
(a) Pre-flash (b) Telefilm
(c) Free cinema (d) Cinema Verité

List-II (Explanation)
(1) Documentary film making movement in Britain
(2) Documentary film making technique
(3) Exposing of raw film to soft light before shooting
(4) Film made for television broadcast

Codes:	(a)	(b)	(c)	(d)
(a)	(1)	(2)	(3)	(4)
(b)	(2)	(1)	(4)	(3)
(c)	(3)	(4)	(1)	(2)
(d)	(4)	(3)	(2)	(1)

69. Match List-I with List-II:

List-I	List-II
(a) Sentinel	(1) Punjab
(b) Udayavani	(2) Andhra Pradesh
(c) Sakshi	(3) Karnataka
(d) Ajit	(4) Assam

Codes:	(a)	(b)	(c)	(d)
(a)	(2)	(1)	(4)	(3)
(b)	(3)	(4)	(1)	(2)
(c)	(1)	(2)	(3)	(4)
(d)	(4)	(3)	(2)	(1)

70. Match List-I with List-II:

List-I	List-II
(a) Tamasha	(1) Kerala
(b) Bhaona	(2) Tamil Nadu

(c) Therukoothu (3) Assam
(d) Theyam (4) Maharashtra

Codes:	**(a)**	**(b)**	**(c)**	**(d)**
(a)	(4)	(3)	(2)	(1)
(b)	(1)	(2)	(3)	(4)
(c)	(3)	(4)	(1)	(2)
(d)	(2)	(1)	(4)	(3)

Read the following passage and answer Question Nos. from 71 to 75:

Psychoanalytic theory tells us that the human psyche is divided into three spheres: consciousness, pre-consciousness, and the unconsciousness. Although Freud might not have discovered the unconsciousness, it is fair to say that he was aware of its significance and used it in his work to an unprecedented degree. He offers a classic description of the unconsciousness in his essay, 'One of the difficulties of Psychoanalysis.'

It was then, and still is, difficult for many people to recognize that there can be contents of their minds of which they are unaware. The three levels of the psyche (Freud's topographic hypothesis) can be represented by an iceberg. The top of the iceberg, which we all see, is consciousness. The part of the iceberg five or six feets below the waterline, which we can dimly make out, is the preconscious. And the part of the iceberg, below the line, which cannot be seen, is the unconscious. It makes up most of the iceberg and, it is important to recognize, the human psyche.

According to Freud, all of our experiences are stored in the unconscious and have an effect on our minds and behaviour. Psychoanalytic criticism suggests that works of art resonate with this unconscious material in our minds. It is likely, psychoanalytic critics suggest, that works of art send messages, in hidden and rather mysterious ways, from the unconscious of creative artists to the unconscious of people who are the audience for their works.

If the people found the idea of an unconscious difficult, they found Freud's notion of the Oedipus Complex outrageous. And it still is a very controversial matter as scholars in many fields argue about whether it exists or was just a fantastic notion of Freud's. He believed that we all experience, when we are young children (around the age of 3), oedipal strivings. That is, we all desire to have the undivided attention and love of our parent of the opposite sex. Freud called this phenomenon the Oedipus Complex because it resembled in important ways the myth of Oedipus, the Greek hero who unwittingly killed his father and married his mother.

Although this theory is very controversial, it is interesting to notice how useful it is in dealing with works of art. The Oedipus Complex has been used by critics to interpret everything from King Kong to the James Bond stories and films.

71. Which sphere of human psyche Sigmund Freud was presumed to have not discovered?
(a) Unconscious
(b) Pre-consciousness
(c) Consciousness
(d) Post consciousness

72. In the example explaining the three spheres of human psyche, which part was identified with pre-conscious?
(a) The iceberg
(b) The topic of iceberg
(c) The portion of iceberg submerged below waterline
(d) The part of iceberg we cannot see

73. How do the works of art send message to the audience?

(a) Through colours
(b) Through human figures
(c) Through unconscious message inscribed in works of art to the unconscious of audience
(d) Through the writings of the critics

74. What did Sigmund Freud believed about Oedipus Complex?
(a) Only female child experience Oedipus Complex
(b) The strong influence of Greek God Oedipus
(c) Young children of about 3 years of age want undivided attention of parent of opposite sex
(d) The unconsciousness in genes of brain

75. How did the critics use Oedipus Complex in the past?
(a) Works of art
(b) Commentaries on Freud's works
(c) In interpreting King Kong, James Bond stories and films
(d) Explaining fantasies in films

ANSWERS

1. (d)	2. (c)	3. (c)	4. (d)
5. (b)	6. (b)	7. (d)	8. (c)
9. (d)	10. (b)	11. (c)	12. (b)
13. (c)	14. (a)	15. (d)	16. (c)
17. (d)	18. (c)	19. (b)	20. (a)
21. (c)	22. (a)	23. (b)	24. (b)
25. (d)	26. (c)	27. (a)	28. (d)
29. (d)	30. (c)	31. (c)	32. (a)
33. (b)	34. (c)	35. (b)	36. (a)
37. (b)	38. (b)	39. (c)	40. (b)
41. (a)	42. (b)	43. (c)	44. (c)
45. (c)	46. (a)	47. (a)	48. (d)
49. (b)	50. (c)	51. (c)	52. (a)
53. (d)	54. (b)	55. (c)	56. (a)
57. (b)	58. (a)	59. (c)	60. (a)
61. (b)	62. (a)	63. (a)	64. (a)
65. (b)	66. (c)	67. (d)	68. (c)
69. (d)	70. (a)	71. (a)	72. (c)
73. (c)	74. (c)	75. (c)	